THE L

The Life and Times of Winnie Mandela

Emma Gilbey has written for the *Spectator*, *New Yorker*, *New York Times*, *Independent*, *Guardian* and *Sunday Telegraph*. She covered the trial of Winnie Mandela for the *Weekly Mail* in Johannesburg. She lives in New York.

Emma Gilbey

THE LADY

The Life and Times
of Winnie Mandela

V

VINTAGE

Published by Vintage 1994

2 4 6 8 10 9 7 5 3 1

Copyright © Emma Gilbey 1993, 1994

The right of Emma Gilbey to be identified as the author
of this work has been asserted by her in accordance with
the Copyright, Designs and Patents Act, 1988

First published in Great Britain
by Jonathan Cape Ltd, 1993

Vintage
Random House, 20 Vauxhall Bridge Road,
London SW1V 2SA

Random House Australia (Pty) Limited
20 Alfred Street, Milsons Point, Sydney
New South Wales 2061, Australia

Random House New Zealand Limited
18 Poland Road, Glenfield, Auckland 10,
New Zealand

Random House South Africa (Pty) Limited
PO Box 337, Bergvlei, South Africa

Random House UK Limited Reg. No. 954009

A CIP catalogue record for this book
is available from the British Library

ISBN 0 09 938801 4

Printed and bound in Great Britain by
Cox & Wyman, Reading, Berkshire

*for my father
and in memory of my mother*

Interviewer   How [do] you find the strength to deal with these kinds of allegations and rumours and the trials and tribulations, is it through a very special love that you have, or is it something else – is it a determination?

Nelson Mandela   No, I don't think I'm in any way better than other couples . . . the whole purpose of a husband and wife is that when hard times knock at the door you should be able to embrace each other. I am very happy that we have found the courage and the inspiration to be loyal to each other.

'Camera 7', M-net television,
South Africa, July 1992

Interviewer   Are you a dangerous woman?
Winnie Mandela   (Laughs)
Interviewer   Capable of frightful things?
Winnie Mandela   (Laughs) I think no–one in his right mind can answer that nonsensical question.

'Carte Blanche', M-net television,
South Africa, April 1993

Prologue

On the morning of Wednesday 6 March 1991, forensic pathologist Dr Patricia Klepp took the stand in room 4E of South Africa's Rand Supreme Court. As she addressed the court in a brisk authoritative manner, Dr Klepp was routine, thorough and unemotional. The details of the post mortem she had conducted were matters of fact. There was silence in court as she spoke.

She began by describing the decomposition. The body had been found in an open patch of grass in high summer. It had lain rotting in the heat for five days before it was discovered, and was infested with maggots. The brain had turned to liquid, the skin was slipping off the bones and all the organs were decomposing. The corpse had been that of a small boy, four and a half feet tall. Blood had poured out of his throat from two penetrating wounds – each the size of a blade roughly half an inch long – in the right side of his neck, and a third wound just under an inch long across the left side. Blood had flowed over his collar and poured down the front and right side of his shirt as he bled to death.

Later Major Claasens of the South African Police would hold up the boy's shirt. The blood stain on it was massive. There had been pictures of seaside resorts on this red and blue striped T-shirt. They were obliterated by blood still vivid though it had been spilled over two years earlier. The shirt had been ripped in two places, and one of its buttons was missing.

As Dr Klepp testified the little boy who had worn the shirt seemed to die all over again inside the courtroom. He had been subjected to a beating so severe that the injuries to his skull alone could have caused his death. Because his brain had liquefied by the time of the post mortem it had been impossible to ascertain actual brain damage, but there had been haemorrhaging within his skull and bruising over the top and sides of his head. He had a cracked rib and his body was bruised all over, especially on his lower back, both buttocks, left thigh and right calf. His throat had been sliced so deeply that the blade had penetrated into his chest cavity, and his lungs had collapsed. There was blood in his stomach, which he had obviously swallowed, Dr Klepp said, before he died.

Considering the awfulness of what she was saying, Dr Klepp

managed to sound quite upbeat – even chatty at times as she took the court through her examination of the corpse of fourteen-year-old Stompie Moeketsi Seipei. The discrepancy between her manner and her subject was compounded by her appearance. Dr Klepp was an attractive young mother, dressed in a light summer dress.

In the press benches three rows of reporters struggled to keep up with her rapid, sometimes technical delivery. In front of them two long tables of black-robed defence lawyers took occasional notes. Listening from the higher level of his bench, less separated than isolated, a judge faced the court. There was no jury.

Nelson Mandela had come to court that morning. He had been free for just over a year now after 27 years as a political prisoner. He was a political leader but he was also a trained lawyer whose respect for the law was well known. Even when the laws of his country had meant little justice for his people, Mandela's concern had been to change those laws rather than break them. He was here in court listening to evidence that his wife had broken the law eight times. The charges against her were criminal rather than political and four of them were serious enough to carry the death penalty. The Mandelas were used to presenting a united front against adversity. That morning – the seventh day of a trial of four counts of kidnapping and four counts of assault – they had been determinedly cheerful on their arrival. But the strain on Nelson Mandela was obvious. He looked his seventy-three years. He had dozed before the morning break. He seemed overwhelmed and exhausted by the proceedings.

In the small dock at the front of the public benches, flanked by three co-defendants, in a room full of family, friends and supporters, sat the focus of the proceedings, the still, silent figure of Winnie Mandela. Her entrance into court caused an abrupt silence before conversations became more animated than before. She was cheerful and friendly to her friends, she was dignified with reporters and at all times possessed of a statuesque poise. Yet there was something intangible about her that caused her to be more isolated than anyone in the courtroom.

It was her stillness. Alone of everyone in court that day, Winnie Mandela seemed uninterested in what it was that Dr Klepp had to say. Alone of everyone in court throughout the trial, she seemed confident as to its outcome. There were occasions when she was so uninterested in the proceedings, that she brought correspondence to court and devoted herself to answering letters. There were other more unnerving times when she may have felt an element of treachery in the evidence being given against her. She was still, then, as she sat staring at the witness on the stand. But she was not calm. Hers was not the tranquillity of a woman at peace.

She came into the courtroom with a reputation. Once extraordinarily beautiful, and with much of that beauty still intact, she had been the adored wife of an idolised leader. To many all over the world she was revered for her courage in fighting apartheid for more than thirty years. Her incarceration, torture, and harassment at the hands of the South African authorities had become the stuff of legend. But in recent years that reputation had changed. Three witnesses due to testify against Winnie Mandela in this court had been found to be credible in an earlier trial, when they said that she had ordered their kidnapping and initiated a vicious assault on them. Now she was feared as well as venerated, hated as well as loved. Now there were those who saw her as a vicious abuser of adults and children alike. She was said to be malevolent, violent and extremely dangerous.

No-one had accused Winnie Mandela of inflicting the stab wounds which had caused Stompie to bleed to death. She was not facing a charge of murder. What she was facing, however, were charges that she had ordered his and three other youths' kidnapping, that she had them brought to her house in her minibus and that she had led at least seven other people in the beating. Even if one took her at her word, even if she was believed when she said she had nothing to do with the incident, the fact remained that it was in her bus that the four were transported, it was in her back rooms that they were assaulted, and it was from her house that the fourteen-year-old child was taken to the open stretch of wasteland where he was later found dead. This was the case against the woman South Africa called Mother of the Nation, and although Winnie Mandela appeared unconcerned, she was far from unaffected.

Chapter One

Nomzamo Winifred Zanyiwe Madikizela was born on 26 September 1934. She was the fifth child. Her father, Columbus, took one look at the newborn baby and saw that instead of a second son, he now had a fourth daughter, and responded without enthusiasm. 'It's a girl,' he said. 'I'm tired of girls. I want a boy.'[1] His mother, known as Makhulu or Grandmother, who was the ruling force of the family, was just as unhappy. 'There are so many girls,' she complained. 'I want a boy.'[2]

In her autobiography, *Part of My Soul*, Winnie said that her mother, Gertrude, 'Must have been crazy for a boy. I remember her asking God every day for a son. This also developed in me the feeling, I will prove to her that a girl is as much value to a parent as a son.'[3] In a tradition which dictated that a mother's property be left to the youngest male she needed a second boy; without another son Gertrude would have no heir.

Columbus and Gertrude Madikizela lived with their children in the Bizana district of the Transkei, about 60 kilometres inland from the Indian Ocean in South African's south-eastern corner. The coastal region was beautiful. It was not a harsh landscape. Soft hills fell towards valleys and streams. Moisture softened the air and added to the atmosphere of gentleness. A vast panorama stretched as far as the eye could see in any direction; the hills, valleys, tracks and streams seemed particularly close to the sky which encircled them. In fact, when the clouds were low it was actually possible to feel that the land was a part of that sky. Then, visibility was non-existent as clouds twisted and swirled towards the ground. However soft or romantic, the landscape discouraged road and rail connections. At the time of Winnie's birth there were still only two main roads – dirt roads – tying it to the rest of the country. People walked, or men rode horses over steep tracks. There was no other form of transport. As a result there was little travel in and out of the region, and new customs were slow to arrive.

The varying shades of green were made up of vegetable patches, maize fields, clusters of evergreen and deciduous trees and large expanses of tall grass. Across the hills, numerous round white huts made of clay and cattle dung were visible, each the size of a room, and each topped by a thatched roof. These were the homes of the Pondos – the people of Pondoland, as the area was known then. Each hut, which was spotlessly clean, had its own function, whether for sleeping, eating, or storage. Though they may have seemed haphazardly scattered across the countryside, the huts were in fact carefully arranged into homesteads, with the area for cattle – the kraal – at the heart of each homestead, just as the existence of cattle was at the heart of this tribe.

For centuries cattle had dictated the social structure. Homes were arranged in order of rank around a cattle kraal in which grain storage pits were located and chiefs were buried, and cattle were exchanged for wives. The collection of mud huts that formed the settlement in which Columbus and Gertrude lived was entirely made up of Madikizelas, descendants of a grandfather who had been a prosperous farmer and trader. But the traditions within the homestead had become confusing. However isolated Pondoland may have been, four hundred years of European settling had had a disruptive effect on the politics, religion and social structures of the Xhosa.

The Pondo people of this area were part of the Xhosa tribe, known to be indigenous to South Africa from as far back as the seventh or eighth centuries AD.[4] They raised cattle, not for their skin or their flesh but for their milk, a diet which gave them glowing skin, white teeth and statuesque bodies. Three hundred years ago, naked or clad in skins, they smeared themselves with animal fat as a sign of their well being. By the late twentieth century their dress was far more European. Early settlers saw a composed, dignified, self-contained, elegant people with an elegant language. The slow sighing and clicking of their speech was lovely to hear, but hard for strangers to understand and still harder to speak.

Europeans first came to the southern tip of the African continent at the end of the fifteenth century in search of a route to the East. During the sixteenth and seventeenth centuries, South Africa's Cape was used as a stopping off point by ships *en route* to and from India. As the journey from Europe to the harbour at Table Bay could take five horrific months of overcrowding, disease and death, the Cape became the final destination for a number of travellers. It was primarily the English and the Dutch who settled along the coast and eventually began to travel inland.

From the start, contact between Xhosa and whites was charac-terised by misunderstanding. Early settlers regarded the indigenous people as savages and were revolted by them. Their habits of smearing themselves with animal fat, eating entrails and their own body lice made the Xhosa bestial in the eyes of the Europeans. The Cape settlers who moved inland were a tough lot who fought, beat and killed the Xhosa they captured. In return Xhosa farmers who prized their herds so highly that they rarely slaughtered their cattle were reluctant to sell off their stock to white settlers and refused to establish trade relations. Farmers who went inland to settle led spartan, nomadic lives. Living off the land and moving camp at night was a harsh, isolated, existence. Only the Bible provided a sense of security and stability. And so it became their lifeline to the civilised world they had left behind. As the rest of their lives became stripped and meagre so did their interpretation of the word of God. They were fundamentalists. By the end of the eighteenth century, when white farmers and Xhosa were competing for land as well as cattle the hostility escalated into full-scale armed conflict.

Geographically isolated from the main body of the Xhosa tribe, the Pondos were for the most part kept out of these violent raids and counter-raids. None the less they absorbed the experiences of their tribal brethren as their own. But not all encounters with whites were violent. It was not unusual for white settlers to cohabit with Xhosa women. Cultural and territorial clashes aside, a certain amount of racial intermingling began to take place. One descendant of such a union was Winnie's mother.

With her long, red hair, her blue eyes, and her very pale skin, Gertrude Madikizela was a renowned beauty. Her mother-in-law never forgot nor forgave her what she considered the white blood in Gertrude. She may have been dazzling, but being 'coloured' she was racially impure.

Makhulu was completely unable to accept the idea of the white man. Coloureds were considered by blacks to be white. Racial conflict thus dominated Winnie's early life. The first time her father brought Gertrude home from the nearby village of Ndunge, the stubborn and outspoken Makhulu announced she did not want a 'mlungu' – white person – around. 'What does she want in the location?' she asked, and from then on never hid her dislike for her daughter-in-law.[5] Makhulu's opinion affected the general treatment of Gertrude in a culture where the deference accorded to a husband's mother was symbolised by the wife spending her first year of marriage cooking for the matriarch. 'How can a mlungu cook for me?' asked Makhulu disdainfully, when Gertrude prepared to carry out her filial duties. 'How can she make the fire?' Simultaneously excluding and humiliating her daughter-in-law, Makhulu began to use Gertrude's sitting-room to discuss confidential matters with her son. She would stride purposefully into the house and send the children and their mother scuttling, with instructions that she was not to be disturbed for the duration of her lengthy private conversation.

Many of Makhulu's generation genuinely hated Europeans, whom they regarded as ravaging thieves. It was tribal land that had been lost to the white man, after all – a loss which limited the grazing areas of the cattle. Gertrude did not only have to face Makhulu's antipathy. To protect herself from gossip about her race, Gertrude was forced to hide her long red hair under a net. But her mother-in-law's aversion and behaviour were extreme; not only was she unable to come to terms with the idea of white blood in her son's wife, Makhulu also abhorred its presence in his children.

If a child misbehaved, Makhulu would tell it not to act like a white person. If a child of Gertrude's cried, Makhulu would say she was unable to take a mlungu's child into her own arms and leave the child in tears, telling it to sit still until Gertrude came. Refusing to comfort a weeping child was standard practice in the Xhosa culture where infant tears were not tolerated; those who did cry were not fussed over, but firmly told to be quiet. What was uncommon, however, was the manner in which Makhulu seized on every opportunity to criticise her grandchildren's mother. Traditionally, a wife was expected to be even more subservient to her mother-in-law than she was to her husband. Gertrude's position in the settlement under these circumstances must have been virtually untenable. Sometimes Columbus joined in with his mother, 'teasing' his wife in front of the children, saying, 'Your mother is a mlungu.' Makhulu's repeatedly insensitive references to Gertrude's race were never forgotten by Gertrude's children.[6]

However, Makhulu's aversion to the children of a mlungu did not cause her to refuse all contact with them. It was the duty – and pleasure – of local grandparents to be the raconteurs of folklore and she enjoyed telling her grandchildren stories as they sat on mats sucking bones, listening to tales of their heritage. She told tales of stealing and plundering, vicious fighting, of witch doctors and ancestors and spirits. She told of how men with blue eyes, pale skin and long straight hair had first arrived in Pondoland, with Bibles in one hand and buttons (money)[7] in the other to steal her people's cattle and destroy their customs.[8] Recounting folklore to her grandchildren was sometimes little more than another opportunity for racial indoctrination.

Makhulu had a personal reason for hating the white man. She had been the first woman in Pondoland to own and run a small trading post – a little shop selling general goods – but had lost it when a newly arrived group of white traders arbitrarily took it away from her.[9] Winnie's grandfather (still regarded by Madikizelas in the area as an extraordinarily clever man, sixty years later) had worked closely and co-operatively with local traders, even at one stage giving them a large piece of his land. It was in return for this land that he had received the trading post, his to own and operate, and on his death Makhulu had taken it over. The management of the post was a source of great pride to this hearty, forthright woman and its loss – when the original white traders left, and their replacements came and 'stole' it – was a tremendous blow.

By the time Winnie was born the racial confusion and violence in her own home mirrored that across the country. South Africa had been a racially exclusive country for twenty-five years and a violent one for more than a hundred. Zulu had fought Xhosa, Boer had fought English, race had fought race. The 1910 Act of Union created the Union of South Africa with a central constitution and govern-ment, but with no place for non-whites. In response, prominent Africans had formed the South African Native Congress in 1912. A year before Winnie's birth, the Congress had been reorganised and renamed the African National Congress. Made up of tribal leaders, lawyers, journalists and teachers, the Congress aimed to promote unity and understanding throughout the country and to defend the rights and privileges of all South Africans – of every race.

The latter part of the nineteenth century had seen the discovery of both gold and diamonds in South Africa – a breakthrough which would cause the migration of thousands of African males from countryside to cities. Some of Winnie's own uncles were part of this transient labour force, rarely returning home and living in indescrib-able conditions in hostels provided by the mines. Miners slept in stacks on shelves between shifts, washed away the day's grime with cold water, and were paid a pittance. Economically, their exploitation enabled the country to become and remain highly competitive in the global mineral market.

Domestically, the ability of Bantus – as blacks were officially designated – to possess land of their own had been drastically reduced in 1913. Over the next half a century, their land-owning rights would continue to be sliced away, as forced segregation prevented them from expanding or moving beyond prescribed areas. Politically, the First World War caused many blacks to become active on their return from fighting in Europe, where they had seen that colour bars – as discriminatory laws were known – were the exception rather than the rule. The ANC began a decades-long campaign against the imposition of the pass law.

Introduced to control the migrant work force, passes had quickly become an effective method of repressing the non-white population. The myriad pass laws, whose terms varied from province to province, would later become weapons to be used against those who opposed the government and its apartheid legislation. At its simplest, a pass, or identity card, valid for one month, was proof that the bearer was employed. At their worst they became an untenable bureaucratic nightmare. Travelling passes, night-time passes, special date passes, passes valid for one area but not another, and passes allowing the bearer to look for work were introduced. The issue and administration of these passes became increasingly arbitrary, and penalties for out-of-order passes grew harsher.

When women had first been issued with passes in the Free State province in 1913, they immediately organised themselves in a political protest of passive resistance. They simply refused to carry their passes, preferring to go to prison than be imprisoned by a pass. Hundreds of women persevered in the seven-year campaign, which ultimately ended in triumph. In 1920, Free State women were finally exempt from the region's pass law. Elsewhere in the country, campaigns against the pass law would be longer, bloodier and less successful. More than any other measure, the pass law would come to represent the oppression of apartheid.

Not only were laws changing, so were customs. Central to the confusion in Winnie's immediate family was her father. Though by birth he was eligible to become headman of his tribe – one of a small group of councillors who advised the chief and acted as deputies in his absence – Columbus had rejected his birthright to become a missionary school teacher. The missionaries had come to the area a century after the farmers. From the early 1800s mainly English missionaries had spread Christianity throughout the Xhosa tribe with an evangelical fervour fanned by a revulsion of the savage ways of their prospective converts. Over the years, Christianity had mingled with, rather than wiped out, traditional beliefs. The result was more confusing than enlightening. Christmas was celebrated, but with the Xhosa ceremony of slaughtering a cow. Polygamy was abandoned by Christians in a village, but not by non-Christians. Some Xhosa chiefs who turned to Christ felt that as they had the tradition of enduring relationships with tribal ancestors they could claim divine kinship with Him. This, however, was frowned on by the emissaries of the true Church. It was the Christian God who was the ultimate power, and it was the Christian God, therefore, who undermined the divine authority of the tribal chiefs. Converts were encouraged to reject almost every one of their own customs. The single-minded Columbus embraced Christianity in what the missionaries would have considered the purest way. He rejected his own heritage.

It is remembered two generations later, as a practical rather than an ideological decision, unusual but not unprecedented.[10] Headmen had to work for nothing and Columbus had a family to support. He had also inherited his own father's considerable business skills and needed a salary to put those skills into practice. Though given his own piece of land to farm, and his own cattle to tend, he needed cash. The mission school in nearby Dutyini had an opening. Columbus took it.

Whatever the decision of her father, during Winnie's childhood the power of the chief in the village and surrounding homesteads was paramount, transcending life. The spirit of dead chiefs was believed to imbue the land with life and strength. It was to them that loyalty and obedience were due. They provided the tradition and structure of the tribe. They were the source of wisdom. Collectively they meant a sense of wholeness. It was by the chief that the most solemn oaths were sworn. Tribal chiefs had authority, but held it democratically. They had power but it was not absolute – it was not theirs to abuse. Acting in accord with, and relying heavily on, the advice of his councillors, the chief governed, not arbitrarily or unilaterally, but according to tribal law custom and history. If he failed to do so he was rejected by the tribe who simply picked somebody else. The process leant itself to healthy debate and a type of legal analysis which rivalled that of European law in its sophistication.

Columbus's decision reflected much of his own racial and religious confusion. He refused to serve officially, but still acted as a leader and would attend tribal court. He embraced the ideas and standards of Europe, and aspired to be European in his behaviour and dress, but harboured a strong sense of the injustice done to his people by European settlers.

Echoing his mother's bitterness at unprincipled white behaviour, Columbus Madikizela was not the most conventional missionary school teacher. He may have worked for the government – mission schools had been consolidated under the Department of Education for almost a century – but he took it upon himself to impart to his very young pupils their 'true' history, abandoning the version in the standard-issue history textbook because it was written by white people and therefore false.[11] He may have taught of explorers such as Bartholomew Diaz and Vasco Da Gama, but as deceitful people who had invaded the country. They had bartered unfairly, stolen land and seized cattle. This was how white men had caused the country's problems, Columbus said. And it was these white men who were trying to condition blacks into believing that whites should be their masters. Instead, he taught, it was the duty of future generations of blacks to get their land back.

And so Winnie, who in her autobiography titled the section on her childhood: 'When My Father Taught Me History I Began to Understand', was brought up to believe that the white man was on one hand a relative of her mother, and on the other a rampaging predator who had exploited and ruined her people. Winnie subsequently described her grandmother as the first racist she knew. With what her grandmother instilled in her at home and her father taught her in school, her childhood, she said, was a blistering inferno of racial hatred.[12]

Like her husband, Gertrude was also a trained teacher. Before her marriage, she had qualified in physical science at the Marianhill Roman Catholic Mission near Durban. Her choice of profession was seized upon and criticised by her mother-in-law. Her son should marry a wife, not a teacher, teachers were men, she complained. Gertrude had a spiritual as well as a physical approach to disciplining her children, and religion became yet another source of conflict between the two women. Gertrude represented the third generation of converts from Xhosa ancestor worshippers and her devotion to Methodism bordered on zealotry. Gertrude inherited her passionate faith in Christianity from her mother, known to Winnie as Granny, an ardent and active Methodist. With both her parents devout Christians Winnie was christened in the Methodist church. She was regularly locked into a room with her mother and forced to pray aloud. And at least twice a day, the whole family would fall to their knees in a special private corner of the garden for set prayers – a practice which made them unique in the settlement. Immediately on their return from school, the Madikizela children prayed with their mother, and only then would they be allowed to go to their chores, their games or their homework. Sundays were devoted to prayer and Sunday School before visiting ill or bereft neighbours.

Gertrude taught her children hymns and biblical stories, and stressed that Christianity was the true way. The children must respect the messengers of the true religion, the white missionaries. She also maintained that the African rites practised by their grandmother, who went among the cattle to pray to their grandfather's spirit, were meaningless voodoo – witchcraft and therefore evil. In return, Makhulu continued to pass on to Gertrude's children the ancestral customs repudiated by their mother and encouraged them to participate in traditional ceremonies, such as sacrificial slaughters in honour of ancestral spirits.

The family discord was set in a life of rural routine against a background of unchanging pastoral beauty. At the age of six, Winnie joined her three older sisters – Viyelwa, Irene and Nancy – and her brother Christopher at the school where their father taught. By then she was already helping with the animals, milking the cows and tending the sheep, raising the crops and playing in the fields. She'd get up with the other small children in the early hours of the morning to do her chores, before going home and getting ready for school. The children rose at 5.00 a.m. at the latest, and quickly ate a breakfast of porridge, heated on a small fire of wattle bark in one of the huts. They fetched water from a stream about a kilometre away for washing and cooking. Those old enough would then milk the cows before leaving for school at around seven. School prayers were followed by lessons until two with a half-hour mid-day break. After school the children returned to work, hoeing and ploughing the maize fields. The girls cleaned the house and prepared the supper. They boiled mealies (corn) or potatoes, cooked porridge and roasted meat. It was common for a mother to feed other children as well as her own, and meals were extended to include those in the settlement who lacked the provisions. In addition to his other activities, Columbus had become a successful farmer. Sometimes as many as twenty other children would be served from the large cooking pots which Winnie and her brothers and sisters helped prepare. Her favourite dish was 'amadumbe', a combination of sweet and ordinary potatoes.

'There are moments of solitude when I miss my childhood very much and the older I grow, the more I realise what effect it had on me; the love of my country. Running through those bare fields bare footed, looking after cattle, sheep and goats – that has never completely left me. Somewhere in my subconscious mind that is the country I am really fighting for.'[13]

Gertrude eventually had two more daughters, Beauty and Princess, and two more sons, Lungile and Msuthu. Winnie continued to spurn the company of her own sex. She wore shorts, climbed and fell out of trees, rode one of her father's many cows or horses bare back, threw sticks, fought, and played ball games with the boys. A weekly highlight for the girls was on Friday afternoon, when their dolls wou¹ ' 'marry'. They brought their wooden dolls to school, dressed in wedding clothes made by their mothers, and all the other activities seemed to stop. Winnie's mother was the envy of all the girls: she was especially skilled at sewing, and made the prettiest dresses and veils. But Winnie never played with dolls, though she did enjoy carving clay toys which she baked in a brick kiln built by the village boys.

She had grown used to tomboyish behaviour. She even looked like a boy. Once when her mother took her to visit the local minister, Reverend Gabela, his wife actually thought she was a boy – a mistake which Winnie later said made her hate her from that day on.[14]

It was becoming increasingly difficult to distinguish between Winnie's boyishness and naughtiness, her disobedience and wilfulness. She was such a tough little daughter. Winnie and her older sister, Irene, were the fighters of the family and often used their fights to prove a point. Arguments generally began when Winnie failed to get her way, or on the rare occasions when someone dared to disagree with her. Her tough tactics were resented by the other children, who felt she had an unfair advantage as the daughter of their teacher. It was understood that only the foolhardy would risk taking her on. However, Winnie didn't pick fights when her older brother Christopher was around; he had no compunction about belting his sister. When the other children realised this, they went to him with their complaints about her bullying.

It was a quarrel with her sister that made Winnie's childhood stand out from those of her brothers and sisters.[15] No longer content to rely on fists, feet or even sticks, Winnie had secretly fashioned a vicious weapon by taking a tin and driving a nail through the bottom of it. When fighting, Winnie whipped out the tin and slugged her sister in the mouth, ripping through her lip with the nail and tearing into the flesh of her mouth. The wound bled copiously and needed stitches. The thrashing Gertrude gave Winnie, in one of their final run-ins, affected Winnie for the rest of her life.[16]

Despite being a girl, Winnie became something of a favourite with Makhulu, who sensed some of her own spirit in her lively granddaughter. Physically Winnie bore more of a resemblance to Columbus than she did to her mother. She loved her grandmother, and responded well to the more relaxed atmosphere of the older woman's house, where there was more time for playing, for sitting around listening to stories, for learning to weave mats and make clay pots, for brewing beer, or cooking traditional African dishes. Life was by comparison an indulgence; cooking, eating and drinking were the priorities, and Winnie was less likely to be put to work or punished for wrongdoing.

Columbus had the attitude that all children should work hard at their tasks, regardless of their sex. While averse to the white man's presence in Africa, he had great admiration for the diligence of the Germans: he frequently praised their industrial achievements to his children. Winnie wrote in her autobiography: 'That's why he insisted on that terrible name "Winifred", which subsequently became "Winnie".' (Although Winifred is in fact a Welsh name.)[17] Her African name, Nomzamo, meaning 'she who must endure trials', was used far less often.

Both Winnie's parents were strict disciplinarians, and both beat her regularly. Gertrude beat her children for their spiritual well-being, Columbus took as his example the discipline of the Germans – or, closer to home, the Boers. Their iron-handed approach was unusual in an environment where unruly children were more threatened with beatings than beaten. Children were not beaten in this community. They were considered precious – beating a child meant ruining a child. Physical punishment, therefore, was normally saved only for the worst transgressions. In this context, Winnie sometimes did deserve a beating – such as when she repeatedly stole, but Columbus regularly doled out lashes, not only to his own children but to all his pupils. Mistakes in algebra, or spelling, playing in class – relatively minor misdeeds such as these – caused the strict schoolteacher to pull out his whip.

Apart from beating them, Columbus rarely touched his children. The local teacher made him, in a sense, the local father, but he was different from other fathers. His lack of physical affection made him stand out. He never touched his children in tenderness. Beating them was his only physical contact: he never hugged or kissed the young children as other fathers did.[18] Aloof and authoritative, he was a stern schoolmaster through and through. Even at home his children rarely spoke to him without the presence of their mother. All of them were scared of him, Winnie included. They were not just intimidated by his anger but by his autocracy. This was a man who not only beat his children, but made them stand to attention when he entered a room and only allowed them to sit with his permission.

From an early age, Winnie was schooled in Latin as well as English, and received a solid grounding in science and maths. Working on slates, and memorising what they were taught, since there were no exercise books, Columbus's twenty pupils learned of China and America, of Portuguese, Dutch and English explorers, of French Huguenots. Schooling was free, though each child had to pay Columbus two and a half cents for a slate. But slates gave Winnie another way in which to assert her authority over the other children. When she broke her slate, she felt perfectly justified – as the teacher's daughter – in commandeering that of another child, for her own use. If a child had no money for a slate, then Columbus would accept an egg, laid by one of the chickens or geese they kept, which he would put in his incubator. The children spent hours at this incubator, and watched breathlessly as their eggs hatched into chicks.

Later, when she had white as well as African instructors, Winnie began to compare her father. He was paid far less than his white counterparts: he was poorer, shabbier and some of his clothes were threadbare. Curiously, considering his mother's influence, Columbus had rejected tribal dress. Unlike the majority of the community who wore Xhosa blankets or any old pair of trousers, he always wore a suit. And he got as much mileage out of his meagre wardrobe of shabby suits and frayed shirts as possible, with the aid of his wife's darning, starching and pressing.

Clothes were extremely significant to Winnie's relatives – and again another cause of conflict. Gertrude's mother was as committed to the West, the wearing of European clothes and the cooking of European food, as her counterpart was to Africa. Not only did Gertrude inherit her mother's devotion to a western church, she was brought up learning western customs. Granny taught Gertrude to bake European bread with dough – instead of grits – and to sew dresses, not skins. So Gertrude not only looked European, she acted it too, practising its religion, and passing its customs on to others in the settlement.

Makhulu found it easier to accept a degree of westernisation in her son. Columbus could wear a suit, be a Christian, and in the employ of the white education authorities; he could even live with a coloured wife, but he never lost his mother's favour. Makhulu complained – often loudly and critically – but remained close to him. He in turn was careful to compromise. To avoid hurting his mother's feelings he did not completely turn his back on Xhosa religious rites. A practising Christian, he still participated in traditional ceremonies.

Gertrude inherited another characteristic from her mother, which

Winnie in turn inherited from her and which ran contrary to her tomboyish behaviour: an obsession with physical hygiene. Granny was inexhaustible in exercising personal cleanliness; her *toilette* took up a large part of each day. The morning *lever* (washing, massaging in specially prepared cleansing ointments, combing and plaiting her hair) and the evening *coucher* (removing and stretching clothes, laying them carefully under the mattress) were protracted rituals. Her grandchildren acted as acolytes when they visited her near Emfundisweni in the school holidays. Winnie was the water bearer, and fetched water from the rivers.

Gertrude was relentless in the maintenance of hygiene in her children and her home, even marshalling the children for a routine physical inspection. Each night they heated water from the river on the fire outside for bathing. Gertrude also forced them to use blackened charcoal to clean their teeth, which they brushed until their gums bled.

Inside the house, Gertrude obsessively checked and rechecked the order of her belongings. It wasn't enough that the house and everything inside it was clean, everything also had to be in its right place. If she sent the children on an errand she would spit in front of the fire and demand that they be back before the spit had dried. She meant it, too. If a child was late he or she would be slapped or forced to miss supper.

From a very young age, Winnie took after her mother in this respect. Her cousins and friends remember her washing the dishes, and cleaning the family huts, inside and out, never finishing, but seeming to start over again. Her older relatives appreciated not just her help, but her company. She chattered away, laughing while she scrubbed for them.

In this way, Winnie's life continued for her first ten years. Her daily and seasonal routines varied little, but her earliest experiences were of harsh discipline, conflict and confusion. When Columbus transferred from the mission school at Dutyini to the local government school 20 kilometres across the hills at Embongweni, Winnie experienced her first major upheaval. A vacancy had opened up at Embongweni, and Columbus applied for and got the job, leaving missionary education behind him for good. The whole family moved house, to less living space and less land, though lack of space was not a particular problem as the three eldest children had now left home for boarding school. On a little plot of land behind the school, Columbus built himself a cluster of mud huts, a little brick school teacher's house, and – with his eye always on business opportunities – a tiny little general store.

Winnie, Nancy, Lungile, Beauty and Princess settled into their new home, while a pregnant Gertrude learned that her eldest daughter, Viyelwa, had contracted tuberculosis. Like all communicable diseases for which there was no cure, TB could be devastating among the poorer urban and rural communities. Viyelwa lay slowly wasting away, nursed around the clock by her mother, who in the absence of any real medical remedy stepped up her prayers, begging God to save her child. But her pleas for mercy went unanswered. Winnie later said this experience did much to shake her belief in her mother's God.[19] For instead of improving, Viyelwa gradually grew worse and when the family returned from church one Sunday, they found her coughing up blood and close to death. She died soon afterwards, as her mother knelt praying for God's angels to come to save her.

Soon after this Msuthu was born, but by this time Gertrude was very ill.

'I was ten years old when my youngest brother was born. He was to be my mother's last child, and the death of her. It was as if she had just been living to give birth to this precious son. She became very ill.'[20]

Like her daughter, Gertrude died slowly, withering away. Winnie said later, 'She lay there, just diminishing daily; for me as a little girl, she was literally disappearing, and she was in great pain, that's all I remember.'[21]

Whether Gertrude – never the same after Viyelwa's death – never recovered from the birth of Msuthu was not clear. In a period when no written records were kept, it is not definite exactly how long after her daughter's death Gertrude died, or of what. At the time of her death she was still breastfeeding three-month-old Msuthu, who escaped whatever disease killed his mother.[22] It is most likely that Gertrude succumbed to TB caught from Viyelwa while she was pregnant with Msuthu, that the stress and exhaustion of nursing then losing one child while carrying another lowered her resistance to infection and eventually proved too much for her. Whatever the immediate cause may have been, the intrinsic rationale – that Gertrude's children killed her – remained constant in Winnie's accounts of the death of her mother.

The death of his wife did little to make Columbus less remote to his children. In fact he made them almost irrelevant to the death bed scene. As Gertrude slowly died, Columbus did little to comfort them. His detached behaviour continued – if anything he became more

17

aloof, barely speaking as he returned home with piles of homework, sitting in silence at his wife's bedside, before shutting himself up in another room where he could correct schoolwork undisturbed for the rest of the evening. His wife prayed constantly as she died, and again she was watched by her daughter as she implored an unresponsive God for help. At ten Winnie was not only old enough to understand what was going on, she could apportion blame. She felt she had good reason to reject her mother's punishing, cruel, Methodist God. This omnipotent Father could have saved Viyelwa – and could now still save Gertrude – but chose instead to deprive eight children – the youngest of whom was still on the breast – of their mother.

Gertrude died in the night. In the final hours before her death, she was surrounded by village elders. Traditionally there was nothing for the children to do, so Winnie hovered nearby, waiting in an adjoining hut, dozing through the night until finally awakened by a screaming Irene who said their mother was dead: 'We flung our arms around each other and wept and it was as if our sorrow would never end.'[23] Her younger sister Princess remembers Winnie crying constantly after their mother died.

Gertrude Madikizela received a Christian burial, though Xhosa mourning traditions were honoured. Black was worn, and heads were shaved, while the walls of the huts were painted with black ochre. Relatives from all over the district came to mourn with the immediate family, and – more importantly – to decide what to do with the children. Traditionally, a mother's death caused the father's brothers and sisters to step in and help care for the young. Columbus's sisters came to the village to take care of the grieving children, and organise the breaking up of the family. The two eldest children, Christopher and Irene, returned to board at their respective schools. One aunt took Nancy away to live with her. For a short time Winnie was sent to stay with her Uncle Gilbert, but was soon allowed to return home, where she would now be the eldest child.

Although Nancy came home regularly, Winnie missed her. But she was losing her childishness and boyishness, as in the absence of a constant female adult presence, she began to take on her mother's responsibilities. The ten-year-old girl became kinder and gentler as she took care of Princess and nursed Msuthu. His mother's death had caused an abrupt weaning and the baby cried all the time. Winnie fed him his bottle and helped him get to sleep, and carried Msuthu and Princess with her when she went to work in the fields – Msuthu tied in her arms, Princess bound to her back.

As well as taking care of the little children, she began to look after her father, laundering his shirts and becoming something of a companion to him. She began to miss him terribly when he made his regular lengthy trips to Umtata for court or council sessions. Though he remained physically undemonstrative, Columbus grew much closer to his daughter, showing his affection in the area in which he was most comfortable – teaching. Already the owner of an extensive and eclectic library, he began bringing home a wide range of literature which he commanded her to 'Read!'

She read everything, working her way through histories, text books and fairy tales, even farming magazines. At school she played less with other children at break times, preferring isolation and escape in schoolbooks. At home, too, she preferred to try to manage on her own in solitude, and when local mothers came to offer their help with the children or the housework, she would thank them and decline.

The fights continued. On more than one occasion Winnie began a fight with a sister or a cousin in the early morning and continued it throughout the day. Mealtimes provided brief respites from these protracted, more rigorous brawls in which she and her adversary punched, kicked, and beat each other with sticks.

Within a year of her mother's death, there was another upheaval in Winnie's life. On inspection by local educational authorities, Columbus's school was found to be overcrowded, and it was decided to disband the top class – in which Winnie was a pupil – and send those students to start secondary school a few months early. The problem lay in finding places at the already crowded local secondary schools. Columbus, who was unable to find Winnie a place, could have kept his daughter at his own school by putting her back a year. Instead he made a curious decision for one so dedicated to education, and declared she should leave the school. For Winnie it must have seemed as if she was leaving school for ever.

The impact of Columbus's decision was crushing. Winnie would later merge her two traumatic experiences into one long disruptive episode, implying that it was her mother's death which forced her to interrupt her education and failing to mention the details of her father's decision.[24]

There was nothing she could do. Winnie accepted Columbus's ruling with stoicism. She continued to herd and milk the cattle, planted and picked the crops, and took full-time care of the family for six months, until she was able to take a place at the secondary school in Gertrude's home village of Ndunge – close but too far for a daily journey. As she entered her teens, she left her father's home for the childhood home of her late mother. During term time she would live with Granny.

One of the reasons Winnie made little fuss when Columbus forced her to leave school was that she was still quite frightened of his temper. As she grew older and they grew closer, she became less intimidated. Eventually she had enough courage to challenge her father when they disagreed. Like her parents and grandparents, Winnie was also becoming authoritative.

Shortly after beginning secondary school Winnie started fighting her father. Their confrontations took place on her return home and were usually over her younger brothers and sisters. In Winnie's absence, Columbus had sent his four youngest children to live with other relatives in the area, though he missed them badly and would frequently take a horse and set off to fetch them, galloping back to the house with a son or a daughter cradled in his arms. Winnie also missed her brothers and sisters. If they weren't there on her return from school, she would fly into a temper, forcing Columbus to go and bring them home. She was quite intractable on the issue, refusing to go back to school without seeing the babies of the family. On more than one occasion, Columbus found himself setting off to get them at her behest.

Within a year, Winnie had changed schools again. Still in the Bizana district, she moved to board at Emfundisweni Secondary School. Now there was no question of her returning home except sporadically. Emfundisweni, on the banks of the Mzintlava River, was not close to any good road, and was a hard 60 kilometres from Embongweni across country.

Columbus himself took his daughter to buy her school uniform, including her first pair of shoes. They were agony – black shoes with laces, causing her feet to swell up so painfully she could only bear to wear them to lessons and would take them off outside the classroom. Columbus also, rather awkwardly, chose an overcoat for Winnie. The huge, man's size, thick, black garment he bought made her an object of ridicule. Winnie hated being laughed at, she left it at home.

She was becoming interested in clothes as she approached puberty. She and Beauty had inherited Gertrude's Singer sewing machine and were able to make their own skirts and blouses even though they frequently fought over what belonged to whom. Actually, Winnie was unusually generous with her wardrobe, often giving away clothes to those who had less than she did. When she found out that one of the local girls in the settlement was staying away from school because she had nothing to wear, she gave her one of her own dresses. Columbus was so proud of his daughter's act of selflessness that, when he found out what she had done and why, he rushed out to buy two more dresses – one for the girl and one for Winnie.

Her first year at Emfundisweni was difficult and unhappy, mainly because there was a great deal of bullying at the school. She found an ally in another new girl who came from the Bizana district, Evelyn Ntombizodwa.

'We were far from home and went home about every six months,' said Evelyn.[25] 'We missed our home. The newcomers in the school were treated very badly by the second years. They would make us make a line and then send us to fetch water. Then they would put a cup into our buckets of water and throw it in our faces – Winnie would cry. Everybody was ill-treated. But when we got to the second year we were just as bad – we had to get our revenge. On Sunday prayers we would take up all the first years' seats and they would come in all shy and embarrassed and wouldn't know where to sit. But the third years would sort it out. Winnie was naughty in the institution, but not only her, all the second years were.'

Despite the bullying and the prolonged absences from home, secondary school seems to have had something of a stabilising effect on Winnie. She became known as a bright and generous student who helped others with their work, and gave sympathy and advice when asked. She was not all bookworm. She enjoyed sports – netball and rounders, as well as skipping and ball games in the playground. But her real passion was the choir. She had a good singing voice and loved both singing and dancing to music. When she did go home she formed her own choir, gathering local children together after school and teaching them how to sing. Once her own choir was proficient, she began organising competitions with other choirs in the area, staging the events at her house, and getting anyone with any free time to come and judge.

All of Columbus's children worked hard at school and all did reasonably well. His belief in the value of education extended to a wish that his sons and daughters be educated beyond secondary or high school. In the course of his enquiries about colleges, he heard of the newly formed Jan Hofmeyr School of Social Work in Johannesburg, which to Columbus seemed particularly suited to Winnie, with what he considered to be her highly developed aptitude for caring for young children. There would also be a certain cachet in having a daughter at this highly prestigious new institute of black education. The Jan Hofmeyr School of Social Work had been founded during the war, initially as a training ground for welfare workers who could then accompany troops to battle. With the war's end, the school had become a permanent college for black social workers, and it was this newly reorganised college that Columbus had heard of and been drawn to.

To get in to the Jan Hofmeyr School, Winnie would have to do exceptionally well in her final school matriculation exams, and for that she needed intensive preparation. Columbus spent a lot of time and energy investigating how best to educate his favourite child, but he did the same for all his children. Christopher had gone on to teacher-training college and like his father eventually became a headmaster. Lungile did well enough in his matriculation exams to be sent to the best college of black higher education in the country, Fort Hare University, and Nancy was also eventually sent to Johannesburg where she trained as a nurse. Overall, the scholastic achievements of the Madikizela children were impressive at a time when it was becoming increasingly difficult to find a good black school.

In 1948 the National Party came to power in South Africa. Apartheid, the segregation of the races, was now official policy. By the beginning of the 1950s, when Columbus was trying to find the best school for Winnie to complete her education, apartheid was more reality than abstraction. In planning for a segregated future, African education came under the reforming eye of the government. Winnie had just left school by the time the Bantu Education Act was passed in 1953. Even so, her final years of schooling were conducted with the understanding that this quality of education was about to end. The Bantu Education Act stated that blacks were now to be educated to a lesser standard than their white counterparts. All African schools were now under the control of the Department of Native Affairs. The Minister for Native Affairs, Dr Hendrik Verwoerd, stressed before the bill became law that, 'When I have control of Native education, I will reform it so that Natives will be taught from childhood to realise that equality with Europeans is not for them.'[26]

Natives may have been taught that racial equality was not for them, but from then on they learned precious little else at school. The imposition of the act signalled the beginning of the end for missionary and private African schools. In turn, the solid classical curriculum they had provided for Africans was placed in jeopardy. As schools came under heavy pressure to place themselves in the administrative hands of the government they lost their autonomy. The new government-prescribed African syllabus contained what the government felt an African needed to learn: manual labour. The alternative was no government administration which meant no government funding, which essentially meant no school.

Columbus managed to find a place for Winnie at the Shawbury High School at Qumbu, nearly 200 kilometres away from Bizana on the main road to Umtata. Founded in 1938, Shawbury was a beautiful series of one-storey buildings set about ten kilometres back from the main road, in a shady cluster of trees. It was surrounded by water, being midway between the Tina and the Tsitsa rivers, and students were able to take advantage of easy access to spectacular waterfalls. There were about two hundred pupils at Shawbury roughly divided between boys and girls. They worked from 8.00 a.m. to 2.50 p.m. with a mid-morning break and an hour for lunch. Winnie arrived at Shawbury in early 1951 and matriculated from there in the public exams of December 1952.

She took her first school exams in May 1951 and did well, coming third out of a class of nineteen with an average of 51.1 per cent (the top mark was 58.1). The pupils were taught both English and Xhosa literature and language as well as Maths, Geography, Latin, History, Biology, Physical Science and Physical Hygiene. Winnie's best subject was Biology (60 per cent), her worst English Composition (40 per cent). Six months later, with two fewer in the class, she only came fifth and her average had dropped to 48.3 per cent.[27]

Back in Bizana, Columbus had a number of local children boarding with him – feeding one or two more made little difference. As well as Winnie's fees he paid for a cousin, Jackson Madikizela, to attend Shawbury. It was not hard for Columbus to afford another set of school fees. The local schoolmaster was a canny businessman as well as a successful farmer and he was sufficiently skilled at marketing his own produce to become the owner of the local supermarket, butchery and liquor store. His family was hardly in the grip of desperate poverty, through this was becoming ever more prevalent among the black communities. The Land Act was now a generation old, and its crippling effects on black farm workers had taken a firm hold. Unable to expand – or even move out of their prescribed territories – Africans had had to endure the effects of overpopulation, overgrazing and soil erosion caused by drought. As successive crops failed, the value of land plummeted, and rural poverty soared.

Over the years public perception of the economic conditions in which Winnie grew up reflected the deprivation of the area, rather than her own immediate situation. In many accounts of her childhood, Winnie would often refer to circumstances of dire poverty – at one stage maintaining that far from being able to provide clothing, housing and schooling for a number of other children, her father could not afford to clothe all his own.[28]

Although her childhood was spent surrounded by destitution, she was never actually indigent. And though there would be periods of her life when she was dependent on the kindness of others for subsistence when money was tight, she was never completely impoverished. But even when she became extremely wealthy, her enduring image remained that of a victim of want, and thus the true representative of a starving, oppressed people. If they were destitute – she appeared so.

After Gertrude had been dead for about ten years, Columbus decided to remarry. He chose another school teacher for his second wife, 34-year-old Hilda Nophikela. Makhulu, Columbus's mother, thought Hilda was a gold-digger who had married her son for his money, referring to her as 'that old hag', and ordering the wedding celebrations cut short. Initially there was a certain amount of resistance to Hilda from her eight new stepchildren, most of whom were grown themselves and used to living without a mother. The eldest child, Christopher had already been married for five years. By the time Hilda arrived, Columbus's children had developed independent lives, and on the whole, she was of little concern to them. In the absence of any lasting feeling against her, she gradually became accepted as a member of the family, especially once she had given birth to Columbus's last child – another daughter.

For the most part Winnie's intellectual and political educations ran parallel, but towards the end of her two years at Shawbury they clashed. By the standards of Verwoerd ('People who believe in equality are not desirable teachers for Natives'), Winnie's teachers could not have been less suitable.[29] There were about ten teachers at Shawbury, mostly graduates of Fort Hare University College, which was a centre of black political activism in the early 1950s. They believed in racial equality. They were intelligent, well educated and militant. For the first time outside her family, Winnie was becoming exposed to different sets of political views. Not only was the school library well stocked with about a thousand books, but students also received daily newspapers – the *Daily Dispatch* and the *Cape Argus* – as well as the *National Geographic, Science Digest, World Digest* and the

South African liberal magazines *South Africa Outlook* and *Forum*. Students were encouraged to read and expected to be active – both physically and mentally. The school had a number of extra-curricular associations, including a debating society.[30]

In June 1952 there was a nationwide campaign of civil disobedience, jointly organised by the ANC and the Indian Congress. South Africa's Indian community had been growing since its establishment in 1860 when Indians had been recruited to work as indentured labourers on the sugar plantations of Natal. Though the terms of the five-year service were as rigid as slavery (a labourer was the property of his master), many Indians had come to South Africa wooed by promises of freedom to settle with full ownership of land after their contracts were up. Those who did settle had prospered to an impressive degree. They grew prodigious amounts of fruits and vegetables, then began trading – first with other Indians in Natal, then expanding to include Africans and Europeans. With their profits they bought land and built extensively.

Commercial success meant Indians were competition for whites. Thus it was only a matter of time before they came under local government scrutiny. The first effects of this coincided with Mohandas Gandhi's arrival in 1893, when a £3 poll tax was imposed on women, children over the age of sixteen and post-indentured men. Shortly afterwards, Natal Indians lost their right to vote.[31] The 23-year-old lawyer had arrived in South Africa in response to a request for legal help from an Indian trading firm with a complicated case in the South African courts. Gandhi agreed to assist in the case, thinking his South African stay would be a year at most. He would remain based in the country until 1914.

As Nelson Mandela was to do later, Gandhi combined practice as a lawyer with work against the laws of segregation. His earliest experiences as an Indian in the country – he was thrown off a train and beaten, and kicked off a public footpath by a policeman – heightened his sensitivity to the Indian predicament, while his legal practice taught him that: 'The true function of a lawyer was to unite parties riven asunder. The lesson was so indelibly burnt into me that a large part of my time during the twenty years of my practice as a lawyer was occupied in bringing about private compromises of hundreds of cases. I lost nothing thereby – not even money, certainly not my soul.'[32]

But passive resistance, also known as soul-force, or *Satyagraha*, and compromise were not especially compatible.[33] In 1952 the Defiance Campaign, as it was known, was a non-violent protest at the 'unjust laws' of the government. In the four years since its rise to power, the government had dissolved the Communist Party and outlawed Communism, introduced both a Registration Act to classify all South Africans into separate racial categories (White, Coloured, Bantu and African) and a Group Areas Act to force members of these different races to live and work in designated areas. Recent appeals to the government by the ANC to overturn the Group Areas Act and the Suppression of Communism Act as well as the pass law had been unsuccessful. The Defiance Campaign was designed to make a mockery of the petty regulations which now governed the lives of non-whites.

Across the country, thousands were organised by the campaign's volunteer-in-chief, Nelson Mandela, to invite arrest by defying 'Europeans Only' notices in railway stations and post offices. Pass and curfew laws were broken after the police had been warned when and where the offences would occur – for again arrest was the aim. Lawbreakers were to choose jail rather than bail or a fine, thus overloading the judicial and prison systems and causing chaos for the authorities. Organised protests continued until the end of the year, resulting in more than 8,000 mainly peaceful arrests and convictions, though there was little impact on the advance of apartheid.

According to Winnie, the Defiance Campaign did have an effect on the politicised students of Shawbury High, who she later said were inspired enough to risk expulsion and stage their own act of defiance. In her version of the history of this episode, a school strike was called for, and Winnie was forced to choose whether she should sacrifice her own education to protest against the government. She said she refused to join the strike. She was due to write her final matriculation exams, her father had exerted himself to send her to this particular school, she had further education to go to, for which she needed to matriculate. If she joined the other students in the strike, she stood to lose all she had worked so hard for. In one account of the Shawbury School strike she aligned herself with the school authorities, never mentioning she had even considered joining the protest.[34]

'I was in my final year of matric, and the students in the rural set-up didn't understand what was happening. They were politicised, but did not know exactly what the Defiance Campaign meant nationwide. They heard "defiance" so they defied authority in the school, they defied us the prefects. "Away with authority" was their slogan, and the school nearly closed down. Very few took exams. We were taking our final exams, but the rest of the school followed the boycott.'

In an interview given for the book *Lives of Courage*, a number of years later, when she was far more militant, she turned this version on its head:

'I first heard the names of Mandela and Tambo in 1953 when I was doing my matric. There was a Defiance Campaign in Johannesburg at that time, and I heard that these leaders had told the country to defy unjust laws. The level of consciousness at our country high school was already far advanced at that time, and our interpretation of that instruction was that we must defy school authority. We didn't even write exams that year because we went on strike because of insufficient food and complaints about the general administration of the school.'[35]

In fact everyone in Winnie's year took exams in 1952, which makes it extremely unlikely that anyone was expelled. While the results were not brilliant, most of her year got low passes. School records show that Winnie came fourth in her class of seventeen in the internal part of the exam which she wrote in September, and that she passed every subject in December except higher Xhosa.

The self-interest which influenced her memory of this episode was to remain – distinct from her kindness, her generosity and her courage – a dominant characteristic throughout her political career. She would do anything in her power to challenge and change the racist order of her country, and it often suited her to do so.

Chapter Two

In 1918 Nelson Rolihlahla (the Xhosa name means 'stirring up trouble') Mandela had been born into the royal family of Thembu at Qunu about thirty kilometres south of Umtata, and 250 kilometres from Bizana. In many ways Mandela's background was similar to Winnie's. Like the Pondo, the Thembu were an independent Xhosa-speaking tribe in which the Mandelas had substantial authority. Mandela's father, Henry, was a councillor – Chief Councillor in fact to the Paramount Chief of the Thembu, but according to Mandela's sister, Leabie, Henry Mandela was deposed from his position for insubordination.[1]

Unlike Columbus Madikizela, Henry Mandela had not converted to Christianity and was polygamous. Fanny, Mandela's mother was his third wife, and he already had a number of children from his first two – including a son. Mandela was the only male offspring of this third union (Henry would go on to take a fourth wife), and he lived with his two sisters in his mother's group of huts. Like Gertrude, Fanny was a devout Christian and Mandela was therefore raised both in his traditional religion and as a Methodist. When not attending missionary school he ploughed the fields, rode horses, herded cattle, played with sticks and listened to tales of his history from village elders. Like Winnie, the stories Mandela heard as a child had a lasting influence on his political development. Some were of white injustice – though told with less festering hatred than Winnie would experience in Bizana. But it was the description of the structure and organisation of early African societies which fascinated Mandela. Always a thoughtful and analytical child, he developed a passion for democratic order, rather than a desire for vengeance against past grievances.

'There were no classes, no rich or poor and no exploitation of man by man. All men were free and equal and this was the foundation of government,' he later said when speaking of his attraction to early African history. 'In such a society are contained the seeds of evolutionary democracy in which none will be held in slavery or servitude, and in which poverty, want and insecurity will be no more. This is the inspiration which, even today, inspires me and my colleagues in our political struggle.'[2]

When Mandela was between the ages of ten and twelve, his father died.[3] Before his death, Henry Mandela had made arrangements for his son to be sent to the court of his nephew, the local Thembu chief, Jongintaba Dalindyebo. Accordingly, Mandela went across Transkei to live as Jongintaba's ward, at the royal household in Mqekezweni. He arrived a shy and lonely boy, dressed in the typical school uniform of khaki shorts and a khaki shirt. The transition was made easier by the presence of Jongintaba's son, Justice. The two cousins were insepar-able. They shared a hut in the settlement before going to boarding school together, and were best friends throughout their teenage years. Together they studied English, Xhosa, History and Geography, and together they spent their youth in the curious mix of Western and African culture common in South Africa. Though they participated in the traditional circumcision ceremony which marked the transition from childhood to manhood for young African males (five weeks of naked seclusion devoted to hunting, tribal history and traditional song and dance) they also spent hours mastering the fox trot and waltz. Throughout this period, Mandela's education and keep were entirely paid for by Jongintaba whose altruism was remembered and appreciated in later years.

After matriculating from Healdtown Methodist High School, the two cousins went as Bachelor of Arts students to Fort Hare University College in the Eastern Cape. It was here that Mandela met his future comrade and law partner, Oliver Tambo. One year older than Mandela, Tambo coincidentally came from Winnie's district of Bizana, though from a much less affluent family than the Madikizelas. Tambo was academically brilliant. He had been educated at the Holy Cross Mission in Flagstaff, before winning a place at St Peter's School in Johannesburg – arguably the best school in the country. He was then awarded a scholarship to study for a law degree at Fort Hare.

Mandela and Justice immediately became involved in politics, joining the Students' Representative Council. While war broke out in Europe, Mandela took on the authorities at Fort Hare, mainly protesting against the students' poor living conditions. Eventually, as the students' representatives grew increasingly assertive, the university authorities hit back and the Council's powers were curtailed, prompting a student boycott of lectures. Those who cut classes were automatically suspended and Mandela and Justice were sent home. Tambo completed his degree in 1941, and re-enrolled at Fort Hare for an education diploma. But by then he too was active on behalf of his fellow students and was expelled in 1942.)

Mandela's suspension was to be a turning point. Jongintaba insisted that he and Justice return to Fort Hare and apologise for their recalcitrance. But Mandela learned that in his absence from home arrangements had been made not only to prepare him for the chieftainship (for which he was eligible by birth), but for marriage as well. A local bride had already been selected for him. Reacting more against the idea of an arranged tribal marriage and a lifetime of rural leadership than of returning to Fort Hare, he decided to run away. To finance his escape he stole from the man who had unstintingly given to him as a parent for the past decade. It was a double betrayal. He defied the man who had brought him up and took from him to do so, selling two of Jongintaba's cattle to a white trader to finance his journey to Johannesburg.[4]

He arrived in a vibrant, bustling city. The beginning of the 1940s was boomtime as Johannesburg expanded its industrial base. Whereas, previously, workers had come to the Rand to go down the mines, South Africa's involvement in the Second World War had caused a shift from mining to manufacturing. Engineering, munitions, chemicals and electronics were growing industries keeping their costs down by hiring cheap unskilled or semi-skilled black workers. Even semi-skills were valuable. For the first time the migrant workforce was encouraged to put down roots. Before, only adult males had gone to the cities, but now whole families moved away from the poverty of the countryside to the promise of a new urban life. Conditions were for the most part still appalling – one in four urban Africans lived under cardboard, hessian sacking, wood or corrugated iron in the newly erected squatter camps[5] – but there was a new vitality in the growing community of non-white city dwellers and a new culture. Street life was brash, colourful and giddy. There was music, poetry and dance. There was crime and drink and brawls and noise. There were jazz bars and dance halls, dark cafés and bright lights. It was heady, exhilarating and dangerous.

It was also increasingly political. The South African government – which had voted to join the war by a narrow margin – found itself in an awkward situation. Non-whites were called upon to join the army not as bona fide soldiers, but as trench diggers and drivers. Racial discrimination, in other words, was continuing in a country which had joined a world war to fight racism, and non-Europeans questioned why they were expected to support such a war. In July 1940, an Indian doctor, Yusuf Dadoo, who would later be a key Defiance Campaign organiser, was arrested for publishing a leaflet addressed to non-Europeans, which put the question: 'You are being asked to support the war for freedom, justice and democracy. Do you enjoy the fruits of freedom, justice and democracy? What you do enjoy is pass and poll-tax laws, segregation, white labour policy, low wages and high rents, poverty, unemployment and vicious colour-bar laws.'[6]

Dadoo was a communist. Until the German invasion of the Soviet Union in June 1941, the Communist Party was highly active, waging a campaign against the government's military recruitment of non-Europeans. With the Soviet Union threatened, the Party did an abrupt about-face and gave whole-hearted support to South Africa's war effort. Other organisations stepped into the breach and kept up pressure on the government. The ANC, in particular, working closely with Indian organisations, tried to win concessions for blacks before it supported the war. Many younger ANC members felt that ANC President-General Dr Alfred Xuma lacked sufficient aggression, and that the Congress should be more militant and more of an instigator, rather than taking its lead from communists and Indians.

Xuma was married to a black American, Madie Hall, whom he had met while studying in the United States. The President-General's wife, herself the first elected President of the newly established women's section of the ANC, was a social worker. Drawing from her experience in America, she believed that black emancipation was a gradual process, only possible through economic independence. It may have been her influence over her husband which caused him to become increasingly out of step with the impatience of the Congress's newly recruited youth. In 1943 they formed their own Youth League – a group far more militant than the main body of the ANC. It was this group that Mandela joined shortly after his arrival in Johannesburg.

He was introduced to politics by Walter Sisulu. Sisulu was born in 1912 in the Transkei, the son of a white father – whom he had never known – and a black mother. He had been living in Johannesburg for ten years before he met Mandela. He worked as an estate agent to become financially independent and was deeply engrossed in politics. Sisulu had been active in campaigning to prevent Africans from joining the South African army – and shortly before he met Mandela he had joined the ANC.

Mandela's arrival in Johannesburg had not been entirely uncomplicated. He was on the run for theft. He had to leave his first job as a mine policeman when he heard he was being looked for on account of the stolen cattle. (Jongintaba found out where he was, telegraphed the mine about the cattle and Mandela lost his job.) Eventually he returned to his guardian to make peace. He left Justice behind with the tribe, but got Jongintaba to agree not only to allow him to return to Johannesburg, but also to resume paying him an allowance while he was there.

Mandela was anxious to resume his education. It was Sisulu who made it possible for him to pursue both education and political issues. Initially, he gave Mandela a job in his estate agency at £2.00 a month plus commission, though when he heard that his new friend wanted to finish his B.A. he paid for his tuition at the Wits law faculty instead. Mandela lived in the Sisulu home in the black township of Soweto while he finished his degree, and he bought the suit for his graduation with Sisulu money. He got a part-time job as an articled clerk through Sisulu connections, and three years after his arrival in Johannesburg he married a Sisulu cousin, a shy, pretty nurse called Evelyn Ntoko Mase.

Mandela was as single-minded about romance as he was about work and politics. He met Evelyn, asked her to go steady within days and had proposed to her within months. Evelyn fell in love immediately.

The two married at the Native Commissioner's Court in Johannesburg in 1944. Their marriage was not consolidated under tribal law because the short ceremony had not included any payment of *lobola*, the Xhosa tradition of purchasing a wife. An important symbol, regarded as the knot tying two families together, lobola legally established a marriage under Xhosa law, and the absence of its payment meant a marriage was not subject to legal tribal intricacies. Lobola worked on the opposite principle to a western dowry. Instead of the bride's father endowing the groom's family with money, gifts or land, he and the bride's other male relations received heads of cattle from the groom. It was a practice disapproved of and discouraged by missionaries who felt it immoral for women to be bought and sold. However, the application of lobola was a far more elaborate custom than the mere acquisition of a human property. It gave a woman security, the right to assistance – should she need it – from any of her male relatives who had received the gift. That security extended to her children who were entitled to whatever was left of the payment once they were adult.

Within a year of their wedding Evelyn was pregnant. Mandela's personal life was taken care of now. They moved into a house close to Walter Sisulu and his new wife, Albertina. While Evelyn's nursing salary paid most of their bills, Mandela continued to study law at Wits.

The newly married Mandelas and Sisulus were among the first to respond to Dr Xuma's 1943 call to the black youth of the country to become more politically active. When the African National Congress Youth League (ANCYL) was formed less than a year later, Nelson Mandela, Walter Sisulu and Oliver Tambo were founding members. By 1948, Mandela had been elected general secretary of the Youth League and had begun travelling all over the country.

At home, Evelyn had given birth first to a son, Thembi, and then in 1948 to a daughter, Makaziwe, who only lived for nine months. Mandela was little support to his wife. He was hardly ever at home. In his place, his mother, Fanny, moved in with Evelyn, providing emotional comfort and practical help. Evelyn, too, was becoming politically active, joining the nurses' union at the behest of her friend Adelaide, the fiancée of Oliver Tambo. Mandela encouraged his wife to find time to participate in the political process as much as possible, making it clear to her how much such involvement pleased him.

With their increasing commitments, the young Mandelas were a busy couple. The Defiance Campaign may not have succeeded in forcing the repeal of laws against which it had protested, but it had created a new unity between anti-apartheid organisations. The ANC and the S.A. Indian Congress had worked closely together in organising the campaign, now they were joined by the Congress of Democrats – a white organisation formed after the dissolution of the Communist Party, which pledged to fight for equal rights for non-Europeans. For the first time, there was a real coherence in the fight against racism between blacks, Indians and whites.

The alliance between the groups began informally. Meetings were nothing more than dinners and drinks in people's homes. This was an intellectual, middle-class group of friends – writers, teachers, lawyers, social workers, nurses and doctors – who shared the same passionate ideology of equal rights for all. As their debates went on into the early hours of the morning, they could not have known they would be banned, arrested, imprisoned, tortured, exiled, and in some cases murdered over the next quarter of the century. This was the group which formed the nucleus of the ANC, which became the umbrella under which all anti-apartheid associations gathered. And it was the multi-racial complexion of this band of friends which resulted in the ANC adopting a policy of non-racism.

These friends of the Mandelas, the Sisulus and the Tambos were devoted to each other, but to outsiders they could appear elitist, and their unswerving commitment to their cause could be intimidating.

Mandela was an immensely popular and admired member of this group. 'It was not only his splendid physique and attractive personality that made him such an outstanding popular leader', wrote Hilda Bernstein, years later. 'He responded to challenge. And when confronted with difficulties his political strength and understanding grew.'[7]

Generally, Mandela would be gone from the house at dawn, either to his part-time job, or to Wits, to meet his political friends. Sometimes it was to box; he had become an enthusiastic amateur boxer. He rarely returned until late in the evening, though once home he joined in looking after the children, helping with the cooking and entertaining. The couple's second son, Makgatho, was born in 1950, and they had another daughter whom they named Makaziwe, after the baby who had died six years earlier.

In the first years of their marriage, during the latter part of the 1940s and the early 1950s, they had a varied and happy life. Mandela enjoyed taking his children out for treats, to the cinema, to watch him box, or just to run and play games. But he was at home less and less. He had been elected one of four of the Congress deputy presidents and was volunteer-in-chief of the Defiance Campaign. This required weeks of travel as he crossed the country, recruiting volunteers and explaining the purpose and procedure, not only of the Campaign but of the ANC. At the same time, Evelyn had temporarily moved to Durban to study midwifery, and was visited by her husband when his work brought him to Natal. It was on her return to Johannesburg at the conclusion of her course that trouble between the couple began.

As the government clamped down in the aftermath of the Defiance Campaign, Mandela was banned for six months under the Riotous Assemblies Act, which temporarily slowed him down. Banning severely curtailed the freedom of an individual, forcing him to obey curfews and report to police regularly. Because they were intended to hamper the activities of the government's political opponents, banning orders also prevented individuals from attending meetings, joining organisations, or being quoted in newspapers. Those who were banned could not go out at night, move house, or leave town. In essence a banning order served as a form of imprisonment without incarceration. Once his banning order was lifted his political and legal work resumed at the same frenetic pace. Though he explained to his children about the many meetings he had to attend and the importance of the struggle, Mandela's lengthy absences were no longer solely attributable to politics. Rumours began to circulate that he was having an affair with Lillian Ngoyi, a self-taught rather than well-educated, charismatic, powerful, founder member of the newly established ANC Women's League. Even Evelyn grew suspicious that he was involved with someone. Later she described this period of growing estrangement:

> I did not believe the rumour at first, but unable to bear it, I turned to Nelson. Who else could I have turned to? He was angry that I questioned his fidelity. The woman was an important ANC leader and that was all there was to it he said. But the gossip continued and there were those who tried to console me by claiming he was bewitched. There was another woman and this one started coming home, walking into our bedroom, following him to the bathroom. What was all this about I demanded, and declared that I would not allow it . . . Nelson was enraged. He moved his bed into the sitting room. He grew increasingly cold and distant. I was desperate. I went to see Walter. I don't think Nelson ever forgave me for that . . . He stopped eating at home and took his washing to a cousin. Then he started sleeping out.[8]

In the end it was Evelyn who left, frozen out by her husband. Mandela no longer loved his wife – he told his cousin Kaiser as much when he tried to patch things up between them. The family life which had been so promising and bright had disintegrated. On the rare occasions when Mandela was at home, he barely spoke to his wife. For a time Evelyn tried to heal what she eventually realised was an irreparable rift. But once she understood she had no marriage left to save, she moved into a hostel for nurses. Mandela never contacted her or went to see her there. Eventually she set up house with her brother. By then eight-year-old Thembi was at boarding school, but Makgatho and Makaziwe divided their time between their two parents. Or to be more precise between their parents' two households: Mandela was often away when the children went back to their original home, so his mother would take care of them. A year after moving out of the house, Evelyn read an announcement in the newspaper: Mandela was divorcing her.

Nelson and Evelyn Mandela had been married for nine years when Winnie Madikizela boarded a train and travelled to Johannesburg. The long journey across the country from Transkei, north to Pietermaritzburg in Natal, crossing into the south-eastern corner of the Transvaal, leaving the Drakensberg Mountain Range to the east, and then travelling directly west to Johannesburg took about three days. The countryside was rich and varied – soaring peaks, followed by miles of flat land – but travelling to Johannesburg by train in 1953 was an experience which made her – as it did so many other rural-dwellers – fully aware for the first time of the limitations imposed on blacks by apartheid. Conditions on South Africa's trains reflected the disparity in living conditions: at the front of the train were the comfortable first-class compartments for whites, while blacks travelled at the back in dirty third-class carriages. 'I was carrying my provisions in a cardboard box . . . I was a country girl, to me there was nothing wrong with carrying a cardboard box on my head.'⁹ The stories she had heard as a child were little preparation for the reality of being treated as a third-class citizen, though racial inequality became an accepted rather than a challenged fact of Winnie's life as she settled into Johannesburg.

On her arrival at the station, she was met by two wives of the directors of the Jan Hofmeyr School who took her to board at the Helping Hand Hostel, a respectable hostel for working women and students. Jan Hofmeyr was roughly divided in half between urban and rural students and Winnie – coming from a country background – was by no means unique. She has said on numerous occasions since that she was the first rural student to be accepted by the college – the exception being made in her case because she was so outstanding.

She did stand out. By the time she arrived in Johannesburg she had turned into a staggeringly beautiful young student, tall and slender, having lost the last of her puppy fat, with enormous, luminous, dark eyes and an air of vulnerability which in an instant could be replaced by a smile and an impish vitality. She was enchanting and seductive.

Men would stand and stare as she walked down the street. Some would whistle, others would call out to her. She and her friend Marcia Fink were protected from any unwanted advances by a married member of their class, Ellen Khuzwayo (later to be a highly respected author), who made sure that absolutely nobody got near her two charges, either in the street or at the clubs and socials where they spent their evenings. If Winnie minded the attention she was attracting, she didn't show it.

Everyday life at the hostel was far more free and easy than it had been at boarding school. The girls lent clothes and make-up and walked in and out of each other's rooms and bathrooms without bothering to knock. There was very little privacy. Winnie found this aspect of her new life intolerable. Rather than dressing and undressing in front of the others – which she found shameful and embarrassing – she bathed and dressed in private. She was ashamed of being naked and felt awkward and unsophisticated in the company of the more fashionable older women. Though her wardrobe was initially fairly basic, she was sent enough money and clothes from home to fit in with the others. But she slept in her petticoat, rather than a nightgown, and would dress hurriedly and furtively each morning. Her obsession with physical privacy was so extreme that the hostel residents grew suspicious and for a time a rumour circulated that she had something wrong with her.

Out in the big city, however, she was neither particularly shy nor reserved. Nor was she terribly interested in politics. Her arrival in Johannesburg coincided with a new period of female political activism, as apartheid began limiting the movements of women as well as men. In this regard the 1952 Defiance Campaign had proved to be a watershed, drawing thousands of women into the ANC. Two years later, Johannesburg was the scene of the launch of the non-racial Federation of South African Women (affiliated to the ANC's Women's League), and the adoption of a Women's Charter, committing women to an active role in the struggle. Much of this zeal for reform was felt at the Helping Hand Hostel, where residents were for the most part ANC members. As at Shawbury, Winnie was surrounded by militancy while she remained comparatively diffident. Her detachment reflected the attitude of her fellow students at the college who paid some attention to the activities of Nelson Mandela simply because he was one of the patrons of their school. But there was no really strong political element at Jan Hofmeyr, and Winnie was not unique in her lack of interest in active political participation. Busy students were encouraged to adopt the philosophy that social workers were peaceful people. Activism, they were told, was for dealing with social problems.

As she studied the theory and practice of a social worker, Winnie was obviously more of a skilled practitioner than an intellect. Capable, but not brilliant at mastering the theory, she shone at practical work. She was, above all, extremely enthusiastic. But she was not the school's star pupil, as many later thought. While it is true that she did well enough to be awarded the Martha Washington scholarship, endowments were plentiful, designed not so much to reward excellence but to help students pay their bills. In the 1949 *Handbook on Race Relations in South Africa*, the Jan Hofmeyr School is mentioned. 'It is financed by annual block grants from the Department of Education (£4,000) and the Johannesburg City Council (£1,000 of free accommodation), bursaries and private contributions.'[10] It was more unusual for a student not to receive any financial help, than to be awarded a bursary.

Winnie's first practical work took place in the Salvation Army Delinquent Girls' Home. It was an unusual experience, she said later, because where she came from there was no such thing as a delinquent girl. At first the girls in the home struck her as being no different from those back in Bizana, though some were obviously deeply disturbed –or as she later put it, 'uncontrollably quarrelsome'. Her way of controlling these girls was to organise them into teams for games. She made them feel involved and they were able to let off steam within an ordered structure.

Winnie played sports with her fellow students too. She stood out for her combativeness as much as for her skill; she was nicknamed Lady Tarzan and the Amazon Queen. Her teachers often noticed her beauty more than her talent. 'She was not a particularly outstanding student, but she was a very nice girl. I would almost say a "dumb blonde". We – the staff and students – all liked her very much. She was a nice kind of country girl, quietly spoken, she had a nice round face and curves,' commented one of her directors. Beryl Unterhalter who taught her first at Jan Hofmeyr and later at Wits University described her as: 'A good student, lively and vivacious, you know, bouncy and bright, and she was remarkably beautiful. She started out shy and unsophisticated but I saw her blossom over time. You began to notice her beauty and she was very charming.'

'I only remember that she was very good looking,' remarked another member of staff.

Winnie would always be extremely proud of her Jan Hofmeyr training. Part of the course included one field trip. For this she was assigned to the Ncora-Tsolo Rural Welfare Centre back in Transkei. The Centre, which had been established by the Jan Hofmeyr School, served a vast area to the south of Pondoland. Winnie was responsible for feeding the starving and treating diseases caused by malnutrition, though her intention was to return to Johannesburg to practise as an urban social worker.

Returning home to visit her family during her field work, she learned to her dismay that a marriage had been arranged for her. Surprisingly, for one who had avoided his own tribal responsibilities and gone to such lengths to provide western education and training for his daughter, Columbus had agreed that she should wed Qaquali, the son of a local chief. Like her future husband, she balked at what she saw as an archaic practice and, disrupting her work, fled back to Johannesburg.

Winnie would have to dodge another offer of marriage soon afterwards. The next proposal came from the chief of Tembuland, Kaiser Matanzima, coincidentally the cousin who had tried to act as intermediary between Nelson and Evelyn Mandela. Tall and elegant, Matanzima was politically at the opposite end of the spectrum from his activist cousin. He was to become a highly controversial, widely hated black leader: his willingness to comply with the South African government in the dismantling of tribal institutions and the establishment of government-controlled Bantu homelands would eventually provoke three attempts on his life. Winnie would say subsequently that she was aware of his rigid, dictatorial manner from the start, though for a while she certainly gave him a great deal of her time and attention.

She first met him at a tribal meeting in Transkei, while on her field trip, but their relationship did not begin until she had graduated from Jan Hofmeyr and begun her clinical training at Baragwanath Hospital in Johannesburg.

When her formal education and training was over, her family marked her transition into the workforce by travelling to Johannesburg for her graduation from Jan Hofmeyr. Despite the odds, she had done well. Others in her family had not been as lucky. Her younger brother Lungile, long thought of as the most brilliant member of the family, had won a place at Fort Hare University College where he begun studying science with exceptional promise. But within a year (shortly before Winnie's graduation) he had suffered a complete mental breakdown from which he would never recover.

No one ever found out what was the matter with Lungile. He went in and out of hospital and from specialist to specialist but without ever being satisfactorily diagnosed. He spent the next ten years at home. 'A mental case,' his sister Princess said. 'I think he was mentally disturbed because our mother passed away when he was very young. So I think it started when he was very young. Our oldest sister, Irene, was also mentally disturbed. Fortunately she got a doctor. He gave her the right medicine, and after two years she was all right.'[11]

According to his stepmother, after his mental collapse Lungile was unable to recognise anyone and became very silent. He was however able to laugh and occasionally told jokes. He would sit quietly in a corner, doing little. He did not need much care apart from when his headaches came on. They were numerous and agonising. Lungile finally died of pneumonia ten years after his breakdown.

So there was all the more reason to celebrate Winnie's success. She had worked hard, she had done well, she was about to take up a position as social worker at Baragwanath Hospital. (She subsequently became widely acclaimed as South Africa's first black medical social worker, despite the fact that black graduates from Jan Hofmeyr had automatically progressed to Johannesburg's largest black hospital since 1947.) She was good looking, took care of her appearance; her early aggression seemed a thing of the past. This was a proud moment for all her family.

Winnie was a remarkably effective and dedicated social worker. Confronting poverty and a host of bureaucracies in a rapidly expanding society required more than the enthusiasm she was known for at college. The patience and resourcefulness she had demonstrated with her younger brothers and sisters were now put to daily, professional use. So was the defiance. No obstacle was insurmountable, nor was any rebuff accepted by Winnie. If college had taught her that social workers should be activists in dealing with social problems, she was able to put that theory into practice at Baragwanath. Much of her time was spent on the paediatric ward, arranging supervision and housing for children whose parents were incapable of caring for them. She would never abandon this role of official surrogate for children in need. Like her father, she eventually provided food and shelter for a number of deprived children herself and over the years would pay many sets of school fees.

Her job also included dealing with the employers of those who were too sick to work. And here she would brook no argument from an employer if a doctor prescribed sick leave for his patient. She began to get a name as someone whose boldness in taking on authorities got results. Encouraged by the admiration of her fellow workers, she grew more inflexible in official matters, an attitude which strongly contrasted with her compassion and gentleness for those in her care. She went out of her way to help those in need, not just waiting for clients to come into the hospital, but bringing them in herself when she found them on the streets. She brought in men and women, boys and girls, badgering doctors to treat the ill and then finding them somewhere to go.

It was during this period that she was re-introduced to Kaiser Matanzima when he came to tour the hospital with a group of VIPs.

Though he had no recollection of having previously met her, this time he was captivated by the young, alluring and dynamic member of the social welfare department. He began taking her out, going to a great deal of effort to make their assignations romantic and memorable. Candle-lit dinners for two were a favourite of his. When he returned to Transkei he began writing to her, and she responded to his letters. But when she heard he had begun arrangements to make her his second or third wife, she got cold feet. It may have been that marriage to Matanzima, like marriage to Qaquali, meant a return to tribal life (something she found intolerable), or that Matanzima was – as she would later imply – too politically inflexible. The most likely explanation for her resistance to her ardent admirer, who – whatever his personal or social limitations – was a considerable catch, was that she was already in love with Nelson Mandela.

They were bound to meet. Winnie had become a good friend of Adelaide Tsukudu who was also a nurse at Baragwanath living at the Helping Hand Hostel. Adelaide's fiancé was Oliver Tambo, who had set up a law practice with Mandela. Through Adelaide, Winnie had already met Tambo and discovered they were both from Bizana. She'd also already seen Mandela once when she had gone to court and watched him act on behalf of a friend of hers. He didn't notice her then, but she had been bowled over by his performance.

In the end they did meet through Oliver and Adelaide, but by accident. She and Adelaide were being driven home from Baragwanath by Tambo when they stopped at a delicatessen for something to eat, realised they had no money, noticed Mandela in the shop and asked him to pay. Tambo took the opportunity to introduce Mandela – who by then had been separated from Evelyn for more than a year – to Winnie. After the brief encounter Mandela rang her almost immediately to ask her out. When Winnie got the call she was so overwhelmed she couldn't work for the rest of the day. 'I was of course petrified – he was much older than me and he was a patron of my school of social work. We had never seen him, he was just a name on the letterheads; he was too important for us students to even know him.'[12] She went through everything in her wardrobe, rejecting dress after dress as too schoolgirlish before finally borrowing something suitably sophisticated – an extremely uncomfortable suit – from a friend.

Their first date set the pattern of their relationship. Though it was a Sunday, Mandela was at work. He sent a friend to pick her up and bring her to his office. When he was finally able to leave, he took her for a quick lunch in an Indian restaurant, where she hated the food and felt completely out of her depth in the presence of the overpowering older man. He was amused at her reaction to the spiciness of the curry, even though her inability to eat it almost reduced her to tears. After lunch he drove her into the country. Walking in the veld he confided, among other things, that he had actually called her to ask for her help in raising money for the ANC. 'Politicians are not lovers,' Winnie said years later when commenting on their first day together.[13]

That Mandela called Winnie so quickly gives some indication of how captivated he was by her, for he had less time than ever to call his own. The National Party government which had been re-elected in 1953 not only passed new legislation mandating how and where urban Africans could and – more importantly – could not live, work and learn, it also began cracking down on those who disagreed with their policies.

Two laws passed in 1953 were designed to limit the activities of the growing anti-apartheid movement. The Criminal Law Amendment Act deemed it a criminal offence to oppose a law by breaking it – thus outlawing passive resistance – while the Public Safety Act for the first time gave the government the power to declare a State of Emergency. With one law intensifying government control while the other closed off the main avenue of opposition, the ANC was forced to adjust the tenor of its campaign against apartheid. It was inevitable in the new climate of legal restrictions that the Mandela and Tambo law office would become a practice devoted to challenging the government's status quo. 'If when we started our law partnership, we had not been rebels against apartheid, our experiences in our offices would have remedied the deficiency', Tambo wrote later. 'We had risen to professional status in our community, but every case in court, every visit to the prisons to interview clients, reminded us of the humiliation and the suffering burned into our people.'[14]

They were busier than ever. More than a year had been spent on the framing of a Freedom Charter – 'The People Shall Govern!' – which called for the setting aside of all apartheid laws and practices and the restoration of the country's wealth to all of its people. The charter ended: 'These freedoms we will fight for, side by side, throughout our lives, until we have won our liberty.' The fight immediately intensified. Within three months of the publication of the Charter, the Special Branch had raided more than 400 homes and offices, seizing books, pamphlets and documents. A year later 156 arrests were made. Mandela, Tambo and Sisulu were picked up, as were ANC President-General Chief Luthuli and the head of the ANC's Cape section,

Professor Z.K. Matthews. Joe Slovo and Ruth First, Ismail Meer, Lillian Ngoyi, Helen Joseph and Lionel Bernstein were also among those charged. Virtually the entire top layer of South African activists finally came to court in December 1956 to be charged with planning the violent overthrow of the government.

The budding relationship between Mandela and Winnie took place against this hectic political and legal backdrop. But Mandela still made time to see her. She met him at his office, she occasionally attended the trial, and she spent a lot of time with him while others claimed his attention. From the start, when seeking Mandela's company, she found herself in competition with the struggle for racial equality, and in that sense she would always remain in opposition to it. Even in the Indian restaurant he was continually pestered by people coming for consultations, none of whom he turned away. Winnie sat there feeling left out. She didn't fit in – not with these people and their considerable problems.

The Treason Trial, as it was known, was to continue from 1956 until 1961, and it fostered and solidified a camaraderie among the defendants, who had spent day after day together for several months by the time they were introduced to Winnie. In the intimate environment of court, friendships were intensifying. Defendants and lawyers were becoming more like family than friends. 'For a time [the trial] had been the focus of attention both inside South Africa and outside, the inspiration for political action, the meeting point for committees and organisations', wrote Hilda Bernstein, whose husband Rusty was one of the accused. 'It was awful, wonderful, inspiring and boring beyond words. For years, attending the treason court was a way of life for those involved.'[15]

This was the well-educated, highly active, multi-racial group in which Mandela had been a central figure for more than five years. It was not surprising that Winnie felt out of her depth in this closely knit band of comrades. She was friendly on the surface; she laughed a lot and seemed warmhearted as well as high-spirited. But with the exception of British-born Helen Joseph who became one of her closest friends, she was never able to let down her guard completely with Mandela's fellow accused in the Treason Trial.

Like Winnie, Helen Joseph (who was twenty-nine years her senior) combined kindness with a determination to have her own way. A graduate in English from King's College, London, Joseph had moved to Durban from England in the early 1930s, married a dentist and lived a life of bridge games and gardening. During the war she had taken a course in welfare information which gave her the ability to lecture women in the Air Force on current affairs. Thus begun a passionate interest in politics and civil rights. When the end of the war coincided with the end of her marriage she left Durban and for the next ten years ran various African community centres in Johannesburg and Cape Town, before working in medical aid. She joined every activist organisation she could (the Congress of Democrats, the Federation of South African Women, the Defend the Constitution Women's league). She was usually a founding member, often a leader – and was quickly targeted by the Special Branch as trouble.

Joseph was like a mother to Winnie. She took Winnie under her wing, listened to her problems, dispensed advice, offered support, and generally made it known that she was someone for Winnie to turn to. Mandela called her Winnie's guardian angel.

Winnie was tremendously influenced by Joseph, admiring her commitment and applauding her defiance. For the first time she began to learn in detail about the aims of the activists in her country's struggle and the effect which that struggle had had on their lives. Though her childhood and her social work experience at Baragwanath meant she was no stranger to the deprivation caused by racial oppression, it was not until she became involved with Mandela and Joseph that she was introduced to the consequences of challenging the government – persecution. Fighting the restrictions of a suppressive state was something she understood and was far more drawn to than any hypothetical discourse or analysis of the country's future. Just as she shone at the practice rather than the theory of social work, so in politics she preferred action to discussion. The child who had settled disputes by using her fists, and still believed that the shortest route to getting her own way was physical, could organise and enjoy a demonstration, a rally or a march, while feeling bored and uncomfortable discussing the ideological motive behind the event. This was why she was so drawn to Joseph who would never take no for an answer.

Meanwhile Mandela and Winnie were falling deeply in love. Physically, they were an outstanding couple. Both tall – Winnie was now 5 feet 8 inches and Mandela was 6 foot 4 – they filled a room by entering it. Electrified by each other's presence, they glowed together. Individually they were each highly charismatic, as a couple they were overpowering. Theirs was an extremely physical relationship. According to their friend Indris Naidoo, they always held hands when they were together, whether in the ANC offices or walking down the street. At meetings they sat together, creating an atmosphere of intimacy in a hall or crowded room. When Winnie was with him, Mandela was unable to take his eyes off her, and she – always conscious of his attention – luxuriated in it with an intoxicating feline sensuality. Her lover was irrevocably under her spell.

And she adored him. She would do anything for him. She remained in awe of him, even as they drew closer. She admired his intellect and his disciplined life-style while responding to his authoritative manner. It was rare for Mandela to consult with Winnie about his intentions, even those regarding her. If he wanted to see her, he would send a car for her or telephone her and tell her to be ready at a certain time. He was too busy to organise their life any other way, and it was not in his nature to do so. One of their earliest dates consisted of Winnie watching him work out at the gym. Often he took her to meetings with him. Winnie willingly went at his bidding. Somehow it made him seem more powerful.

Life with Mandela was not all work, however. Both were great lovers of jazz; the couple often spent their Sunday evenings at Uncle Joe's café in Fordsburg listening to musicians Dollar Brand, Kippie Moeketsei and Dudu Pukane. They ate out when they could, continuing to indulge Mandela's love for prawn curry which Winnie gradually got used to and eventually learned to cook.

In many ways Mandela was like a father to Winnie and she was intelligent enough to realise it. She described an incident on their first date: when walking in the veld the strap on her shoe broke and she had to walk back to the car barefoot. 'He held my hand as my father would hold a little girl's hand', she later wrote.[16] The sixteen years showed, both physically and in the way they behaved towards each other. Winnie was a young 23-year-old when they met, and Mandela, who was nearly forty, acted his age. He became her teacher, expanding her cultural horizons, introducing her to his friends, instructing her in the finer points of the struggle against apartheid. He even tried to teach her how to drive, but gave up in exasperation when her inability to do exactly as he said led to ferocious arguments between them. Winnie hadn't entirely given up her spirit: she was still capable of flying off the handle. Mandela laughed at her volatility and often joked that he was the only man who could tame her. He found it attractive. It was, after all, another aspect of her passion.

Chapter Three

'It's this week's No.1 social announcement. Attorney Nelson Mandela and social worker Miss Winnie Madikizela are holding a party today to announce their engagement. The party is being held at the home of Mr and Mrs P. Mzaidume at Orlando West. Winnie is the third daughter of Mr K.K. and the late Mrs Madikizela of Bizana, Transkei. The wedding is being planned for June 14.' (*Golden City Post*, 25 May 1958.)

They were married within a year of their first meeting. Mandela was still banned and on trial, so there could be no protracted celebration or honeymoon. Writing in the same newspaper of the forthcoming ceremony, columnist Arthur Maimane commented that Mandela would be: 'The first bridegroom I know of who won't be able to make the usual – and often boring – "my wife and I" speech at the wedding reception. He is banned from addressing public gatherings.'[1] There was no lengthy sentimental proposal either. With his divorce granted, Mandela assumed that Winnie would answer yes to any question of marriage. So he took her out and showed her the house of a dressmaker he knew. Winnie should go there, he said, to arrange her wedding dress, asking as an afterthought how many bridesmaids she would like. She was too much in love to query his method of proposing, she later said, feeling they had an understanding which transcended discussion.[2] Whether her nonchalance was feigned or genuine, it outmatched his when she responded to the news that she was getting married by calmly asking what time the ceremony would start.

Whatever understanding they may have had, Winnie felt unable to ask Mandela certain questions. She had been aware he was separated when she met and started going out with him, but she had never actually felt up to asking him what he was doing – if anything – about obtaining a divorce. In keeping with his aversion to personal discussion he kept the details of his divorce to himself, presenting his intended second wife with a *fait accompli* when his first marriage was finally dissolved.

Mandela then arranged for Winnie to be driven to Pondoland to tell her family that she was to be married. She spent a full day at home before she could pluck up the courage to tell Columbus her news, and even then she couldn't tell him herself but asked Hilda to tell him for her. Her apprehension was well founded. Whether or not Columbus had previously known anything of his daughter's involvement with Mandela, he was shocked and not altogether happy at her decision to marry him. The father of three children, on trial for high treason, was not his notion of the ideal son-in-law. When he sent Winnie to Johannesburg he had not envisaged her future tied to a man who could be put to death or sentenced to life imprisonment. Unlike Winnie, Columbus was not caught up in Mandela's charisma. However, he recognised that Winnie was so in love she felt invincible, and therefore he went along with the marriage despite his serious misgivings. But he spoke of those misgivings at the wedding.

Mandela's second wedding was very different from his first. The elaborate nature of the ceremony not only reflected the intensity of his love for his second bride, it also indicated how the pressures of a life awaiting trial while banned made traditional ritual more important to him. Winnie too, wanted her wedding to be traditionally correct and insisted on getting married in Pondoland, feeling that her husband should have first-hand knowledge of her background.

Mandela paid lobola for Winnie. As he was unable to leave Johannesburg without permission, Winnie's lobola was negotiated by a cousin. And in keeping with tradition, Winnie never knew how much her husband paid for her. He was allowed to leave Johannesburg for four days to go to Pondoland for his wedding. He and his bride left at midnight on 12 June and reached Bizana in the afternoon of the next day.

The excitement of her wedding was too much for Winnie who arrived home with a badly upset stomach. She was met and put to bed by the women of the village, including her grandmother, Makhulu, who was firmly of the opinion that the stomach upset was a direct result of Winnie's being invaded by spirits. The ritual celebration of spirits combined with the worship of a Christian God for the two-day wedding ceremonies, reflected the religion of Nelson and Winnie's childhoods. The actual wedding service was Christian, and took place in the Methodist church in Bizana, though the language of the hymns had been translated from English into Xhosa.

There was not enough time to complete every aspect of the festivities before Mandela had to return to Johannesburg. The newly-wed Mandelas were unable to take part in a reciprocal ceremony in Mandela's own village, which meant that the sharing of a tier of wedding cake among Mandela's relatives never took place. Winnie wrapped the top tier and took it back to Johannesburg with her, intending that she and her husband would visit his family when they next had time. They never would. Over the years this piece of cake would assume tremendous symbolic value for Winnie. She took it with her when she was banished to Brandfort, and told visitors that miraculously it never crumbled. It seemed to represent her own resilience in adversity. No matter what was done or how long the groom would be absent, his bride and his wedding cake would remain as he left them. It was an impossible dream.

Following their wedding the Mandelas returned to Johannesburg, and the Soweto township became Winnie's home for the first time. Not all of Mandela's friends welcomed Winnie warmly. Many of the women were still friendly with Evelyn and resented her replacement. Though Mandela had been separated when he met Winnie, she was regarded as the reason his first marriage ended, which technically she was, because he divorced Evelyn to marry her.

In many ways her day-to-day life with her husband was similar to that of her predecessor. Mandela left the house before daybreak and returned late at night. He worked through every weekend. But there was a marked difference in his attitude at home. He wanted to be with his wife. He and Winnie shared a happy house, full of passion and laughter. Having lived in a hostel for six years, Winnie was all the more appreciative of being mistress of her own home. And with the additional security of marriage to the man she adored, she relaxed. She understood that the limitations of their relationship were not of her husband's design, but had been imposed by the demands of the political situation and so she accepted them. For the first time, however, she began to be personally affected by the activities of the Security Police, for now when they tried to disrupt Mandela's life by banging on his door in the early hours of the morning, it was her life that was disrupted too. When they searched for illegal books or documents, it was her belongings they rifled through, tore up and smashed and left strewn across the floor. Her desire to keep a spotless, tidy home was constantly thwarted. And she, who had been so anxious to maintain a level of personal privacy, suddenly found that there could be no such luxury in her new life. Winnie had no control over these constant intrusions. She described the trauma of the first police raid:

There were these coarse Boer policemen thumbing through our personal belongings, pulling books off shelves, turning drawers upside down, reading our letters, rough handling our possessions and all the time passing derogatory and derisory remarks about kaffirs. It was horrible. And it was all for nothing. They couldn't find anything incriminating. After they had gone we tidied up the mess and I made coffee before we went back to bed. Nelson warned me that I would have to get used to raids like that, but afterwards they never seemed quite so traumatic as that first time.[3]

In the early days, with Mandela there to help restore order to the house, talk to and soothe her, there was at least a sense of a trauma shared. Later she would have to cope with these numerous raids alone. She had learnt her assurance from Mandela, and with him developed a determination that she would not be distressed by these assaults. The couple always insisted that the Security Police treat them as equals and with respect. The difference between the Mandelas was that Nelson always tried to keep from losing his own temper. Winnie's was not so easily controlled and she had no compunction about shouting at or lashing out with her fists against those policeman who abused her.

She had other problems to deal with as she adjusted to married life with Mandela. He was used to bringing home any number of guests for dinner with little or no warning. The constant visits and dinners she had to prepare at a minute's notice sometimes reduced her to tears as she tried to stretch the small amount of food in the house. Money was tight, and she liked to do things properly. Her husband did not acknowledge any difficulty, feeding friends hardly seemed a problem compared to everything else he was dealing with.

As he had done with Evelyn, Mandela encouraged Winnie to play an active role in politics. It wasn't enough to attend meetings at his side. There was a burgeoning women's movement she could make a contribution to or even play a leading role in. And so, four months after her marriage and in the early weeks of her first pregnancy, Winnie joined the next major anti-pass law demonstration organised by the ANC's Women's League.

'It was the government threat to subject women to the provisions of the pass system which . . . brought them into Congress in large numbers about the time of the Defiance Campaign', wrote ANC President-General Albert Luthuli in his 1961 autobiography.[4] 'Women concern themselves, by and large with fundamentals. It is the fundamentals at which the Nationals have struck. Their Abolition of Passes Act imposed the pass system on them. The intensification of measures which shatter families has made it harder than ever before to keep families together, or to be sure of earning anything with which to feed children . . . The involvement of African women in the struggle in the last ten or fifteen years has made them a formidable enemy of the oppressor. The things they live for – the security of their homes and families, and the well-being of their children – have been savagely assaulted.'

Nearly 2,000 women gathered at the pass office in the centre of Johannesburg to protest against the pass law in late October 1958. Roughly 1,200 of them were arrested – as they had expected to be – for contravening the Criminal Law Amendment Act. More than one-tenth of them had brought their babies, which they carried tied to their backs as they were bundled into vans and taken off to Johannesburg's Fort Prison. It was Winnie's first arrest. As with earlier Defiance Campaigns, the number of detainees overwhelmed the resources of the prison system as intended. Conditions were so cramped that women were barely able to sit, let alone lie down, on the filthy stone floors of the restricted squalid cells. There was much pushing and shoving as the prisoners attempted to ease their own discomfort.

During her incarceration, Winnie started to bleed. If anything could prevent her losing her first child while in detention it was the presence in her cell of a trained midwife and friend – Albertina Sisulu. When Albertina noticed that Winnie was ill she immediately took charge, making her lie on the floor, covering her with an overcoat and forcing her to take some food. Winnie's haemorrhaging slowed then stopped and the threatened miscarriage was averted.

Albertina Sisulu had already been something of a guide as Winnie grew used to the life of a political activist's wife, though the two women had less in common than their circumstances might have suggested. The same age as Nelson Mandela, Albertina Sisulu was also from the Transkei. Her mother died when she was fifteen, causing her to leave school and take charge of her six-month-old baby sister. After two years at home, she was sent to boarding school by her grandparents, who decided she should take up nursing to help support her four younger brothers and sisters. Accordingly, Albertina, who had wanted to become a Roman Catholic nun and teach, went to Johannesburg General Hospital, trained as a nurse, and became involved in politics. After her marriage to Walter Sisulu in 1944, Albertina combined her own role as a wife and as a mother with that of an activist. Initially she attended ANC meetings and worked closely with Lillian Ngoyi to improve conditions for working women. Eventually she was the sole financial supporter of her family. Money was a desperate problem for the family, as Sisulu began spending more time in prison than out. In the decade following the Defiance Campaign he was imprisoned eight times.

Unlike Winnie, Albertina Sisulu was untemperamental and un-glamorous, more conciliatory than controversial. Both women were courageous and resilient, possessed strong maternal instincts, could be practical and were capable of extraordinary kindness, but Mama Sisulu, as she was commonly known, had a composure which friends and dependants found comforting. Both women became extremely forceful and influential activists, but those attracted to Winnie were more likely to encounter stimulation rather than the reassurance and solace they got from Mama Sisulu.

The women spent about a fortnight in prison before being brought to court *en masse*, found guilty and sentenced to imprisonment or a fine. Many wanted to spend the maximum amount of time in jail but a decision had been taken by the male leaders of the ANC, including Mandela and Sisulu, that the women should be freed and that no others should invite arrest. Whether the decision sprang from a patriarchal theory that an active role in the struggle was men's work, or whether the attitude of two key leaders was affected by their wives being incarcerated, or whether the ANC leadership was forced to bow to overwhelming pressure from countless other husbands and fathers anxious to release their wives and daughters, the fact remained that after this incident the women felt sidelined. Much to their chagrin, their fines were paid and they were released.

Winnie Mandela came out of prison to find herself unemployed. Her role as a demonstrator had caused Baragwanath Hospital to dismiss her in the first of many retaliatory employer actions she would face as an activist. The loss of income was a blow as the couple prepared for the arrival of their first child together, for Mandela had less time than ever to cultivate his legal practice. Two years of preliminary examination before a magistrate in Johannesburg's Drill Hall had ended in the number of accused in the Treason Trial being reduced from 156 to 91 and the case had come to court in Pretoria in August. The accused may have been fewer but the case was still mammoth. The prosecution produced dozens of witnesses and thousands of documents, including statements recorded at various activist meetings around the country in an attempt to prove that those on trial were guilty of plotting the violent overthrow of the government.

Mandela spent each day at court in the Old Synagogue with his fellow accused. He would get up early, put in a couple of hours at the law office, drive the 60 kilometres to Pretoria, spend the day listening to evidence, prepare for the next day and then drive back to Johannesburg. Friends helped out with loans and gifts as much as they could, and Columbus sent his daughter some money. But as 1958 drew to a close money was extremely tight.

The following year was to be their one full year of married life together. Their daughter Zenani was born in February when Mandela was up in Pretoria at the trial, though he made up for his absence by bringing a profusion of gifts to mother and daughter on his return. Winnie adored motherhood and Mandela adored her for it. His love for Zami – as he called Winnie – and Zeni bordered on the reverential. Becoming a mother made Winnie even more assertive. She stood up to Mandela's mother who came to stay after the baby was born and wanted to look after Zeni in what was by Winnie's standards an outdated and unhygienic way. She had members of her own family to stay. Nancy and Princess came to Johannesburg to study and lived with their sister, providing her with emotional and practical support. She now had a definite role in the family, with a child whose daily needs had to be her priority. Conscious of how easy it would be for her to lose her own individuality as Mandela's wife she was determined that this shouldn't happen. She became pregnant again. But the second pregnancy, which followed shortly after the first, was not successful, and Winnie miscarried. She continued her activities as a social worker on an *ad hoc* basis, helping friends with ill children to get doctors' help and medical supplies. But her biggest step was to begin informal public speaking lessons, writing her own speeches and going to classes with other women who criticised each other's speeches and delivery. As the Mandelas celebrated Christmas 1959 with their friends at Helen Joseph's annual Christmas party, they looked back on what they felt to have been a happy and rewarding year. They had three months of such married life left together.

The two years in which she had known Mandela had actually been very difficult. In addition to sacrificing a full wedding ceremony, Winnie had had one child and a miscarriage, lost the job she had been so proud to get, and was struggling to make ends meet. Married to a man who was married to a political cause had made her something of a single parent. And her husband was still on trial – she had never known him not to be, and she continued to live with the unrelenting pressure that he might be found guilty and put to death. Verwoerd had become Prime Minister and made territorial apartheid a reality, creating independent bantustans or homelands, one of which included Pondoland.

The creation of homelands was denounced by the ANC, and many tribal chiefs, but welcomed by Columbus Madikizela. For his deference to the new order, he and many others received money and power. Commercial pragmatism outweighed any moral restraints Columbus might have had. He became a member of the Transkei cabinet, 'elected' to the position of Minister of Agriculture and Forestry. It was potentially an extremely powerful position in a rural economy. But for Winnie her father's position was politically untenable. He had literally sold out to the authorities. She wrote to tell him of her feelings and demanded that he resign, prompting a stream of furious letters between father and daughter. Their relationship would be strained for the rest of Columbus's life.

1960 was a watershed in South African history. The previous year had forced the ANC to take a stand against a new, less compromising political movement – pan Africanism. Africa for the Africans (the concept at the heart of the movement) had once been embraced and advanced by Mandela, Sisulu and Tambo, during the 1949 Youth League conference. The three modified their views to democracy for all as they worked closely with whites and Indians, but the idea of Africa for Africans continued to attract a hardcore of militants.

On 6 November 1958 (the same day that hundreds of women were released from the Fort Prison after the pass law demonstration) *New Age* newspaper ran a front-page article under the headline 'Good Riddance: Africanists Routed At ANC Conference'. The story continued: 'Last week-end's Transvaal ANC conference soundly defeated and drove out the Africanists, restored unity and an elected leadership to the province, and endorsed the present ANC policy as expressed in Chief Luthuli's words: "The label of Europeans Only must be replaced by Democracy For All."'

Those routed were not defeated. Instead they formed their own organisation, the Pan African Congress. The leader of the movement, 34-year-old Robert Sobukwe, shared many of the same qualities his older former ANC colleagues had possessed at his age. A highly intelligent, radical graduate of Fort Hare University College who believed that blacks could only rely upon themselves in the struggle, Sobukwe spent 1959 travelling the country enrolling the disaffected.[5] Once again, the pass laws were the most contentious issue. Sobukwe organised a number of anti-pass law PAC demonstrations, culminating in an incident when thousands of men, women and children, massed outside the police station in the township of Sharpeville, fifty miles south of Johannesburg, expecting to be arrested for not carrying passes on 21 March 1960.[6]

Eyewitnesses described policemen firing continuously and indiscriminately into the crowd as men, women and children were shot and killed. 'Before the shooting I heard no warning to the crowd to disperse', wrote Humphrey Tyler, then editor of Drum magazine. 'There was no warning volley. When the shooting started it did not stop until there was no living thing in the huge compound in front of the police station. The police have claimed they were in desperate danger because the crowd was stoning them. Yet only three policemen were reported to have been hit by stones – and more than 300 Africans were shot down'.[7]

The police panicked. Reports afterwards established that they were alarmed at the size of the crowd and worried that if the fence surrounding the building collapsed, the police station would be attacked. Once the first shot had been fired (it was never established by whom and on whose order – if anyone's) guns blazed without stopping. Sixty-seven were killed at Sharpeville and 186 wounded.

The brutal and immediate police response was followed by intensive police retaliation after the event. Later that day, when news of the massacre had spread across the country via radio, police baton-charged a crowd of thousands of men who had congregated in the Cape township of Langa, to protest the pass laws, provoking a week of intensive rioting and stayaways (strikes).

The Sharpeville massacre set the precedent for those that would follow over the years. Organised peaceful, political activity resulted in gun fire.

In the days following the massacre, there was a state crack-down of unprecedented harshness. As millions of rand left the country and shares on the Johannesburg stock exchange plummeted, doors were knocked upon, houses were raided and activists rounded up. Though he had had nothing to do with the events at Sharpeville, Mandela was one of the first to be taken into custody.

Opening his door in answer to a thunderous knocking, in the early hours of 30 March, he and Winnie watched as their house was ransacked by police. Mandela was then told to pack his bag. The police took him without a warrant, refusing to let him call a lawyer. Winnie had no idea where or why he was being detained. In the weeks prior to his arrest, she had had less and less time and attention from her husband. His political activities and his Treason Trial defence had, for the most part, excluded her, as Mandela began spending many nights up in Pretoria, rather than making the journey down to Johannesburg for a few hours each day. He had stopped telling her what he was doing and where he was going – he didn't have the time. Increasingly, he had merely been coming home to bathe and change, then immediately leaving the house to return to work. Winnie later wrote that she had to force him to stop and eat on these occasions and even then the phone would constantly ring with people needing to speak to him. She didn't complain but she missed her husband desperately, and would talk about him to her sister, Princess.

The relationship between the two sisters had grown closer after Princess briefly moved in with Winnie when she was attending school in Johannesburg. Columbus, however, complained that he needed a daughter at home, and demanded that Princess return. He had behaved in the same way when Msuthu went to live with Winnie on leaving school. Msuthu had arrived in Johannesburg without the requisite permit, which led to his arrest and a charge of illegal entry. Columbus was furious and wrote to Winnie, telling her to send Msuthu home at once; he was an embarrassment to the Transkei government and to the family. Winnie hadn't complained. Instead she sent her brother and her younger sister back to their father rather than risk his wrath. She then had Princess brought back for occasional visits to stay with her.

Sharpeville brought the world's press to South Africa and Winnie found herself the focus of media attention. With her husband in custody, and Winnie keen to commit herself in print, she became a good story. Her role began to shift. This time she had watched her husband being taken away in the middle of the night; she could organise and lobby the authorities on his behalf. Winnie was not excluded from what was happening to her husband: her role as Mandela's wife assumed an official dimension, incorporating both public representative and spokeswoman.

Confusion arose when Winnie's remarks did not exactly reflect the positions held by her husband and his colleagues. 'Suddenly I wasn't speaking for myself any more. If I uttered a word it was "MANDELA'S WIFE SAYS". Not only was Mandela's wife speaking but "THE POLICY OF THE AFRICAN NATIONAL CONGRESS SEEMS TO HAVE SHIFTED FROM . . ." and I hadn't the slightest idea what they were were talking about. I couldn't handle the situation at first. I couldn't handle myself.'[8]

She was always more militant than the ANC, in fact her rhetoric and activities were more in keeping with those of the PAC, whose position – that the way to success in the struggle was to turn the outrage of the masses into massive insurrection – was very close to her own. She was an Africanist, who believed in the popular consciousness of Africans. Key words and phrases railing against 'white domination' and vowing that this was 'a revolution' and that it was imperative to 'continue the fight' and 'keep the freedom flame burning' became staple ingredients in her speeches from the early 1960s and scarcely changed for the next thirty years.

In April 1960, less than a month after Sharpeville, both the ANC and the PAC were declared unlawful organisations by the South African Parliament. A State of Emergency was imposed throughout the country. Oliver and Adelaide Tambo fled South Africa to begin more than thirty years in exile. Mandela was still in jail, where he would remain for five months until the Emergency was lifted in August. Alone in Johannesburg, Winnie realised she was pregnant again. Her family back in Pondoland could be of little help or support to her: they were facing dangerous problems of their own. Not all the consequences of Columbus's decision to co-operate with Pretoria had been beneficial. He and others who had sold out to the government – including Winnie's former admirer, Kaiser Matanzima, now the Transkei's first prime minister – suffered numerous attacks on themselves and their property. Assaults on Columbus were unrelenting. On one occasion a band of locals came searching for him, prompting him to flee from his house through a tiny back window, and go into hiding. The group only left the property when Christopher fired at them with a shotgun. On another occasion the Madikizela house was burnt to the ground – the family lost everything they had and for a time had to sleep outside on the ground under the trees. Columbus's mother was beaten up, his store was broken into, and his money stolen. Although he was provided with alternative accommodation in Bizana by his government and went to live in town, he eventually resigned from the cabinet and went back into business full time.

In addition to the numerous pressures she had to cope with, Winnie was having a difficult pregnancy, struggling against constant nausea. Just prior to Mandela's release in August he had given evidence in his own defence at the Treason Trial, so Winnie went up to Pretoria and back each day to listen to him and show support. Once free, Mandela resumed the lengthy trek to and from Pretoria each day with little time to spend at home with his pregnant wife and small daughter. He was exhausted and missed them both. When he was in detention the other detainees listened as he talked about Winnie at length, worrying about what might be happening to her. But with so many demands upon him, as he regained his freedom, he had little time to do more than see her occasionally and reassure himself that she was coping.

In December she was far from all right. Mandela had gone to visit his older children in Qamata. Makgatho was ill and Mandela wanted to bring him back to Johannesburg for medical help. He was to be gone a day and a night, not risking a longer stay as he was breaking his banning order by leaving at all. But in his absence Winnie went into labour, and began a long, complicated delivery. 'My husband was never there, when both our children were born,' she later said, confusing the reason for his absence. 'He was either in prison or out gathering information about the Treason Trial.'

Their second daughter, Zinzi, was born by forceps delivery on 23 December, but infection had set in. Winnie had puerperal fever and was in obvious distress.

Fatima Meer later described how Mandela dealt with the problem:

Nelson reached home in the early hours of the morning with a sick boy, the news of Zinzi's arrival, a sick wife and a police raid in full blast on his house.

His first thoughts were for Makgatho. He took him to Dr Abdullah, and then, leaving the boy in the care of [his sister] Leabie, rushed to hospital. He found Winnie weak but recovering. She was out of the tent, but his tiny new daughter was now running a temperature.

Nelson's anxiety came to an end: Evelyn took over their son and the hospital cared for his wife and baby.[9]

Three months later, just more than a year after the massacre at Sharpeville, Justice Rumpff pronounced that the remaining Treason Trial defendants in the dock were not guilty. They were all discharged. The court went wild. People were crying and shouting, Winnie and Mandela kissed and danced. Mandela and Counsel Bran Fischer were carried outside on people's shoulders, where a vast crowd had begun singing 'Nkosi Sikelel'iafrika' (God Bless Africa), the African national anthem. That evening there was a big celebration at Fischer's house in Orchards, where all the accused celebrated till the early hours of the morning, dancing and drinking.

Before that, however, Mandela had to confer with his advisers and he sent Winnie back to Johannesburg without him. He had called a meeting to discuss his political future: he was about to disappear into the underground world of opposition politics, and Winnie would resume her life alone. She later described what happened with varying degrees of bitterness.

> He was outside the gate, but I couldn't reach him, there were so many people wishing him well – everybody was excited. I packed his bag but by the time I took it out he wasn't there. He was gone. Someone else came to fetch the bag about an hour later . . . That was the last time I saw my husband as a family man, legally at home. There had been no chance to sit down and discuss his decision to commit himself totally.[10]

> The day the trial came to an end, the leaders of the African National Congress came home. They came to celebrate the results of the trial and the fact that they had been acquitted. My husband did not even enter the house. They were all jubilant and they were standing outside. Joe Modise . . . walked into the house and asked me to pack a few things for my husband. I did, and I gave him a suitcase. And all I was told was that I would be seeing him in a few days. I never really knew much about the nature of his work, because I think they felt it was better that way. He left with the rest of the leadership that day. That was the last time I saw my husband at home.[11]

Asked to pack a bag for her husband, told that he was going on a long journey which he was unable to tell her about, she complied without fuss like other wives of other activists.

With Mandela's descent underground, a far more militant ANC strategy took shape. It had been obvious for some time that passive resistance wasn't working. The Sharpeville massacre had taught that the bigger the protest the harsher the response. Other than that nothing was going to change. If non-violence had no effect on the regime, then the time had come to use violence.

Another element affected the decision. South Africa was preparing to leave the British Commonwealth and become a Republic. It was clear that conditions for non-whites would deteriorate under the new regime. An All-In African Conference held in March 1961 called on Africans not to co-operate with the proposed Republic. Mandela was elected leader of a National Action Council which was to organise a strike and a campaign of non-co-operation. The strike took place on the last day of May, the same day that South Africa became a Republic. In his analysis of the strike, Mandela showed how much more militant he had become. 'We shall fight together tooth and nail, against the Government plan to bring Bantu authorities to the cities . . . Non-collaboration is the weapon we must use to bring down the Government. We have decided to use it fully and without reservation.'

In June 1961, Mandela proposed in a meeting of the ANC's National Executive committee that violence should now be used. His proposal was accepted. However, Luthuli, who remained a committed pacifist, added the rider that terrorism should not be organised under the ANC as such, but under a new organisation. Working from underground, consulting with both ANC and SACP (South African Communist Party) leaders, Mandela then founded the terrorist wing of the ANC – Umkhonto we Sizwe or MK (The Spear of the Nation). The idea was to have three phases of operations. Phase one would be to sabotage the country's infrastructure. Railway lines, power stations, government buildings were to be blown up. If nothing changed, military bases and police stations were to be added to the list. Finally, if all else failed, all-out guerrilla warfare would be used to overthrow the government.

The make-up of MK reflected that of the ANC proper – women were eventually allowed to participate but only up to a point. The few who did join and went to training camps outside the country were originally prevented from carrying guns. They washed their male colleagues' clothes, they performed secretarial duties and they were put into communications and intelligence. They did not become leaders. As there had been in the passive campaigns waged by the ANC, there was a certain amount of resistance to the involvement of women at all.

Inside the country, women were invaluable to MK as couriers, purveyors of intelligence and inspectors of potential bomb sites. Stashing weapons and hiding terrorists allowed them to be included in ANC activities without overstepping the bounds of their roles as housewives. Their clandestine activities required considerable courage – and considerable discretion. The government's reaction to the establishment of MK had been to set up a new organisation of its own. Republican Intelligence – later the Bureau of State Security, or BOSS – was an ultra-secret section of the Security Police with the task of infiltrating and destroying MK and the ANC. Teeming with informers, it was the omniscient eye of a seemingly omnipotent force.

In the early days of MK, before cells and training-camps were founded, there was an amateurism and a cronyism to the proceedings. Friends taught each other how to manufacture makeshift bombs and practised blowing up public lavatories. But more than explosive techniques had to be mastered. ANC members and MK operatives had to learn how to operate in secret. All initial attempts at subterfuge were clumsy and inadequate, but discretion and clandestine operations would never be fully grasped by Winnie.

Having rented a farm called Lillisleaf in the suburb of Rivonia outside Johannesburg, MK and the ANC worked together planning the campaign of sabotage. Winnie brought the children there to see their father, and the Mandelas pretended to have a normal family life surrounded by a number of domestic and farm employees – all of whom could testify as to what and whom they had seen. There was nothing discreet about Lillisleaf.

Although he became known as The Black Pimpernel for his skill at disguise and uncanny ability to avoid capture by the government, Mandela himself took enormous risks. He slipped in and out of the country, in and out of hiding, and was on his own for large stretches of time. He lived in great discomfort, setting up MK cells and consulting with ANC leaders, and he seemed impervious to danger. 'It was part of the amateurishness that it was thought that a man of his vulnerability, given how much he was targeted, could go to meetings in a different part of the country of quite big groups of people and that nobody would know anything about it,' said Harold Wolpe, a founder-member of MK.[12]

To know when Mandela was around, all the police had to do was mount a watching brief on Luthuli and Winnie. On one occasion, when a scheduled meeting with Winnie fell through, Mandela was so disappointed that he simply got into a car and drove off to look for her. He eventually managed to see her after going to someone else's house and getting a friend to telephone her.

Adding an extra sense of drama to the period, Winnie later said she was always blindfolded when she was taken to see her husband, but others took less precautions. Amy Reitstein, who worked for the ANC in the early 1960s, was also taken to see Mandela while he was in hiding. 'I knew the person who was his main security,' she said. 'He said, "Would you like to come and meet him?" They took me because I didn't know where I was, because I didn't know Johannesburg. I only know he was living in this flat on the first floor . . . We rang the doorbell and he looked through the eyehole and let us in. He had on a pair of shorts and a T-shirt, or a vest. It was quite late at night. He was very happy to get up and chat. He needed some typing done, so I went for the next couple of days and spent the whole day with him and typed for him.'[13]

Outside South Africa Mandela made no attempt to keep a low profile. He toured North, West and East Africa soliciting support from fellow African leaders. He went to London to mollify Liberal and Labour party leaders concerned at the establishment of MK, pointing out that Luthuli remained committed to non-violence. His task became easier when Luthuli was awarded the 1961 Nobel Peace Prize at the same time that MK committed its first acts of sabotage. While Mandela travelled extensively outside the country, he made it clear he was not about to go into exile. It was only a matter of time before he was captured. The fact that he remained at large for as long as he did – seventeen months – may have had less to do with the government's incompetence or Mandela's skill at disguise than the value of keeping tabs on him and his associates.

He was arrested on 5 August 1962. The circumstances surrounding the arrest were curious. It took place after a briefing to Luthuli and others about his trip to London, when he was stopped at a road block in Natal by Security Police. For years after the arrest, it was said in ANC circles that the CIA had informed South African security as to Mandela's whereabouts. But exactly who the culprit had been was unclear.[14] Whoever the informant, there was no doubt that the CIA had successfully infiltrated the ANC and was extensively involved in African politics.[15]

In addition to the burden of having her husband back in custody, Winnie had been having a hard time finding work. The government had reacted to the disappearance of Mandela by slapping a banning order on his wife and the consequent restrictions she had lived under for two years made it extremely difficult for her to hold down a job. For a time she had worked as a social worker at the Child Welfare Society, juggling her duties to fit in with the terms of her banning order as best she could. But then her ban was made stricter, preventing her from moving anywhere other than her house and her office, and she had to leave. Over the years there has been confusion about how Winnie was paid at the Child Welfare Society. To a certain extent, the society was a government-subsidised operation, paying the salaries of a number of white, black and coloured staff. Some said that the government refused to pay for Winnie's salary, but that the society paid for her from its already over-stretched budget out of a desire to help her. But this was totally untrue, according to Mary Uys, who was Director of the Child Welfare Society during Winnie's time there. In fact there were a number of unsubsidised posts, and Winnie's was one of those.

It was while she was at work at the Child Welfare Society that she got the news that Mandela had been captured. 'Part of my soul went with him at that time', she wrote in her autobiography.

I was on my way out, going to do field work in the Soweto area. I went down in the lift, and, as I was getting out, I bumped into one of his friends – the way this man looked! He was white like a ghost, his hair was standing on end. I noticed he hadn't shaved and was wearing a dirty shirt and trousers as if he'd just jumped out of bed; you could see something drastic had happened. This was one of the men who used to be along the line when I was taken to see Mandela underground.

I associated him so much with my husband that I found myself asking, 'Is he alright?' The first thing that struck me was that Nelson had been injured. And I thought, my God, he could have run into a road block and the police could have fired. And the reply was, 'No, we think he'll be appearing in the Johannesburg court tomorrow.' Then of course I knew what that meant.

Winnie drove home in a state of shock. Mandela was charged with leaving the country without travel documents and inciting Africans to strike. Some of the glamour of The Black Pimpernel had extended to his wife. On the opening day of his trial it was Winnie who made front-page pictures dressed in traditional Tembu Dress. The article about her on an inside page debated whether tribal costume such as she was wearing promoted tradition rather than tribalism.

'We are not going to rub off our culture and traditions because of the fear that the Nationalists will make propaganda use of them,' she said posing with a Tembu pipe held to her mouth. 'We are Africans and need not regret that we were born Africans. Our children must not forget who we are and where we came from.'

In her husband's absence, what Winnie did, what she wore and what she said were beginning to get their own share of attention and praise. Letters were written about her to newspapers: 'When Mrs Nelson Mandela was invited as a guest of honour to a recent national conference of the Indian people, she honoured the dignity of the occasion by appearing in Indian traditional dress', ran one letter.

'Knowing how Africans themselves display sensitivity about their own traditions and culture she sought to convey the same sentiment of respect for the culture of a minority oppressed people. One would venture to say that if she had made her speech in any of the Indian languages, an even deeper sense of appreciation would have been evinced.'[16]

'All honour to a very brave lady', said another. 'Any husband with a wife like Winnie would be proud indeed . . . She is fighting for the nation . . . The African nation should be proud of women like Mrs Winnie Mandela.'

Mandela was sentenced to five years imprisonment in November 1962. He was forty-four years old. That day Winnie attended court, singing national songs with the crowd at the trial, with 'the smiling courage that has characterised her since her husband went underground and before that during the long drawn-out treason trial'.[17]

She told reporters that Zeni and Zinzi were too young to know what was happening. All Zeni knew, she said, was that her daddy was taken by the police one day. Her comments showed how her rhetoric had begun to take shape.

'I feel fine,' she said. 'I have never been so confident about the future in store for the African people.' And: 'What has happened should take none of us by surprise, for we are faced with a vicious oppressor. I will continue the fight as I have done in the past.'

I shall certainly live under great strain in the coming years, but this type of life has become part and parcel of my life for some time. I married Nel in 1958 . . . He was then a treason trial accused and I was aware that even a death sentence was hanging over his head. I do not think that people should worry that he has been sentenced to five years' imprisonment. Their worry must be that we are prepared to allow the Nationalist Government in power that long. That is what people must worry about. The greatest honour a people can pay to a man behind bars is to keep the freedom flame burning, to continue the fight.

The arrest and locking up of my husband must be taken as that of Dr Nkrumah of Ghana, who was freed from prison before he finished his prison term and took over the premiership of his country. It must be taken as that of Dr Fidel Castro who stayed in the mountains for six years and then came down after the revolution to lead the Cuban people. It must be taken as that of the Ben Bellas and other great leaders of Africa who have suffered for their people.

The Makanas must not be forgotten, the great leaders of the olden days who fought with spears against the cannon. People must have these events ringing in their heads so that Mandela will not be imprisoned for more than a year.

We must recognize and acknowledge that our struggle is against white domination and is in Africa, and that the brunt must fall upon us Africans.

My husband correctly said suffering in jail is nothing compared to suffering outside jail. Our people suffer inside and outside of the jails. But suffering is not enough. We must struggle. (*New Age*, 15 November 1962.)

In July 1963 the government raided Lillisleaf farm. Smashing down on Umkhonto we Sizwe, the State charged nine people including the imprisoned Mandela, Walter Sisulu and Govan Mbeki with sabotage and attempting to cause a violent overthrow in the Republic. This time the stakes were much higher. A conviction could carry the death penalty, and, having avoided the death penalty in the earlier Treason Trial, the chances of escaping it now had decreased. The State took five months to present its case, introducing 250 documents as exhibits and parading a variety of witnesses before the court. Confined to Johannesburg, Winnie had to get special permission to attend the trial in Pretoria and it was difficult for her to attend regularly. She was not allowed to wear national dress – or to dress in any way which might lead to an incident. 'Whenever she attended court, the police watched her with lustful eyes,' said Hilda Bernstein, the wife of another defendant.[18] Under their scrutiny it was impossible for Winnie to exchange even a few words with Albertina who sat with her in the black section of court. Both women were banned and therefore prohibited from speaking to each other.

Knowing that he was fighting for his life, Mandela's defence was political. He read a lengthy statement before a packed court in which his wife sat next to his mother. Mandela said he had done what he did because of his own proudly felt African background. 'During my lifetime I have dedicated myself to this struggle of the African people. I have fought against white domination and I have fought against black domination. I have cherished the ideal of a democratic and free society in which all persons live together in harmony with equal opportunities. It is an ideal which I hope to live for and achieve. But if needs be, it is an ideal for which I am prepared to die.'

These words probably saved him. It was not in the government's interest to create martyrs. Instead of being sentenced to death, Mandela got life imprisonment. So did eight of the nine accused, including Walter Sisulu and Govan Mbeki. Winnie didn't cry as her husband was sentenced on 12 June 1964, though some said there were tears in her eyes. She had Zeni and Zinzi with her and took them to wait outside Pretoria Central Prison to wave goodbye to their father for the last time. As she waited in the crowd a Security policeman approached her to remind her she had to be back in Johannesburg by noon. She ignored him but not without kicking him first.

Situated just off the Cape Coast in the middle of Table Bay, Robben Island had been a penal colony since the seventeenth century, and a home for political prisoners for more than one hundred years. Uncompliant Xhosa chiefs had been imprisoned on the island by the governor of the Cape Colony, Sir George Grey, in the late 1850s. It was bleak, barren and wild. Prison life on Robben Island was extremely harsh. The authorities hoped that with poor treatment they would shatter the morale of political prisoners. 'From the security police to the prison authorities, they tried to instill into our minds that we would be forgotten in a few years' time,' said Ahmed Kathrada.[19] Confined to a special isolation block, the Rivonia inmates slept on a cement floor. Each had three blankets, thin enough to be seen through. While Indians and coloureds were given long trousers and socks as part of their prison uniform, blacks had to wear shorts, and were not given socks or underwear. Each day they would be sent out to perform hard labour, smashing stones with hammers, working in the lime quarry in their shorts, sandals and calico jackets. The routine never varied. Day after day, season after season, rain or shine, the convicts would be outside working, and Robben Island could get bitterly cold. Work began at 7.00 am and continued until the light started to fade at 4.00 pm with a one-hour lunch break. At the end of the day convicts were forced to strip down and wash with cold water. They would be driven to and from work by guards with Alsatians. Some of the guards had swastikas tattooed on their wrists.

'I used to work in the quarry where I could only see the sky,' said Nelson Mandela describing his life on Robben Island. 'Then . . . I was moved to another lime quarry – but at least I could see Cape Town. Then in November 1971, I was put on to collecting seaweed. This is the most popular job – you can see the sea, and feel it, and watch the ships coming and going.'[20]

Black convicts didn't just wear inferior clothes, they ate inferior food. Unlike the other inmates, they did not receive bread with their meals, nor were they ever given milk. Their diet was maize porridge with half a teaspoon of sugar for breakfast, boiled grain for lunch, and porridge with stale vegetables in the evening. In the absence of any other real bargaining tools, food became an important issue. The political prisoners went on hunger strikes to try and change prison conditions and the warders themselves would deprive prisoners of meals for a day on the flimsiest pretexts, or put them on a diet of gruel.

Prisoners were constantly assaulted. Not only were there regular beatings and rough strip searches, at the whim of a warden some prisoners might be placed in strait jackets or put into solitary confinement. On one occasion, Nelson Mandela was stripped and made to stand to attention, stark naked, for an hour. 'This is no way to treat someone of my standing,' he later commented.

Letters were confined to two a year for the first several years: reforms gradually increased the number to two a month. Often, however, letters in and out of the prison would 'go astray', never to reach their destination. When Mandela complained to Winnie that she had stopped writing, she was amazed. Six letters in a row had been kept from him. When he asked for them, they were given to him in a bundle.

Prisoners were allowed two visits a year, and visitors had to apply each time for permission to go to the island. Here, too, permits would often be delayed or lost until after the designated visiting day, forcing relatives to wait another six months before they could try again.

Those who did make it to the prison were allowed to see the inmates through a thick glass window and talk through headphones. Conversation was to be limited to personal matters and was closely monitored. Harassment of visitors was relentless and Winnie Mandela's treatment was possibly the worst of all. During the boat trip from the mainland to the island she would be kept apart from other prison relatives, and on one occasion was not even allowed to sit up on the ferry deck: she was forced instead to spend the forty-five-minute journey in the tiny foul-smelling cabin down below, where she became sick from the diesel fumes. Another time she was forced to sit alone on the deck despite the fact it was raining and cold.

She was once arrested for failing to give her name and address to a policeman in Cape Town after a visit. She had already written down her address on a form at the police station and then confirmed that it was correct. She was also made to write it in the book at the ferry. When she was asked for her address again as she got off the ferry she lost patience, told the policeman to leave her alone and drove off. For this crime she was sentenced to twelve months' imprisonment, suspended for three years, except for four days. She was given leave to appeal and released on R20 bail.

Both Nelson and Winnie Mandela strongly believed in the importance of never showing how affected they might be by their treatment. But in the early days Nelson found it easier to stick to this principle than Winnie. It wasn't just his temperament that helped him to cope. He had less to cope with. The prison routine was exceptionally harsh but it was constant. Winnie never knew what to expect next.

Chapter Four

With Mandela and other leaders in prison and Tambo in exile a question arose over who was to keep the ANC alive within the country. Winnie assumed that the leadership role was automatically hers. 'I was ready to deputise for Nelson', she wrote. As Mandela's wife she was his heir. She had already achieved a high profile of her own. She had spoken on his behalf and on behalf of the organisation. It was only natural that she – as a Mandela – should assume responsibility.

Leading, as far as Winnie was concerned, meant telling other people what to do. It did not involve discussion, argument, or the heeding of advice. Leaders were well educated and well born – background was more important than age and political experience. The gap that had existed between her and others in the ANC because of their difference in age extended to their difference in upbringing. Winnie did not see the poorer, self-taught ANC members as her equals. They were the rank and file. She was well born and well educated. She was a chief.

Her attitude made her unpopular among her peers, particularly among other wives. Winnie made little effort to become more friendly with other women in positions similar to her own. She saw herself as superior to them. The only women she really trusted as equals were her own sisters. Trust was becoming a rare commodity in a world where a house was less a home than a series of hiding places against the inevitable time when there would be a knocking at the door and the police would burst in. Telephones were assumed to be tapped, conversations either had to be inconseqential or in code. Meetings had to start on time at places kept highly secret. Windows had to be covered to prevent the lone police officer permanently outside the house from seeing everything that went on inside. Banning orders confined people to their houses from 6.30 p.m. to 6.30 a.m. on weekdays, and throughout weekends and public holidays. They forced them to report to a police station every day, confined them to their own residential area, and prevented them from speaking to other banned people. Life became increasingly isolated under this rigid system. Individuals were forced to spend large amounts of time alone, not knowing whom they could trust.

Winnie's isolation made her vulnerable. She was devastated by

Mandela's sentence and had a difficult time dealing with her own loneliness. But instead of turning to the ANC for comfort and support, she turned to other men. Winnie never said that any of these liaisons were romantic. Sometimes she denied a specific allegation outright, usually she ignored the rumour. Men who were close to her often doubled as drivers, secretaries or factotums. It stood to reason that they should accompany her on trips or spend time with her at home when they worked for her. But some of these men had wives who resented Winnie for taking their husbands away from them. One was Miriam Somana. She eventually divorced her husband, Brian, and even cited Winnie in the divorce action.

The case of Brian Somana indicated how easy it was for the Security Police to set Winnie up by assigning an informer to become close to her. Somana was a young black journalist who began to help Winnie out by driving her around after Mandela was arrested. The first indication that he might be more than a driver came in March 1964 when he was arrested at Winnie's house during a 5.00 a.m. raid. A year earlier Somana had been detained in solitary confinement and it could have been during his detention that he agreed to co-operate with the authorities.

When she divorced her husband a year later, Miriam Somana said he had committed adultery with Winnie. He had fallen in love with her at the end of 1963 and had moved in with her from May to December 1964. Before that he had accompanied her on trips to Cape Town and Swaziland. Winnie denied this. In an affadavit before the Johannesburg Bantu Central Divorce Court she said she was being named by Mrs Somana in order to 'harm us' – herself and Mandela. The Somanas had brought the action before the court, 'Not for the purpose of resolving their differences but for the purpose of damaging my reputation. I deny emphatically that I committed adultery with Brian Somana.' Winnie told the court that her husband had asked Somana to assist her while he was in prison. It later became generally known that Somana was a police informer. Winnie claimed Somana had associated with her to dispel those rumours and had threatened her with violence if she refused to help him. Essentially, she said, she had stuck by Somana out of fear.

It was an implausible scenario, but much about her continuing relationship with the Somana family was strange. In January 1965, Brian Somana's younger brother, Oscar, was charged with arson and causing malicious damage to property following a fire at the garage attached to Winnie's house. Giving evidence, Winnie told the court that a feud had developed between herself and the Somanas after a business partnership between herself and Brian Somana collapsed, 'Because of rumours that it was financed out of reward money offered by the police for the capture of Walter Sisulu.' Somana's enmity towards Sisulu apparently went back several years to a time when Sisulu persuaded him to give up a highly-paid insurance job for lower-paid employment as a journalist for *New Age* newspaper – a publication which was banned shortly after he joined it.

During Oscar Somana's trial, Brian admitted to the court that he was 'in love with Mrs Mandela'. The court also heard that it had been Oscar who told Miriam Somana about the 'alleged love-affair' between Brian and Winnie. Oscar was acquitted in June: the magistrate concluded that Winnie was trying to frame Oscar. There probably had been an affair between Mrs Mandela and Mr Brian Somana, the magistrate said, and Mrs Mandela may then have had a grudge against the Somanas. The idea that Winnie had burnt down her own garage to frame the brother of the man she was supposed to have been involved with made little sense. The magistrate, Mr R.D. Bax, attempted to justify it by saying that 'Transkeian Xhosas were fond of burning their neighbours' properties'.

The car that was damaged in the fire belonged to another male friend, photographer Peter Magubane. Both Winnie and Magubane said they were never more than friends, although Magubane was also found in Winnie's house during a pre-dawn raid – hiding under her bed. Their friendship lasted for several years, and Magubane often helped Winnie with Zeni and Zinzi. Government harassment extended to the Mandela daughters, and Winnie was having a hard time keeping her girls at school. Under the terms of her banning order she was forbidden to take her own children to school. When she got friends to drive them, her friends were harassed. She wrote in her autobiography that Zeni and Zinzi kept being expelled once it was discovered who they were. This was probably a reference to the time she enrolled the girls at a coloured school. An ironic decision given the acrimony she had experienced as a child about her own mother's race. When the police discovered the Mandelas were pupils at the school they were forced to leave. Technically they were prohibited from attending because they were not coloured.

In addition to dealing with the government's harassment of her daughters and friends, Winnie had to contend with endless threats to her own liberty. A routine was established. Winnie would be arrested and charged in the lower, or magistrates court. She would be found guilty, sentenced, but allowed to appeal. The higher appeal court would either overturn her conviction, suspend her sentence, or give her a low fine. The final outcome was less important to the authorities than the enormous amount of time and energy Winnie had to spend in dealing with the law. She continued to lose patience. She wrote in her autobiography of one occasion (she gave no date) when a policeman walked into her bedroom when she was half dressed and put his hand on her shoulder. 'All I remember is grabbing him, and throwing him on the floor, which is what he deserved. I remember seeing his legs up in the air and him screaming, and the whole dressing-stand falling on him. That is how he broke his neck (he did recover).'

As she went from low-paid job to low-paid job, hounded out of employment by a police force who kept up their raids on her house, Winnie became increasingly worried about her daughters. Apart from Magubane she had a number of other friends she could turn to for help, and she decided to ask a local shebeen (pub) owner, Elijah Msivi, if he knew of a way of sending the girls to school in neighbouring Swaziland. If they were out of the country for most of the year, they would not only be safe, they had a chance of getting a decent education. Columbus's influence in that area was still extremely strong. This innocent request for her children's protection was to lead directly to her own lengthy detention.

In early 1968, 29-year-old Mohale Andries Mahanyele's career was in the ascendant. A highly intelligent young man, he had completed high school and was employed at the United States Information Agency as an assistant librarian while studying for an economics degree. By black South African standards he was extremely well educated. Soon after he had started working at the agency Mahanyele was visited by his friend Elijah Msivi, who told him that Winnie wanted to send her two daughters out of South Africa, away from the continual harassment the family suffered at the hands of the security police. She knew of a good private school the girls could go to in Swaziland, but needed to find somewhere for them to live. It had occurred to Msivi that Mahanyele, through his American connections, might be able to help. Was there anything he could do? Mahanyele promised to try. A few days later Winnie came to see him. It was an innocuous enough beginning.

As they worked on finding accomodation for the girls Mahanyele and Winnie became friendly. She was grateful for his help and her gratitude made her charming as she chatted away about her life and family. Eventually Mahanyele succeeded in finding somewhere for

Zeni and Zinzi to stay while they attended school in Swaziland, but his relationship with Winnie didn't end there. Instead it grew more intense. She knew Mahanyele had a car and began asking him to drive her from place to place, meeting to meeting. Then Mahanyele began attending these underground cell meetings of the ANC. In the early days he would be asked to leave at a certain point in the meeting, but soon he was accepted enough to be allowed to sit all the way through. Winnie began confiding in Mahanyele more; she would talk to him about political speeches she wrote and made at the funerals of activists. After the funerals, she'd tell him how the speeches were received, who had listened and how they had responded.

Occasionally they debated the merits of communism versus capitalism – Mahanyele always paying careful attention as Winnie expressed her views. She called him 'Capitalist' for working for the Americans, disapproving of the US government's attitude to communism. In return, because of her communist views, he began calling her the 'Big C'. She talked continuously about the need for black liberation and again Mahanyele constantly pinned her down on details. How should liberation occur? he would ask her. What steps needed to be taken? And always he would get the same answer. Force, she would say. All other attempts had failed in the struggle to end oppression and force was the only avenue left unexplored. The only remaining option she felt was available to the ANC was the violent overthrow of the white government. As they drove past a crowded football stadium together one weekend she commented on what a waste of time football was. So much more could be achieved if the spectators were employed as soldiers in the struggle.

By March 1968 Winnie felt confident enough in her relationship with Mahanyele to ask him another favour. Among the office facilities at USIA were two roneoing machines used for running off official information pamphlets on US government policies. Winnie wanted to use them. She asked him to help her make copies of ANC information pamphlets using the machines. The pamphlets were intended to convey ANC opposition to government-controlled local black elections. Mahanyele refused. But she asked him again and again, begging him for the use of USIA facilities, saying that no other offices could be used, the pamphlets were secret. He continued to repeat that he had no permission to use the machines, but he was weakening. Eventually, on a Sunday morning when the agency offices were closed, Mahanyele drove Winnie, Joyce Sikakane and Rita Ndzanga through the deserted streets of Johannesburg to the empty premises of the USIA. Sikakane and Ndzanga carried a large leather bag full of white paper and a typed prepared stencil. The three women all wore rubber gloves as a precaution against leaving finger prints. Mahanyele showed Ndzanga how to use the machine and for two hours the women ran off pamphlet after pamphlet, until thousands filled the cardboard box on the floor. When they had finished Mahanyele drove them home. They had been careful, but not careful enough – a wax sheet from the typed stencil was subsequently found and would be used against them.

Mahanyele took advantage of this incident to ask Winnie more questions. Before allowing the machines at USIA to be used, he questioned her closely about the intended destination of these pamphlets. She replied evasively, merely saying there were people who would deliver them to the right places. Later he asked a couple of questions about what had happened to the pamphlets. This time he was told not to probe too deeply.

A few weeks later he was asked – and agreed – to open up USIA premises again for the same task. The routine was the same as before, with Sikakane and Ndzanga running off pamphlets while Winnie Mandela supervised. Mahanyele left the women to it and sat at his desk in an outer office, waiting until they were finished. Then, as before, he drove them home.

Mahanyele was married and his wife, Ntsiki, began to resent the amount of time he was spending with Winnie. Not only would he be out most nights, ostensibly driving Winnie around and attending meetings with her, he was also gone at the weekends, attending to her needs. Ntsiki confronted him about it one evening and told him this had to stop. Mahanyele ignored her.

It wasn't long before other employees at USIA began to notice that there was something different about Mahanyele. The amount of mail he received, for example – overseas mail. For Mahanyele and USIA were now being used as a mail drop for the ANC. Winnie had asked Mahanyele to give her his full name and his office mailing address at USIA and he had complied, even though she had refused to tell him why she needed the information.

Mahanyele's behaviour on receipt of the first letter was curious. He opened an envelope addressed to himself which had UK postage stamps on it. Inside he found another envelope – sealed – addressed to 'Winnie'. He opened that too. The letter was stapled at each end. He removed the staples, read the letter and took out two postal orders which were folded inside it. He noted the amount of the postal orders

– one was £10, the other £5. He tried to make sense of the letter which began 'My Dear Sister' and was signed 'Zoya', but even though it was written in English he couldn't understand it. He finally gave up, deciding it must be in some kind of code. But he looked carefully at the handwriting so that he would be able to recognise it again.

He did not give the envelope and its contents to Winnie. Instead he put the bundle into his desk drawer at work and left it there. A few days later, Winnie asked him if he had received anything for her. It wasn't until he had actually been asked for the letter that Mahanyele handed it over. Winnie told him there would be more letters and asked him to hand any future ones to her immediately without opening and reading them first. Before changing the subject, Mahanyele had one question. Who was Zoya? A friend abroad, Winnie said. What kind of friend? From where? But he wasn't told. It was a personal matter, replied Winnie, and that was the end of it.

It was not the end of the letters, however. Soon Mahanyele was receiving letters every week from the UK – an unheard-of practice for someone of his level at the agency. Others at work commented on it and his employers became suspicious. Especially when strangers started showing up at USIA on Mahanyele's days off and asking questions about his mail.

Ntsiki somehow found out about the letters and was unhappy that now, on top of everything else, her husband was being used as a mail drop. She told him so, precipitating another fight between them. When Mahanyele mentioned his wife's unease to Winnie the letters stopped arriving at USIA, but Mahanyele continued picking up ANC mail. Now he would drive Winnie to a post office in the Braamfontein district of Johannesburg and collect whatever was in her mail box there. She didn't want the security police to know that the box was hers, fearing they would begin intercepts there too. As an extra precaution she had Mahanyele keep the key to the box himself.

It was his taking the key home that finally brought Mahanyele's relationship with Winnie to an end. Ntsiki found it and, on being told by her husband whose key it was, threatened to take it to the police. Not only was she going to take the key to the police, she told him, but she was going to tell them everything about his relationship with Winnie Mandela, everything. Mahanyele managed to calm her down, but the damage had been done and it was irreparable.

The next ANC cell meeting he attended had one item on the agenda – Mahanyele's wife. Ntsiki's threats had come to the ears of ANC members and they wanted to know if she intended going to the police.

74

about Winnie. They also wanted to find out whether Mahanyele knew about any relationship between USIA and the South African security police. ANC distrust of the Americans went back to Nelson Mandela's capture. The suspicion was that all information between the two governments was shared. Mahanyele's employment at USIA meant that others in the movement had never trusted him. Though he worked for the Information rather than Intelligence service, the difference between the two agencies was seen as cosmetic by the ANC.

Mahanyele's refusal to answer the questions put to him made him too dangerous to be useful and for the time being his relationship with the underground movement was over. Within a year his associates – including Winnie, Joyce Sikakane and Rita Ndzanga – had been arrested. When they came to court in 1969 charged under the Suppression of Communism Act, Mahanyele was a key state witness against them.

That the charges were brought under the Suppression of Communism Act may explain the role played by Mahanyele as an employee of the United States government. Certainly, at the time, the fact that charges were brought under this particular act struck Winnie's lawyers as peculiar. No country continued to be more aware of the dangers of communism in Africa than the United States. The South African Communist Party and the ANC were closely allied, particularly in carrying out clandestine terrorist operations against the government – a directly threatening aspect of communism.

In early 1966 the US Ambassador to South Africa, William Rountree, had discussed communism in detail in a lengthy, friendly meeting with Prime Minister Verwoerd. It was Verwoerd's contention, Rountree wrote in a cable describing the meeting, that the United States and other Western nations were not doing enough to combat communism in South Africa. South Africa was the strongest anti-communist country in Africa, yet it was the object of attack from Western nations on issues (such as apartheid) which actually went some way towards fighting communism.

Rountree said he had told Verwoerd that, 'Not only did we endeavor to counter communism through our political relations with governments concerned, through our information programs, and through other such means, but we had committed very substantial aid resources to enable African countries to develop their economies and to create systems that would be solid blocks against communist penetration. While we continued to be concerned with efforts of international communism in Africa, we were by no means discouraged by events of the past several years. There was growing recognition in most African countries of the dangers of communism and the road was none too bright for either Russian or Chinese communists . . . One aspect of the differences between us to which Prime Minister had indirectly alluded was the question of race relations. It would be my purpose to try to understand to the best of my ability the attitudes and motivations of the South African Government and report objectively to my government.'[1]

Verwoerd was assassinated later in 1966 (by a white parliamentary messenger who was subsequently judged insane), but the United States fully expected his successor, John Vorster, to continue executing his policies. Known to the Americans as a ruthless and defiant defender of the Afrikaaner, Vorster had quickly indicated he was prepared to maintain South Africa's dialogue with the United States.[2] The United States was aware that Vorster had pro-Nazi leanings, yet felt that as a more practical, accessible man he might, in fact, be easier to deal with than his predecessor. A White House briefing memo, written on the day of Verwoerd's assassination, anticipated that, once sworn in, Vorster would lead the white minority in a shrill, probably violent witch hunt to suppress any attempts by black Africans to take advantage of the killing.

'They will probably look for a "communist conspiracy" euphemism for the seeds of black rebellion. They will probably resort to mass arrests, absolute suppression of dissent, and other emergency measures.'[3]

The memo suggested that the United States should informally 'do our best to keep the lid on black African hopes for a change in Southern Africa . . . This process should be carried on in the capitals as well as in New York. It will be hard, and we will be branded reactionary and colonialist. It may even have some effect on our own elections. But it seems to [be] the only reasonable course.'

Winnie was arrested at two o'clock in the morning of 12 May 1969. Awakened by yet another thunderous knocking on the doors and windows of her house, she was told to pack her bag and go. It was a night of mass raids as the Security Police swept into homes across the country, detaining hundreds as they went.

This was her first major period of detention. Like the other detainees, Winnie was held under the 1967 Terrorism Act – a recently passed law which was notable for its absence of judicial restraint. The act gave the police unprecedented power. It enabled officers to detain offenders indefinitely without trial, in solitary confinement, and it denied them legal representation outside visits. Its purpose was two-fold. As well as taking activists out of circulation it gave the police an opportunity to obtain information. Detention under the Terrorism Act invariably involved interrogation and torture.

Those taken away knew that the prospect of their disappearing without trace was real. In an attempt to avoid such a fate it was extremely important to get word to a lawyer. As she left the house, Winnie managed to tell Princess to instruct the attorney Joel Carlson to represent her.

Joel Carlson was an old friend of the Mandelas and a well-known human rights lawyer based in Johannesburg. A gruff man who passionately hated the apartheid laws of the country, he had worked hard and for little pay on behalf of the oppressed. His clientele was mainly black. Maintaining such a practice wasn't easy. Carlson was subjected to his own share of harassment from the Security Police. His phones were tapped, his offices watched – his house would even be firebombed. But he continued – with a certain measure of success – to take on the authorities.

Carlson was telephoned at dawn. It took him until midday to get confirmation that Winnie had actually been arrested. He then had to find out which prison she had been taken to. He also had to field a number of calls – some of them suspicious – asking about her, and take several more from families of other detainees. Twenty-one others were eventually arraigned with Winnie before a magistrate in Pretoria – but that was five and a half months away.

While Carlson was left to explain to relatives that bail and visits were not allowed, the detainees were driven to Pretoria Central Prison and placed in solitary confinement cells. Locked behind three separate doors, they were surrounded by brick walls in spaces of five feet by ten. They lay on single thin mats or stinking, infested blankets on cement floors with cement ceilings overhead. Single light bulbs covered with wire mesh burned day and night. Cell windows were small, narrow and high, and they were also covered with wire mesh and protected by iron bars. The only necessities provided were a sanitary bucket, a plastic bottle of water and a mug.

Prisoners spent twenty-four hours a day, seven days a week in these cells. They were brought out only for brief, intermittent periods of exercise and for interrogation. Questioning would not begin for a few days. The initial period of isolation proved to be an effective way of inducing anxiety and a desire to co-operate.

Collaboration meant victory. To that end, interrogating officers had developed a number of elaborate, extraordinarily brutal techniques.[4] The most basic – beatings, kickings and punchings – were accompanied by verbal abuse. Many prisoners were forced to remain standing for long periods, sometimes on their toes with their arms stretched high, or balancing on bricks. Some had to hold chairs or other objects above their heads, others might have to crouch or sit in an imaginary chair. Some would be suspended, their hands and feet hog-tied to a broomstick placed on two chairs, or made to undergo prolonged periods of forced gymnastics ending in physical collapse.

Though torture had been introduced as a way of extracting information, at the time MK was formed it was still in its early stages. The most sophisticated and sadistic methods – electric shocks, strangulation and suffocation – were generally not used on women. Such unusual consideration did not last, however, nor did it extend beyond the confines of the interrogation room. Menstruating women were denied sanitary pads. Instead they were given toilet paper or told to use their 'big fat hands'.

Interrogation sessions were lengthy. Prisoners would be collected in the morning, taken to the interrogation cells, questioned all day and returned to their cells at night. Some were repeatedly kept through the night for days on end.

When Winnie was first taken from her cell on a Monday some days after her arrest, she was relieved that the claustrophobic uncertainty and insecurity of her first time in solitary confinement was over. The next stage of her ordeal was worse. For five days straight she was questioned non-stop by a number of policeman, including the most notorious, Major Theunis Swanepoel.

Joel Carlson had come across Swanepoel in an earlier case and described him as 'A heavy man, broad across his shoulders, and the most outstanding thing about him was his ugliness. His face was pockmarked, blotchy pink and purple. His nose was flabby with wide, flat nostrils. His ears stood out from his head beneath his close-cropped ginger hair and his head sat on his shoulders as if he had no neck . . . His fingers, fat and short, moved a little uneasily but he seemed self-possessed . . . I saw the essence of the man in his eyes; they were cold, oily and frightening. I had seen the evil of the man's soul and it made me shudder.'[5]

As Winnie was questioned, it was clear that the police already had a great deal of information about her. They had letters she had written, knew of meetings she had attended, said they had statements from men she had associated with. Their challenge lay not so much in finding out what she knew, but in breaking her spirit. Working in shifts around the clock, they made use of a variety of techniques. They shouted at her, then they offered her food. They threatened her, then they were gentle. They offered her incentives to co-operate, then described the hell she might expect if she didn't. She hated them but she was also exhausted and disoriented.

The police wanted Winnie to make a statement – not just in court, but over the radio. She was to instruct the black people of South Africa to abandon all illegal struggles and co-operate with whites, claiming there was hope for them under present law. If she did this, they said, they would move Nelson Mandela from Robben Island and give him special privileges. They'd even release him and eventually allow him to resume a normal life. If she refused to co-operate, she could expect to spend the rest of her life in prison.

As the days passed, her health – both mental and physical – began to break down. Forced to sit upright in a chair, her body became swollen, while the stress of the interrogation gave her palpitations. When she was taken to the toilet and watched by a wardress as she urinated, she passed blood. She started to become dizzy, then she fainted. When conscious her mind wandered. Deprived of sleep she began to hallucinate.

Finally she capitulated, broken by the sounds of screams from an adjacent room. She admitted she was guilty. She had written every letter and attended every meeting. She confessed to everything they asked, until finally she was returned to her cell, delirious.

It had been an appalling experience, but others endured worse. Rita Ndzanga and her husband had also been arrested on 12 May, forced to leave their four young children alone in the house at two o'clock in the morning. Ndzanga suffered two torture sessions. First she was beaten and forced to remain standing until she eventually made a statement. She was then left in solitary confinement for several weeks, before they came for her again.

A white security policeman began to hit me; I fell down; I then began to scream; they closed the windows; I continued screaming; they dragged me to another room hitting me with their open hands all the time . . . In the interrogation room the security police asked me what makes me not speak. They produced three bricks and told me to take off my shoes and stand on the bricks. I refused to stand on the bricks. One of the white security police climbed on top of a chair and pulled me up by my hair, dropped me on to the bricks, I fell down and hit a gas pipe. The same man pulled my hair again, jerked me and I again fell on to the metal gas pipe. They threw water on my face. The man who pulled my hair had his hands full of my hair. He washed his hands in the basin. I managed to stand up and they said, 'On to the bricks.' I stood on the bricks and they hit me again while I was on the bricks. I fell, they again poured water on me. I was very tired, I could not stand the assault any longer.[6]

The strategy was to arrest and interrogate everyone. On the basis of the statements they received, the police decided who would be defendants and who state witnesses (Ndzanga ended up a defendant) but the difference was semantic. Everyone remained in detention. Witnesses would be prosecuted at a later stage. The police varied their techniques. Joyce Sikakane, who would also be a defendant, was given special privileges in an attempt to persuade her to co-operate. As details of her treatment were leaked to other detainees, this also served a divisive purpose. Prisoners believed Sikakane had turned against them and was co-operating.

Of the twenty-two accused, one man died and three others went mad. Winnie began talking to herself to pass the time. Suffering from insomnia, she found the nights as long as the days. She played with ants – if she had an ant or a fly in her cell she felt she had company for a day – undid her blanket and the hem of her dress, scraped paint off the wall, and did exercises. Eventually she was allowed a Bible. In her autobiography she described it as a meaningless document in the circumstances. Elsewhere she said getting it was the most unforgettable moment of her detention, it gave her a wonderful feeling of floating, as if she had taken a drug.[7] After the interrogation, her only outside contact was with white Afrikaans wardresses. They left her food, took her for exercise periods and came to inspect her. Inspection took place every day. Forced to strip, prisoners had to stand naked while every particle of their clothing was minutely inspected. Their bodies were also checked. Winnie wrote that although they never succeeded with her, other female prisoners had their vaginas inspected daily.

Hygiene was minimal. By the time Carlson was allowed to see the women in late October, they had not had baths or showers for more than 160 days. Water for washing was sporadically left in filthy buckets. The food was unsanitary, vegetables were covered with mud, raw porridge had strange lumps floating in it. The women could only eat it when driven by hunger. Many of them – Winnie included – suffered from malnutrition. Exercise was at best a ten- to twenty-minute walk round the prison yard accompanied by wardresses. At worst, it was non-existent. Prisoners were forced to remain in their cells with no exercise for days at a time. In the circumstances, Carlson was struck by how well his clients had held up.

When the accused finally came to court to be charged at a preliminary hearing in October there was some confusion as to who their lawyer actually was. None of the defendants had been able to instruct Carlson personally. Nor had he been given a copy of the indictments. He had no idea of the charges that were about to be brought against the twenty-two accused. He was unsure whether he really was their representative. All he had was signed power of attorney from a relative of each defendant. The situation was complicated by the presence of a second lawyer. While in detention, Winnie had been persuaded to sign her power of attorney over to a lawyer called Mendel Levin. In addition Levin claimed to have been given Peter Magubane's power of attorney before his arrest. Levin was determined to remain Winnie's representative.

'This is a serious matter your Worship,' he said. 'No person can claim that he actually acts for a person, unless he holds the power of attorney, or is personally instructed by that person. Now, my instructions insofar as Mrs Mandela [sic], are through her own authority and the lady is in Court and therefore, I want to make it perfectly clear that I am acting for her and untill her mandate is cancelled, I will continue to act for her.'[8]

With defendants represented by a lawyer recommended by the Security Police, the idea of a fair trial threatened to become farcical. But it was not to be that simple. After a brief recess so the matter of representation could be sorted out, Levin came back to court somewhat crestfallen:

'At all relevant times I held the power of attorney signed by Mrs Mandela personally and powers of attorney signed by relatives of certain of the other accused mentioned today,' he said. 'This morning in court when I saw Mrs Mandela, I asked her to confirm whether I was acting for her or not. She confirmed this. I saw her in the cells a few minutes ago and she informed me that she would make a statement in court as to the question of her legal representative.'

It seemed, Levin said, that Mandela himself had sent word to his wife, through her relatives, that no-one other than Carlson should act for her. He admitted he had no power of attorney for any of the other

81

defendants. In fact, he said, Mrs Mandela had mentioned to him that all the accused would be instructing Carlson. Levin then asked permission to withdraw.

And so it was settled. Carlson was accepted as lawyer for the twenty-two defendants. The trial was set for 1 December, and the hearing adjourned. The defence had a mere five weeks to prepare its case.

If that wasn't demanding enough, it proved to be extremely difficult to have regular consultations with the women prisoners. Many of the accused were shattered after their experiences of the previous few months and needed considerable encouragement to speak. The prosecution was slow to co-operate in providing copies of documents, and refused point-blank to hand over the statements given under interrogation. Counsel needed to be found and briefed (Carlson was an attorney and couldn't appear in the Supreme Court) and someone had to pay the bills.

The first ray of hope in the case came with the appointment of Judge Simon Bekker – a straightforward, relatively unbigoted man – to the case. Surprisingly, the indictments themselves were also cause for optimism. Though detained under the Terrorism Act, which carried the death penalty, the twenty-two accused had only been charged under the Suppression of Communism Act, whose maximum sentence of ten years could be suspended.

Again, this may be explained by the role of the United States. The United States was highly critical of what it described as the 'atrocious' Terrorism Act. In statements made at the United Nations the US frequently criticised the South African government's use of it during this period. It was quite clear that indictments brought under this act would not have the United States backing that could be expected under the Suppression of Communism Act. If a US government employee was to testify as a state witness in this trial, it would be preferable that he give evidence against a communist conspiracy.

Overall, the indictments did not reflect the time and energy put into them. The accused were broadly charged with wrongfully and unlawfully taking part in the activities of the ANC, and in some cases with furthering the organisation's interests. Details of the wrong and unlawful acts were sparse: The accused had established groups and committees, administered and/or taken the ANC oath, recruited members or encouraged each other to recruit members, arranged, attended or addressed ANC meetings, and encouraged each other to listen to radio broadcasts by the ANC in Tanzania.

They were also charged with planning to blow up trains and railway stations, corresponding with oversees branches of the ANC, visiting ANC members in prison to obtain information, obtaining post boxes and cover addresses for ANC mail, and propagating the communist doctrine in discussions, speeches and lectures.

There was no mention of how, when or where. When pressed to be more specific, the State provided further particulars which in some cases merely repeated the indictment. When asked, for example, what proof, the State had that the accused acted in concert and with a common purpose, the response was: 'Their participation in the said common purpose is inferred from their having taken part in the activities mentioned in the Indictment and particularised in this reply.'

However incomplete the charges were, a thorough defence had to be provided for each one. With the judicial scales tipped heavily in the prosecution's favour, it could not be enough to claim insufficient evidence.

Wherever possible in the indictment, Winnie, identified as accused number three, was specifically described in leadership terms. She was alleged to have addressed meetings, sent people on assignments, instructed others to recruit, received pamphlets and inspected trains. She was even charged with visiting her own husband on Robben Island during 1967 and 1969 – visits that had been approved by the State. Whatever illegal activity may have occurred during these visits, all of which had been monitored by the State, was not specified.

In his opening remarks, the prosecutor, J.H. Liebenberg, an elderly, astute lawyer, made a point of targeting Winnie.

'The accused, through the instrumentality of number three, maintained regular correspondence with the London headquarters of the African National Congress. She was required to report on matters affecting the African National Congress, the members, the distribution of pamphlets and any problems requiring solution,' he said.[9]

David Soggot, George Bizos and Arthur Chaskalson were retained as counsels for the defence. All three had solid track records as human rights lawyers. Chaskalson and Bizos had worked together as part of the defence team at Mandela's Rivonia trial and Bizos in particular was an old friend of Winnie's. It was Bizos who represented Winnie when her numerous brushes with the Security Police took her to court. A wartime refugee from Greece, Bizos was known to be a fearless adversary when taking on the government. Hopelessly overworked, like Carlson, he never became a rich man from his law practice. Most of his briefs came from the poor and oppressed, who came to Bizos with an unshakable faith that he could work miracles against the system. He couldn't, but he did what he could.

The pre-trial period quickly passed. Prisoners were interviewed during the day, counsel was briefed at night. Winnie was not afraid to lose her temper. After she had been charged, some of her restrictions eased slightly. She was allowed more clothes, for example. She described coming back to her cell on one occasion, after she had been consulting with Carlson, to find her suitcase of clothes had been flung on to the floor. The cosmetics and cold cream she had been given had been opened and thrown on top of her clean clothes. She was so angry she saw red, she said, taking her anger out on the chief wardress when the woman came to strip her. 'I don't know how she escaped that cell,' Winnie later commented.[10]

The trial affected the British as well as the United States government. One State witness mentioned in two counts of the indictment, Philip Golding, was a British subject who had been arrested and tortured into co-operating. He was being held in detention until the trial began and there was intense pressure from the British government to release him. As a result he was the first to take the stand. The fact that a British subject, whose testimony would be closely monitored by international observers, had been tortured, gave the defence an idea of what strategy to employ.

The old synagogue in Pretoria, converted to a courtroom, was packed on 1 December. Family, friends, reporters, foreign observers, students and church members sat in the public gallery, surrounded by police. Security Police also flanked the room: they cocked their guns as doors to the court were closed: then doors opened and the long line of prisoners walked in.

Winnie had managed to dress in ANC colours. All of the prisoners had been given clean clothes for the trial; Winnie's were adorned with green, gold and black.

'With due respect my lord,' she said, when asked to plead. 'I would like to draw your attention to the fact that I have been under detention in the past six months in terms of section six of the Terrorism Act, an Act which I regard as unjust, immoral, soul corrosive and physically destructive. Twenty-four days after my detention I lost a colleague of mine, who could not go through the ordeal we have already gone through behind bars and that was Caleb Mayekiso, a colleague. My lord, I find it difficult to enter any plea.[11]

Mayekiso had been detained in the mass arrest in May, but had died shortly afterwards while in detention. When pressed to enter a plea Winnie continued, 'I find it difficult to enter any plea because I regard myself as already being found guilty.'

'I think you are wrong in that assumption,' returned Judge Bekker mildly, entering the not guilty plea on her behalf.

Winnie showed no fear. In that sense she stood virtually alone. When Philip Golding began to give evidence he was obviously terrified. He stood with Major Swanepoel to his right, testifying inaudibly. Though constantly interrupted and told to speak up, he seemed too frightened. Not that what he said was particularly incriminating. As a former trade unionist, he testified, he had offered his money and expertise to various banned ANC members as a way of rebuilding South African unions. As part of that effort, he had been asked to approach ANC members in London to solicit their help and had failed. That, testified Golding, concluding his evidence for the State, was the extent of his involvement.

If a state witness and a British subject like Golding testified that he had been tortured, every other allegation of police brutality would significantly gain in credibility. If each State witness and defendant who had given a statement testified that that statement had been taken under duress, the spotlight would undoubtedly move from the dock to the table where Swanepoel and his fellow security officers sat. As David Soggot stood to begin his cross-examination, his aim was to get Golding to admit he had been brutally treated.

Obtaining the admission was hard work, for Golding's fear was largely based on his having no idea whether he was to be released or returned to detention. In the circumstances, he was understandably unwilling to antagonise the police. He admitted he had spent two days in the interrogation room, but when asked what had happened to him when he didn't talk, he replied that he really couldn't see the relevance of that line of questioning.

None the less the questions kept coming and Golding finally acknowledged that he had been kept standing for those two days. But he was still uneasy. When asked if it had been an emotional or physically painful procedure, he answered carefully, 'I wouldn't say emotionally, particularly.'[12]

Eventually Soggot got what he was after. 'I was punched,' admitted Golding, and, 'Kicked a bit . . . on my back.' When pressed he said he had been kicked four or five times. After that he clammed up. He was then allowed to leave the witness box, released and given permission to leave the country.

Mohale Mahanyele was not asked if he had been tortured. The

extent of his influence on the trial had already been shown in the charge sheet. Specific references had been made to the copying and distribution of illegal pamphlets, the receipt of letters and money from activists in London, the collection of mail from post office boxes in Braamfontein, and the attendance of underground meetings. When he came to testify he was forthcoming and thorough. Of all the State witnesses, he was unique in having a memory that never faltered. While others failed to remember conversations or discussions, Mahanyele not only recalled them in detail, the substance of his recollections was highly incriminating.

'I had spoken to accused number three on various issues regarding politics and she felt that all other avenues had been exploited unsuccessfully and the only alternative was for the African people to take it upon themselves to free themselves,' he said at one point during his evidence in chief. 'They were to use force in order to free themselves.'[13]

While the defence was aware that torture had occurred, counsel had to prove it. But fear was pervasive and it was hard work coaxing descriptions of brutality from frightened witnesses. George Bizos's gentle and persistent questioning of Eslina Klaas, a married woman from Port Elizabeth who had tried to help the families of prisoners, elicited another inadvertent admission of brutality.

Q. For how long have you been in custody now?
A. Seven months.
Q. And you were kept at a little police station called Addo, were you not?
A. That is correct.
Q. And Accused Number 21 [Livingstone Mancoko] was brought there by the police once?
A. Yes.
Q. What was your condition when Accused Number 21 was brought there?
A. There was nothing the matter with me.
Q. Didn't you have injuries on your face?
A. No.
Q. You needn't be afraid before his Lordship.
A. I am not afraid.
Q. Did anybody tell Accused Number 21 to tell you to make a statement?
A. I beg your pardon?

Q. Did anybody tell Accused Number 21 to tell you to make a statement?

A. When he was brought there, he was accompanied by two policemen and he asked me, that is Number 21, to make a statement.

Q. And did he in the presence of the policemen?

A. In their presence, yes.

Q. And was it clear that it was at the request of the two policemen?

A. I don't know.

Q. None the less he was in their company?

A. Yes.

[*Court intervenes*] Had you by then not made a statement yet?

A. I had not.

Q. And how long had you been detained by that time?

A. I was arrested on 14th May, and they came and saw me on 4th June.

[*Mr Bizos*] And on how many occasions had you been requested to make a statement?

A. On seven occasions.

Q. And wasn't your lip cut when Accused Number 21 saw you?

A. No.

Q. And didn't you have bruises on your face?

A. No.

Q. What were the people who were asking you to make a statement doing when you refused?

A. Nothing.

Q. Were they just nice, polite requests?

A. I was standing, I was asked to make a statement. They just spoke to me.

Q. And for what period of time were you standing?

A. From Monday to Thursday.

Q. All the time?

A. Yes.

Q. Night too?

A. Yes.

Q. Were you kept standing from Monday, Monday night, Tuesday, Tuesday night, Wednesday, Wednesday night and Thursday?

A. Until Thursday, yes.

Q. Without sleep?

A. Without sleep.[14]

When Shanti Naidoo was produced as a witness there was enormous shock. Naidoo's brother, Indris, was in prison with Mandela on Robben Island; her mother and family were in court when she appeared, to show their support for the other defendants. Since Shanti was not listed among them they had not expected to see her. In fact, they had no idea what had happened to her since her detention in mid-June; she had simply disappeared.[15] Shanti was as surprised as anyone when she heard she was expected to testify, and immediately refused. Her friendship with Winnie and Joyce made it impossible for her to speak out against them, she said.

Judge Bekker was understanding but unyielding. 'It obviously must be an unpleasant task that she is called upon to fulfil where two of her friends may be implicated as a result of her giving her evidence,' he said. Still, he would have to commit her to a period of imprisonment if she refused to co-operate. With a prison sentence for contempt hanging over her, Shanti did not hesitate to describe the mitigating circumstances lying behind her statement to the police.

'I was forced to make certain admissions because I couldn't stand the strain of standing on my feet for hours and hours,' she said. (She had been interrogated for five days without sleep.)

'My mind went completely blank at times, and I went to sleep standing and I had a sort of dream in which I was actually speaking to the officers who were interrogating me, in my sleep.'[16]

Naidoo was sentenced to two months' imprisonment for refusing to testify. Her sentence was positively received by her counsel. As a convicted prisoner, she could begin to serve a finite term in the main body of the prison and out of the control of the Security Police.

In its determination to isolate Winnie, the State did not limit itself to forcing friends to testify against her. Princess Madikizela, then in her early twenties, had been arrested soon after Winnie and threatened with ten years' imprisonment unless she testified against her sister. She had been kept in detention for the seven months between her arrest and the trial. On the stand – with Bizos's help – she made her discomfort clear.

Q. It can't be pleasant to stand in a witness box and speak about what your sister and her friends were doing?
A. That is so.
Q. And you must have made a statement to the police?
A. I was practically forced to. They said you are not going to leave

88

this office unless you make a statement.

Q. Who said this? Miss Madikizela, I want to give you this assurance, or perhaps I am putting it too highly, that you can speak freely before his Lordship, and as far as the Court is concerned, at any rate, I don't think that you have anything to fear anymore.

A. I understand.

Q. How did [the police officer] come to say that you would not leave that office unless you made that statement?

A. I told this person that it is difficult for me to talk about my sister.

Q. And what did he say or do about that?

A. He then remarked that even a male person cannot leave here unless he makes a statement and this applies to you to.

Q. And for how long did you hold out?

A. Well I was brought there during the early hours of the morning and in the afternoon I made my statement.[17]

Princess had been interrogated on three separate occasions. She claimed that she was no longer able to differentiate between her own recollection and what had been suggested to her in interrogation. More threatened with torture than tortured, at one point she had been shown a pile of bricks and told that Joyce Sikakane had stood on them when she refused to talk. 'She couldn't walk when she left,' Princess testified she had been told.

Although she appeared forthcoming, the amount of good she did for the State's case was negligible. Whenever she was asked an incriminating question, she grew confused or her memory failed her. She was asked to identify Peter Magubane which she did. She confirmed he was a friend of her sister, and that he sometimes called at the house. But, she said, she never listened to what they talked about.

Later she admitted attending the funeral of an activist but she couldn't remember where it was or what was said there. She did remember that no songs were sung at this funeral and no slogans shouted. Clenched fists were raised, though, by everybody.

Just before court recessed for the Christmas break, the defence team decided they would attempt to bring Mandela to the trial. He had, after all, been named as a co-conspirator. They were well within their rights to call him as a witness. Before going off on the two-month hiatus, they advised the authorities that they intended to subpoena him.

It may have been the prospect of giving Mandela unwanted publicity or it may have been the damage done by the exposure of police brutality, but the defence never got to present its case. When court re-adjourned in February 1970, the Attorney-General, Kenneth Moodie, was present. He was withdrawing the prosecution, he told Judge Bekker. Legally, this meant the defendants were to be acquitted.

There was no explanation for his decision and no forewarning. Judge Bekker seemed as thunderstruck as everyone else in court except for the police. While most of the courtroom stood stunned, they quickly forced the defendants into vans and took them back to prison. They had the power to re-detain them immediately under the Terrorism Act and they did so. The twenty-two accused, their lawyers, families and friends were back to square one. Instead of freedom, acquittal had led to more statements, more torture, more charges, more pleas, and another trial.

The first anniversary of the arrests came and went with no indication of when fresh indictments might be brought. The women continued to have a more difficult time than the men. Gone were the rights to visits, clothes and cosmetics they had won while they were on trial. The prison wardresses were, if anything, more tyrannical – taunting and harassing their charges with renewed vigour.

On 18 June the defendants were re-charged under the much harsher Terrorism Act. Winnie did not appear in court. She was in the prison hospital suffering from malnutrition. Her gums had started bleeding and she was having fainting fits. The problem for the State lay in bringing fresh indictments against defendants who had now been in prison for more than a year. Thus the second charge sheet, while alleging that a different law had been broken, bore an overwhelming similarity to the first. It was this virtual reproduction of the original indictments which finally brought the ordeal to an end.

At the start of the second trial in October, defence counsel, Sidney Kentridge, called for an acquittal. The grounds for his plea were straightforward: if the first set of charges had resulted in an acquittal, then so should the second, virtually identical set. Producing the two charge sheets he painstakingly compared them – an exercise which took three days. It paid off. All charges were dropped. The defendants were free to go. This time they were not detained again.

Chapter Five

Winnie had changed by the time she emerged from prison in October 1970. Incarceration, she wrote in her autobiography, had made her feel more liberated. Her soul had been more purified by prison than by anything else[1]. Yet however uplifting she claimed the experience might have been, it had taken its psychological toll. 'It is in fact what changed me. What brutalised me so much that I knew what it is to hate,' she said, recalling the experience twenty-two years later.[2] 'I still don't hate my oppressors as much as they hate us. Because to have that degree of hatred of a fellow human being because he shares an ideal you don't share, an ideology you don't share – you must have a very special kind of make-up within you, that would induce you to kill because a human being does not agree with you politically.'
Elsewhere she said:

> What I went through – that personal experience hardened me so much that at the end of my interrogation, looking at my interrogators and what I had gone through, I knew that as I sat in that cell, if my own father or my brother walked in dangling a gun and he was on the other side – and I have a gun too in my hands – in defence for the ideals for which I had been tortured, then I would fight. There was no way you could talk any language of peace to vicious men who treated defenceless women and children in that manner. I realised then that the Afrikaaner had closed the chapter of negotiations, and that the decision taken by my leaders in 1962 was arrived at with difficulty, but that there was no other way . . . The white man had hit us for too long. Our patience had been tested and had endured for too long. I knew then that there had to be a political crisis in this country for us to reach the ultimate goal.[3]

The fact was that she had been broken in detention. She had tried to hold out as long as she could under interrogation, but ultimately she had capitulated and told the police everything they wanted. Though she may, as she claimed, have been careful to place the blame on no-one but herself, by co-operating with the police at all she had sold out. By her own standards she was a traitor. On the surface there was no sign of inner harm. Perversely, isolation and torture had made her more beautiful. Joel Carlson thought she was enchanting – much thinner, with hollowed out cheeks and enormous, wounded eyes, but still extremely vivacious. At the party he threw the night of the release, the group of former prisoners, lawyers and friends didn't seem to have a care in the world as they celebrated freedom. Winnie had the same carefree attitude in the weeks that followed.

Even when she was re-banned a fortnight after her release (an administrative error caused the two-week delay) and once again forbidden to attend political, social and instructional gatherings, as well as prohibited from leaving her house at night or at weekends, she remained relentlessly cheerful. Occasionally she would moan about not having enough money to pay the rent or telephone bill, but she was far more likely to laugh at her predicament. Not that she found her situation amusing, no-one could have. Her laughter stemmed from a relief at being out of prison, no matter how difficult the conditions of freedom, coupled with a determination that she would not crumble, not even in front of friends.

In an interview she gave before the new ban, she was stoic. 'I don't really consider this freedom,' she said. 'The conditions under which I was detained are still the same. I expect the same thing will happen to me again. I am not frightened of re-arrest. I believe in the cause of the African people and am prepared to face whatever difficulties I come up against.'[4] She added that while she didn't expect to see Zinzi and Zeni until the Christmas holidays – they were still at school in Swaziland – her immediate plans were to visit her husband, whom she hadn't seen for nearly two years.

When her first application to visit Mandela was turned down, prompting Winnie uncharacteristically to burst into tears, there was a storm of outrage. A month later, the second application was handled personally by Justice Minister Pelser and immediately granted. Carlson accompanied her to Cape Town where they managed to lose their police tail for a brief period. It was a rare moment. Winnie and her lawyer drove all over the city without being followed and even managed a short trip to the beach.

At Robben Island, Winnie was allowed thirty minutes with Mandela who, pragmatic as ever, had brought a written list of things to discuss with his wife. Mandela had found his wife's prison ordeal extremely hard to bear. He later described it as a desperately distressing experience. He could never get used to the idea of Winnie in prison, he said, and had sleepless nights at the thought of the children alone at home in the holidays.[5]

All of this was proving too much for Winnie to cope with. On her return to Johannesburg she was taken ill with what was described as a mild heart attack. Stories of her poor health persisted over the next few months. As well as suffering from palpitations and high blood pressure, she contracted a severe case of bronchitis. But she continued to put on a brave front, even as the effort took its toll on her body.

Adjusting to life outside prison, she and Joyce Sikakane were initially helped by a white clergyman, Cosmas 'Cos' Desmond, who drove them around and let them use the telephone in his small house in Parkhurst to call prospective employers. This was really more for Joyce than for Winnie, who knew it was unlikely that she would be hired by anyone except friends. They also became friendly with a young scientist called Renfrew Christie who lived in one of Cos's rooms, and he, too, began helping out when he could. In return, Winnie prepared huge curry dinners for Cos's household.

Angela Cobbett, a wealthy white activist, whom Winnie met at Cos's house, offered her own home in Rosebank as another place where Winnie could meet with friends. Cobbett's husband was furious at his house being used for these meetings, and eventually reported his wife to the Security Police. Her husband wasn't the only member of the household to be less than enthusiastic about Winnie. Cobbett's maid complained that Mrs Mandela was disliked by the staff for being so cold towards them.[6]

Eventually Angela was divorced from her husband and had to move. Without a house to offer, she began to see less and less of Winnie, only bumping into her at rallies and meetings. Winnie grew increasingly distant and the deteriorating relationship left Cobbett somewhat embittered at being used and then dropped.

Until Cos was banned, Winnie went to see him every day. When his parents came to stay at his house, she made a point of visiting them too. It was an enjoyable time. Cos's parents thought Winnie was marvellous. She called them 'Mum' and 'Dad' which they loved. For the rest of her life, Cos's mother carried a picture of Winnie taken with her husband, showing it to everyone she met. Even when dying in hospital, nearly twenty years later, she showed it to all the nurses.

When Cos was banned, too, the government did not tell him why – they didn't have to. He knew there was official unhappiness at his dealings with blacks. Although some of the dinners continued, they had to be surreptitious. It became more difficult for Cos to help Winnie.[7]

His life became much more difficult too. His house was attacked, police shot bullets and threw bricks through his windows. Winnie's house was also attacked. First, an armed man was seen skulking under her back window. Then her front door was broken down when she refused to open it to men claiming to be Security Police. On one occasion a shot was fired through the door.

The day after that shot was fired, Renfrew Christie, Angela Cobbett and Chris Wood took Angela's Alsatian dog, Henry, to Winnie for protection. With Winnie unable to receive visitors, an elaborate pantomime ensued in the street. The dog was put through his paces and Winnie, standing at a distance, learnt his commands. Henry was well disciplined yet sweet-natured, trained to respond to simple commands. 'Watch' prompted a charge at an attacker, teeth bared and ready. 'Sit' was his command to stop. After the rehearsal the dog was persuaded to jump from the street on to Winnie's property, without any of her visitors having to take him to her. As no-one was on her property, no-one was violating the banning order.

At that point the police arrived and arrested Cobbett, Christie and Wood. All three were duly arraigned before a magistrate for being in a Bantu urban area without a permit. They were found guilty and sentenced to ten days' imprisonment or a twenty rand (£4.00) fine. Christie paid, but Cobbett and Wood were determined to serve their time. If by going to prison they intended to draw attention to the absurdity of their situation, they were successful. By virtue of being a wealthy white Northern suburbs housewife, not at all the sort of person the police liked to be seen jailing, Cobbett got huge press coverage. Someone – no-one ever found out who – paid her fine, much to her fury, and she was released. Wood served his time and the police took the opportunity to cut his shoulder-length hair short, gloating at the symbolic triumph of grooming a rebellious student.[8]

After their prosecution, Christie, Cobbett and Wood were subpoenaed to appear before a magistrate to give evidence against Winnie. Magistrates were beginning to force friends to testify against one another by means of section 29 of the Criminal Procedure Act – or face a jail sentence. Increasing numbers were forced to choose between betrayal and freedom, or imprisonment. The three reluctant witnesses dealt with their quandary by handing in written statements, which if admitted would presumably free Winnie.

They were admitted. But Winnie still had to go to trial. She was charged with violating her banning order and receiving visitors when taking possession of Henry. Though Christie, Cobbett and Wood had not been on her property, the police tried to prove that talking over the garden fence constituted receiving a visitor. It was a tenuous case at best and once the statements of her three friends were taken into consideration Winnie was acquitted.

She wasn't always so lucky. At the beginning of 1971 she was again charged with violating her banning order, when her sister Beauty came to the house with her husband, two children and brother-in-law to pick up a shopping list. Bizos defended Winnie and argued that the nine-month-old baby and two-year-old toddler could hardly pose a threat to State security. 'They can't conspire to form an illegal organisation,' he said.[9] But for receiving three adults and two children in her house Winnie was sentenced to six months' imprisonment. For receiving the banned Peter Magubane – who was found hiding under her bed by a policeman – she was given a year. The sentences were suspended for three years on appeal and the convictions were eventually overturned.

Winnie and her friends adapted their lives to accommodate their restrictions, making the police who pounded at Cos's front door wait on the doorstep while the banned people inside dispersed. When Cos was arrested for visiting Winnie, Winnie claimed he had not been visiting her at all, but had come to the house to give religious instruction to Princess. Yet each victory triggered another battle. Despite residing in Winnie's house for ten years and attending school in the neighbourhood, Princess was suddenly arrested for illegally being in Johannesburg, cautioned and discharged. Carlson then had to make a special application for her to continue living in Winnie's house.

Winnie continued to associate with other banned people as she resumed her political career, and among other things it led to the end of her relationship with Joel Carlson.[10] Well aware of his susceptibility to her charm, Carlson had none the less taken his responsibility for Winnie very seriously. He knew she needed work, he wanted to keep an eye on her, and he liked having her around so he offered her a clerical job in his office. But he made it absolutely clear that she must do nothing to discredit his law firm. She wasn't to use his telephone (which he assumed was tapped) to plan clandestine meetings. No political nor romantic activities were to be conducted from his premises.

Winnie refused to listen. When Carlson warned her against resuming a relationship with Peter Magubane, she chose to accept Magubane's interpretation of such advice – Carlson was simply jealous. He may have been, but he was also extremely anxious about the effects of her behaviour on his law practice.

He learned not to trust her explanations, never knowing whether they were based on fact or imagination. When Carlson told Winnie that his clerk had said she was having affairs, her response was that not only was it untrue, but that the clerk was a spy. Another legacy of her prison experience was that direct criticism seemed to trigger paranoia. Unable to evaluate it rationally, Winnie saw it as a personal betrayal. Her critics became traitors, spies, informants and sellouts. At the same time she was blind to those who were truly treacherous. She ignored several warnings from anxious friends about those who really might have been selling her out.

In his exposé of the Bureau of State Security, Gordon Winter recounted that during this period a rumour was planted by the Security Police, claiming Winnie herself was a traitor to her cause, and had been recruited by the recently established BOSS. Attempting to explain her constant ability to win acquittal on State charges against her, a story was spread that, as a BOSS agent, she was protected by the government as one of their own.[11] It is true that there was always a certain amount of suspicion about Winnie, which grew throughout the years. She did her own credibility the most damage, however, making it harder rather than easier for people to trust her. She took risks, she was indiscreet and she associated with dubious characters. It was sometimes hard to understand what her objectives could really be.

Carlson didn't actually have a job as such for Winnie and had to find things for her to do. Winnie didn't particularly care what she did, as long as she got out of the house and into the city. She did some clerical work and a a bit of translating, but she was bored and soon became difficult. She and Carlson started having rows. He was terrified at the potential impact of her activities, not just on his business but on his family. For it had soon become clear that Winnie had gone against his wishes and was engaging in underground politics again, using his office as her base. She even came in to use the telephone on Saturdays although Carlson had forbidden it as unsafe. She said that, since she was a national figure, Carlson should expect her to be involved in the struggle and she never tried to understand his own trepidation.

In the end he told her to get out and not come back. Her initial response was dignified, she left immediately without a word. But she didn't remain silent for long: Carlson began to hear rumours about himself, attributed to Winnie, to the effect that he was a thief and an adulterer. Carlson wasn't just under attack from Winnie. Police attacks on his house made him fear for his children's lives. Soon after this Carlson decided that he and his family should leave South Africa. He left for New York to make his home in the United States without seeing Winnie again.

Winnie found that other work was hard to come by, especially when employers were harassed by the Security Police. Over the years Winnie lost a number of jobs because of police intervention. At one point she worked in a dry-cleaners, another time she was employed for a few months as a debt collector in a sleazy operation run by a man who sold encyclopedias to working-class whites.

But Winnie showed a chameleon-like ability to adapt to the ways of those around her. With the activists she was militant; with the mothers of young activists she was maternal; with Ray Carter, wife of an Anglican priest, she prayed.

Winnie had become friendly with the devoutly religious Carter through Helen Joseph, and she began worshipping with her at St Mary's Cathedral. Carter took her relationship with Winnie very seriously. Her worldly contribution was to write to the government on Winnie's behalf, urging the Minister of Justice to stop his persecution. On the spiritual side, she rang Winnie every night as late as possible, to pray. They shared a a belief, she felt, that in all the evil and all the darkness, God was the true light. Knowing that her telephone was tapped, Winnie would respond, 'It doesn't matter who is listening, Ray, it can only do good.'[12]

It was Winnie's devout faith, Carter believed, which made her the lovely person she was and gave her the strength to cope with her suffering. The two women established an additional routine, promising to pray for each other every evening at 7 o'clock. Carter continued to pray for Winnie, even after they lost touch. Their friendship lasted for more than fifteen years, ending in the mid 1980s when Winnie suddenly stopped replying to Carter's letters. After that, Carter wrote to Nelson Mandela in prison, and he always wrote back.

Although Winnie used St Mary's Cathedral for worship, evidence was heard in the August 1971 terrorism trial of the Dean of Johannesburg, Gonville Aubie ffrench-Beytagh, that she also used it as a pick up point for funds. The British priest had been arrested on 18 January 1971 for allegedly storing and distributing literature of the ANC and SACP, inciting people to terrorism, receiving funds from IDAF (International Defence and Aid Fund) and planning to blow up buildings. He was convicted and given the minimum sentence of five years, released on bail pending his appeal which subsequently set aside both his conviction and his sentence. Ffrench-Beytagh then left the country rather than run the risk of being re-detained.[13]

During the course of this trial, a security policeman, identified only by his nickname of 'Pistool', testified for the State that he had infiltrated the ANC and, masquerading as Winnie's driver, had witnessed her collecting money from the Cathedral. Another State witness, Alinah Ndala, whose evidence was of dubious value once she admitted she had only co-operated with the police 'because there was no other way out', testified that as a member of the ANC she took orders from the organisation's leader, namely Winnie. On more than one occasion, she said, Winnie had instructed her to collect money from the church to be used in her ANC activities. Ffrench-Beytagh was convicted of two counts of inciting people to violence, and two counts of receiving funds illegally from the banned IDAF. He was found to have received 51,400 rand (more than £10,000) from the organisation, R1,000 of which was said to have gone to Winnie for rent, maintenance, car upkeep and travel to Robben Island. She was never prosecuted. Presumably it would have been impossible to prove that she knew the money she picked up from the church was illegal.

The following year Winnie unwittingly began spending time with another spy, the journalist John Horak of the *Rand Daily Mail*. According to Horak, who later told the truth about his duplicitous role, he used journalism to infiltrate left-wing circles. His effectiveness must have been questionable, as it was common knowledge among journalists that he was a spy. Visitors to the *Daily Mail*'s newsroom were even warned to be careful of him. He was allowed to continue as a journalist, however, as the general consensus was that it was better to know who the spy in the newsroom was than not.

Winnie couldn't see Horak as anything other than a friend who earned her trust by doing what she wanted. She went so far as to ask him to lie on her behalf on one of the many occasions she was charged with meeting Magubane. To maintain his cover, Horak gave a preliminary false alibi to Bizos, but stopped short of appearing in court on the instructions of his police handler, Major Johan Coetzee.

In October 1972, Winnie and Horak were detained together by the Security Police, taken to John Vorster Square, questioned separately, then released. The arrests received wide press coverage, doing much, the police felt, to increase Horak's credibility among activists. But just how effective his 'detention' had been remained unclear. He had been released with no more than a warning and those who escaped prosecution were always regarded with suspicion.

Winnie trusted Horak enough to use him as a driver for Zeni and Zinzi, taking them to and from school in Swaziland. When there were fears the girls might be kidnapped, the school was instructed by Winnie that only Horak was authorised to collect them.[14]

The two girls were not having an easy childhood. While both their parents had been imprisoned they had spent their time shuffling between boarding school and a selection of relatives and friends. Zinzi described life at Our Lady Of Sorrows as 'awful', a place where nobody cared for anyone.[15] Once they resumed spending their holidays with their mother, they had to endure the never-ending Security Police raids. At home for the 1972 Christmas holidays, twelve-year-old Zinzi spoke to reporters after a white man kicked the door of their house down.

It had begun with two sets of African policemen knocking on the door, asking to see her mother, she said. Then a man in a blue safari suit knocked. 'He told me to open the door when I said my mother was in the bath and then he kicked it open. The man shouted and swore at my mother through the bathroom door and then went away.' He later returned with other white men, Zinzi said, and denied kicking the door down.[16]

Of the two girls, it was Zinzi, rather than Zeni, whose stand against the police was more defiant. An intelligent, precocious child who was growing to look remarkably like her mother, Zinzi showed a singular resolve in coping with harassment. After the door incident she wrote to the UN Committee on Apartheid, and in surprisingly adult langauge called on them to press the South African government to provide personal security for Winnie.

You have expressed concern over my mother's safety. I would like to appeal to you to ask the South African government to ensure she is protected.

The family and mummy's friends fear that an atmosphere is being built for something terrible to happen to mummy. As you know, my mother has been a victim of several attacks, and we believe the attacks are politically motivated.

Hardly a month goes by without the newspapers reporting some incident concerning mummy, and her friends and family feel that the public is being conditioned to expect something terrible to happen to her.

I know my father, who is imprisoned for life on Robben Island, is extremely concerned about my mother's safety, and has done everything in his power to appeal to the Government to give her protection, but without success.

As you know, my mother is forced by her restriction orders to live alone and this makes it very easy for attacks to be made on her.

Her family and friends are now becoming really frightened about what may happen to her unless she receives proper protection.

Everything possible has been done in South Africa to appeal for her protection, but without success. Our only hope now is to appeal to the United Nations on her behalf.

At the end of this sophisticated letter, Zinzi said she was writing on her mother's behalf because 'If my mother wrote, you might not have had it as most of her letters to her friends don't reach them.'

From then on Zinzi played an increasingly public role. She spoke to reporters about her parent's plight. She lobbied members of parliament and human rights groups, and she began writing poetry, some of which described her life as a Mandela child.

She contacted the UN again the following year just before Winnie went back into prison to serve a six-month sentence for yet another illegal meeting with Peter Magubane. This time having 'Lunch with her children in a Combi [minibus] in the presence of a banned person.' The original sentence of a year in jail was reduced to six months on appeal. It was inevitable that the numerous violations of her banning order would result in some prison time and at the end of September 1974 Winnie went back inside. Appealing for his help in securing the release of both their parents, Zinzi and Zeni had sent a joint telegram to UN Secretary General, Kurt Waldheim. In return they received assurances that the Special Committee on Apartheid would redouble its efforts on their behalf.

On hearing that her mother was going to prison again, according to one story of this time, Zinzi burst into tears in court. Winnie turned to scold her for giving the police the satisfaction of seeing her cry, a weakness that was never to be shown again.

This prison experience was very different from the previous one. In prison proper, a convicted felon rather than detained under the Terrorism Act, there was no interrogation or torture. While serving her six-month sentence in Kroonstad Prison, Winnie's own courage impressed her cellmates, Dorothy Nyembe and Amina Desai. Her forbearance was in some measure due to their companionship, for the absence of solitary confinement was a real relief. Sunday visits from the girls when they were at home made her feel less cut off from her family too. Overall, conditions at Kroonstad were much easier than they had been in Pretoria Central Prison. There were proper washing facilities, and after the intervention of the Red Cross the food improved and inmates ate meat and vegetables every day. Spending their days sewing, discussing politics, and telling each other about their families, the three women grew close. Winnie especially felt a real solidarity existed between her and the much older Nyembe, who was half way through a fifteen-year sentence for harbouring MK guerrillas.

On her release in March 1975 Winnie went to work in the credit control department of Frank and Hirsch, merchandisers and distributors of electronic equipment. She stayed there for nearly two years. Her job involved following up the payments of those who owed money, compiling lists of creditors, sending out invoices and checking credit security of those who wished to make purchases. Helmut Hirsch had given Winnie the job at the request of the Institute of Race Relations. He was a brave man, whose act resulted in immediate and intense police scrutiny.

Winnie was an enormously popular employee and a good advertisement for the firm, although at first customers and some of the employees were shocked that she had been hired. She tried to diffuse the tension her employment had caused by chatting to those who walked past her desk, and making a point of greeting her fellow workers each morning. Among the staff of three hundred, she was more successful at winning the friendship of black employees than whites, many of whom saw her as a communist subversive. One young English immigrant actually resigned rather than work with Winnie, though she subsequently asked for her notice to be withdrawn when her husband told her she should be ashamed of her attitude.

Although staff members were afraid to associate openly with Winnie after the police made it clear that they were monitoring the company closely, many black employees spoke to her as a social worker. They asked for her advice as well as her political opinions, they discussed problems with passes and the repossession of houses. She always tried to help or to suggest other places that could help, but any aid she gave was mitigated by the problems that associating with her caused. With tips from informants, the police always knew who she had been talking to. Those who had dealings with her were contacted, warned, then deliberately harassed.

Winnie's bonhomie was never much more than superficial. While generally agreeable, she made no real friends at Frank and Hirsch. Her colleagues were fellow workers and she didn't see them outside the office. She spoke little of her own problems, though she was forthcoming when asked about the events of her life. Her reserve was accepted by the staff, who assumed that people in Winnie's position had to be very careful with whom they spoke.

For a brief period life seemed easier. The banning order which lapsed at the end of September 1975 was not re-imposed, nor was the house-arrest order renewed. Free to speak and move at will for the first time in thirteen years, Winnie immediately gave three interviews to South African newspapers, attended a terrorism trial, and made a major speech.

'As long as our people are imprisoned and as long as Whites continue to do what they are doing, my life will remain unchanged,' she told the *Star*, showing that her rhetoric had also remained unchanged. As she had done many times in the past, she predicted disaster. This time, however, she was unwittingly prophetic.

'Black people are now becoming impatient,' she said. 'It is becoming harder for them to understand why Whites allow this situation to continue. Nobody really wants violence. No mother wants to see her children die. But Black people are asking what they can do in an already violent situation. Is it possible that Whites are not aware of the agony of the Black people? Can they be unaware of how explosive the situation in South Africa is?'[17]

The situation she prophesied had been looming for more than a year, following a government announcement that, from the beginning of the 1975 school year African secondary school students would be taught in both Afrikaans and English – the two official languages. The new policy only affected white, urban areas, as education in the homelands continued to be conducted in English alone. There was no objection to English from students in any area, but aside from ideological objections to the enforced teaching in Afrikaans – long regarded as the language of the oppressive minority – there were practical disadvantages to this new directive. Teachers were not trained in the language. Every teacher-training college but one taught solely in English, and previously African teachers hadn't even needed to be competent in Afrikaans to qualify as educators.

African education experts expressed concern about Afrikaans as an enforced medium of instruction, saying that with so few teachers trained to teach – especially in subjects like maths and science, it was ridiculous to increase the shortage by an insistence on Afrikaans. Why couldn't the universally spoken English be the language of education, with Afrikaans taught as a subject? Why should an African child be forced to learn through the medium of not one but two European languages?

The inflexibility of the government, as its directive filtered down through various school boards, was recognised though not accepted by black students. Some explanations for the policy were patronising and insulting. One inspector was recorded as saying that 'The education of a black child is being paid for by the White population, that is the English and Afrikaans-speaking groups. Therefore the Secretary of Bantu Education has the responsibility towards satisfying the English and Afrikaans-speaking people.'[18] Schools were told they could apply to be exempt from the Afrikaans rule, but exemptions were rarely granted and this lip service to flexibility only heightened student rage. Afrikaans was to become a political rallying point of the youth. As protest after protest was ignored at school upon school, so the continuing protests grew increasingly violent, resulting in an outbreak of devastating riots.

Initial protests came from adults, not children. School boards and principals' associations were the first to speak out against the policy, with teachers' associations joining later. The government's response to statements of protests issued by these various groups was to tell them to mind their own business and not interfere with policy.

By 1975 students were actively organising against Afrikaans. Symbolically, it represented everything that African students in Soweto who were looking for alternatives to the government hated. Especially as there was a new focus on black pride in the country. Taking a cue from the United States, Black Consciousness was the order of the day, with Black Consciousness groups coordinating the mobilisation of students. Black Consciousness took the Pan-Africanist creed of 'Africa for the Africans' one step further. First expressed in the late 1960s, the movement rejected cooperation with whites, believing that whites were an intrinsic part of the black man's problem. 'Black man you are on your own,' said the South African Student Organisation (SASO) President, Barney Pityana, in early 1971. While identifying with and taking much of their tone from black American activists, such as Malcolm X, the South African black student leaders took pains to remain on good terms with American authorities within South Africa and stressed that Black Consciousness in no way meant unwillingness to be friendly with whites on a personal level.[19]

Winnie had embraced Black Consciousness wholeheartedly. Black pride was a cause she could sincerely identify with. The trial she had attended following her unbanning was that of twelve student leaders whom she described as 'a source of real inspiration and the leaders of tomorrow',[20] and she subsequently met and had talks with Steve Biko and other student leaders. As a result she was identified as a Black Consciousness activist by the government, although her position did not reflect that of the ANC, which continued to be a multi-racial concern. In her reaction to the energy of Black Consciousness she may not have reflected the position of the ANC's imprisoned and exiled leaders but she was very much in step with the feeling spreading among black youth across the country.

Chapter Six

By the middle of May 1976, 1,600 students at four Soweto schools were on strike against being taught in Afrikaans. At this stage students were not receiving much support in their militancy from parents. Most felt their children should continue with their studies while the matter received attention. But the matter did not receive attention as the government continued its policy of ignoring the students.

When students and teachers arrived at Pimville Higher Primary on 24 May, they were greeted by a poster which read: 'To hell with Afrikaans. No assembly today.' In front of the principal's office lay a heap of Afrikaans science books. Commenting on the strike, the Black People's Convention – another Black Consciousness group – applauded the students saying: 'The black child has long realised and accepted the challenge. It is true that the child is the father of the man.' This was not a tribal struggle, said the BPC, but a national struggle. It was a struggle which was daily becoming more political. In response to the BPC statement, Mr C. Ackerman, regional director of Bantu Education accused the organisation of provoking riots.

By now many black leaders were fearful that the protests would lead to unbridled violence. In a letter to Prime Minister John Vorster, Desmond Tutu, then Dean of Johannesburg, wrote of a 'growing nightmarish fear that unless something drastic is done very soon then bloodshed and violence are going to happen in South Africa almost inevitably . . . A people made desperate by despair, injustice and oppression will use desperate means. I am frightened, dreadfully frightened, that we may soon reach a point of no return, when events will generate a momentum of their own.'[1]

In the absence of official action, the students became increasingly militant. On 27 May, an Afrikaans teacher at Pimville Higher Primary, Mrs Karabo Tshabalala, was stabbed in the neck with a screwdriver by a student. Police coming to arrest the youth were stoned by other students at the school. When students at Belle Higher Primary (age 12–16) started drifting back to classes on 4 June, retribution was immediate. Those still on strike picketed the premises, padlocked the gates and buildings and stoned the pupils.

Police were now regularly visiting the increasing number of striking schools, and just as regularly getting stoned. Pupils were being detained by the police and those who were still at liberty and on strike refused to write their June exams. Police vehicles were set on fire. At one school tear gas was used to disperse the students, without effect. Pupils continued to hurl stones at police as the windows of the principal's office were broken and phone lines were cut.

Still the government took no action. Ignoring the school children in Soweto meant ignoring one fifth of the total population of the township. Out of an official population of roughly 800,000, 170,000 were at school.[2] And on 16 June 1976, 10,000 of those students decided that it was time to march.

The first shots were fired just after 8.00 am. A reporter for the *Rand Daily Mail* watched as two students carrying placards were attacked by police who shot at them as they ran down the street across Soweto at White City. The first death occurred as students converged outside Orlando West Junior Secondary School in the middle of that morning.

Eye-witnesses estimated that the crowd of marching children numbered 30,000, ranging in age from seven to nineteen. They gathered at different points in the township as they prepared to march to Orlando West, with seniors warning their various groups not to be violent. The march was to end at Orlando Stadium where a mass meeting was scheduled. By the time the police arrived at Orlando West, 10,000 students were already massed and stood giving the power salute, singing songs, and waving their placards.

Fighting began as soon as – without warning – the first tear gas canister was thrown by police into the crowd. Children scattered in all directions, some dazed and blinded by the gas. They swiftly regrouped and, when police re-charged, hurled stones in defence. The police opened fire, shooting directly into the crowd of students. The first child killed was thirteen-year-old Hector Peterson, who had been shot from behind. Other schoolchildren fell wounded to the ground.

The mood was now war-like. A police dog was let loose among the students – to be stabbed with knives. It fell writhing to the ground and was beaten with bricks and stones. Another dog was hacked to death and set alight. In immediate retaliation for the shooting, two white officials from the West Rand Board, Soweto's administrative body, were dragged from their vehicles and hacked and clubbed to death.

Police circled to advance among the students. Meanwhile children rushed into the school to ask those teachers huddled inside if they could drive the wounded to hospital. The teachers refused. A local Soweto doctor, Aaron Matlhare, began taking the injured to

Baragwaneth hospital. He would later be detained, tortured and used as a State witness for his role in the uprising.

To try to hold the police back, the unarmed children set up road blocks, stoning cars and forcing drivers to give the power salute and shout Amandla! before they were allowed to pass. Police vehicles were set on fire and some police forced to run for their lives through the rampaging crowds. Police helicopters hovered overhead, assessing the damage and spraying teargas as 25 armoured vehicles drove in black and white police reinforcements. The army went on standby, prepared to take on the children. Rioters commandeered buses from the local bus company and stoned trains running into Soweto before setting one on fire. Government buildings in the township became a major target, and as Soweto burned, the Johannesburg Fire Department said it was too dangerous to send in emergency vehicles, unless escorted by police or troops.

Journalists were also attacked, especially photographers as students objected to their pictures being taken while they rampaged. But the photographs worked in their favour as news of the shootings spread. A picture of the dead body of Hector Peterson flashed all over the world and the students began to receive additional support. Approximately 200 students at the liberal Wits University took part in a spontaneous picket outside the university campus in Jan Smuts Avenue, as a gesture of solidarity. Students there carried placards saying; 'Don't start the revolution without us'.

Black and white leaders in South Africa began to express outrage at the killing of children. Winnie's statement mirrored the radical mood of the students. 'The language issue is merely the spark that lit the resentment that is building up among Black people,' she said. 'Every car that looked like a White man's car was burned. That had nothing to do with Afrikaans.'

Desmond Tutu's statement reflected more of the anguish of the adults. 'I and many people want to know why the police should have tried to quell with guns a riot by schoolchildren,' he said 'Could they not have used water hoses to drive them back and dampen their enthusiasm? Would they have used guns and dogs on a similar group of White schoolchildren?'[3]

Interviewed on television that night, the Minister of Justice, Jimmy Kruger, who controlled the South African Police, defended police action. 'I believe the police used as little force as possible in the circumstances,' he said.

The rioting continued at the same level of intensity throughout the second day while whites in Johannesburg queued outside gun shops. The ramifications were beginning to reverberate way beyond Soweto. Overseas, South African shares plunged. Protesters massed outside the South African embassy in London, blocking the building and shouting 'murderers out', while a British foreign office spokesman expressed 'deep concern' at the news of serious incidents and heavy loss of life in Soweto. In Sweden, Prime Minister Olof Palme condemned the South African Police for firing on the students, calling the action 'an appalling manifestation of the brutality of an unjust society'. And while South African Prime Minister John Vorster prepared to leave for a weekend of talks on Southern Africa in Germany with American Secretary of State Henry Kissinger, the Soweto riots were hastily added to the agenda by the United States.

However informal Winnie's relationship may have been with the students – and until 16 June she had been more of an adviser than an active participant – in the days immediately following the riots her role expanded. With the foundation of the Black Parents Association Winnie became officially involved. It was the first time she had been given a leadership position in a political organisation solely in her own right. But she was loved by Soweto students far less for being Nelson Mandela's wife than for echoing their own positions against the system. For the first time, she, as a leader, perfectly reflected the mood of the masses. The situation in Soweto had been created from a grassroots level by young militants who, exasperated at having to tolerate the status quo, had taken the law into their own hands. Its dynamics finally crystallised Winnie's political position and gave her a blue print for future activism.

When she later described the events of the uprising, her language indicated this position. 'It was more of a war situation,' she said. 'That was a military zone. The government security forces were on that side, and the schoolchildren were this side.'[4]

The idea behind the formation of the BPA came from student leaders who needed parents as mediators rather than insurgents. They realised the value of a recognised parents committee to negotiate and act as intermediaries between themselves and the government. Many parents were horrified by the anarchic turn of events and anxious to restore order. Students had no shortage of volunteers. As soon as parents heard there was an organisation they could join, hundreds offered their services.

The BPA acted as a mouthpiece for the students, organised funerals for those who had been slain, and raised money for medical and burial expenses. Winnie was an automatic focus of attention. She was a unique combination of parent and radical, admired by the students for saying whatever they wished her to say with no fear. Her courage – especially towards the police – won her many fans. She marched in and out of police stations, shouting and throwing things, accusing the police of murder, issuing long lists of demands. Unflagging in her efforts to help, she organised meetings, drove people about, and pressured others into offering their services.

The BPA's first task was to organise the burial of the dead. Mass burials needed permits from the Johannesburg magistrate but the denial of permission came from the Minister of Justice himself. Kruger issued a statement justifying his decision on the grounds that a mass burial for those killed in the riots would be more an exercise in political agitation than an effort to assist the bereaved with the laying to rest of their dead. In a veiled reference to Winnie, he said, 'It appears that known Black Power organisations are affiliated to the Black Parents Association and that well-known political agitators are actively concerned with this organisation.' With no permission for a mass burial, the BPA called instead for a day of prayer and alerted the press to attend individually organised funerals.

Hector Peterson was one of the first to be buried. His funeral, which Winnie attended, drew large crowds, but although Security Police helicopters hovered overhead throughout the burial, it passed off without incident. Meanwhile the atmosphere in Soweto remained tense as schools were shut and meetings banned. Police continued to make arrests in connection with the riots and those they picked up were tortured to reveal what they knew. They were also tortured to sign confessions implicating those whom the police wished to hold responsible for the riots. Winnie was a natural target of the investigation. Not only was she actively involved in the BPA, she was also a leader of the ANC.

The Soweto riots had given a much needed injection to the ANC. Some student leaders were already in touch with members of the underground organisation, which was eager to take advantage of this new young generation of revolutionaries. ANC pamphlets circulated in Soweto in the days following the riots and ANC members who were secretly in the country actively recruited and worked together with the students, adding political objectives to their demands in an attempt to expand the language issue as the unrest spread.

Although Soweto schools reopened on 22 July, attendance was low and protests continued, with schools all over South Africa targets of arson. As the weeks passed, students in Soweto encouraged mass stayaways and work-stoppages to put pressure on the authorities. They called for the abolition of the entire black education system and eventually demanded the resignation of various members of the government-controlled black Urban Bantu Council. The council, which had no administrative powers and could only act in an advisory capacity, had long been scorned by most Africans, who felt it was a tool of the white authorities. The issue now involved far more than just language. There was now a whole range of demands with which the students, the Sowetan community and the ANC could identify.

The ANC's support of the students was not just internal. Many schoolchildren – some as young as ten years old – fled South Africa, crossing the borders to neighbouring countries. Some became ANC members before they left. Those who joined the movement inside South Africa had their passage out of the country arranged. On becoming members they would immediately be provided with money and transport to the border. Others would cross the borders independently and would be recruited by the ANC outside South Africa when they requested political asylum. Many students took advantage of the ANC's offers of safety from the South African authorities, especially when in doing so they received an education and a formal structure to their cause.

Much of the education was in fact guerrilla training in camps in Angola, Tanzania and Zambia. By the end of 1976, more than 6,000 young activists had left the country, according to South African Police records. The police closely monitored the mass exodus and knew that Winnie was one of the leaders heavily involved in recruiting. In addition to holding her responsible for the riots, they watched her use her influence in its aftermath to reinvigorate the ANC. A new law enabled them to stop her.

She was detained in August 1976 under the Internal Security Act. The government could now imprison people with no more excuse than wanting them taken out of circulation. It was preventive detention. Although 135 were detained under the act before the end of the year, the first to be rounded up were more figureheads than real leaders. The true student leaders – Sowetan teenagers as yet unknown to the authorities – were thus able to carry on organising.

Her house had been petrol-bombed a few days earlier, on the same morning that the BPA announced plans to seek a meeting with Minister Kruger. Whether or not the petrol bombing was intended to dissuade Winnie or any BPA member from being too confrontational with the Minister, again the true targets were missed. The BPA was only intending to act as a courier and present Kruger with a memo written by Soweto student leaders. Those who had actually written the memo, calling for the immediate release of all students in police custody and the scrapping of the Bantu education system, were to remain unidentified and protected.

After her arrest Winnie was taken with ten other women to Johannesburg's Fort Prison, where she remained for five months. During the school holidays, Zeni and Zinzi stayed with Helen Joseph, who took them to visit Winnie every week, bringing her fruit, clothes and newspapers. Zinzi later wrote that several families refused to take her and her sister in but that her father sent word that they should go to Joseph. 'She accepted us with warmth, happiness and with no strings attached. We felt at last that we had some home again.'[5] Many BPA leaders were detained, although the organisation continued to dominate the headlines. From prison, Winnie and her old friend and fellow BPA member Nthato Motlana brought an urgent application against an Urban Bantu Council member, Lucas Shabangu. They claimed that at an 8 August meeting at the home of Soweto's mayor, T.J. Makhaya, they had both been targeted by Shabangu as leaders of the BPA. One of those present at the meeting, Sidney Mkwanazi, described in an affidavit what had happened.

The meeting had started at about 8.15 pm, he said, and about fifty people attended – all members and former members of the UBC. Each person who entered was ordered to give his name to a man at the door, who was identified as a sergeant in the police force. A decision was announced that in future, any child who stopped workers from going to work or questioned workers returning home should be killed. Also, permission had been applied for and received from the government to 'remove the dirt' – a reference to student activists. Those present were told they had the co-operation of the police force in whatever they decided to do. Shabangu then called for attacks on various BPA members, including Winnie and Dr Motlana.

As details of this meeting became public, Shabangu and Makhaya fled into hiding. Justice Coetzee granted the Mandela and Motlana applications against Shabangu and ordered him to pay costs.[6] Winnie continued to be targeted. On the whole, women who were detained with her at the Fort Prison were not tortured or questioned about her role in the uprising. But as many of the true leaders were gradually rounded up, interrogation and torture continued with the line of questioning rarely varying. One former student leader later described the process:

The first thing that the police did was to try to suggest to us that all this had happened because of her. Basically trying to say that we just couldn't have decided on all those things that we did – she must surely have had a hand. She must surely have suggested these things. She must surely have been involved in getting us to know how to manufacture petrol bombs – which we denied, because it wasn't true of course. Which in my view was basically reflected of the mentality of our rulers, that [black] people are not capable of independent thought. We always need things to be suggested, to be instructed or commanded by other people. But the fact is that whatever happened in Soweto had nothing to do with her.[7]

In the minds of those subjected to this process, there was no doubt that the police were looking for an 'evidence' implicating Winnie to take to the government-appointed Cillie Commission investigating the riots. After they had been released, a number of students told Dr Motlana that the authorities had pressured them to blame both Motlana and Winnie for the uprising. Even if Winnie had not been involved in detailed planning, she was regarded as inspirational and as a role model. If the police were to smash the students' organisations successfully, Winnie had to be removed from the centre of action. Only if she were to be far from Johannesburg – not in prison, where she had a record of rallying other prisoners and encouraging defiance, but isolated in some remote spot – could she be neutralised. Banishing her was the only way to stop her. However much or little the events of 16 June were caused by her, by bringing about her banishment, the riots would change her life. She may have contributed to the general perception that she had been more involved than she was. When she described what had happened years later, she exaggerated her role and the size of the massacre, while protesting at the government's inflated idea of what she had done.

[Before the Soweto uprising] I was very involved in organising the people and conscientizing them about the extremely dangerous situation that was developing . . . I met with a few leaders here and suggested that we form the Black Parents Association to encompass the entire country, because it was obvious then, that the outbreak of anger against the state wasn't necessarily going to be confined to Soweto. The government regarded me as having played a major role in the formation of these organisations and in generally encouraging the students' militancy toward the state. Although it would be wonderful to imagine that I have such organisational powers, it was madness to think I was responsible for these things. This was a spontaneous reaction to the racial situation in the country – an explosion against apartheid.

I was present when it started. The children were congregated at the school just two blocks away from here. I saw it all. There wasn't a single policeman in sight at that time, but they were called to the scene. When they fired live ammunition on the schoolchildren, when Hector Peterson, a twelve year-old child, was ripped to pieces, his bowels dangling in the air, with his little thirteen-year-old sister screaming and trying to gather up the remains of her brother's body, not a single child had picked up even a piece of soil to fling at the police. The police shot indiscriminately killing well over a thousand children.[8]

Once again they came in the early hours of the morning. Throughout the night of 16 May 1977, as she had sat up studying – she had begun to work by correspondence course on a social work degree at the University of Southern Africa (UNISA) – she had heard strange noises. But when the raid started there was no doubt as to who had come and why. At first she thought she was being redetained under the Internal Security Act, but after several hours at Protea police station in Soweto, surrounded by heavily armed guards, she was told that this time she was not being charged or detained. Instead she was to be taken to the Free State. Her period of banishment had begun. Zinzi went with her. She had been at home when her mother was taken to the police station, and as she waited a large truck arrived at the house and policemen started loading furniture and belongings into it. Then they took her and the truck back to the police station, picked up Winnie and left.

Ilona Kleinschmidt, former wife of the head of IDAF, Horst Kleinschmidt, and a close friend of Winnie, got a call from her in the early hours of the morning to say she was being taken away. Again Winnie was terrified at disappearing without trace. Many others had been taken off into remote places without any means of communication and disappeared in recent years. Touching base with Ilona meant that someone somewhere knew where to come and look for her.

In 1977 Brandfort was in the middle of nowhere. Later, when the toll road was built, it was four hours' hard drive from Johannesburg, with the landscape gradually broadening out as the houses fell away, until finally nothing remained on the horizon between the ground and sky. The colours of the Free State in which Brandfort sat were not rich and vibrant like the Transkei but more a mix of gentle pastels – any lustrousness was dusted down with a wash of sand. In contrast to the muted tones, the temperatures were extreme: There were freezing cold nights in the winter months and baking hot desert-like days in the summer.

The white section of Brandfort seemed on first sight to be an idealised heartland town. It was clean, well-ordered and fresh. The mid-size houses were low and wide with well-watered, manicured lawns and neatly kept flower beds. The citizens of Brandfort were neatly kept too. It was a small town. In its entirety, Brandfort was smaller than one northern Johannesburg suburb. There was one main shopping street – at one end stood the police station with its well-tended fences and its smiling officers, at the other end was the township.

The poverty in Brandfort's township was chronic. Those who could looked for work forty miles away, in the city of Bloemfontein, taking employment in any form of unskilled labour. There were few jobs in and around Brandfort, though it was possible for some to work as manual labourers for local white shop owners or farmers, or to join the police force. Work tending cattle as farm labourers barely paid a living and depended on the vagaries of the seasons as well as the landowners. There was no question of saving money in the township. Whatever money was earned was needed even before it came into the house. Those who couldn't find work starved. Township buildings reflected the poverty. Houses were little more than makeshift shacks, bits of nylon acted as curtains and doors, piles of bricks became tables and shelves. Iron beds doubled as couches during the day, taking up most of the space in the one room.

As they arrived in Brandfort's black township and were dropped at house no. 802, Winnie and Zinzi could not believe what they were now facing. As MP Helen Suzman subsequently described it, Winnie was to be 'cooped up in a dreary little Free State dorp, in an even drearier black township'. They had not been allowed to pack – the police had done that for them, when they loaded the truck, grabbing all their belongings and stuffing them into bundles. Everything they owned had been brought with them, but less than one third would stay. As the police tried to cram furniture, electrical appliances, clothes and books into the tiny three-roomed house, anything that couldn't fit through the minuscule front door was taken away to be stored in the local police station.

When Ilona Kleinschmidt arrived the next day she found the two had practically nothing. Nor had the house. There was no water, no electricity, and the floors were covered with earth. Prior to their arrival the house had been used as a dump by local builders. There was no bed – Winnie and Zinzi had spent their first night huddled together on a mattress.

This was how Winnie and Zinzi Mandela found themselves as Brandfort moved towards winter. They were nowhere with nothing. They couldn't even speak the local African language, Sotho. Not that they would have been in a position to communicate if they could – Security Police had already visited the township and warned local inhabitants that Winnie was a dangerous criminal. Residents were instructed to have nothing to do with her. Any local curiosity about her was therefore outweighed by fear – not just of her and of what they had been told she might do to them, but of what the authorities might also do to them, if it was discovered that they had been in contact with her.

If Ilona Kleinschmidt was shocked at the three-roomed shack which was supposed to be Winnie's new home, she was impressed at Winnie's resilience. On her arrival in Brandfort, not knowing where to look, she eventually found Winnie carrying a bucket of cold water back to the shack, knowing she had no way of heating it. She might have been despondent, but it didn't show. Instead she looked superb, wearing a smart skirt and jersey, a fashionable pair of boots, and a silk hat on her head. Kleinschmidt was amazed at her strength of character. Winnie was determined to be strong for Zinzi, for she was desperately aware that however bad the predicament might appear to her, it must seem that much worse for her sixteen-year-old daughter.

Kleinschmidt made a list of things Winnie and Zinzi needed and went back to Johannesburg, leaving mother and daughter behind. Winnie wasn't keen for Zinzi to stay but Zinzi wouldn't go, unable to bear the thought of leaving her mother there alone. Back in Johannesburg, Kleinschmidt spread the news of Winnie's banishment, and soon carloads of Winnie's friends were making the long, slow journey to the Free State.

Priscilla Jana, an associate at Ismail Ayob's law firm who handled most of Winnie's legal business at that time, was one of the earliest visitors. She brought Winnie a little black and white battery-operated television whose batteries could be recharged at the office of a local attorney, Piet de Waal, whom Winnie had swiftly retained as her local legal representative. Jana also took down cosmetics, fresh fruit and vegetables. Others who came collected Winnie's clothes for dry cleaning and took them up to Johannesburg, either returning them themselves on their next visit or giving them to someone else to take back. If her shoes needed mending, they too would be collected and taken back to Johannesburg for repairs. People brought gas heaters, quilts, books, pictures – anything they could think of to make the tiny house more inhabitable. Winnie might have been gone, but she was never forgotten.

But there was no doubting her loneliness. Her infrequent visits to Mandela took place under the same difficult conditions. The couple continued to correspond. They had now been separated for more than fifteen years but Mandela's letters to his wife remained romantic and lovesick. He wrote of the tenderness and intimacy that existed between them and of how much he loved and missed Winnie. He often referred to her beauty and the physical nature of their relationship, though he hadn't touched her since 1963. Mandela constantly referred to incidents that had taken place during their brief time together, saying that touching Winnie's hand, hugging her, tasting her food and spending hours in the bedroom with her were the things he could never forget. Her love and devotions, he wrote to her, had created a debt he could never repay.

Winnie's visits to Mandela gave her rare opportunities to leave Brandfort, for not only had she been banished, she had also been banned. One friend, who theoretically could not visit her, still regularly made the long journey to Brandfort. Helen Joseph had been distraught when she first heard the news of Winnie's banishment and immediately wanted to rush down and visit her. But at seventy-two she was unable to make the long journey alone. She confided her distress to a member of her local church, Barbara Waite, wife of the famous South African cricketer John Waite. Waite was a nurse and, as a member of the women's group Black Sash, actively involved in working for human rights. She had already met Winnie briefly through Joseph and didn't mind acting as Joseph's driver to the Free State, although she hadn't particularly taken to Winnie. Waite and Joseph began making the trip to Brandfort once a month, sometimes going together, sometimes taking Father Leo Rakale, an Anglican priest.

White people were not allowed into the township, so visitors would call ahead from Johannesburg to the telephone box at the local post office at prearranged times to let Winnie know they were coming. Then, as laden cars drew up to the boundary between the township and the white section of Brandfort, they would find her waiting, overjoyed.

The rules governing Winnie's movements, including the one preventing her from speaking to Helen Joseph, were rigidly enforced. On many occasions the two women did not even speak to each other, despite the fact that Joseph had driven so far to see her friend. The Security Police daily sent a policeman from Bloemfontein to watch Winnie and arrest her whenever she made an infringement of her banning order. In the early days it was Sergeant Gert Prinsloo, who took his job exceptionally seriously. He spent most of his day parked on a low hill opposite Winnie's house, watching her through binoculars, but sometimes he would come closer. He was difficult to those who came to see her, and seemed especially dedicated to harassing her friends.

He had the opportunity to make life difficult for Waite and Joseph when Joseph decided she wanted to go down to Brandfort as a surprise for Winnie's birthday. Having telephoned ahead to Zinzi to let her know they were coming and to tell her to bring Winnie out to the township boundary at a certain time, the two women set off with the car full of presents and a birthday cake. Arriving in Brandfort, they sat at their prearranged spot and waited for what felt like hours – but no-one appeared. It began to drizzle. Reluctant to sit parked in the same place for too long for fear of drawing police attention to the car, Waite started driving around, looking for anyone who could go into the township to fetch Winnie. Eventually they saw a man on a bicycle and asked him if he would please go to tell Mrs Mandela she had visitors. Finally Winnie emerged, not knowing who or what to expect. Zinzi had completely forgotten to give her the message.

As soon as she saw who was in the car Winnie was thrilled. She ran up towards them and as Joseph got out she threw her arms around her and hugged her tightly. It didn't matter that they were breaking the law, she embraced her friend and told her how glad she was to see her. She greeted Waite effusively too, ignoring the fact that she was now contravening two parts of her banning order – first by talking to someone listed, and second by attending a 'gathering' of more than one person. On that rainy birthday in 1977, it didn't matter what she was allowed to do. Her friends had come to visit and she was delighted. Both Joseph and Winnie began talking together as Joseph filled Winnie in on details of Steve Biko's death. Biko, who had been detained on 19 August, had died of multiple head injuries just days before, on 12 September, having been driven for 750 miles naked and manacled in the back of an open truck.

What happened next would have been farcical if its effects hadn't been so devastating to at least one of the women present. There was a rustling of leaves in a bush behind where the three women stood, and, like some evil pantomime character, out jumped Officer Prinsloo. He had crept into the bushes to spy, remaining hidden as they stood chatting.

Prinsloo requested that Waite and Joseph accompany him to the police station to make a statement. He wanted them to commit to paper the circumstances of this meeting with Winnie. All three present were aware of the implications. Joseph and Waite knew that if they made such a statement, Winnie could go to prison for violating her banning order. For Joseph this was routine. After a lifetime of harassment, being taken off to yet another police station in an attempt to be forced to make yet another statement held no threat for her. Rather, she enjoyed the challenge, and promptly refused to make a statement on principle.

For Waite it was entirely different. She had not spent her life dodging the Security Police as an anti-apartheid activist. Her activities with the Black Sash movement may have had an element of danger, but on the whole she had been protected from this kind of exposure by her social background. She was a liberal white nurse and housewife living in the security of Johannesburg's northern suburbs. Unlike Angela Cobbett, who came from the same background but enjoyed the idea of confrontation, Waite was a retiring woman. For her, this was an extremely distressing situation.

Once Prinsloo had made his presence known and demanded statements, Winnie and Helen Joseph automatically slipped into a well-worn pattern of behaviour. First there was the refusal to make a statement to the police on principle. They said that there was nothing to make a statement about. Nobody had done anything wrong, nothing had happened. Waite found herself swept up beside them. She knew that, trivial as it might seem, something had happened. Winnie had contravened her banning order. The law, however much they might hate its pettiness, had been broken. She couldn't let the authorities know that, but she was an unskilled liar who considered telling untruths a sin. She couldn't and wouldn't fabricate an entirely innocent encounter. So, from a combination of loyalty and fear, she too refused to make a statement.

Waite and Joseph were allowed to leave Brandfort but told they could expect to hear more from the police. As they drove out of the town, they passed Desmond Tutu on his way in. He too was coming to visit Winnie. They told him what had happened and then drove on back to Johannesburg. That night Waite got a phone call from Tutu. He asked her why she had refused to make a statement, she could have made one saying nothing had happened. He had spoken to Winnie, and apparently nothing had in fact happened. Waite told him that that wasn't true and that she dare not make a statement – but it wasn't to be that easy.

She and Joseph were subsequently issued with subpoenas to appear in court in Bloemfontein. Waite received a sentence of one year's imprisonment for refusing to make a statement. She was given leave to appeal and released on bail. Waite then contacted Counsel Sydney Kentridge to handle the appeal for her. Like everyone else, he asked her why she didn't make a statement now. She'd made her stand, he said. But Waite was really terrified of lying. Still, Kentridge managed to get her sentence reduced to two months. Joseph was only sentenced to twelve days because of her advanced age, and began her sentence feeling honoured at the opportunity to serve time for her friend.

Going to prison was the worst thing ever to happen to Waite. Knowing that her imprisonment wasn't a resolution, that she would have to face the situation once more on her release, she remained frightened. She had been told she would be asked to make the statement again on completion of her sentence, or face another spell in prison. As she sat, day after day, desperately weighing up her lack of choices, Waite finally realised she had chosen the path that had been urged on her from the start. She could, and now she decided she would, lie. The day she was let out, she went straight to Kentridge and fabricated a statement. She then went to Tutu and told him what had in fact happened, even though the Bishop made it clear he really didn't want to know. After that she shunned Winnie. She couldn't bear to have anything to do with her, especially when she heard that Winnie was telling people she had no idea why Waite had refused to make a statement – nothing had happened and she could easily have said so.

Winnie's version of the incident was slightly different. Waite and Joseph, she wrote in her autobiography, were forced to spend four months in prison for refusing to give evidence.

Helen Joseph and Barbara Waite, used to bring me some food – that was early in 1977. Father Rakale usually brought them and notified me of their arrival. This time he couldn't come, so they sent me a telegram from the post office and I rushed to town. There were warm exchanges and I was careful to greet one at a time. I parked a few yards away from them. We took the groceries from Barbara's car to mine. It started raining. So Barbara was sitting in the back of the car, Helen Joseph in front. I stood next to the car and spoke to Barbara.[9]

Other friends of Winnie went to prison for refusing to make statements about her, as the State continued its attempts to discourage visitors to Brandfort. Ilona Kleinschmidt and a friend of hers called Jackie Bosman went down one weekend, and had the same treatment from Prinsloo. Once again he was hiding in the bushes, as had become his habit, watching every interaction. As the two women prepared to leave at the end of the visit, Prinsloo approached their car and requested their names and addresses. They thought nothing of it – he always did that. Nothing happened for a couple of months, but then two subpoenas were issued. Kleinschmidt and Bosman were to make statements. Having been asked general questions they refused on principle to make statements without knowing what it was that the police were looking for. The impression they received as the police asked who was there, what had been said and whether Winnie had contravened her order was that they were looking for a reason to arrest Winnie for breaking her banning order and hoping her friends would provide it.

Like Waite, Bosman and Kleinschmidt received a sentence of one year's imprisonment for refusing to co-operate with the police. But these women laughed, it seemed so ridiculous. One year! For refusing to make a statement to the police! It was ludicrous. They appealed againt their sentence and won, but their euphoria was shortlived when two weeks later they were re-subpoenaed under a newly written section of the Criminal Law Amendment Act. They went back to court. This time Bosman was given four months' imprisonment and Kleinschmidt three – the dropped month a magnanimous acknow-ledgment by the authorities that she had a five-year-old daughter to take care of. The two women finally went to jail at the end of 1979. They were allowed to spend three hours a day together and passed the time reading and knitting. Soon after their release they made the journey to Brandfort again.

Winnie had sent a series of loving messages to both women as they went through their ordeal and they were concerned that she would feel guilty about what they had done for her. They wanted to reassure her that she was not the cause of what had happened to them. It was not her fault, and she should not take responsibility for them. From then on, the episode was never referred to again.

Even Winnie's doctor was subpoenaed in 1979 in an attempt to harass her. Joe Veriava used to visit sporadically from Johannesburg to deal with Winnie's various ailments. Winnie suffered from high blood pressure, and a lot of what Veriava described as 'stress-related' complaints. His subpoena was eventually dropped, and the State acknowledged that interfering with a doctor-patient relationship was going to be hard to hold up in court.

It was accepted by those who were harassed that the only relevance of their predicament lay in its ability to upset Winnie. The message being sent to her friends was that if they came to see her they would end up in a situation they could not win. If attempts to isolate her by sending her to the middle of nowhere had failed, then making public examples of her visitors might be more successful. For a while the strategy worked. For a brief period at the end of the 1970s Winnie's friends became anxious about the prospect of driving to Brandfort, affected by what had happened to the four women. It was in this, perhaps her loneliest period, that Winnie turned her attention to the town in which she lived.

Despite the constant hounding by police, she began to make a life for herself in Brandfort. Though she was consoled in the early months by having Zinzi with her, it soon became clear that having her around was a mixed blessing. Zinzi was just as much a target of Security Police harassment as her mother.

Just five days after her mother had been banished in May, Zeni – by now eighteen, and eight months pregant – had married Prince Thumbumusi, son of King Sobhuza of Swaziland. The two had met while Zeni was studying in Swaziland at Waterford School. Because of the terms of her banishment, Winnie had initially been refused permission to attend Zeni's wedding, the decision only being reversed on the intervention of her former admirer, Kaiser Matanzima of the Transkei. After Zeni had given birth to Winnie's first grandchild – a girl – she travelled to Brandfort for the christening. She was soon to leave South Africa for good for the United States. Now Zeni was a member of the Swazi royal family, intending to study in America, Winnie knew she was safe from the South African authorities. But Zinzi was still vulnerable to persecution.

In theory Zinzi was free to move around as she wished, though the fact that she had not been banished, nor served with a banning order, was no deterrent to police. Friends who tried to visit her were either prevented from doing so by police or questioned extensively and aggressively about their meetings. Consultations she had with doctors and lawyers were interrupted, and the police never ceased in their attempts to intimidate Zinzi herself. On one occasion, when local friends had come to the house, they burst in, using the informal gathering of teenagers as a pretext to arrest Winnie.

Both Winnie and Zinzi were defiant in the face of their treatment. On the first anniversary of the 16 June student uprising, Winnie took Zinzi to a Whites Only boutique in Brandfort to buy her a black mourning dress. When the saleswoman pointed out that they were breaking the law by being in her shop and tried to throw them out, Winnie lost her temper and started shouting. The ensuing fight resulted in yet another arrival of the Security Police.

Not long after her mother's banishment, Zinzi began to break down. Before leaving Johannesburg she had sought psychotherapy. Now, in the absence of that treatment and with the constant pressure she lived under, she became severely depressed. Her skin became infected and she went to see a local doctor who told her that her condition was pyschosomatic. She couldn't sleep at night and wept continuously. During the day she was listless and despondent. When she tried to tell the lawyer Priscilla Jana what was happening to her, she was interrupted by the police to such an extent that the two women eventually sought refuge in Jana's car and drove out into the veld for their meeting – only to be followed there by Prinsloo.

In September 1977, four months after the banishment to Brandfort, it was clear to Winnie and Nelson that something had to be done about Zinzi. From prison on Robben Island, Mandela brought an urgent application for an interdict against the Security Police to restrain Prinsloo and Sgt Zakia Ramalthwane from intimidating or harassing his daughter. Affadavits filed before the judge, Mr Justice De Wet, described the treatment Zinzi had received. Zinzi's own statement gave details of police bursting into her house while she had friends over, demanding names and addresses, issuing threats and evicting everyone present, then visiting the teenagers in their own homes and detaining them for questioning. As a result, she claimed, people were terrified of coming to see her. For a while, she said, she tried leaving the door to her house open, so that the police could see she was entertaining guests alone. But that didn't work either and eventually she resorted to talking to friends for a few moments at a time over the fence or in the yard.

Affadavits from two local teenagers described being interrogated, arrested, assaulted and threatened with imprisonment if they continued to have anything to do with Zinzi Mandela. One of the friends claimed he was asked by the Security Police to work for them as an informer against the Mandelas. In granting the order against the police and awarding costs, Mr Justice De Wet stated that, even though her mother was restricted, Zinzi had the right to receive visitors in her house. Any allegations that the visitors were in fact there to see the mother had to be supported by at least some evidence, he said.

But Winnie had had enough. The pleasure she derived from having her daughter with her was dissipated by the anxiety she felt on her behalf. It was not right that a teenage girl should live like this, she said. Zinzi must concentrate on her own life. This kind of treatment was not going to stop and it would be better for Zinzi to go away from it all. She sent her back to Johannesburg to live with Helen Joseph.

Zinzi's departure from Brandfort left a huge gap in Winnie's life. Not only were friends' visits dropping off, she now had no family member there for support and nobody in the township would talk to her. Even when she went to fetch water from the municipal tap, she was shunned. Nelson Mandela had known she would be deeply distressed by Zinzi's departure. He was fully aware that Zinzi was Winnie's last link with any kind of happiness in Brandfort, and he worried about her loneliness. He wrote letters of support to both women.

Norah Moahloli, who lived a few doors down the street from Winnie, would see her standing at her gate watching the children play. Children were allowed to speak to her, and Moahloli began sending her small son up the road with a pumpkin or some vegetables for Winnie as a gesture of friendship. In the early Brandfort days, Winnie had very little money and – prevented from working – was dependent on the charity of others to survive. Friends from Johannesburg who brought down groceries often included an abundance of oranges. She started giving them to the children who played outside her gate, and slowly they got used to her and would come over to her, at first shyly and then with increasing confidence.

As always Winnie's popularity base was with those younger than herself. In Brandfort it was the children who first accepted her and the children who were most influenced by her. She started going up to the school in breaktimes and handing out fruit and sweets. Children would go to her house and she taught them to read with books that friends from around the country sent to her. They would sing songs together and play games.

As the months passed, the people of Brandfort gradually grew more used to her. It was the habit of those in the township to greet one another as they went about their daily business, and soon they found themselves greeting Winnie, too. She asked the women about their organisations and if there was anything she could do to help with cooking or sewing. There was some resistance to her to begin with, but she took the initiative, saying she knew of outside organisations that could be of assistance to them and she would contact them for help. It wasn't long before a large parcel of black material arrived, sent from an 'outside organisation', to make uniforms for the school-children. The material was followed by a sewing machine, the sewing machine by food, blankets and vegetable seeds.

Winnie contacted Operation Hunger and food supplies began to be delivered to Brandfort on a regular basis. This infuriated local whites who had enjoyed a lucrative practice of selling soup, sandwiches and old clothes to the elderly residents of the township, coming to sell their wares on days when pensions were issued, and there was money around. Now, not only was Winnie cornering their market, she was making them appear greedy and corrupt. On the same day they were trying to sell their products, she came with the food from Operation Hunger and gave it away. She made a point of telling those who took the food that she was giving it away free whereas the whites were selling it.

She spent evenings reading and continuing with her UNISA course work. Much of the course was conducted by correspondence, but she was occasionally allowed to travel to Pretoria to attend seminars. Part of her social work degree included the study of anthropology and her written assignments showed how seriously she took the work. She took care over the presentation, carefully underlining all headings, writing lists in neat columns. Each four-part paper took her between two and three hours. The layout was better than the substance. On one question in an August 1978 assignment, where she was asked to name the geographical races of the world, she mistakenly only listed African races – for which she received 0/6 and an admonition in the margin to 'Please read the questions carefully'.[10] Discussing concep-tions of the supernatural in April 1979 she wrote as an introduction to an anthropology essay for which she received 50 percent: 'It is generally accepted that although many individuals believe in the supernatural, this belief seems more pronounced in non-literate people and very often the belief is intertwined with religion as part of people's culture. That is why magic is invariably included in discussions of religious systems. The Anthropologist view point concentrates on determining what kinds of supernatural beings and powers the people believe in.'[11]

The most enlightening remarks were her own, written in the space on the back of each paper where students could comment on the assignment. In May 1979, she wrote: 'I was extremely impressed by the tutorial we attended at UNISA on 11 & 12 May which enlightened me on how to handle your assignments though I may still have problems in sorting out the relevant information.' She then wrote in the section for other suggestions: 'For far away students like me with no study group around it would have been so helpful if there was some kind of workshop group with our lecturers and similar students besides the large impersonal tutorial once in a while if possible.'[12]

'I may not be able to write always because of all the adverse pressures I have to cope with all the time', she wrote to Ray Carter at the end of 1978. 'But one thing you should always know is I regard you as the Angel God has sent to be with us spiritually in Brandfort, to cheer us at difficult times and to help us pray and be grateful that we are still there when others have had to give up their dear lives in the names of principles that are dearer than life.' She added that she still prayed for Ray at 7.30 each night.

In comparison with his wife's situation, life had become easier for Mandela and the other Rivonia trialists. Many of the political prisoners who had been imprisoned in the mid 1960s had completed their sentences. They were being replaced by the new generation of activists, the student leaders, the young radicals who brought their militancy with them to Robben Island, taking on the prison authorities. These inmates finally caused conditions in prison to improve.

In 1973 Mandela told a journalist he never got depressed. 'On this island we abound in hope,' he said. 'I can say I have never had a single moment of depression, because I know that my cause will triumph.'[13] Even if the statement was made for its public relations value, many of those who were imprisoned with Mandela said that the long period of incarceration had done nothing to bring down his spirits. He continued to be calm, optimistic and confident about the future. Interviewed after a 1970 visit to Mandela on Robben Island, MP Dennis Healey said, 'I was relieved to find that intellectually, morally and physically he was fighting fit. He wasn't in any way cast down by his experiences of the last eight years.' Healey had noticed that Mandela was held in 'obvious respect' by his warders, attributing their deference to the possibility that Mandela could quite easily make a transition from prison to the Presidency.[14]

By the time his wife was sent to Brandfort, conditions on Robben

Island had improved dramatically. Newspapers were allowed, letters had increased, prisoners were allowed to mingle more freely and to study formally through UNISA. The most valuable prison education, however, was an informal imparting of ideas and opinions among inmates. When Murphy Morobe, Dan Montsisi and Seth Mazibuko – three student leaders from the Soweto uprising – went to Robben Island, they were amazed at the knowledge and understanding of their elders, some of whom had learnt whole books off by heart so that they could 'read' them to other inmates. Those who came in were extensively debriefed on life and the political situation outside. It was the best opportunity inmates had for keeping abreast of what was happening in South Africa and beyond.

As he entered his fifties, Mandela welcomed a new batch of prisoners on to the island. The Soweto student leaders were imprisoned in 1979, and from them Mandela was able to learn much – about the uprisings themselves, about the role his wife had played and about how keen the authorities had been to blame and punish her for what had happened. He listened to the students and discussed the riots and their implications with them. There was a camaraderie and understanding which meant that, for some, these were the happiest days of their lives. In Brandfort, Winnie received the news of her sister Nancy's death and mourned for her alone.[15]

Chapter Seven

As the years of banishment passed, the impression left on Winnie became indelible. She strove to remain uncowed by her isolation and was determined to keep the struggle going – even if the venue had changed. But with Winnie, fighting apartheid was always more of a battle than a struggle, and the battle was always extremely personal and highly emotional. If friends who visited her were amazed by her resilience and calm in the face of her exile, those who lived around her witnessed an ongoing active defiance, a refusal to surrender, to relinquish control of her life. They watched as her attempts became more and more imperious, hysterical and ultimately frightening.

The battle between the State and Winnie had always been over who would have control of her. A state-controlled Winnie would have been a highly effective and prized trophy. Not only could she have undermined – and informed on – every aspect of the anti-apartheid movement, her own effectiveness as a leader would crumble. Sometimes it was hard to believe the police had any agenda at all other than to persecute for persecution's sake. Their pettiness as they hid in her bushes, burst into her house on any pretext, and invented new 'rules' which she had to obey, were no more constructive than the slow removal of the wings from a fly. One raid on the tiny house, when Helen Suzman was present, lasted for three hours. Police removed posters, books, household documents and everything in the ANC colours of black, green and gold, including a bedspread.

Winnie never forgot that there was a point to all of this, that the attention the police gave her over the years had a purpose. She rationalised the threat that she posed to the authorities. Their relentless pursuit of her must in some way be a measure of the extent of her power. If they were threatened, she must be threatening – and if she was threatening, she must be powerful. It was not a hard logic for her to accept.

The early incident in the dress shop with Zinzi had quickly set the tone for Winnie's pattern of behaviour. If she was different from the natives of Brandfort, and was to be treated differently, she would act differently too. It wasn't difficult. She was doing what she wanted, she believed in what she was doing, and she was used to getting her own way. But this time she had more to gain, more to prove and less to lose by taking on the entrenched racism of this little town. There was a whole community here she could wake up and activate.

Her imperiousness was soon established. She started shopping at more local 'whites only' shops, including the supermarket. When the Afrikaner housewives inside the shops saw her, they would leave. But blacks would follow her in and start shopping too. Winnie would take her time over her shopping, knowing that the whites outside were waiting for her to finish. 'I would deliberately take an hour to get whatever I needed – even if it was only a bar of soap – and I enjoyed seeing these women waiting outside.'

If white shop keepers complained about her presence or asked her to go to the non-white side of the store, she would explode, loudly and abusively stating her right to shop just where she wanted. No 'white dog' or 'cunt' or 'pig' or 'white bastard' was going to order her around, she'd shout, giving the power sign.[1] The blacks were impressed – especially the children, who now spent much of their free time following her around or over at her house, often staying the night there if the evenings grew too late. She taught them what it meant to be politically aware, and told them of the background to the ANC, telling them why it existed and what it stood for. She taught them freedom songs, how to toyi toyi (a dance usually performed by activists at rallies and marches) how to give the power salute and shout Amandla! Soon the children followed her everywhere as she drove around the township – she had had a Volkswagen sent down from Johannesburg – with her window rolled down and her clenched fist raised. It was as if she was trying to recreate the situation she had left behind in Soweto. While studying so hard for her own degree, she told the children not to go to school, saying they were being fobbed off with an inferior standard of education and they must protest against it. The teenagers told the younger children what she said, and instead of going to school, everyone ended up at Winnie's house for cold drinks, sweets and singing.

This was not Soweto and the inhabitants of Brandfort's township were unused to activism. Many parents became anxious about Winnie and her influence over their children, but didn't know how to intervene. Unlike the children, the majority of the adults were frightened of her, both politically and personally. Her frequent losses of temper with the police and the local whites had given her the reputation of a firebrand. As a result there was a reluctance from those in the township to take her on. They didn't want abuse hurled at them if they disagreed with her. Besides which, she was so influential. What effect could their remonstrances have against such a colourful, charismatic woman who had food, drink and presents for everybody? Brandfort parents who disapproved of Winnie swallowed their resentment. If they had a complaint to make, they made it to their sons and daughters – whenever they saw them. Their complaints went unheeded and they knew it. But there was nothing else they could do.

Previously, those who had come into contact with Winnie had been divided between fans and critics. In Brandfort that division became more extreme. She had a polarising effect on the community. Although many parents were frightened of her, several others owed her an enormous amount and spoke of her years later with gratitude and love. These were the working mothers of the pre-school children, for whom Winnie started a crèche. Before she came it had been standard practice for mothers to leave their children to play in the streets when they went off to work. There was no awareness of day care in Brandfort, of what it was or of what value it could be. Some of the children who had played outside Winnie's gate in the early days had been left to fend for themselves as their mothers went off to work, and it was in conversations with them that she realised she could do something positive. She approached the local Methodist minister, explained what she wanted, and asked if the kitchen next to the church could be used as a school. With his permission she recruited four women to work at the centre and to spread the word that the facilities were available.

The crèche opened with about twenty children. In the early days there was little for them to play with, but they would sing and have stories and prayers. Later, as the number of children grew so did the toys and clothes. Only women who were employed sent their children to the crèche, paying R10 (£2.50) a month so that food and toys could be bought for the children. What money was left at the end of each month was divided between the women as a salary, giving them up to R20 a month each to take home. Perhaps the most important aspect of the crèche was that children who attended were given breakfast and lunch as well as constant supervision.

The crèche was a resounding success, eventually growing from the original 20 children to 76, and acquiring its own building and sophisticated equipment along the way. Soon donations were no longer only from friends. They came from the foreign embassies, private individuals and the relief organisations of numerous countries as word of Winnie's day care centre grew. But as with so much that Winnie did, the truth of the crèche was not quite the idealised picture portrayed to the rest of the world.

She never worked there. She couldn't have – it would have violated the terms of her banning order. But that didn't stop her from leading people to believe she went there every day to take care of the little ones. Not only did she not work there, she very rarely went up to the crèche. Those who worked at the day care centre were there from early in the morning until late at night. As a result they could never go to see Winnie at her home. In all the years she spent in Brandfort, Winnie never really got beyond cursory greetings with the women who ran her day care centre.[2] Their good will was taken for granted. Money might have been coming into the township for the day care centre from all over the world but it rarely made its way into salaries for the helpers. They continued to be paid minimal amounts, often having to wait for more than a month for any reimbursement at all.

Elsewhere in Brandfort, other beneficial effects of having Winnie as a resident were being felt. For the first time in anyone's memory, there were hot regular meals in the township. What wasn't donated by Operation Hunger or by the increasing number of visitors was bought locally. Those who came to visit her were now asked to bring vegetable and flower seeds. Winnie had begun planting her own garden with trees, flowers and shrubs, and as curious neighbours watched she would give away vegetable seeds with instructions on how to plant. Not only did the growing vegetables go some way to solving the terrible food shortage in the township, the seedlings provided some colour and signs of life in the drab, dusty unpaved streets. Watering was a problem when water was scarce, but Winnie had a hosepipe and remained oblivious to any drought. When a policeman went to tell her to turn it off one day she simply turned it on him, drenching him from head to toe.

Every aspect of her social work training and experience were brought into play. As well as dealing with the problems of food, clothing and child care, Winnie began to look at medicine. The standard of health in Brandfort's township was not high. There were the usual infectious diseases, stomach upsets, bladder infections and coughs and colds. Many suffered from illnesses stemming from malnutrition, some of them fatal. The problems lay in how to treat the ill-health. There were very few medical supplies in the area, and no money with which to buy them. Many of those who became ill had no hope of recovery.

In search of a solution, Winnie turned to a couple of doctors: her own physician, Joe Veriava, who was registered at Coronation Hospital in Johannesburg, and a friend and fellow doctor, Abu-Baker

Asvat, whom Joe had brought with him on one of his visits. Asvat was a young, extremely politically active Indian, whose medical practice was in Soweto. He had been a member of the Black Consciousness movement at the time of the student uprising, and when the movement regrouped in 1978 to form the Azanian People's Organisation, Asvat joined AZAPO.[3]

He was already in the habit of driving long distances with a caravan attached to his car packed full of medical supplies. He usually went to squatter camps, making it a priority to treat those who had no other chance of receiving medical attention. After his trip to Brandfort with Veriava, he added the Free State township to his list. It was Asvat rather than Veriava who became the township's doctor. On his first few visits his wife Zhora travelled with him, as a companion and helper on the long journey. He paid for all his petrol, medical equipment and supplies himself, but never mentioned it and his patients never knew that he was personally and financially their sole source of medicine. Those who needed a doctor's treatment saw him, others with less serious complaints would be treated by Winnie with supplies he left behind. Asvat's 'mobile clinic' was such a success that Winnie eventually decided to build a structure for it in her small back yard. The two-room building would house the bathroom she still longed for as well as including space for a waiting area and an examination cubicle. There was room to store medical supplies and the grain from Operation Hunger.

When the 1980 'Release Mandela' campaign began, Winnie's stage expanded beyond community activities and battles with the Security Police. She entered the world arena as a symbol of all that South African resistance represented – the good work she was doing in the face of tremendous adversity resulted in the donation of thousands of dollars and the support of prominent leaders all over the world. She became an icon removed just a little further from reality.

The campaign was officially launched in March 1980 with a front-page headline in the Johannesburg *Sunday Post*, demanding that the government 'Free Mandela'. The ANC had spent the years since the student uprising training its flood of recruits, and was now ready to re-emerge – bigger, better and much more effective. The new-look ANC was a more efficient, sophisticated version of the old organisation with more money, more manpower and more than one method of continuing the struggle. The Release Mandela campaign was the cornerstone of the new strategy. It provided a focus and a rallying

131

point for those against apartheid, while attempts to destabilise the government increased. The newly expanded Umkhonto we Sizwe, with its better lines of communication, its more sophisticated cell structures and its heightened presence in the townships, began attacking government installations. In the early months bombs went off at a number of power stations, the most effective explosion occurring at the Sasolburg refinery on 1 June.

But something more was needed than selective guerrilla attacks and the calling for the release of a leader who had been imprisoned for eighteen years. The movement needed a figure within the country who could act cohesively as a symbol to draw the elements of the campaign together. Winnie came to be chosen because in the abstract she was the ideal choice. Here was someone in a tragic situation who was sympathetic and charismatic, who was courageous, outspoken and to top it all was the beautiful wife of their leader. On paper she was perfect. But she was not perfect, and the exiled leaders were well aware of her imperfections. She was too headstrong, she wouldn't take orders, and had a history of doing what she thought best or what she wanted to do rather than what she was told. She was brave, but sometimes her courage was too defiant. She took advantage of every single encounter with the authorities to show her resistance, when it might have been more prudent to pick and choose. And was she trustworthy? Her wilfulness could easily endanger the lives of others around her. Was she worth the risk? The answer was yes. Winnie's advantages outweighed her problems. She came across well in the media, and she was the best of what they had. The ANC decided to use her.

Although neither Winnie nor Nelson Mandela could be quoted in South Africa because of the terms of their respective banning orders, the campaign began in the press. Visitors to Brandfort could describe Winnie's life in exile there and write in detail about her heroic attempts to make something of it. She was sewing school uniforms, planting seeds, bandaging limbs, cooking food, studying and, whenever she could, making the long journey to Robben Island to see her husband. White liberal journalists, such as Benjie Pogrund and Allister Sparks from the *Rand Daily Mail* came to visit, to see what her life was like, and they became close friends with her. Sparks wrote long, glowing accounts of her life in Brandfort, while Pogrund – during his stint as the newspaper's editor – regularly sent her its review copies of books for her library. He also sent reporters to describe, among other things, the well-stocked library in her small lounge.

Her old friend from the Jan Hofmeyr School, Ellen Khuzwayo, who was now a writer, visited her and wrote about the experience.

When I saw her by chance in 1982, I was gladly surprised and impressed by her very pleasant disposition, her calmness and complete composure. Her charm, her singing laughter, her un-changing face and her ever-present dignity are those of the Winnie Nomzamo of the 1950s when I first met her. Those who see her often confirm that she still practises her profession in this com-munity. Her small home, I learn, radiates hope for the deprived of Brandfort. It is used as a relief half-way house for the hungry and destitute: a soothing, healing place for the sick: and a place of light and learning for the ignorant. Her vegetable gardens are said to be a model for the whole township of Brandfort, in her effort to arrest the high rate of malnutrition. A woman who teaches by example.[4]

The sad life of the exiled wife was a good story, especially overseas. Pogrund wrote it up for the *Boston Globe*, Sparks wrote it up for the *Observer*, and soon other representatives of news organisations came to see for themselves what life in Brandfort was really like. But life in Brandfort was not really like what they saw. Locals watched as Winnie began staging events with the police for the press. Little run-ins became more frequent and more antagonistic – especially when there was a foreign camera crew around.

The UN Security Council issued a resolution calling for the release of Nelson Mandela and other political prisoners. Instead of being released, he was transferred, leaving Robben Island for the mainland prison of Pollsmoor in Cape Town in 1983. The story of the Mandelas aroused interest and support – much of it financial – from all over the world. Winnie's role as benefactress was heavily publicised and she became known as the Mother of the Nation. From then on she began receiving cheques and letters of support from academic institutions, labour organisations, churches and individuals at an unprecedented rate. Much of the money went to her lawyer, Ismail Ayob, who then handed on to her whatever she needed, thus controlling her spending power. But some cheques went directly to her. Some were still there fifteen years later, lying in boxes of forgotten belongings, uncashed and unneeded.

The Security Police kept tabs on everything. Her bank accounts were monitored, her conversations recorded, her friends watched. Miles away in Pretoria, photocopies of her letters, bank statements and credit slips were filed away. No amount was too small for police attention. A cheque for £80 cashed in June 1983 from Sylvia Marshall – a sympathetic admirer in England – was noted, as was the R15,000 Anglo-American's chairman, Harry Oppenheimer, sent for the clinic in early 1985. Over the next few years she was sent a fortune. According to police records, the UN special committee against Apartheid sent her $100,000 for her home and clinic in 1985. Her total deposit for the previous month had been $44,000. Another UN collection gave her $22,000. Money came from Canada (one embassy cheque was for R13,800 for the clinic), Australia (embassy cheque – R8,800) and Germany (Action for World Solidarity – 5,200 Deutschmarks). One human rights gift she received in August 1986 was for R253,164.56. Two months later she got a Cuban cheque for $70,000.[5]

She had several personal bank accounts, mainly in Johannesburg, though she also opened one in London which was also monitored. From the mid 1980s her balances were solidly in the thousands of rand. In May 1988 one account had over 100,000 rand in it, another had 15,000. She borrowed cars, then she was given them – or given the money to buy them herself. She was given toys for the crèche and Abu Asvat continued to pay for his medical supplies himself. She said that whatever money she had came from the proceeds of her auto-biography, *Part of My Soul*, which was first published in Germany in 1984 and sold steadily around the world. One royalty instalment from the book's editor, Anne Benjamin, was for 10,000 Deutschmarks at the beginning of 1986.

In an *Observer* story that ran in January 1982, Sparks quoted Brandfort's mayor, Jurie Erwee, who also ran a local liquor store as saying, 'She comes in here to buy things: champagne, Cinzano, stuff like that.' The 'stuff' amounted to R3,000 worth of liquor a month, according to M.K. Malefane, a young stylish Rastafarian artist who was introduced to Winnie by Zinzi and subsequently moved into her house. Until she lived in Brandfort, Winnie had not drunk much alcohol. Drunkenness was a feature of life in the township, though, and she quickly became aware of it. The township bar was occupied from the moment it opened until it closed at 8 p.m., with children joining their drunken parents when they came back from school. Bored and depressed, like many of her fellow township residents, Winnie began drinking as a way of getting through the endless days.

Malefane was not the first young man to move in with Winnie in

Brandfort. Oupa Seakamena, Zinzi's boyfriend and the father of her first child, (a daughter – Zoleka) also lived with Winnie for a while. He had initially moved in to be with Zinzi, but stayed in Brandfort with Winnie after Zinzi returned to Johannesburg. He helped her plant her garden and worked around the house – apparently with the approval of his parents. When he left he was replaced by Malefane, who stayed with Winnie for the rest of her exile. Malefane felt he was more than Winnie's lodger and a friend of the family. He was later described as her agent, who assisted her in the running of her projects and represented her when the terms of her banning order prevented her from attending community meetings.[6] It was the handsome, dread-locked Malefane who told Ismail Ayob how much money they needed and settled their local accounts. It was Malefane who bought their supplies – including most of the alcohol. It was Malefane who drove to and from Johannesburg and Bloemfontein, and anywhere else he was needed to go to fetch and carry at Winnie's behest. And it was Malefane who on 3 July 1983 watched Winnie assault Andrew Pogisho – a nine-year-old boy.

When she appeared before Brandfort's magistrate, J.H. Meyer, after Pogisho's mother had laid a complaint against her, Winnie denied hitting Pogisho with her belt buckle. She said he bumped his head on a cupboard while trying to get away from her, after she had accused him of stealing a tricycle. The tricycle was part of equipment she now kept at her house for children to come and play with. In a subsequent hearing Pogisho testified that Winnie had accused him of the theft and then hit him with her belt buckle, causing a deep gash on his forehead. While maintaining that she had never hit the child, Winnie told the magistrate that she had the right to chastise him. If she could not discipline children who played on her premises, she said, then she would have all the toys removed and it would be the community's loss.[7]

Malefane was never called as a witness. He never told the court that he had watched as Winnie removed the belt from the waist of her denim skirt, that he had seen her wind it round and round her wrist, that he had watched the blood spurt out of Andrew Pogisho's forehead as the heavy buckle first struck him. He never informed the magistrate that the incident took place in the morning or that Winnie had already been drinking when she hit the boy. Nor did he say that he watched her strike Pogisho a second and then a third time while cries for her to stop were ignored. Finally Malefane never testified that he threw himself on top of Winnie to prevent her from continuing the

135

assault, causing a physical fight to break out between the two of them. There was no evidence in court to this effect and, in its absence, Winnie was acquitted of assault on 8 December 1983.

There was another assault in November the following year, one for which she was convicted. The details on her police record registered her as committing assault with a bottle and a shoe. The woman who was assaulted had to receive hospital treatment as a result of Winnie's attack.[8] It has proved impossible to find out more details of this assault. The prosecutor in the case, J.P. Olivier, went to practise law in Bloemfontein and was eventually disbarred, having been convicted of fraud. No-one in Brandfort would speak of either assault, and the police said both dockets [case files] had been destroyed.

As her own violence increased so did her paranoia, especially after a suspicious death early on in her stay in Brandfort. Dr Chris Hattingh, a doctor with a practice not far from Brandfort, had offered Winnie a job in 1978. It took her six months to get permission to work for him, during which time he began to be followed by Security Police. Then, on the day she should have begun work, Hattingh mysteriously died in a car accident. The police maintained a cow had run into the road causing Hattingh's car to overturn on the spot, but those who knew he had been trailed as he drove around the Free State remained unconvinced. Winnie was extremely upset by Hattingh's death. She felt his giving her a job had killed him.

She never stopped missing her life in Soweto and longed to return. She was allowed to make an emergency trip home in June 1984 when Zinzi was attacked by her boyfriend and rushed to hospital. Patrick Moshidi, the father of Zinzi's second child, Zondwa (also known as Gaddafi), punched, kicked and stabbed Zinzi in the hand and head because, she said later, he was threatened and insecure.[9] He then dragged her up a hill and, after she lost consciousness, left her for dead. She was found and taken to hospital where she spent several days in intensive care (a scan revealed possible brain damage) and had thirty stitches. Attempts to protect Zinzi's privacy by saying she had been hurt in a car accident were thwarted by the police who leaked the true cause of her injuries.[10]

In general Winnie was allowed to leave Brandfort only to visit Mandela, to attend seminars and to receive medical treatment. It was when she was seeing doctors in Johannesburg that her house was raided for the final time by police. The incident had begun in the morning of 6 August when a group of school children boycotted school and then raided the local bottle store. The crowd proceeded to

Winnie's house and demonstrated outside, stoning police who arrived on the scene. The police retaliated by throwing tear-gas grenades and firing rubber bullets, forcing a number of the children to run inside Winnie's house for protection. They were pursued by police (who later claimed to have found petrol bombs and gasoline canisters in one of the rooms). In the process, windows and doors were broken and Winnie's belongings strewn about the floor. A reporter later found blood on the walls.[11]

A week later – while Winnie was still in Johannesburg – her house was attacked again. This time the damage was far more extensive. Petrol bombs thrown inside started a fire, which gutted the premises. The small clinic behind the house was burnt to the ground. Police denied responsibility for the attack, blaming it on a gang from a neighbouring town. Whoever was behind it had achieved one thing. With nowhere to live, there was no way Winnie could return to Brandfort for the time being.

Twelve United States Senators contributed 13,000 rand to pay for the house to be rebuilt. While repairs were done Winnie remained in her house in Orlando West – technically in defiance of her banning order – and although she returned to visit, she never lived in Brandfort again.

Tension remained in Brandfort long after she had gone. It may have been created by the uneasy disparity between the comparative wealth of the town and the abject poverty of the township. It may have been that the region as a whole became more politicised during this period. Many felt, though, that the legacy of Winnie's years in the township was a continuing palpable anxiety which resulted in a tremendous reluctance to discuss her. There was a fear that talking about Winnie to outsiders would result in some kind of unpleasant retribution. That she – omniscient and omnipotent – would reach out from Johannesburg and punish the offender.

Whites unhesitatingly blamed her for the tension. Their feeling was that before she came everyone knew his or her place. Blacks didn't make demands. They worked, they were taken care of, and they were grateful. They weren't resentful. Winnie had made them want rights and after that no-one knew what to expect.

In the township a hardcore group of ANC supporters remained loyal to her memory, drawn in by the magnetism of her warmth. They appreciated her efforts on their behalf, they admired her courage and pitied her loneliness. She had made them feel special. Others continued to resent her airs and graces, her fancy clothes and her obvious wealth long after she had gone. They disliked what they had felt to be her condescending patronage and they hated the constant Security Police presence that her life in the township had brought. She was a disruption, they said, destructive, and they just wanted to forget her.

The Security Police wrote to Winnie at the beginning of November 1985, telling her that her house was now repaired and she was to return to Brandfort. Their timing couldn't have been worse. The deadline they gave for her return was 4 November, but on 3 November Mandela was operated on at Volks Hospital in Cape Town and his prostate gland was removed. Winnie had flown to Cape Town for the operation, staying in the Mount Nelson Hotel while Nelson was in hospital and visiting him daily. Rumours about Mandela started to circulate. Could this be the opportune time for the government to release him?

The *Weekly Mail* reported that Minister of Justice and Prisons, Kobie Coetsee, had raised the possibility of Mandela's release at a cabinet meeting, arguing that the government now had an opportunity to free Mandela on compassionate grounds. The suggestion was opposed, but the day after the reported cabinet meeting, Brigadier Fred Munro, the commanding officer of Pollsmoor Prison, went to see Mandela in hospital and stayed for two hours. Mandela then sent for Winnie, told her he needed to have an urgent consultation with their lawyers, and asked her to make immediate arrangements for them to fly from Johannesburg to Cape Town.[12]

His urgency increased speculation that a release was impending. From Lusaka the ANC issued a statement that the organisation would accept any plan which might fly Mandela to freedom in another country. But the day after he met with his lawyers Mandela returned to prison, though the rumours had grown so intense that the government was forced to respond. In a statement shooting down the mounting excitement, the Deputy Minister of Information, Louis Nel, announced that reports of the release of Mandela were 'nothing else but a continuing campaign of disinformation by propaganda experts behind the Iron Curtain'.[13]

With Mandela's health in jeopardy and a growing faction within the government lobbying for his release, Winnie felt able to ignore orders for her return to Brandfort. Defying a police order to report to a magistrate, she remained in Cape Town with her husband until he was sufficiently recovered to be transferred back to Pollsmoor Prison. She then returned to Soweto and her home in Orlando West, knowing that she faced arrest.

Even though an arrest for the violation of her banning order remained a very definite possibility, Winnie was prepared to risk it. More important to her was the chance that she would not be arrested, that she would be allowed to remain at liberty in Soweto, that the talks between her husband and the government might be of benefit to her. Public interest in her continued to be enormous. Her presence at a funeral of 12 residents in the township of Mamelodi outside Pretoria on 3 December caused mob scenes. (The victims, the youngest of which was a two-month old baby, had been killed by police fire.)

Diplomats from the United States and Great Britain attended the funeral, which attracted crowds of over 50,000 mourners. Security Police filmed Winnie as she addressed the enormous crowd, and then investigated the possibility of arresting her for addressing a public gathering in violation of her banning order. Her speeches could not be quoted in South Africa, and technically she was still prohibited from attending public meetings and from being with more than one person at a time, but in the four months she had spent in Soweto since August she had addressed crowds on several occasions without a reaction from the police. She had spoken at a wedding, at a memorial service, attended rallies and press conferences, all without retaliation. The only attempt the police made to silence her at Mamelodi was to dismantle the public address system before the speeches began.[14]

Her rhetoric had become more extreme in the years she had spent away from Soweto. No longer was it enough to say, 'We are here as testimony to the fact that the solution to our country's problems lies in black hands. This is our country.' Now she added, 'In the same way as you have had to bury our loved ones, our children, today; so shall the blood of these little heroes we buried today be avenged.'[15]

Winnie was not speaking alone. The ANC had also become more revolutionary in the years since the Soweto uprising. At the 1985 policy conference in Lusaka the mood had moved away from negotiation in favour of a 'people's war' – armed mobile combat units prepared to incur civilian casualties. Present at this conference and rising swiftly in the ranks of Umkhonto we Sizwe, was Chris Hani, a highly educated, charismatic young radical who quoted *Hamlet* and believed in the political assassination of ANC enemies.[16] Hani and Winnie were close friends and political allies, their words often echoed each other and they drew their followers from the same hardcore group who had come to political life in 1976. But while Hani attended conferences and influenced policy, Winnie operated from the sidelines of the organisation. Even after her return to Soweto her positions were her own, her speeches made without consulting other political leaders.

Winnie's banning order was finally amended just before Christmas on Saturday 21 December 1985, with an announcement from Law and Order Minister Louis le Grange that he had relaxed some of her restrictions. Although still prohibited from attending political gatherings and students' meetings, not allowed to be quoted within South Africa without Ministerial permission, prevented from sitting on the board of any educational institution, not allowed to teach or distribute publications, banned from membership of political organisations and prevented from communicating with other listed and banned people, Winnie no longer had to report to police stations and was now allowed to attend social events.

And there was one major concession. She no longer had to be confined to Brandfort. In fact she could go anywhere she wanted within South Africa – with the exception of the magisterial districts of Johannesburg and neighbouring Roodeport. Effectively, Winnie could go anywhere she wanted to except home.

Counsel Denis Kuny was at his house on the Saturday her banning order was amended. He received a phone call from a lawyer in Ismail Ayob's practice who asked Kuny if he would go with him to Winnie's house in Orlando West. The police were there trying to get her out and she needed help. Kuny drove with the lawyer to Soweto where, outside Winnie's house, they found the police waiting on the street in a virtual state of siege. The police wanted to go into the house and arrest her for refusing to leave Johannesburg, but she wouldn't let them in. It was a chaotic scene – Winnie in a towering rage, the police adamant that she had to go and the entire contretemps watched by a group of journalists, including six foreign correspondents.

When they realised they had an audience, the police asked if the journalists had permits allowing them to be in Soweto. On hearing that they had not, the police took the journalists to the police station, and detained them for half an hour before letting them go.

Kuny was at the house to act as a mediator and he shuttled backwards and forwards trying to negotiate an agreement between the police at the gate and Winnie inside. Both sides refused to give in. The police were polite, formal and unyielding – Winnie was not allowed to be there and they had come to make her leave. Winnie was less restrained. She was furious at the prospect of being forced out of her home days before Christmas. For more than an hour, Kuny tried reasoning in an attempt to reach some kind of compromise and at one point he lost patience with Winnie, 'You are a difficult woman!' he said to her in exasperation. The enraged Winnie took tremendous exception. She was not a difficult woman, she said. She agreed that she might be stubborn, but she was definitely not difficult.

Eventually Kuny persuaded the police to allow Winnie to leave without arresting her and he got her to agree to go and see Mandela in Cape Town and tell him what had happened. On the understanding that the police would take her to the airport, Kuny waited until the fuming Winnie left with her escort, then he went home.

The police drove Winnie to the Holiday Inn at Jan Smuts airport. She had no money and no luggage; at some stage during the altercation she had sprained her ankle – and she was still furious. She borrowed enough money from hotel staff at the Holiday Inn for a third-class train ticket back to Soweto and promptly returned home. She remained at her house for a day, until just before noon on Sunday morning when the police arrived again. This time there were no negotiations. Eyewitnesses who watched the arrest described how Winnie was dragged 'kicking and screaming' from her house. She was taken to Krugersdorp Police Station where she was detained under the Internal Security Act and kept overnight.[17]

The reaction to Winnie's arrest was immediate, universal and outraged. In Great Britain the *Sunday Times*, *Sunday Telegraph* and *Observer* had all carried the story of Saturday's altercation on their front pages; Sunday's arrest was the lead story of all major radio and television broadcasts. The President of the Anti-Apartheid movement, Bishop Trevor Huddleston, sent telegrams to President Reagan, Mrs Thatcher, French President Mitterrand, West German Chancellor Helmut Kohl and UN Secretary General Javier Perez de Cuellar asking for their urgent intervention in releasing Mrs Mandela. Speaking on BBC radio on Sunday afternoon, British Foreign Office Minister Malcolm Rifkind described the arrest as both disturbing and damaging. In the United States, White House spokesman Larry Speakes issued an unusually strong statement. 'The United States Government deplores the South African Government's action in arresting Winnie,' he told reporters. He said the United States had made a formal protest about the arrest to South Africa's embassy in Washington as well as sending an observer to monitor court proceedings in Johannesburg. France condemned the arrest as an attack on human rights, and classified it as 'extremely regrettable'.[18]

Winnie appeared in court on 23 December and was released on R500 (£120) bail. About fifty police and soldiers, some in riot gear, surrounded the court as spectators waited for her to emerge from the police cells. Her sprained ankle was bandaged, and on leaving the dock surrounded by a crowd of hundreds – reporters and supporters – she limped heavily to Ismail Ayob's offices. Released on bail, Winnie did go to Cape Town and spent Christmas week visiting Mandela, who was still recovering from his prostate surgery in the hospital wing of Pollsmoor Prison. Zinzi went with her, taking her two small sons. It was not an easy visit. Neither Nelson nor Winnie was feeling particularly well. Nelson hadn't yet fully recovered and Winnie was exhausted and suffering from high blood pressure. She wanted to see Dr Veriava on her return to Johannesburg, but did not know whether she would be allowed to remain there long enough to be treated.

The family group that arrived back at Jan Smuts airport on Monday 30 December was tired and irritable and less than enthusiastic at the sight of 50 journalists waiting to see if there was to be another altercation with the police. There was, though not at the airport but on the highway to Soweto. Security Police swept down on the car, forcing it to a stop, and wrenching young Zondwa Mandela from Winnie's arms as she was re-arrested. In the jostling – all of which was watched by journalists – the little boy's head was bumped against the car door. Later Zinzi claimed her son had swollen lips and pains all over his body because of the attack.[19]

Once again, Winnie was not remanded in custody, but allowed to remain at large. Wherever she went she was followed by police and reporters as well as a large crowd of ANC followers. When she visited a friend in Kagiso township on 2 January 1986, the house was surrounded by a crowd of 1,000 well-wishers, singing ANC songs in praise of her. Police took down names of journalists and gave them five minutes to leave, declaring the area a place of emergency. With the press gone, tear-gas was fired into the crowd. It was only on the intervention of a catholic nun, Sister Bernard Ncube, that the crowd dispersed.[20]

By the time Winnie appeared in court on 22 January on charges that she had violated her banning order, it was fairly obvious that she was not going to leave Soweto. As well as the high level of international attention her case still commanded, she was receiving increased organised support from the ANC, and local community groups were now organising consumer boycotts in support of her. The government had to find a way of giving in to the situation gracefully, while saving face.

At the request of the State prosecutor she was not asked to plead to the charges against her. Her case was then postponed for a month. When, a week earlier, Ismail Ayob had brought a civil suit against the government, challenging the validity of her new banning order, his suit had been dismissed, but permission for an appeal had immediately been granted. Clearly the government was looking for a period of limbo.[21]

Meanwhile, negotiations for the release of Mandela continued. At the beginning of February, George Bizos flew to see Mandela in prison to consult with him on the conditions and mechanics of his release. As with Winnie, the government was reluctant to have Mandela anywhere near his power base. One condition of his release was that he must spend a 'cooling-off period' outside the country. Mandela refused, insisting that his release be unconditional, and that he be released on to South African soil. Privately, sources within the Mandela family and the government were telling reporters that they expected a release in a matter of weeks. Ismail Ayob even began making enquiries about office space in Johannesburg. In this climate of negotiations it was unlikely that any action would be taken against Mandela's wife for refusing to obey a directive as to where she should live.

At the end of March, Ismail Ayob announced that Law and Order Minister le Grange had agreed that Winnie's case could be indefinitely postponed. Earlier that month, the country's Appeal Court had ruled on a similar case that these kinds of banning orders were not valid. The ruling had broken the ground for a victory in Winnie's civil suit. Unwilling to concede total defeat, a spokesman for le Grange said that Winnie's restriction order had not actually been lifted. Ayob then clarified his own statement. The State Attorney, acting on behalf of the Minister of Law and Order and the Commissioner of Police, came to an agreement 'That he would abandon judgment,' he said. State Attorney P. Kleynhans promptly denied that any deal had been made, but he did admit holding talks with Ayob where the possibility of the State not opposing Winnie's appeal in her civil suit had been discussed, though final agreement on anything had still not been reached. It was a confusing time. In one day le Grange issued an initial statement to the effect that Winnie was still banned, then followed it with another one saying her banning order was under review. By nightfall he was locked in discussion with his law advisers over 'the entire matter of banning restrictions'.

Winnie was finally allowed to stay in Soweto though the government remained concerned that she would have an inflammatory effect on her fellow residents, particularly the youth. (As a precautionary step le Grange warned newspapers in the country that they quoted her at their peril.) Fellow residents were uneasy at the return of this flamboyant neighbour. The tension which surrounded her in Brandfort had followed her back to Soweto. So had the ostentatious wealth. Within a year work had begun on what became known as the 'Mandela Mansion', a large detached house in an area known as Beverly Hills. The house was vast by Soweto standards and mystery surrounded it. No-one knew where the money for it had come from – Winnie still pleaded poverty – and why it was being built. Nor was it clear who exactly Winnie represented when she spoke on behalf of the people. When she eventually opened an office in Soweto to deal with the 'endless streams of people who need help', Winnie stated that it was 'definitely not an ANC office. It is an advice office, a welfare office, specialising more in community work than dealing with political issues . . . The public compelled me to open this office. Now the people can at least reach me. They do not have to roam around looking for assistance.'[22] However, she said that she had no capital to run the office.

During Winnie's exile, an alliance of more than six hundred independent organisations had come together under the umbrella title of the United Democratic Front (UDF) to resist apartheid. Previously, unionists, church and community leaders, politicians, students and human rights workers dealing with day-to-day issues as they arose and working in small ways against the system had been unable to confront the State head on. The idea behind the UDF was to link the smaller struggles to the one main struggle so that, as UDF leader Azhur Cachalia later put it, 'The struggle for the washing line became the struggle for the vote.'[23]

With the coalition of the UDF, anti-apartheid groups had the advantage of grass roots support and a national coherence. UDF leaders did not lead in the abstract. They were elected from their own organisations. In order to become a leader of the UDF one had at least to be a member of a smaller group.

Because of her absence in Brandfort, the formation of the UDF had passed Winnie by. On her return to Soweto she belonged to no elective community-based group. She saw herself as an independent entity who didn't need a mandate to do and say as she pleased. Some said that the appointment of Albertina Sisulu as a UDF President infuriated Winnie and made her determined not to have anything to do with the UDF. In many ways the lives of the two women had followed parallel lines – much as their husbands' had – but after their early detention together in 1958 they had grown apart. They had little in common and disliked and disapproved of each other.

Albertina's life had been extremely harsh. She too had been detained and held in solitary confinement in the 1960s. She had been tortured and interrogated, banned and then placed under house arrest for ten years. While Winnie was in Brandfort in the early 1980s, Albertina was in prison. Unlike Winnie, Albertina had to endure the torment of having her own children placed in detention. Her eldest son, Max, was first arrested in 1964 at the age of sixteen. Her daughter, Lindiwe, went into exile after a year's detention during which she was assaulted and tortured. Another son, Zwelakhe, was also detained for a year.

In theory the formation of the UDF should have passed Albertina by as well – she was still in custody in 1983. But she had kept strong professional and community ties (she still worked as a nurse) and was elected unopposed as Transvaal President. Winnie may have become an international figure with donations flowing in from all over the world; Albertina had remained local and poor. When she acted or spoke, it was truly on behalf of her community. Her support – like Winnie's – stemmed from the grassroots up. Her supporters, however, included parents as well as children. Albertina was trusted and respected rather than worshipped. No-one – except perhaps Winnie – resented her new position.

Not long after her return to Soweto, Winnie gave the most controversial speech of her career. In the past she had spoken of the need for violence without going into detail. By becoming specific, the damage she did to herself was far greater and more lasting than than that meted out to the regime she condemned. In early April 1986, having travelled back to Brandfort to speak at a funeral, she was militant but still vague.

'We no longer come to the funerals of our young heroes to shed tears,' she told the crowd of about 3,000 mourners. 'The time for crying is over. We can no longer waste our tears. The time has come where we must show that we are disciplined and trained warriors.'[24]

A week later, at a rally at Munsieville on 13 April, her threat became tangible. 'We have no guns – we have only stones, boxes of matches and petrol,' she said. 'Together, hand in hand, with our boxes of matches and our necklaces we shall liberate this country.'

Whereas talk of an armed struggle in the abstract had become commonplace, no-one was prepared for this speech. Necklacing – ramming a tyre round the neck and over the shoulders of a victim, filling it with petrol and setting it alight – was a particularly barbaric method of killing, used in townships mainly against suspected police informers or collaborators. There was no escape from burning to death when necklaced, burning tyres were impossible to remove. There were almost 400 necklace murders between 1984 and 1987. Not only was it on the increase, it was becoming a symbol of political violence. When Winnie spoke of liberating the country by using the necklace, her implication was clear – whites were to be burnt. Deputy Minister of Information Louis Nel said her speech constituted 'a call for violence in South Africa against the white community'.[25] Many in the government felt vindicated in their suppression of the ANC. Reports of the necklace speech proved to the world that the ANC was indeed a dangerous terrorist organisation. Under those circumstances, le Grange even allowed portions of the speech to be quoted inside the country.

Nel wasn't the only one to interpret the speech as a call for violence against whites. Winnie's comments were widely reported in Britain and the United States where they caused considerable alarm. 'Her rhetorical gifts and her symbolic leadership status give her an obligation to show responsibility,' ran an editorial in *The Times*. 'To judge by the past week's performance this is an obligation she has not yet appreciated.' Newspapers in South Africa also criticised her.[26] The ANC was horrified and sent her messages to keep quiet for the time being, although until then no-one in the ANC had actually spoken out against the necklace. Later in the year Oliver Tambo said he was not happy with it, but felt unable to condemn those who used it because of the brutality of the South African government.[27]

Increasingly defensive, Winnie claimed to have been misquoted, but her remarks had been captured on videotape and there was no escaping them. So she said she had been quoted out of context and tried to explain what she had really meant.

The country has suffered years of institutionalised violence which has led blacks to react in irrational ways like using matches and necklace.

We mine the wealth of this land and we man the industry of this country. We even bring up their children. We could have killed them if we wanted to.

I said we accept the challenge from Pretoria that the Government has 'declared war' on the people of this country. The regime has taken the struggle to this stage. We have no AK47s to defend ourselves. War has been declared on defenceless and unarmed masses.[28]

'I wasn't advocating violence,' she said to a crowd of 20,000 at a May Day rally at the Orlando Stadium in Soweto. 'The panicking racists say I advocated violence. I have not done so yet. The time will come when I will call on you to defend yourselves with the same might that Pretoria is unleashing against people. I want to call on you to close ranks and prepare for that violent onslaught. That day when you are called upon to fire back, you must do so in a disciplined manner.'[29]

The words wouldn't go away. Year after year they came back to haunt her, brought up by interviewers at home and abroad who persisted in asking what she had meant. On a trip to the United States in 1990, Phil Donahue questioned her about the speech.

'Insofar as necklacing is concerned,' she said to Donahue, 'no sane human being would condone that type of – that method of eliminating any opponent. It is brutal and barbaric, and to my knowledge, no-one has ever, ever, given green light or stamp of approval to that method.'

'So this "we shall liberate" quote then, that is not what you meant at all?' Donahue asked.

'That was absolute nonsense. What I had been trying to say then was that our children had been so oppressed and they had met up with such violence from the government that they had resorted to that form of method of eliminating their enemies. And that was not the form of method approved of by the ANC,' she said.

'No sane person would ever, ever approve of that,' she repeated. 'It was quoted completely out of context. I would have no reason whatsoever to believe in that form of – the elimination of our enemy when in fact we have the armed struggle. As I pointed out, we belong to a disciplined organisation. Now when it comes to the question of violence, whether we approve of violence, I'm afraid we have no violence to renounce. The method used by the oppressor determines your own reaction.'[30]

When the subject came up in a South African television interview in 1992, she was far less restrained.

Interviewer. You have been quoted as saying that 'with necklaces we will free this country', I can't imagine a worse torture than to die by the necklace . . .

Winnie. I haven't a single victim on my hands. I haven't a single victim I have shot at myself. I haven't.

Interviewer [interrupting]. But surely such a statement is incitement . . .

Winnie. Whatever I have – that was quoted out of context in the first place and we are not dealing with that now. We must deal with the reality of this thing. Even if that statement had been made a million times, I will tell you that you are justifying the deaths of over 11,000 of our people who have died at the hands of the racist minority regime. Are you justifying that? Are you really seriously trying to tell me that there is anything more cruel than what we are seeing today? Our children butchered, our babies shot at the backs of mothers.

Interviewer [interrupting]. No. What I am trying to . . .

Winnie . . . where a government is in fact intent on killing our people.

Interviewer. You say to me that you cannot understand that kind of cruelty. Then my counter-question is how can you, in whatever context, say that necklaces could be allowed, could be a way of . . .

Winnie [interrupting]. We are not discussing that now, whether or not it was quoted out of context. We . . .

Interviewer [Interrupting]. Could we discuss it?

Winnie. No. We are not going to discuss that now. That is not the terms of the interview in the first place. But there is nothing whatsoever to justify the killings of our people. What statements were made, statements that were not actualised – that is in fact nonsense to try and suggest to me that in the light of statements like that, the government is justified in killing our people.[31]

She may have claimed not to have been advocating violence, but in endorsing the necklace Winnie was saying exactly what one section of the black population wanted to hear. By 1986 considerable numbers of township youth were forming criminal gangs, as deteriorating urban and economic conditions led towards township anarchy. The continued imposition of apartheid had led to South Africa's isolation. British and American firms had begun disinvesting. The European Community (and eventually the United States) imposed trade sanctions, oil-producing nations prohibited sales to South Africa. In addition South Africa had been expelled by the Olympic Committee and was boycotted by artists and actors. As the rest of the world turned away, violence and poverty had spiralled. Left alone, inflation and unemployment soared and the rand fell.

The government's response was to crack down on the impoverished and angry. In 1984, troops had been sent in to the townships, ostensibly to curb 'black-on-black' violence. In October army units joined the police in patrolling Soweto. During 1985 alone, 35,000 troops were used in townships around the country. But evidence showed that the South Africa Defence Forces (SADF) were in fact themselves perpetrators of violence particularly directed against the youth. The Detainees' Parents Support Committee (DPSC) reported soldiers picking children off the street at random and holding them for several hours in police vehicles or in remote areas of veld. The children were beaten with fists and rifle butts, whipped with sjamboks and subjected to electric shock treatment.[32]

By mid-1985 thousands of unaffiliated youths lacking direction or cohesion, many of them badly affected by their experiences in detention, saw themselves as soldiers in the liberation struggle. They formed groups of street patrols hunting down other troublemakers, hooligans and vandals. Initially they confined themselves to situations they came across as they patrolled the streets. Then disputes were brought to them to 'judge': The effect of these gangs on the community, particularly in Soweto, was extraordinarily destabilising. As evidence began to emerge that the police both tacitly and actively showed support for these gangs, the fear they generated increased.

Older township residents were horrified by the disorder and the challenge to their authority from these young thugs. Gang control replaced people's courts, which in their non-violent form had long been a traditional form of dispensing justice in the black community. Previously street committees made up of respected residents – almost without exception men – who were elected by members of the few streets or blocks that they represented settled domestic and minor disputes. At their best they gave a direct, speedy and local participation in the pursuit of justice. Now they became personal fiefdoms and small power bases using extreme forms of punishment. It was in this climate that Winnie made her necklace speech and it was in the same climate that she formed her own personal vigilante gang – Mandela United.

Chapter Eight

In the 1820s Mma Nthatisi was the Regent of the Sotho-speaking Tlokwa people. Forced to contend with famine and death, she uprooted her followers and began a period of nomadic wandering, sustained by plundering. Her people fought, they stole and they killed – to such an extent that the mere name Mamantee became synonymous with violence. Those who were turned out of their homes and ruined by Mma Nthatisi shouted the news of their plight to neighbouring tribes from mountain tops. This made many tribes so apprehensive that any approaching multitude was thought to be Mma Nthatisi's. As the damage wrought by this infamous troupe grew more widespread, so the rumours about their leader became more fantastic. A woman of genuine courage, Mma Nthatisi had at one time been described as tall, very handsome, inclined to stoutness in middle age, affable, sociable and very popular with her people. In time, however, that description became phenomenally distorted. Mma Nthatisi was eventually transformed into a terrifying giantess with one eye in the middle of her forehead, who in true mother-of-the-nation fashion fed her army – numerous as locusts – with her own breast milk, and sent an advance party of hornets before her as she strode across Africa spreading ruin and devastation.

In 1986 Mandela United was formed in Soweto. As the damage done by this disparate group of youths became more widespread, so the rumours about their leader became more fantastic. Some people were so frightened they would not say her name. She became known as 'The Lady'. According to Winnie, however, when speaking at her trial in 1991, there was nothing sinister about her followers or their behaviour. [1]

Winnie's version, which has been strongly disputed by fellow members of the community is as follows: on her return to Soweto in 1986, she felt unsafe because of the petrol-bombing of her house in Brandfort. The Sowetan community took no formal steps to help her or welcome her back but informally they were kind, often dropping in at her house with offers of help. Young people – mostly male – would come round, often spending the night in the rooms at the back of her house. Some would be on the run from the police, some would be in need of a place to stay and would be referred to her. She fed them and she sent many of them to school, even paying their fees. Her home became a natural place of refuge for the local youth.

Schooling was intermittent, because a State of Emergency was in existence, and she suggested that in the absence of any other organised activity those staying with her should perhaps formalise their street games. Acting on her suggestion, the boys formed a soccer club and called it Mandela United, the girls a netball team, called the Mandela Sisters. Winnie played no role in the formation of the clubs, but she didn't object to the use of the Mandela name. In fact, she approved of the whole idea. It was common to name football teams after political figures at this time – there was already a Sisulu FC in Orlando.

She was a generous benefactress to the seventeen or so members of the teams, staying at the back of her house, not only feeding, housing and educating them, but giving them money when they needed it. She assumed she wasn't their sole financial supporter, but had no idea what their other sources of income might be.

She didn't know who they all were either, although she knew that the people at her house now came from all over the country, and that they were not all soccer players. But she assumed that those who didn't play stayed with her because they needed to. She didn't question them further, she didn't exercise control over who stayed in her rooms or pay too much attention to who was there and what they might be doing. She was happy to shelter political refugees and never thought her house might be a refuge for criminals.

Shortly after Mandela United was formed, some of the players came to her and told her they had found a coach who lived a few blocks away. His name was Jerry Richardson. Winnie didn't know Richardson, but approved of the team having a coach.

With the money they received, Mandela United and the Mandela Sisters bought themselves gold tracksuits with a black and green trim – the colours of the ANC. When not worn the tracksuits were kept in a garage on Winnie's premises, but some of the refugees needed to wear them all the time, as they had no other clothes.

Winnie maintained that Mandela United only lasted as a football team for a couple of years. By November 1988 it had been disbanded, although one or two of the original members still lived in the back rooms and still wore the tracksuits. Winnie continued to keep open house and several non-playing refugees came and stayed on her premises. There was an understanding that those who lived with her should respect her privacy, just as she respected theirs. She never went to visit them in the outside rooms and they never came into the main house. She did become aware, at one stage, that they had begun some kind of sentry duty, but she thought it was more for their own self-protection than to guard her house. Many had been harassed by the police in the past and everyone at the time feared detention. She had the impression that they were patrolling on a shift basis, taking turns to guard themselves and her.

According to Winnie, her contact with the youths was minimal, apart from going to organised activities with Mandela United and providing them with money, education, food and shelter. She would see them in the street outside her house and in her yard and would greet them when she saw them, but she was a busy woman, deeply involved in community affairs. Every day she went to her office in Orlando East where she and her various employees worked long hours taking care of local social problems. At home she had Zinzi and Zinzi's children to take care of. She didn't have the time to spend with the boys in the back rooms.

The players did begin accompanying Winnie to funerals and meetings, but never in any formal capacity, like bodyguards. They were comrades, after all, they had every right to attend such organised activities; anyone who was around could go along. They did wear the Mandela United tracksuits to these events because it was the custom to wear decent clothes and their own clothes might be a little tattered. The tracksuits were neat and attractive; there was nothing inappropriate in wearing them to a funeral.

Winnie's cousin, Wordsworth Madikizela, described the occasion when Mandela United accompanied Winnie from Soweto to Bizana for the funeral of her brother Christopher.

> The night before the funeral we always have a vigil where people sing hymns and it is very religious and quiet. Winnie came with her soccer team and they took over. They were arranging the seating of people and handed out the programmes. During the vigil they led the singing from the front and they made everyone sing political protest songs, which were not the right songs to sing. The people of the area – mostly Madikizelas – felt snubbed and were very upset about it. It might be how they have funerals in the townships but she comes from here and she knows how funerals are held here. And Christopher was a man of the area, he was a school teacher and had nothing to do with politics.[2]

Jerry Richardson's account of the football team placed more

emphasis on sport than ceremony.[3] He said that in January 1986 he was approached by some young boys who told him they were going to form a team called Mandela United. An enthusiastic player, he offered his help, saying he would be prepared to be the team's coach. According to him, the club was never officially registered, and in fact only lasted for about six months until July 1986, when 13 of its members were arrested and it was forced to disband.

Former members of the football club and parents of children who joined Mandela United tell a third version.[4] They say that on her return to Soweto Winnie became aware of how active and how organised the youth of Orlando West was. The comrades there were politically motivated, as people were throughout Soweto, but they were also anxious to work with the street committees. They were violent, and they could be vindictive, and they had become used to harassing people, sometimes simply for something to do. But they believed in the power of organisation, especially as the situation in the township became increasingly anarchic. For Winnie they were a ready-made power base.

As in Brandfort, and as in Soweto ten years earlier, there was an affinity between Winnie and the youth. She told them what they wanted to hear and appeared a dependable yet sympathetic authority figure. She had money, food and a place for them to stay. Whereas in Brandfort she had encouraged students to stay away from school, in Soweto she did the opposite. By the beginning of 1986 the ANC was actively encouraging students to return to school, on the premise that even a poor education was better than no education at all. Not only did Winnie provide the sole opportunity for many youths to receive an education, she attended class herself, enrolling as a Social Anthropology Political Studies student at Wits University. She was a somewhat irregular attender of lectures and tutorial, but no worse in that regard than many other students. She still took care over her essays which were considered competent but not brilliant. As in the past, education was not an area she tried to grandstand in, but something she took seriously and worked hard at. She was popular among this peer group. A relaxed and friendly fellow pupil, she was even elected class representative in International Relations.

Although unassuming and industrious, she did attend class accompanied by bodyguards. Those who accompanied her carried her briefcase – a practice which became famous in the university when on one occasion the bodyguard dropped the briefcase on the floor and a gun fell out. Often Winnie's bodyguards joined in her classes, one in particular was remembered as being especially bright.[5]

So not only did she symbolise a real resistance to apartheid to the youth she came across in Soweto, she offered them more. They could be her boys. And that is what they became, calling her 'Mummy' and obeying her rules. Her rules were strict. The boys had to be in at a certain time each night, signing in and out of the house in a special register. Failure to sign in meant a whipping – by the other boys as well as by Winnie.

Residents of Soweto were never able to believe how quickly Mandela United became so powerful. Nobody could have dreamt it would become what it did. It seemed that Winnie had only just returned from Brandfort when the football team started mushrooming from nowhere. Parents were aware of their children's excitement about the club, with its double attraction of soccer and the Mother of the Nation. But some questioned her motives even then. They wondered how someone who was supposed to be so involved in the struggle could spend as much time as she did with the footballers. They didn't mind their sons playing football for Winnie or spending time at her house, but like the parents in Brandfort they took exception when their children stopped coming home. More and more children spent the night over there. One day they were playing soccer, the next they had moved into Winnie's house. Again, like the parents in Brandfort, the Sowetan parents were reluctant to confront Winnie. They were frightened of her. There was something about her, some uncontrollable quality which they didn't trust.

Ordando Macubu's mother took exception to her son living at Winnie's house and went to see Winnie. She told her that although it was very kind of her to house the homeless children and provide them with food, the fact was a number of the children staying at her house did have a place to live – in the same neighbourhood. There was really no need for them to live at Winnie's house. But Winnie disagreed. She believed that she, as a surrogate mother, was better for Ordando than his real mother. She claimed that all the children living with her had been starving, including Ordando. His mother didn't feed him but she did, and that was why he stayed at her house. Fuming, Mrs Macubu left Winnie's house in Orlando West without further discussion, and without her son.

It wasn't long before those who had flocked to join the club became less friendly with other boys in the township. Then they became somewhat menacing. They would roam around the township recruiting members, saying that those who didn't join would be regarded as police informers. It was at this point that the feud between Winnie and Dudu Chili took root.

Dudu Chili was a local single parent, the mother of four boys. She didn't just run her own household, she was also a local leader, active at both a community level and political one. Township residents came to her with their problems, not least because she had a car and a telephone. Much of her spare time was spent ferrying those who had been shot by the police to hospital.

Dudu was also used as a local dispute-solver, embodying the most informal kind of people's court as she dispensed advice, helped recover stolen property, and lectured recalcitrant teenagers. She was not frightened of Winnie. When her son Sibusiso came home clearly worried, saying that the threats against him by Mandela United members had reached a stage where he felt he had no choice but to join the football club, Dudu went to see Winnie, and asked her straight out why she wanted Sibusiso to come and live on her premises. Either he is a sell-out or he isn't, was Winnie's response. If he refuses to join the soccer club, the boys will have no choice but to believe he is a police informer. Dudu was no fool: like her son, she was well aware of the implicit threat, knowing what happened to sell-outs, but she was not prepared to let it rest there. She went to a cousin of hers, a woman who had been very friendly with Winnie in the past and asked her to intercede. Dudu's cousin visited Winnie and for a while afterwards there was a lull and Sibusiso was left alone. But then boys started running away from Winnie's house and the feud between Winnie and Dudu Chili really began.

Members of Mandela United were not supposed to leave the house at all without permission. People said it was because Winnie feared that they would spread the word of what was really going on inside the house. Rumour had it that that was the reason behind the register, with its rule about signing in and out. But boys did leave the Mandela house, some in fear of their lives, and many talked. The rumours about what was happening at Winnie's house increased. She was said to be drinking more and more heavily, and under the influence of alcohol. One couple who had her to dinner were embarrassed when she became too drunk to stand.

It was what she was said to be doing to the youths in her house that was so shocking. Numerous stories were told of people being beaten up, whipped, even murdered – some were hacked to death. One rumour circulated that each day corpses would be loaded into a car, taken out and dumped; another was that every morning soccer club members would scrub the blood of victims from the floor and walls. Everything was done with the knowledge of and at the instigation of

'Mummy' who, it was said, kept body parts in her fridge for use in tribal spells.

Dudu Chili and Albertina Sisulu set up an escape route for boys who ran away. There was no question of being allowed to resign voluntarily from the club: those who wanted to leave had to leave the entire area, and in some cases the country.

There were so many missing boys and so many reasons to disappear at this time that parents didn't know where to start looking. A missing child could have been detained, he could have been shot by the police, he could have been recruited as a member of Mandela United, he could have been recruited as an Umkhonto we Sizwe cadre by the ANC, he could have been killed by Mandela United or by any other of the vigilante gangs. However, the level of anxiety of a number of parents was so high that they took their fears about Mandela United to the police, despite the fact that they regarded the police as an enemy.

The Security Police and the Murder and Robbery squads in Soweto had heard the rumours of what was going on in Winnie's house from shortly after her return to Soweto. What they found disturbing was that the rumours didn't vary, they were always about disappearances, allegations that youngsters were taken to her home and never heard from again. But they subsequently claimed that there was never enough evidence to prosecute her – if there was any evidence at all. Some parents complained to the police that their children had been recruited by Winnie against their will, forced to become Umkhonto we Sizwe soldiers and sent out of the country to receive training, but there was really no way of knowing whether such recruitment was voluntary or involuntary. Police estimates were that between twenty and thirty recruits were leaving the country each month to be trained by Umkhonto we Sizwe. Those who left were absolutely forbidden to get in touch with anyone. No letters, no messages, no form of communication was permitted – recruits just disappeared, for their safety and the safety of the underground movement.

Parents who didn't believe their children had been recruited but thought they had been killed by Mandela United had no proof – there were never any bodies. So the police took no steps against Winnie. Their inactivity resulted in another set of rumours. Why wasn't anything done? Why was her football club allowed to conduct this reign of terror? Lack of police action against Winnie made her extremely suspect in the eyes of Soweto residents, but it also made her appear invincible.

As well as recruiting members for Mandela United, some of whom did go on to receive Umkhonto we Sizwe training, Winnie also housed the occasional terrorist who came back into the country. But her residence was not a popular choice for cadres who knew it was under constant surveillance. Staying at Winnie's house greatly increased the risk of blowing a cover. As the rumours about what was going on inside the house circulated, stories of Winnie's involvement with Umkhonto began to increase. Some of them she spread herself. She was as indiscreet as ever, and thought nothing of boasting that her house was used as an arms stash. People began to say that she was the centre of a cell and every member of Mandela United was actually an ANC terrorist. The police, who had informers inside the house as well as surveillants on the street outside, did not take these stories too seriously. Nor did they ever take action against Winnie on these grounds. It served their purpose to allow her house to be used as an occasional refuge. It helped them keep tabs on what was going on in the ANC and in Umkhonto we Sizwe. Her house wasn't used as a weapons arsenal. The only weapons to be stored there were those which belonged to individual cadres, who were trained to take responsibility for their own arms. (The organisation's code said it was an offence to be negligent 'in handling, using or storing . . . of weapons'.)

Cadres were also trained to be solid citizens. The code also said it was an offence to engage in conduct that weakened people's trust, confidence and faith in the ANC and Umkhonto we Sizwe. Theft, looting and forcible seizures of property were offences, as was the abuse of authority and/or power, cruelty, assault, rape, disorderly conduct, the use of insulting or obscene language, bullying and intimidation or any other form of shameful behaviour. Members of Umkhonto we Sizwe who transgressed could be punished by anything from a reprimand or rebuke through imprisonment with hard labour, to 'the maximum penalty' of death.

Mandela United's terrifying habits were not confined to recruiting new members. They were an active vigilante gang, summarily dispensing what they called justice – acting as arbitrators, mediating in domestic disputes and recovering stolen property. They expressed their opinions with the aid of fists and whips, and they arbitrated with AK-47s.

The age of the football team members ranged from early teens to early twenties. Most of them had already been detained by the Security Police, picked up off the streets or from their houses and held for questioning – sometimes for months without being charged. Arrests were unquestionably violent. An arrest from home still meant a group of armed white police officers, banging and kicking on the door and shining bright lights through the windows, usually in the early hours of the morning. On entry they would search the house, kicking over any furniture in their path, shouting at and hitting their victims.

Those who were arrested on the street at a march, a funeral, or even in a random sweep, would be surrounded by white Security Police dressed in riot gear. They would be beaten with rubber truncheons or shot at with pellets and forced into a police vehicle. At the police station, interrogation would begin, but not before the youth had been left alone for a period of time – the initial spell of isolation was considered a valuable inducement to talk. If – as was common – the victim had at an earlier age already witnessed the removal of one of his parents or an older brother or sister, the effects of his own detention were that much worse. Children of tortured parents suffered from intense fear and depression, feelings which came flooding back as their own cell door slammed shut.

By the mid 1980s new and increasingly brutal forms of torture had been developed. It was now not uncommon for interrogation to take place at gunpoint. Detainees were threatened that other family members would be arrested or killed (one woman was made to listen to a tape police said was of her young daughter being raped). They were also forced out of windows while held by the ankles or made to lie down among corpses. Any pretence that these sessions were to elicit the truth had long gone. As well as having to endure false accusations prisoners were ultimately forced to sign false statements.

Many who endured this process suffered long-term physical effects. Some couldn't walk properly, others became impotent, some even suffered brain damage. The psychological damage caused insomnia, memory loss, an inability to concentrate and increased tendency to alcoholism and drug addiction. Upon release former detainees were disorientated and anxious and needed to regain some sense of control of their lives. They felt inadequate after their long periods of helplessness in the face of physical and psychological attack. More than ever they needed to keep face, to prove themselves, to prove that the system hadn't won. This last need was important to others living in the community. They had to know that their safety was not in jeopardy, that they hadn't been betrayed. Release meant facing distrust, which in a climate of violence and fear might never really dissipate.

Prisoners were often told that others were talking. They would be told they had been implicated by a specific person in the township and asked in turn what they knew about his activities. They were also promised that unless they co-operated they would be detained again and again. In the circumstances, many did co-operate, forging uneasy relationships with the authorities and informing on what was happening in the area. The police didn't bother to keep their contacts particularly secret. Overt communication between police and township residents didn't just provide information, it helped destabilise the community. Some who couldn't face such an existence went on the run. Displaced youths came flooding into Soweto, fleeing from police in other parts of the country.

By far the most widespread and far-reaching effect of this continual abuse was in the loss of innocence suffered by the thousands who were victims of it. For these children there was no youth, no childhood. They had to look out for, and look after, themselves. With no homes and no formal, continuous education, and the only constant authority presence in their lives that of the Security Police, the police became something of a role model. Vigilante gangs aped many of their characteristics as they roamed the streets in packs, armed with guns, picking up suspects and taking them off to be interrogated.[6]

Thousands of children, some as young as nine years old were detained by the police. At home, most of the Security Police who were married with families of their own provided a more orthodox example of behaviour to their own children. One high-ranking officer even had a plaque on his desk which read: 'Anyone can be a father – not anyone can be a Daddy.' In its treatment of young black children, however, the State had become an abusive parent.

So had the Mother of the Nation. Acting in her name, Winnie's boys would burst into a house with much clamour and show of force, before compelling an intended victim into a vehicle and driving him off to the place of interrogation – Winnie's house. Once there, a mutated form of police questioning would occur, with verbal abuse, kicking, punching, whipping, beating and slapping. Instead of mock executions at gunpoint, victims would be hung from the ceiling; instead of being hooded or blindfolded, they would have plastic bags placed over their heads, and have their faces shoved in buckets of water. Instead of electric shocks, their flesh would be carved and, as cited in one case, battery acid would be smeared into the wounds. And instead of being dangled out of a window by their ankles they would be thrown high up in the air and left to hit the floor – a practice known as 'breakdown'. Finally, amid threats of what would continue to happen to them if they did not comply, they would be forced to 'confess' to whatever crime it was they had been accused of – stealing a car, taking too much property in a divorce settlement, being a sell-out. Those who were released after their ordeal took no action against Mandela United – what could they do? But the word spread and so did the fear.

The line between crime and politics was becoming blurred in Winnie's mind. Her followers were activists not criminals. It was appropriate, she thought, to attend the trial of her friend Lindi Mangaliso, accused of murdering her husband, because Lindi's mother was an activist and 'I felt I could not turn my back on her because of her facing murder charges.'[7] When Winnie flew down to Cape Town at the beginning of December 1986 to attend the trial, she found a crowd who thought otherwise waiting for her. She arrived at court to shouts of 'We don't need you here', 'Go home', 'You're not supposed to be here', 'You know our children are being necklaced and still you come and associate with a murdress' and 'You are a public figure and now you associate with a murdress'. She ignored the crowd (estimated by some accounts to be more than 500) and went into court.

When she came out again the incensed crowd pelted her with eggs, cans and handfuls of sand, forcing her to flee into a nearby restaurant to take shelter. When she emerged to get into a taxi they threw sand on top of her head. The incident got a great deal of press coverage, especially in the right-wing *Citizen* and on government-controlled television. Furious at being seen at such a disadvantage, Winnie called a press conference. First she attacked the South African Broadcasting Corporation (SABC). 'I heard them say there was a mob of about five hundred. There were no more than thirty,' she said. Then she attacked the State, whom she accused of orchestrating the whole thing. 'These are the government's usual measures,' she said. 'We are not surprised.'

'The people who participated in that incident were the same hooligan element we find among our own communities here, the people who are vigilantes, who take advantage of democratic, peaceful demonstrations and make it appear we have black-on-black violence.'[8]

She could have been describing her own football team. She began using this type of defence more and more. Forced to defend or explain her increasingly erratic behaviour, she would deny any personal wrong-doing, at the same time accusing her accusers of exactly the thing she was supposed to have done. She gave every sign that she genuinely believed what she was saying was true. Just as she believed that she took good care of those to whom she had become a surrogate parent. She never acknowledged a fault. When put on the defensive she would strike back.

Nominally the coach of the soccer team, Jerry Richardson ran Mandela United as an agile lieutenant to Winnie's commander-in-chief. His background was shrouded in mystery and he never escaped the rumours that he was an agent for the Security Police. He did in fact act as an informer.[9] He was the classic victim who fell prey to the authorities. He had a low intellect. He had an inability to cope with stress: stressful situations made both his speech and his reasoning deteriorate. When he felt inadequate he hid his feelings by either pretending to be bored or by becoming increasingly aggressive. He often pretended to be macho and sophisticated.[10]

Richardson was born in 1948 in Soweto. He never really knew his father, who died when he was six years old. His mother then became the family's sole supporter until her death in 1969. She left two boys and two girls. The young, aimless Richardson left school at twelve, never developing any particular aptitude for anything except football. Soccer was the only thing he was good at – he was a particularly skilled left back – and would fantasise that he was a soccer hero. He married a local girl at seventeen, but never felt any real affection for his wife. In fact the most important relationship of his adult life was with Winnie. He adored her, he idealised her, he revered her and her approval not only meant that he was accepted, it gave him self esteem. Like the others in the team, with whom he strongly identified, he was dependent on her, not just for food and shelter, but emotionally. He always called her 'Mummy'.

When Richardson and his wife bought a house together in Carr Street, Mzimlophe, in Soweto, he began to get involved in local street committees in the area, eventually becoming chairman of his own Carr Street committee. He had a great deal of time to devote to local social issues, because as far as anyone could see he never had a job. His unemployment became the reason his neighbours distrusted him, but they already disliked him. He was a pompous and domineering committee member, always wanting his own way. There were times when the Carr Street committee was forced to take action against its own chairman. The first occasion arose shortly after his election, when he was alleged to have abducted his girlfriend's daughter, prompting intervention from a delegation from the committee. Richardson released the little girl, but he continued to cause trouble and arouse suspicion.[11]

Local residents were suspicious of Richardson's frequent meetings with white people who used to drive him around in what looked like unmarked police cars. As he didn't have a job these meetings couldn't be work-related. The matter of Richardson's 'friends' aroused such anxiety in the neighbourhood that it was discussed at a street committee meeting, and another delegation was sent to visit Richardson. But when they got to his house a group of police there chased them away. Committee members decided to exclude Richardson from their meetings, but even that was problematic. He always seemed to know when and where meetings were scheduled and often turned up unannounced.

His wife had left him, taking their two children with her. Virginia Richardson later said she was forced to leave her husband after he made several attempts to kill her. He had begun bringing other women home and would kick his wife out of the bedroom so he could sleep with them. 'One night he came into the lounge where I was sleeping. Luckily I heard his footsteps and woke just before he stabbed me. I pleaded with him to spare my life so I could leave the following morning. He agreed. But he emphasised that I was not to come back.'[12]

Suspicion, distrust and dislike of Richardson came to a head on 9 November 1988 when his house was attacked. The circumstances of the violent raid confirmed to many who witnessed it that Richardson must indeed be in league with the authorities. It was this attack which caused him to move into Winnie's house.

It was a hot South African summer's day on 9 November. Outside the house, Jerry Richardson was watering his flowers and tending to his garden. Inside the house sat two Umkhonto we Sizwe cadres, who were taking refuge with him for a couple of days. Overhead, a police helicopter hovered. Neighbours described what happened next.

'Police sped on to the street and approached the house. A calm-looking Richardson lifted his arms to the air, signalling surrender. Police approached Richardson, handcuffed him and put him in one of the private vehicles. They then proceeded to launch a grenade and gunfire attack on the house. The shootout was long.'[13]

Two hours long was the estimate of some eyewitnesses. At the end of the attack, Jerry Richardson's house had been substantially damaged. The two Umkhonto we Sizwe soldiers and a white police officer lay dead.

Seated on the back seat of the police car, Richardson was driven out of the township by two white officers. He was detained for two weeks then released without being charged. He returned to Soweto with crutches and dark glasses, but on the third day of his return he walked again, abandoning his crutches and appearing fresh and healthy. He then went to Winnie. He asked for her help in giving him somewhere to stay and repairing his own house. She agreed and Richardson joined the rest of the soccer team in the back rooms.

At the inquest, Richardson gave a statement in which he gave his version of the background to the incident at his house.

During 1988 (August) I was requested by Winnie to give my house for a sleeping place to two men she knew. She never told me who these people were but I said it would be fine if these men slept at my house. However I heard nothing again from Mandela about these two men. One night after 22.00, after about 3 months have passed, on 4 November 1988 Winnie showed up at my house. She was escorted by two men. I know the one by the name of Shakes only and the other one was introduced to me as Sipho. Winnie then said that Sipho was the man she told me about during August. She further requested me to do anything Sipho asked and that the other man she requested a sleeping place for is on his way. Winnie and Shakes then left. Sipho had a maroon bag with him and I then showed him to his room. In the room Sipho put his bag on the bed and told me he was a dangerous man. He asked me if I had ever seen an AK47 rifle, to which I replied in the negative. He then removed an AK47 rifle wrapped in a yellow towel from the bag and handed it to me to feel the weight. Hereafter he put it back into the bag and kept the bag and kept the bag underneath the bed. Sipho then explained to me to be careful not to let his presence be known. He also told me that another dangerous man, Thebogo, was on his way to my home. Several days passed in the meantime. On 6 November 1988 Sipho showed me another article looking like a fuse of some kind. He told me it was very dangerous and only needed an apple. I later learned that this item was indeed a detonator for a hand grenade.

During November 1988, Thebongo arrived at my house at plus minus 21.30. He greeted me by name and also said hullo to Sipho. He too had a bag of clothes with him, but showed me there was nothing else in it. Both Sipho and Thebogo slept on the same double bed in the sleeping room, whilst I slept in the sitting room. Several days passed again, whilst both my guests were talking about 'suitable targets in the surrounding cities like Johannesburg and Krugersdorp'. They also left the house occasionally.[14]

Richardson never at any stage claimed this statement was fabricated or that it had been tortured out of him. He never maintained that it was anything but the truth and voluntarily given. His motive for giving it appeared at his own trial. After he had gone through the statement, line by line with the prosecutor, he said 'This policeman did not like this lady and I was told by this policeman that if she can be in trouble then I will be safe.'[15]

John Morgan was an elderly Sowetan who sometimes acted as Winnie's driver. He had known her since her marriage when he had been a neighbour of the Mandelas in Vilakasi Street, and had belonged to the same boxing club as Nelson Mandela. Morgan suffered from a number of health problems over the years, mainly stemming from his diabetes. When necessary he would go to Winnie for financial help. In return he drove her whenever she needed him. From the time of her return to Soweto he regularly drove her about. He was also a driver for the soccer team.

On the night of 26 May 1987, two teenage boys were asleep in their uncle's house when three men approached and banged on the door. All of them wore stockings over their heads, and one of them was carrying a gun. When the uncle opened the door, the three demanded the boys, held them at gunpoint, swore at their mother and then forced them into a car. The attackers were subsequently identified as Isaac Mokgoro, Absolm Madonsela – and John Morgan.

Once inside the car, Peter and Philip Makanda were forced to lie on the floor in the footwell below the back seat. Madonsela and Mokgoro then got into the car and, sitting on the back seat used the boys as floor mats. John Morgan drove them to Winnie's house, the two boys were hustled into one of the back rooms where a third badly beaten and bleeding youth was already being held, tied to a chair. One of the members of the football team in the room was asked if these were the right boys, to which he replied, 'Yes, they are.' Winnie was then fetched. As she came into the room, one of the men said to her, 'Here are the boys, we have brought them.' She turned to Peter and Philip and greeted them. Gesturing towards the third youth – who has never been named or found – she said, 'If you don't want to be hurt like this boy you must tell the truth.' She then left.

After Winnie had left the room, the accusations began in earnest. The charges were that the two brothers had sold out, that they were informers. They were told that others had died because of what they had done. Peter denied being a sell-out, and was hit. Both boys were beaten, and Peter was hung by the neck with a plastic rope from the roof until the rafters broke and he fell to the ground. A plastic bag was then placed over his head and his face was pushed into a bucket of water. The boys were told that there was a vicious dog on the premises and unless they confessed it would be brought in to rip them to pieces. Some of the players in the room carried guns and constantly threatened both boys. They were told that a failure to confess would result in their being shot. And then someone said, 'Let's stoep [carve] them.'

Philip was first. While Peter and the third youth were forced to sit on a mattress and watch, Philip was made to sit in a chair with his hands tied behind his back. Using a pen knife, a large 'M' for Mandela was sliced into his chest and 'Viva ANC' was carved thickly down the length of one of his thighs. Someone then fetched a car battery and battery acid was smeared into the wounds. Then it was Peter's turn. He was held down and 'Viva ANC' was carved across his back – not one, but several strokes were used.

After the carving the boys were beaten up some more before being told to lie down on the floor and sleep. In one of the more bizarre aspects of the case, Winnie came into the room after a couple of hours and served them with tea and cakes. The third boy told the players about someone else he claimed was a sell-out, prompting Mandela United to set off to fetch the youth. It wasn't long before the fourth boy was bundled into the back room. If he didn't want to look like the three boys lying there, he was told, he must tell the truth.

Suddenly one of the soccer team members keeping watch sounded an alert. A police car was cruising outside and it was no longer safe to keep the four boys in this back room. John Morgan said that all four could be taken to his garage, and they were loaded into his van, driven to his house and put into his garage. After a while, Peter and Philip worked out how to open the garage door from the inside and managed to escape, leaving the other two boys behind. They never saw them again.

Peter and Philip ran straight to the Meadowlands police station where they made statements about what had been done to them. Their case was then consolidated as part of a conglomerate case which the police was investigating under the Internal Security Act. Morgan, Mokgoro and Madonsela were subsequently arrested and charged with kidnapping and assault.

The case came to court the following year. A lawyer who was involved in the case saw the Makanda brothers just before their trial and noticed that their scars were still vivid. Johannesburg attorney

Kathy Satchwell represented the three defendants. Her job was comparatively easy. The two boys had had to pick out their assailants at an identity parade with no two-way mirror to protect themselves. They had to sit in front of the line-up and point to whomever they recognised, while being watched and listened to. In the circumstances, the Makanda brothers were too intimidated to be effective witnesses. They contradicted each other's testimony as to who the perpetrators of the crime were, making it impossible to get a conviction. Acquitting the accused, the magistrate commented, 'The experience must have been so frightening that their powers of observation were affected and their minds were more on how to get through the ordeal alive.'[16]

Winnie was never charged in connection with this crime, nor was she called as a witness, nor was she ever questioned.

Chapter Nine

The case of the battery acid assaults was consolidated with another case under the Internal Security Act. The Security Police were already investigating another entirely separate case under the same Security Act umbrella, which also involved the Mandela premises at no. 8115 Orlando West. Because this new case had taken place at Winnie's house they felt it made sense to have the same investigating officer, Captain Andre Kritzinger work on it, even though it was a common crime rather than a security offence. The case already under investigation had as its central figure a trained Umkhonto we Sizwe soldier who had spent one night tearing up Soweto at the beginning of 1987.

Thirty-two-year-old Oupa Alex Seheri lived in Soweto. In recent years he had spent time in various Umkhonto we Sizwe camps outside the country. His specialty was the use of firearms; he regularly taught youths in the township how to handle guns, and on 24 January he had a date to teach a group how to operate a Scorpion pistol. On 23 January, the evening before the scheduled gun lesson, Seheri attended a night vigil for the funeral of a friend.[1] Night vigils were a common occurrence in the community. Friends and relatives sat watching over the body of the deceased through the night before the next day's burial. Vigils had recently become occasions for violence. It was easy for a rival group to find out when and where a vigil was planned, go to the sitting targets and kill those keeping watch. Vigils were also convenient meeting places for those in the underground movement. Under the formal cover of mourning, terrorists could meet and exchange messages and make plans.

While at the vigil, Seheri met up with Vuyisile Tshabalala – another ANC cadre. Tshabalala introduced Seheri to a friend of his, Setimbiso Buthelezi (no relation to the Inkatha leader) who at that time was Zinzi Mandela's boyfriend and a member of Mandela United. At the end of the evening Buthelezi, who was driving a maroon Audi belonging to Winnie offered to give Seheri a lift home.[2] The men left the funeral together.

The next day, Seheri got a message from Tshabalala. The pistol he was to use at that evening's gun lesson was waiting for him at Winnie's house. Seheri took a taxi to Orlando West, taking his own AK-47 with him, carefully wrapped in a green raincoat. On his arrival he recognised the maroon Audi of the previous evening and asked if he could see the driver. He was then taken to Zinzi's bedroom where Buthelezi was sitting around with some other members of the soccer team. Buthelezi showed him the package which had been left for him – a black bag with a Scorpion pistol inside. It was indeed the gun Seheri had been waiting for.

Seheri couldn't carry two bulky weapons around with him without arousing suspicion, so he asked Buthelezi if he could leave his AK-47 behind. Buthelezi was extremely reluctant to agree and only allowed Seheri to hide his gun under Zinzi's bed after Seheri promised it wouldn't be for long, that he would return immediately after the lesson. Seheri then set off to meet his two pupils at a shebeen in Zola in Soweto.[3] He sat for some time drinking – he got through six beers and a bottle of brandy – and smoking, before realising that no-one was now likely to arrive. He then left to spend the night at the house of a former girlfriend of his – Lindiwe Mkhonza – who owned a shebeen nearby.

When Seheri arrived at Lindiwe's shebeen, he found a party already well under way. Among the youths present was Xola Mokhaula, who was drinking with his brother, Bobo, and a group of their friends. When Xola got up to go to the toilet, he brushed past Seheri. He didn't know it, but that action was to end his life.

The ensuing massacre began on the flimsiest of pretexts. As Xola had moved past Seheri, Seheri's cigarette had either by accident or by design touched Xola's trousers, burning a small hole at the knee. 'You're burning me,' said Xola flinching. Seheri, by now drunk and belligerent, refused to apologise. Instead he blamed Xola's clumsiness. 'You burnt yourself,' one witness heard him say. An annoyed Xola promptly hit Seheri on the nose, which began to bleed.[4]

'Outside,' said Seheri, and, followed by a sizable audience from inside the shebeen, the two went into the yard to settle the dispute with their fists. From the start Xola had the better of Seheri. He quickly grabbed him by the throat and wrestled him to the ground. He then sat on him, hitting him in the face. The struggling Seheri tried to grab the Scorpion from inside his coat, but Bobo saw the gun, rushed over and pulled it away. The fight was over. All that mattered to Seheri was that he had lost possession of his firearm, in violation of the Umkhonto we Sizwe code. He begged the youths to return it, but they refused. Taking the Scorpion with them, they left the shebeen.

Seheri and Lindiwe arranged for another youth in the shebeen, Ben Dlamini, to give them a lift in his yellow Rekord. They drove over to

Winnie's house so that Seheri could pick up his AK-47 and use it to get the Scorpion back. In addition to collecting his rifle, Seheri picked up seven members of Mandela United. Travelling in Dlamini's Rekord and Winnie's Audi, with Lindiwe giving directions, the expanded group set off to find Xola.

Meanwhile, Xola's group had gone to Xola's parents' house where they had given the Scorpion to his sister, Faith, to hide. They wanted to get the police to come to remove the gun, but they couldn't find a phone to use at that late hour, so decided to hide the gun overnight and take it into the station the following day. While the rest of the group – about seven in all – sat outside drinking beers and guarding the house against Seheri, Xola went to his friend Tutu's house to sleep. He knew there was no way it could be safe for him to remain at his own home that night. Faith hid the gun under the dining-room table and went back to bed. For a brief period everything was quiet.

The first car to drive slowly past the front of the house was the yellow Rekord. Ten minutes passed. Then both cars swept by, Seheri firing his AK-47 out of the Rekord's window. The group on the verandah immediately scattered. One of them, Jeremiah Nkosi, was shot in the back of the head as he ran away. Managing to keep moving, he circled back towards Xola's house to see what had happened. Xola's mother spotted him. 'Go away, they'll kill you,' she hissed. Nkosi set off again but, weak from loss of blood, fell in the street and passed out. He was later found and taken to hospital.

Colin Dlamini, who had fallen asleep on the verandah, woke at the sound of the gun shots to find Seheri standing in front of him brandishing his AK-47. 'Where is the thing?' he demanded, referring to his Scorpion. 'I don't know what you're talking about,' replied Colin and began to run. He was shot by Seheri in the chest, arm and leg, but got away.

All Xola's friends escaped except one. As Seheri came towards the house, Mlando Ngubeni was too frightened to move and just stood where he was on the verandah. Inside the house, Faith and her mother huddled together in the dark when they heard a knock at the kitchen door. 'Who is it?' they whispered. But it was only Mlando, asking to be let in, so they opened the door and switched on the lights. In burst Seheri, Ben Dlamini and Charles Zwane (a soccer team member) pushing Mlando before them. Both Seheri and Zwane were armed. Seheri demanded his gun. Mlando started babbling that Faith knew where it was, and Seheri should shoot her instead of him, he didn't know anything. Faith remained silent.

Seheri made both Mlando and Faith look down at the floor, then shot Mlando in the hip. Mlando crawled into the bedroom where he bled to death, while Seheri asked Faith if she would like the same treatment. But she continued to deny knowing where the gun was. When Seheri aimed his gun at her she looked straight at him. 'I have three children,' she said. 'If you want to kill me, you must start with my children.' Seheri decided that he would look for Xola instead. He warned Faith to leave the doors unlocked for his return, and left the house with his gang. The minute they had gone Faith grabbed the gun from under the dining-room table and ran outside and dropped it into the coal box. Then she went back into the house and waited.[5]

Lindiwe knew that Xola and Tutu were friends. She took the youths to Tutu's house, where – as she had expected – they found both Tutu and Xola. 'We have come to kill you,' said Seheri. He pointed his gun at Xola's temple, while someone else pulled Xola forward by the front of his trousers. A third person grabbed Tutu's neck and forced him to walk, while a fourth, carrying a long spear, brought up the rear. In this way, the awkward procession made its way back to Xola's house.

They marched straight back into the kitchen where Tutu was forced to kneel on the floor next to Xola's mother. Xola asked his mother where the gun was, but she didn't know. He looked at Faith, then at the floor. Faith asked Seheri what he would do if his firearm was returned. She made him agree that if he did get it back he would leave Xola alone. She did not tell him she had hidden the gun but said she had heard a noise outside earlier, somewhere in the vicinity of the coal box. It might have been someone hiding the Scorpion. She stood at the kitchen door and showed Seheri towards the coal box. Seheri handed his AK-47 over to one of the members of Mandela United, went to the coal box, opened the door and saw his gun. 'Here it is!' he shouted, pulling it out and jumping up and down. Then he turned towards the house, and aimed the gun. 'Look! I'm shooting!' he called.

Faith screamed. 'You can't shoot me, I have a child, I'm carrying a child,' she cried. 'Get away, move away,' replied Seheri, aiming at Xola. Xola ran into the bedroom, followed by Seheri and two of the others and fell to his knees. 'What have I done? I have given your gun back,' he pleaded. Faith put her baby down and pleaded too, grabbing hold of Seheri, begging him to forgive her brother. Her mother was begging Seheri for mercy. 'If you have to shoot him. just cripple him, don't kill him,' she implored.[6]

Instead of shooting Xola, Seheri fired his gun at the wardrobe. He then went outside to where Lindiwe and the others were waiting by the cars. Faith also went outside and watched them. She heard Lindiwe and Seheri in conversation. 'You have killed him?' asked Lindiwe. 'I have taught him not to be forward,' replied Seheri. 'Go and kill the dog,' instructed Lindiwe. 'And wipe out the evidence.'

Seheri turned and went straight back into the house. Re-entering the bedroom he looked at Xola. 'I have come to kill you,' he said. Then he called the women to come and watch. 'Look,' he said and shot Xola in the head. The bullet entered at point blank range. Seheri shot again; blood and brains splattered all over the room.

Lindiwe wanted Seheri to find Bobo and kill him too, but Bobo had run off much earlier, so the group left and returned to Winnie's house, where the Scorpion pistol was returned to its black bag and hidden under Zinzi's bed.[7]

Storing the weapon at Winnie's house made it a potential embarrassment to the Mandela family. As the police began to investigate the murders of Mlando and Xola, it wasn't long before the trail led them to look under Zinzi's bed. There they found the black bag, with the Scorpion still nestling inside it. They had no option but to take in Zinzi for questioning. But the police were now ambivalent about meddling with the Mandelas. Their uncertainty was reflected in a *Business Day* story in which only Zinzi's identity was confirmed.[8]

Police are investigating the possibility a Soviet-made Scorpion machine pistol, found in the home of a prominent Soweto woman, was used in recent terror attacks in which two people were killed. Secrecy still surrounds the woman's identity. Police have confirmed that the woman in whose home the gun was found on February 27 was detained for questioning that day. She was later released. On the same day Zinzi, the daughter of the jailed ANC leader, Nelson Mandela, was detained for a few hours for questioning and released without charges being laid against her. Police, however, would not confirm Mandela was the woman concerned.

Most of the information came to the police from the five who were eventually accused in the case, Seheri, Lindiwe, Ben Dlamini, Setimbiso Buthelezi and Charles Zwane. The possibility of Zinzi and Winnie being accused was swiftly rejected. Although it was technically an offence to house a weapon, police and prosecutors were well aware that it would be extremely difficult to prove that Winnie knew of the Scorpion's presence in her house. None of the available evidence linked Winnie directly to the gun, and in the absence of anything concrete, she was left alone. Any suggestion that she should know that her house was being used as an arms stash, and could possibly be prosecuted on those terms, was ignored. It would be impossible to prove.

Both Winnie and Zinzi provided the police with statements, but Winnie never went to the police station. She gave her information to her attorney, Ismail Ayob, who passed it on. Both Mandelas were down on the list of potential State witnesses when the case came to the Rand Supreme Court in November 1988, but at the last moment neither was called to appear. The prosecution was anxious to have their evidence, because they had confirmed in their statements that Buthelezi was the regular driver of the maroon Audi, that he was a member of Mandela United, and that both Buthelezi and Zwane lived at the Mandela residence. This information would corroborate what Buthelezi and Zwane had confessed in police custody. It would prevent them from claiming – as was common – that the police had fabricated their confessions.[9]

State prosecutors knew that Winnie and Zinzi were reluctant to testify. None the less the prosecutors made it clear to Ismail Ayob that they intended to call Winnie and Zinzi and expected them to be co-operative. But just days before their scheduled appearances, an unusual event occurred which made them unnecessary. Buthelezi and Zwane summoned their lawyers and said they wished to make a series of admissions. Buthelezi admitted that he was the driver of the Audi, that he had driven it to Xola's house and back again, that he had hidden the AK-47 under Zinzi's bed before the shooting and hidden the Scorpion pistol in her room after the shooting. Zwane admitted that he was present at Winnie's house on the night of 24 January, when Seheri arrived, that he was a passenger in Winnie's Audi which drove to Xola's house and was present when shots were fired, and that he had given the Scorpion pistol to Buthelezi to hide. Both men implicated themselves by these admissions. On the basis of his admissions Buthelezi was found guilty of possession of a machine gun and rifle. On the basis of his admissions Zwane was found guilty of possession of a machine gun.[10]

Buthelezi and Zwane were sentenced to four years' and one year's imprisonment respectively. Zwane's year was wholly suspended for five years, but he would be arrested again within four months, this time charged with nine counts of murder and eight counts of attempted murder. Buthelezi went to prison for three years. Ben Dlamini was acquitted on all counts and Lindiwe Mkhonza was found guilty of the murder of Xola Mokhaula, for which she went to prison for ten years. The judge found that she had associated herself with the murder of Xola, by deliberately inciting Seheri to kill him. Her house in Soweto was subsequently burnt to the ground.

Oupa Seheri was found guilty of two counts of murder, two counts of attempted murder, one count of illegal possession of a machine gun, one count of illegal possession of a rifle and counts of illegal possession of ammunition. He was sentenced to death.

Others besides the police raided Winnie's house on 27 February 1987. Local residents reported that earlier in the day shots were fired when members of a rival football team arrived at the property. A couple of days earlier, the house had been stoned by the same footballers – students from Daliwonga High School in the Dube section of Soweto – as another local feud involving Mandela United began to escalate.[11]

The fight between members of Mandela United and pupils at Daliwonga High School had begun literally as a turf war. At issue was the use of the local Riverside football field. Members of Mandela United had arrived at a match being played by pupils from Daliwonga High and told them to leave so that they could play there. The fight which broke out only ended when Mandela United produced guns and forced the Daliwonga pupils to flee. The stoning of the Mandela house was a direct revenge attack by the Daliwonga players for being forced off the football pitch. In the process, they managed to cause R1,000 worth of damage. They also captured two members of Mandela United and took them back to their school where they beat them up until teachers intervened.

Conflict between the two groups continued intermittently for the next eighteen months, until a local girl who was both a member of the Mandela Sisters netball team and a pupil at Orlando High School was gang-raped by students from Daliwonga High as she returned home from a discotheque. It was now July 1988. She went to Mandela United, told them what had happened and who had done it. The revenge attack was almost immediate. The Daliwonga students were identified, collected, taken to the back rooms of the Mandela property, charged, found guilty, beaten up and then released. As far as Mandela United was concerned, the score had been settled. But the Daliwonga pupils went back to their school, and began to rally support from other students for a counter-strike.[12]

On Thursday 28 July, a greatly expanded group from Daliwonga High went to the Mandela home. Eye-witnesses described a sea of students coming down the street, a mob of teenagers approaching. They climbed the walls to the house, smashed the windows and doors and, with a great deal of commotion, set the house on fire. What was so strange about this attack – and made it so different from the attack on the house in Brandfort – was that this time no-one came to help.

According to an account of the arson attack, written by Nomavenda Mathiane for *Frontline* magazine, the street outside Winnie's house was soon full of people – though neither Winnie nor members of the soccer team were at home when the fire started. However, no-one watching lifted a finger to help. The crowd watched as the house was destroyed. Local residents did nothing. The police arrived and did nothing, the ambulance came – its driver and assistant did nothing, the fire brigade came, but the firemen could do nothing – they had no water in their tanks. All these people stood and watched in silence as Winnie's house was completely destroyed.

Someone else watched in silence too. At some stage Winnie drove up slowly towards her burning house. By then, as well as residents, policemen, firemen and medical personnel, the street was full of reporters, who raced towards her for a comment on the destruction of her home. She ignored the crowd, she looked at her house, and then she left.[13]

Those who went to see Winnie later that same day found a woman in deep shock. Her old friend Amina Cachalia went to her offices, and found her sitting behind her desk staring blankly. Amina thought she seemed absolutely devastated. Zinzi was there, and an American businessman with whom she had become friendly, Robert J. Brown, was self-importantly dictating who was and who wasn't allowed into the room. The football team sat around. When Amina asked Winnie what on earth had happened Winnie stopped staring and looked at her. 'I don't know what is happening to my life,' she said.

Albertina Sisulu, who went to Winnie's house to view the damage later, told Amina that she had found stacks of burnt cash strewn about the floor. Bishop Peter Storey from the Methodist Church also went to Winnie's house. His obvious assumption was that the house had been burnt down by the government and he wanted to commiserate with her. Her neighbours told him otherwise. The disclosure that the fire was actually caused by members of the community left him shaken. He drove on to Winnie's office for what was to be his first encounter with the football team. Mandela United were barricading the building with people, and a young thug stood on the gate controlling entry. Storey was asked aggressively what he was doing by the player guarding the gate, to which he responded that he was not answerable to him, he had come to see Mrs Mandela and would he get out of the way.

When Abu and Zhora Asvat went to visit Winnie that evening, they found her still in a state of silent shock. She said nothing. She didn't cry, she just sat staring without moving and without expression. No-one else in the room – Brown and Zinzi were still with her – spoke either. The Asvats stayed for about half an hour and then left.

Everything Winnie cherished had been burnt. All the Mandela family records were destroyed in the fire, all the letters, all the photographs and all the gifts they had been given over the years. Also destroyed was the slice of wedding cake that Winnie had been keeping for Nelson's release. The symbol of her resilience, of her unchanging courage and patience had gone up in smoke.

No charges were laid against the students at Nelson Mandela's request.[14] Instead, from prison, he asked for a powerful group of community leaders to convene to control the situation before any more damage could be done. An immediate task was to disband the football team. And so the Reverend Frank Chikane of the South African Council of Churches, the NUM's Cyril Ramaphosa, COSATU's Sidney Mafumadi, FedTraw's Sister Bernard Ncube and Aubrey Mokoena of the Release Mandela Committee met with Winnie and Mandela United in the first of many meetings of the aptly named Crisis Committee.

But the damage caused by the fire was only one of Winnie's misfortunes. After she had gone to Pollsmoor Prison to tell Mandela about what had happened he stopped eating. Then his speech became slurred. Eventually, on 12 August, Mandela was taken to Tygerberg Hospital. He had acute tuberculosis. When Winnie and Zinzi went to see Mandela he was initially unable to recognise them. He was heavily sedated, having had two litres of fluid removed from his left lung, and couldn't speak properly. He had lost an enormous amount of weight and for the first time looked his age – seventy years old.

Mandela never returned to Pollsmoor Prison. He spent the next few months recuperating (his tuberculosis had been caught in the very early stages). In early December he was transferred to a warden's house in the grounds of Victor Verster Prison, near Cape Town. More than ever, it looked as if he might be released.

Back in Soweto, Winnie refused to disband Mandela United, in spite of requests from her husband and the Crisis Committee. While her old house was rebuilt she moved into a house in another part of Soweto. It was Robert J. Brown who found the house in Diepkloof-Extension, which had a number of back rooms and Jacuzzi. He negotiated payment and arranged for her to move as painlessly as possible. Brown had already given Winnie $30,000 to build the controversial mansion. So he was now paying for both the house she was renting and the house she was building.[15] But Brown proved to be a mixed blessing for the Mandelas. In the days following the fire he was regarded as an opportunist trying to take advantage of a tragic situation. Brown hailed from North Carolina. Originally a liberal democrat, his political career in the United States had begun with civil rights sit-ins under the banner of Martin Luther King. Brown worked on Bobby Kennedy's 1986 Presidential Campaign. He had also worked for Richard Nixon, becoming a Republican in the process.

In 1986 he was considered for position as US ambassador to South Africa by the Reagan administration. In the year that sanctions were imposed, the idea of sending America's first black ambassador to South Africa was appealing and Brown's nomination was supported both by conservative Senator Jesse Helms and Atlanta mayor (and former US ambassador to the United Nations) Andrew Young.[16] He had considerable business experience on the African continent, especially in South Africa where his PR clients included Nabisco and Sara Lee.[17] But Brown had to withdraw his name from consideration when background checks revealed that his business and political past would prevent his winning confirmation.[18]

According to an article in *Business Day*, in 1987 Brown obtained an agreement from Mobil Oil to give Winnie $50,000 for building and other purposes. A first instalment of $20,000 was hand-carried to South Africa by Zeni when she visited her mother in December.[19] Brown fund-raised heavily during this period, using his opposition to sanctions as a way of attracting thousands of dollars from huge corporations. As well as Mobil, Caltex, Johnson & Johnson, Pfizer, Combustion Engineering and Control Data all gave money to the Coalition on Southern Africa (COSA) – a church-based group opposed to sanctions with strong ties to Brown.

But a second *Business Day* article in March 1989 claimed that of $765,000 given to COSA in September 1987, less than 5 per cent had gone to charitable concerns. In fact the only money definitely known to have reached South Africa was Winnie's $20,000. Brown's company had received $65,000, and a consulting company – Pagan

International – which had founded COSA with Brown had received $229,000. Draft contracts obtained by *Business Day* showed that Pagan International and Brown initially hoped to divide up the entire $765,000 between them, with $500,000 going to Pagan and $260,000 going to Brown.

Giving money to the Mandela family (*Business Day* also claimed Brown paid Zeni's rent in Massachusetts and arranged scholarships for her and her husband at Boston University) was something of an investment. Brown realised he could make a fortune from the family, and proposed marketing the Mandela name to prevent others ripping it off. Winnie had already sold the rights to a movie about her life to Camille and Bill Cosby for a contract worth $110,000.[20]

It was to get Mandela's agreement to this proposal that Brown had accompanied Winnie down to Pollsmoor Prison when she told Mandela about the fire. His aim might have been less than altruistic, his timing might have been terrible, but Brown remained undaunted when Mandela refused to see him. Instead he stood triumphantly on the steps of the prison as if his effort had been successful and announced he had the power of attorney for the Mandela family.

Although Brown had Winnie's backing, Mandela was outraged by his attempt to control the name Mandela – a name Nelson Mandela felt belonged to the movement more than his family. He quickly and publicly moved to distance his family from Brown, drafting a statement which Ayob issued saying that Brown did *not* represent the family. 'If the family name needed protection it could be protected by the African National Congress', Mandela's statement said. Reverend Chikane openly questioned why Brown had gone to the prison, when his visit had not resulted in a meeting with Mandela, and the Crisis Committee said in a signed statement that the Brown 'controversy added more pain to the family in the light of the burning of the house'.[21] It was an isolating moment for Winnie. Not only had someone with her personal backing been rejected by the community, but in a choice between his movement and his wife's wishes, Mandela had chosen the movement.

When Winnie moved into her house in Diepkloof-Extension she took many of Mandela United with her. The football team moved into the back rooms of this new house just as they had in the old. Nineteen-year-old Mandela United member Lerotodi Ikaneng, who had returned to his parents' house after the fire, did not move back in with Winnie, but stayed at his own home. It was soon made clear to him that he had made the wrong decision.

Winnie sent a group from the football team to fetch him to a meeting of Mandela United at her house. As soon as he arrived, Ikaneng realised he was at a special disciplinary committee meeting. Winnie, Zinzi and about twenty soccer team members were present, including Zinzi's current boyfriend, Sizwe Sithole. Winnie began the meeting by demanding to know why Ikaneng was not living with her. Ikaneng replied that he had decided to stay with his parents for a while. Zinzi then spoke up. Ikaneng was an informer, she said, accusingly. It was the only conclusion they could draw from his decision not to stay with them. Winnie agreed. Unless Ikaneng came back to live with them, they would have to believe he was a police informer, a sell-out. No action was taken against Ikaneng, however. The meeting closed and he was allowed to leave. It was obvious that he was expected to return.[22]

Ikaneng didn't want to return so he stayed where he was. A few weeks later he had another run-in with the gang. On a Saturday night he and his friend Tole were on their way to a night vigil in Soweto. They had set off together from Tole's house with Tole dressed in khaki, just as if he were a member of the SADF, it was later said. Tole had recently been released without charge from police detention. His friends still didn't know why he had been detained nor what he had been questioned about, but his detention and release had made him a target of suspicion. He was believed to have co-operated with the authorities. As Tole and Ikaneng drew close to Beki Mhlangu's shebeen they saw a group of people standing around in the yard by his gate. It looked as if there had been a fight. Tole suggested they go and see what had happened. For a while they stood and chatted to a couple of the fighters, then Ikaneng noticed the arrival of Sizwe Sithole and another member of Mandela United, Mothile.

Sithole was drunk. He lurched around with his coat swinging open, revealing the AK-47 he had strapped inside. He came up to Ikaneng's group, demanding to know where Dudu Chili's son, Dingos, was. He said Dingos had stolen a toy gun from Sithole's younger brother Javu and he wanted it back. By chance Dingos Chili arrived at the shebeen while Sithole was speaking. (Dudu Chili and Jabu Sithole were also there.) When he saw Dingos, Sithole took out his AK-47 and aimed it at him, insisting that Dingos tell him where the toy gun was. Dingos said he didn't know what Sithole was talking about. To prove he was serious Sithole fired a shot in the air. While Beki Mhlangu came running out of the shebeen to try to stop the second fight of the night, Sithole aimed at Ikaneng. Tole had suddenly disappeared and Sithole wanted to know where he'd gone. Ikaneng didn't know.

Sithole and Mothile set off to look for Tole down the alley that ran alongside the shebeen. Ikaneng, Jabu Sithole and Dudu Chili decided to follow them. As they entered the alley, they heard a shot. Ikaneng then saw Mothile grab Tole. The three started running towards Tole as he and Mothile struggled on the side of the road. But as they got close, Sithole suddenly lurched forward with his semi-automatic aimed straight at them, so they ran off in different directions. Ikaneng jumped over a fence into a neighbouring yard. He heard another shot. Running back to the street he saw Tole lying in the road. There was no sign of Sithole and Mothile – they had run away. Tole had been shot dead.

The next day the distraught trio of Ikaneng, Dudu Chili and Jabu Sithole decided to phone Winnie about what had happened. When Winnie came to the phone she pre-empted Ikaneng by asking him whether it was true that Tole was dead. It was true, Ikaneng told her. He and others were extremely upset about it and wanted to talk to her. Winnie told him to wait where he was, she would send a car.

A car duly came and the three set off for Winnie's house. On their arrival, Winnie called the football team together and a meeting began. Ikaneng demanded to know why Sithole had shot Tole? He had to, replied Winnie. Tole had given evidence to the authorities while in detention. In the circumstances they had no choice but to kill him. She added that Ikaneng now had to go into hiding. It was possible the police would try to question him about Tole's death. Another soccer team member added threateningly that if Ikaneng refused to go to the hiding-place Mandela United had arranged for him, they would believe he was interested in telling the police what he knew about how Tole had died. Ikaneng sat in silence while everyone waited for his answer. Eventually, when it was obvious that no response was forthcoming, he was told by Winnie to go away and 'think better'. Winnie then gave Ikaneng, Dudu and Jabu money for taxis and they went home.

Ikaneng did not sleep at home that night. He went back to his parents' house the following day. Sure enough the police had been looking for him, they did want to interview him as a witness to the death of Tole. At that point he made a decision. He went to the police station and gave them a statement, telling them what he knew. Then he went home. Nothing happened for a week or two. By now it was October 1988 – springtime in South Africa. On a hot day Ikaneng went with a friend to the swimming pool at Orlando West. While there he was approached by a member of the soccer team, who had a message for him from Winnie. She wanted to see him immediately in her office. The office was quite close to the pool, so Ikaneng went straight there. On his arrival he was met by Winnie and Zinzi, both of whom glared at him menacingly. In icy tones, Zinzi said she had heard what he had told the police about Sithole. Stalling, Ikaneng asked her what she meant, what had she heard? She knew what Ikaneng had said, she repeated. 'Yes, Rotodi,' said Winnie. 'This is what you wanted in the Mandela family?' And she stood up. Coming towards Ikaneng, she grabbed him by the shirt and pulled him up from his chair. She started to punch and slap him. Then she called a couple of Mandela United players and ordered them to take Ikaneng to the Diepkloof house. They took Ikaneng outside, but while they were opening the car door he slipped out of their grasp and ran.

Ikaneng ran home, where he found his grandmother and sister. Breathlessly he told them what had happened and that the football team was now after him. The three of them crept outside to see if Ikaneng had been followed. As they looked, a beige Mazda 323 pulled up. The windows were dark, but Ikaneng could tell that it was full of members of Mandela United. He specifically recognised Shoes – the player who had come to him at the swimming pool and had been told to take him to Diepkloof. Without stopping to think, Ikaneng jumped over the fence and started running through the streets to the railway station. He knew he had to leave Soweto.[23]

Ikaneng went to stay in Sharpeville for the next few months, only returning home once for money and clothes. He thought that if he laid low for a while he might eventually be safe. When he did finally return to Soweto, on 3 January 1989, he found the football team ready and waiting to kill him.

Chapter Ten

In all the different versions of the events of 29 December 1988, only one detail is consistent: that on that Thursday evening, four males went from the Orlando Methodist church house of the Reverend Paul Verryn, where they had been staying, to Winnie's house in Diepkloof-Extension.

Whether they were forced to go or went voluntarily, whether they had already been threatened with 'discipline' from the football team, whether Winnie was present on their arrival at her house, whether she participated in the assaults on them – these questions were subsequently at issue. It was unclear why these particular four had been taken, or why anyone at all should be abducted from Verryn's house. In the past one of the four, thirteen-year-old Stompie Mocketsi Seipei, had been accused of being a police informer, one reason he may have been picked up. Twenty-nine-year-old Kenneth Kgase was supposed to have been taken at the last minute, because he was 'clever' and could cause trouble by raising an alarm if left behind. But the reason for abducting Pelo Mekgwe and Thabiso Mono remained unclear.

It was hard to get at the truth when so many people involved in the case lied. Whether directly, by omission, by suppressing evidence, by implication, about trivial details, whether once, twice or continually, whether from fear, from political expediency, or by direction, the lying was pervasive, the truth distorted or destroyed. There were no heroes in this drama either. Its cast was divided between villains and victims.

The Reverend Paul Verryn ran a Methodist church house in Orlando East in Soweto. He was, in fact, the first white minister the Methodist Church had placed in a black township. The Church had chosen him not just because of his record of courage but because of his sensitivity and understanding with the young. When the Church decided that it would be appropriate, symbolically and practically, to have a white man tending to the black community, Verryn was regarded as a good choice, especially since he had a certain amount of psychological training.

A small, red-haired, bespectacled man with a moustache, Verryn was extremely popular both with the black community in which he lived and among liberal whites with whom he socialised. He was known for his insight, his humour and his loyalty. He was indefatigable in his efforts on behalf of the oppressed, even though in the course of his career he had once been held up in his house for eighteen hours at gunpoint, had had a brick put through the bonnet of his car, endured police raids, and in one week received about twenty-three death threats on the telephone.

His small three-bedroomed house, or manse, was generally overcrowded (he sometimes had as many as forty people staying). Most of those who came to stay were young males in their teens and twenties who were on the run from the police. Youths, in fact, not unlike those in Winnie's back rooms a few houses away down the same street. It was even said that Verryn, like Winnie, had the occasional Umkhonto we Sizwe cadre to stay. But he put up anyone who needed a roof, and no-one was forced to stay with him. Like Winnie, Verryn had an inflexible rule that those staying with him had to report in each night. If people were not going to be there he needed to know. Otherwise he might confuse voluntary absence with detention, and if a resident had been detained Verryn needed to get moving on it as soon as possible. He made it quite clear that anyone who did not obey this rule would not be welcome in his house, and when Maxwell Rabolou persisted in staying out without telling Verryn where he was, Verryn asked him to leave.[1]

Unlike Winnie, Verryn had no back rooms. As a result, not everyone who stayed with him could get a bed for the night, and it was common (as in most houses in most townships) for beds to be shared by two or three people. Some slept on his couches, some didn't get above the floor, but everyone got refuge and shelter. Many who came to Verryn's house spent more than one night there. For some people it became their home.[2]

It became the home of twelve-year-old James (known as 'Stompie', meaning a hard, unyielding thing) Moeketsi Seipei's home in 1988, a year after his release from detention under the State of Emergency. Stompie had a confusing reputation. In Tumahole he was known as a brilliant young activist who had led hundreds of other boys to marches and rallies, could recite chunks of the Freedom Charter off by heart, and liked nothing better than a political exchange. In Johannesburg he was regarded as more of a charming little imp who liked watching television and playing with toys, couldn't concentrate on lessons, and was always running out of school. Many in both places, though, agreed that while in police custody he had become an informer.[3]

Those who worked in Priscilla Jana's office knew Stompie well and loved him. Jana had acted as Stompie's lawyer and arranged his release from detention. After his release Stompie hadn't wanted to stay in Tumahole, fearing continuing police harassment, and had come to Johannesburg with Jana. When not at school he spent his days at her office, running errands, photocopying, or drawing pictures. The women there adored him. They bought him presents, made him sandwiches and took him to school. He was such a bright little scrap, he was lively and had a good sense of humour – it was a pleasure to have him around.[4]

Initially Stompie stayed with one of Jana's employees, Matthew Chaskalson, son of the human rights lawyer Arthur Chaskalson. But when Matthew left Johannesburg, Stompie had to go elsewhere. He ended up at Verryn's house, where he was thought to be less of a delight.[5] He was obstreperous, bossy, boastful and argumentative and frequently got into fights. He found it difficult to do what he was told. He created tension. He also never washed.

At roughly the same time that Stompie moved in, Verryn's manse became the home of a 35-year-old East Rand woman and her two children. Whether Xoliswa Falati just turned up at the house uninvited and was there when Verryn got home one evening, or whether he asked her to live with him when he learned that her own home had been fire-bombed was later disputed. As was the role Falati played within the house. She claimed she was a mother figure – called 'Mama' by the boys – who as house-mother bought food, took clothes to the dry cleaners, gave money for transport, cooked and cleaned.

'Now that we don't have homes, let's make this house a home. We should have discipline, help each other, have respect, have that togetherness as comrades,' was how she described herself, addressing the men and boys who were her fellow residents.[6]

Others described Falati as a bossy, interfering troublemaker who threatened those who didn't help with the housekeeping with discipline from Mandela United. They said that rather than protecting Stompie from other boys who were ill-treating and isolating him, she was his main antagonist.[7] It was hard to understand why, if she had felt sorry enough for Stompie to bring her son Mlaxndo to the house as a playmate for him, as she claimed, she and her daughter, Nompumelelo, beat him up after the two boys got into a fight.

Another unresolved question concerned the Reverend Paul Verryn's sexuality. Rumours about Verryn had been circulating Soweto for months and had already been brought to the attention of

Verryn's supervisor in the Methodist Church, Bishop Peter Storey – and to Winnie. Verryn himself told Storey of the rumours – and so did Winnie. She expressed her concern that Verryn might be abusing a position of trust by trying to have sex with the youths who stayed in his house.[8]

Verryn's house was less than five minutes' walk from the house Winnie lived in until it was burnt down. It was in one of the nicer parts of Soweto. The houses were painted and had colourful little gardens – down at the bottom of the same dusty, sloping street was Archbishop Tutu's bungalow. As her neighbour, Verryn was impossible for Winnie to ignore: it may have been that he – like Dudu Chili – seemed like a galling rival with his own houseful of youths. As a white Methodist priest he may have appeared to represent the influence of the establishment on young blacks. His manse might have been thought of as an opposing power base rather than a place of refuge. But for a long time the relationship between the two houses was easygoing. Winnie even referred a number of youths looking for a place to stay to Verryn. And some who stayed with him eventually moved in with her.

Maxwell Rabolou went to her when Verryn asked him to leave in 1987. She later said that when he came to see her he complained that Verryn had made advances to him. She raised the matter with the Reverend Frank Chikane, who was skeptical about her allegations, but promised to look into them. Rabolou told her he was too scared to return to the manse, and stayed in her back rooms for a couple of months. But by the beginning of the following year he had returned to Verryn's house.

In mid-September 1988, the youth was back at Winnie's. His relationship with Verryn had remained uneasy, and again he had been asked to leave. It had happened again, Rabolou told her. Verryn had made more sexual advances towards him. Again he wanted to stay. This time he said he was never going back to the church house. Winnie contacted Chikane again. He had received other similar reports about Verryn and said he was going to hand the whole matter over to Bishop Storey.[9]

Verryn and Storey met to discuss the rumours in October 1988. Storey was sympathetic. He realised that as a single man and a minister, Verryn was vulnerable to this kind of personal attack – and that rumours of this kind could be started by anyone with an axe to grind. He talked to Verryn about steps he could take to protect himself. The rumours had stemmed from Verryn's allowing, even encouraging, youths staying at his house to sleep in his bedroom and his bed (Verryn usually shared his bed with two other males, and more than one person had claimed to have been intimately touched by Verryn during the night). Storey said it would be a good idea to make his whole bedroom completely out of bounds. He felt Verryn needed an area of privacy within the house anyway. He also advised Verryn to involve local congregational leaders in helping him with the young people and approved of the idea of having Falati and her children in the manse. But Verryn disregarded his advice and continued to share his bed with those who came to stay.[10]

Things came to a head over Christmas 1988. Paul Verryn had been away in Pretoria on vacation. He was about to leave on another trip to Potchestroom, but needed to stop in briefly at the manse on his way through Johannesburg. He had received a message that his residents had been threatened with a visit from Mandela United. He wasn't unduly concerned. Fights at the overcrowded manse were fairly common. He usually settled them at house meetings and thought he could do the same with this one. First he heard heated complaints from Falati that some of those staying weren't pulling their weight in keeping the house clean, that they were refusing to wash their dishes. Then he heard from Thabiso Mono and Pelo Mekgwe that Falati had threatened them with a disciplinary visit from Mandela United because they hadn't helped with the washing up. Verryn spent several hours at the manse, attempting to defuse the situation, and finally left in the early afternoon of Wednesday 28 December believing he had been successful.

Two opposing narratives told the story of what happened the next day. The first version, offered by Kgase, Mono and Mekgwe, was largely corroborated by police statements given by John Morgan and Katiza Chebekhulu – a somewhat unstable fifth resident at the manse. Kgase, Mono, Mekgwe and Stompie were taken against their will by Jerry Richardson and members of Mandela United to the back rooms of the Mandela house, where they were accused of having had sex with Verryn, Stompie was accused of being a police informer, and all four were assaulted. The assaults as described by Kgase, Mono and Mekgwe were prolonged and vicious and were begun by Winnie.

She began by telling them, 'You are not fit to be alive,' then punched Kgase on the face before turning and punching Stompie. After Stompie she punched Mono and Mekgwe. She also questioned them, asking them why they slept with Verryn. She accused Stompie of being a police informer, and punched him when he denied it. Other members of the football team soon joined in, causing pandemonium. Each of the four was attacked by at least two other youths, beaten, punched, kicked, and slapped. They were beaten on the knees with shoes and bottles, and as they lay on the floor their bodies were trampled upon. Kgase described Winnie humming a tune as she whipped him. Some of the soccer team went and fetched plastic supermarket shopping bags and wanted to put one over Stompie's head, but Jerry Richardson stopped them.

After that, Stompie was thrown up into the air and dropped to the floor three times, then the same was done to each of the others. While they were being thrown up and dropped, the soccer players shouted out 'Break Down!' At some stage during the assaults, Winnie left the room. Richardson was then in charge. When the attack was finally over, he ordered the four to go out and wash in an area where there were three basins and a big tin bath. All four were bleeding, their clothes were ripped and blood-stained, and Richardson wanted them to clean up. For Kgase, Mono and Mekgwe the assaults had ended, but not for Stompie. He was put into the bath, and while water was poured over his head, he was punched and hit by Richardson and a soccer team member called Slash. He then 'confessed'. He had sold out, he said. He had told the police about four comrades in Parys. He was an informer.

Following Stompie's confession, Richardson gave out blankets to make up beds on the floor and told the four youths to lie down and go to sleep. He warned them not to try to escape. Any thoughts they might have had of doing so evaporated when Richardson and Slash spent the night in the same room. Kgase, Mono, Mekgwe and Stompie lay on the floor, frightened and in pain. Stompie seemed especially bad, silent except for the occasional groan. They spent the next morning in the same room, guarded by Richardson who told them the rules of the house: they were not to call Winnie anything other than 'Mummy', they were not to try to escape, they were to behave well and as a reward for good behaviour they might be sent into exile where they could work as comrades. Richardson said that Stompie had done something very bad and the other three should take note. Because of what Stompie had done, it was likely that he would have to be 'dumped'. After Richardson's talk, the four captives were made to clean the room in which they had slept as well as the areas outside, with specific directions to get rid of their own bloodstains. There was blood on the walls inside the room, blood on the paving stones outside and blood on the Jacuzzi. Stompie was made to wash all bloodstained clothing. That evening he was beaten up again. By now his face was swollen, his eyes were swollen, he had a lump on his head and he couldn't see properly.

Outside the room another effect of the previous evening was being felt. Katiza Chebekhulu, who had accompanied the football team to collect the four youths and joined in the assaults on them, had become hysterical. So hysterical, in fact, that Winnie had to take him to the doctor. According to the record book and medical card completed in Dr Asvat's surgery, Katiza was brought to see him on 30 December, the day after the kidnapping and assault, and was treated for his nerves with a mild tranquilliser. The date in the record book was written by Albertina Sisulu, Asvat's nurse. The date on the card was stamped with a date stamp.

By Sunday 1 January, Stompie was vomiting when given food. All four boys remained captive in the same room, with Richardson their constant companion. Members of the football team came in and out, but none of the four had seen Winnie since the first evening. According to Katiza Chebekhulu, Dr Asvat was summoned to examine Stompie and found that he was permanently brain-damaged, whereupon a decision taken to kill him was taken.

Stompie was taken away sometime after sunset. Richardson came into the room wearing overalls and told Stompie he was going to take him home. He handed him a piece of paper and told him to write down his address. A little later, another member of the soccer team, Jabu, came in with another piece of paper and Stompie had to write his address down again. Finally Richardson returned alone, told Stompie to collect his belongings and go. The two left the room together. In his police statement, Chebekhulu said that Winnie herself helped tie and gag Stompie, after which he was put in the boot of a red car and driven away by Richardson and another football team member. It was the last time Stompie was seen alive.

At the beginning of January 1989, Lerotodi Ikaneng finally decided it was safe to return to Soweto. On 3 January he, a friend and a couple of girls went out for the evening. Ikaneng and his girlfriend were on their way home when a gang of youths stepped into their way. He immediately recognised Jerry Richardson and Slash from Mandela United, but there were others with the football team who were unfamiliar to him. They were Kenneth Kgase, Thabiso Mono and Pelo Mekgwe.

Earlier that day, Richardson, Slash, Isaac and Killer had come into the room where Kgase, Mono and Mekgwe were being held and given them running shoes. Richardson told them they were going to do 'a duty' and would be leaving as soon as he had got some money from Zinzi Mandela. The group of seven then went into Diepkloof where they caught a taxi to a garage in Orlando West. Kgase, Mono and Mekgwe still didn't know what they were supposed to be doing, and were too frightened to attempt to escape. Slash, who seemed to be looking for someone, went into a shop next to the garage, but whoever it was wasn't there. So the group left the garage and continued the search.

Once they had found Ikaneng, Richardson told him he needed to talk to him. Accompanied by the rest of the group, Richardson took Ikaneng into a neighbouring shebeen where Ikaneng was told to sit down. Richardson had a quick conversation with some of the football team players before returning to Ikaneng. 'Let's go,' he said and grabbed Ikaneng by the arm, pushing him outside.

Ikaneng began to protest. 'What did I do? Why are you grabbing hold of me?' he asked. There was no answer, so he tried again. If allowed to walk on his own, he wouldn't try to run away, he told them. But the moment his arm was released he ran through an open gate, jumped over a fence into the neighbouring street and sped away. It was a futile attempt. It was only a matter of minutes before he was recaptured and frog-marched through the park at Mzimhlope, across the main Sowetan freeway and into an open veld. Once in the veld, he was tripped to the ground and held down. He did not hear Richardson tell Slash that this was the ideal place to kill him. Someone produced a pair of garden shears, and Richardson told Isaac to open them up and separate the blades. Kgase, Mono and Mekgwe were each helping hold Ikaneng, as instructed by Richardson.

Richardson sat on Ikaneng's chest while Isaac struggled to separate the shears. After a while, Slash got impatient, grabbed the shears from Isaac, wrenched off one of the blades and handed it to Richardson, who sliced across Ikaneng's neck. He then took the second blade and stabbed him again. The group were instructed to pick up what they believed to be the lifeless body of Ikaneng and throw it into some neighbouring reeds. Then they returned to the Mandela house.

Although badly wounded, Ikaneng was not dead and was in fact able to get up and go for help. He had a gaping wound on his throat – his neck had been slit from ear to ear. He managed to stagger back across the freeway where he banged on the door of a house, then collapsed on the grass. He was taken by ambulance to Baragwanath Hospital, where he remained until 16 March.[11]

Having satisfactorily completed their duty, Kgase, Mono and Mekgwe had been accepted by the members of the football team. The other youths started to talk to them, calling them 'Comrade' and telling them the past had been forgotten. Richardson warned them again not to try to run away. If one of them should manage to escape, he said, the consequences for the remaining two would be dire. But he and the others trusted them. They demonstrated their trust by assigning the three to help guard the house. It was a system known as 'posting', where two youths at a time would circle the house for two-hour stretches, guarding it from intruders and watching for other surveillance. The three detainees were not yet sufficiently trusted to be allowed to guard the house together. They were separated and put on duty at different times. While guarding, or sitting around in the area outside the back rooms, they would occasionally see Winnie coming and going, but they didn't speak to her.

As new members of Mandela United, Kgase, Mono and Mekgwe got to accompany Winnie to a local funeral. The day after the attack on Ikaneng they were given Mandela United tracksuits and driven to the funeral of a local friend of Winnie's, Sipho Mabuse, who had died on the day of their abduction. Driven by John Morgan, they went with Richardson and other members of the soccer team to the Mabuse home, where they mingled with the mourners. Winnie went separately. During the church service, the soccer players formed a guard of honour, standing around the coffin with raised, clenched fists. They accompanied the coffin to the grave and, once it had been lowered into the ground, helped heap earth on top of it. They all then joined in the singing, dancing and toyi toying before leaving and returning to the Mandela house. Three days later, Kgase escaped.

The opportunity for Kgase to get away came during his night shift on sentry duty. He was guarding the house with Isaac. Richardson had instructed them not to spend the entire time together, but to split up so that one could cover the house and the other the street outside. Kgase was assigned to patrol the house. Once he got round to the back, he realised that he was completely out of Isaac's sight. Everyone else was asleep, so now was his opportunity to get away. He took off his shoes, jumped over the fence and fled.[12]

David Ching was not just the pastor at the Central Methodist Church in Johannesburg, he was also its caretaker and lived on the premises. At about 6.30 on the morning of 7 January 1989, he was awakened by a knock on his door. It was Kgase. On leaving the Mandela home, Kgase had made his way to the taxi stand at

Baragwaneth Hospital where he took a taxi into Johannesburg. On his arrival at the Central Methodist Church in Pritchard Street Kgase was incoherent with fear. He asked Ching to lock the door behind him, then tried to explain what had happened. But he was so upset and his speech was so rapid and so disjointed that it was hard for Ching to understand him. Ching did notice his face was swollen and one of his eyes was very bloodshot. Kgase showed him his knees, which were swollen, and his back, which was marked. Ching phoned Verryn.[13]

Paul Verryn rushed to Pritchard Street the moment he heard that Kgase was there. On his arrival, the first thing he understood Kgase to say was that he had learnt to kill. Kgase was referring to the incident involving Ikaneng, whom he presumed was now dead, but Verryn didn't know what he was talking about. His main concern was to take Kgase straight to a doctor for a medical examination and then to a lawyer. Kgase told him that although Mono and Mekgwe were still at Winnie's house, he did not know where Stompie was and presumed he was dead.[14]

Verryn took Kgase to be examined by Martin Connell, a close friend of his with a private medical practice in the attractive suburb of Melville in Johannesburg. Connell examined Kgase at his house and made a note of his findings. Kgase's back was covered with scars. The skin was broken in five places; he was heavily bruised —one bruise on his back was 15 cms large. He had bruises on his left shoulder and hip, his chest, his right arm and his face. His face, in fact was so swollen that it was asymmetrical.[15] Connell did not notice Kgase's swollen knees. Kgase's emotional state reminded the doctor of soldiers who had been subjected to mortar fire. He was very frightened, especially about what might happen to Mono and Mekgwe.

After Kgase had been examined by Connell, Verryn arranged for him to see his friend Geoff Budlender, a lawyer at the Legal Resources Centre, to make a statement about what had happened to him. Budlender did not agree to act for Kgase without giving his decision some thought. The case sounded really offbeat to him – this was not something he had ever done before. On the other hand, he realised that this was such an unusual case, it was unlikely he could have done anything like it. Finally he agreed to become involved because he felt that the premise of the Legal Resources Centre was to protect people from an abuse of power. True, most of their cases involved an abuse of State power, but if there were private individuals who also abused power, then it was the job of the Centre to offer legal protection. Human rights had been seriously abused, if Kgase's story was true, and his case was right for the Centre on those grounds too.[16]

The Methodist Church now started to take official steps to find out where Stompie was and to try to release Mono and Mekgwe. Their steps did not involve contacting the police. Bishop Storey – who was coordinating church and community attempts to free the missing youths – was sympathetic to the fact that the police were not regarded as friends by the people of Soweto. And for all he knew, the police might take advantage of the situation to try to pursue some agenda of their own. He was anxious that his church should not be manipulated by the police – or by any State agency. He was worried that any kind of heavy-handed approaches to those in the Mandela household might jeopardise the safety of those being kept there. And he was well aware that this situation – involving the wife of Nelson Mandela – could have implications way beyond the immediate condition of the missing three youths. That final reason alone was compelling enough to merit a delicate approach to Winnie.

The first attempt to obtain the release of the youths had come even before Kgase escaped. For news of the abduction had spread fast: others staying at Verryn's house were terrified for their own lives as well as for the lives of those who had been taken, and they had quickly raised the alarm. A member of the Crisis Committee, Aubrey Mokoena, had gone to question Winnie on 4 January. Winnie saw Mokoena but denied that the young people were at her home. Two days later – just hours before Kgase escaped – Dr Nthatho Motlana went to see Winnie. This time she admitted the youths were there but refused to give him access when he asked to examine them.

At some stage during the first two weeks of January, the police began receiving a string of anonymous phone calls. The first one, from an unidentified black male, simply said that Stompie had not disappeared but had been killed. A later call described a place where his body might be found. But when the police went to search the area they found nothing. His body had already been picked up and was lying, unidentified, in the local morgue. A local woman had stumbled across his remains in the exact place described in the phone call, on 6 January, and had reported it. Senior members of the police force believed that if the Methodist Church had not been involved in this case, Stompie's body would have remained permanently unidentified. Apart from following up the information received in this phone call, the police would take no further action in this case for a month.[17]

By 11 January, thirteen days after the kidnapping, Bishop Storey and the Reverend Frank Chikane had met, discussed what they felt to be a hostage crisis in Mrs Mandela's house, and agreed that the church and community would co-operate closely in attempts to discover the whereabouts of Stompie and obtain the release of Mono and Mekgwe. The relationship between the Methodist Church and the Crisis Committee was in fact to be so close that the two ministers decided that no person or group should act alone. From then on, any visit to the Mandela household, or to Nelson Mandela in prison, resulted in a full briefing to those who had not been present. The situation was regarded with the utmost seriousness, with fears for the lives of Stompie, Mono and Mekgwe at the top of the list of concerns.

On 11 January, Chikane, Mokoena, Sister Bernard Ncube and Sidney Mafumadi went to the Mandela house. This time Winnie claimed that she was protecting the youths, that they had not been abducted, that they were staying at her house at their own request. The group asked to see the youngsters and Winnie agreed to allow them access. But then she changed her mind. She told them to return the next day and once again members of the Crisis Committee left the Mandela house without seeing the captives.

It was at this point that the possibility of Paul Verryn's life being in danger became of real concern to the Crisis Committee and the church. The homosexual allegations against Verryn seemed to develop in response to pressure from the community to release the youths: the greater the pressure, the more sensational the allegations. As in the past, Winnie's defence was to accuse her accuser of abuse: it had been Verryn from whom young people needed rescuing.

The following day Chikane left on a trip to London. While overseas he was to contact Oliver Tambo and brief him on what was happening, and also arrange for Nelson Mandela to be briefed on the situation. Meanwhile his colleagues returned to Diepkloof-Extension. On their arrival they were met by Zinzi, who told them that one of the youths had 'escaped' – a word which they felt had crucial implications. And then, finally, they were allowed to see the youths. Mono, Mekgwe and Katiza Chebekhulu were led into the room and allowed to be questioned and examined. But before being brought in they had been instructed by Richardson as to what say. They were not to speak about the assaults, he told them. Instead they were to state they had left the church manse because Paul Verryn had tried to have sex with them.

Mono and Mekgwe's injuries were immediately apparent to the

Crisis Committee when the youths came into the room. Chebekhulu, on the other hand, did not seem to be hurt. Chebekhulu's role in this drama was ambiguous. He had been a resident at the manse who had gone with the others to Winnie's house, but of his own volition, and had taken part in the subsequent assaults. He said Verryn had tried to have sex with him, and seemed genuinely upset by the experience. But his allegations were confused and rambling. He was an intelligent teenager, who at times seemed emotionally disturbed. His mental ability to stand trial would later be questioned.

Mono, Mekgwe and Chebekhulu each said they were staying with Winnie of their own free will and that they had sought refuge with her from Paul Verryn's continuous, unwarranted sexual advances. But one of the three broke down when he was alone with the committee, and confessed that they were being held captive and had been told what to say about Verryn. 'I am going to die anyway,' he said. 'So I may as well tell the truth.' The committee left the house without disclosing that they had been given this admission.

In the absence of calling for police help, the Methodist Church considered its legal options. Fink Haysom, a partner in the human rights law firm Cheadle, Thompson and Haysom advised the church on possible courses of action. There were two alternatives, neither of which would be easy. The first was to obtain a writ of habeas corpus compelling a release, but in order to take such a step church members had to find, and obtain authority from, the parents of the captives – a potentially difficult and time-wasting process. However, Ismail Ayob told Winnie that the Methodist Church was considering bringing such an application against her in the hopes that the knowledge of potential legal action might induce her to let the boys go. It did not. The second option was to get an interdict against Winnie, preventing any further act of violence being perpetrated on the youths in her house. The problem here was that in order to get such an interdict, the members of the Crisis Committee who had seen the injured youths would have to give evidence as to what they had seen, and none of them was prepared to testify against Winnie.

The reluctance of the Crisis Committee members to give evidence went to the heart of the dilemma which the abduction of the four youths – five if Katiza Chebekhulu was to be considered taken against his will – created in the community. Here was a heroine, a larger than life, almost mythical figure, who for whatever reason had been given enormous stature by a community which was now forced to challenge her. It wasn't just that challenging Winnie in her own right was a task that individual members of the Crisis Committee felt unequal to. They also had to consider potential damage to the anti-apartheid movement as a whole. It would not look good to the rest of the world if one of the most influential South African activists against oppression was known to be keeping young men hostage in her house. Especially when some of them bore marks of a recent assault, and one of them had completely disappeared.

For the time being legal action was abandoned. Convinced that Winnie was building a case against Paul Verryn, the Crisis Committee felt that the youths in her house were relatively safe – they were needed to give evidence. Bishop Storey felt it was extremely important that the black community, not the Methodist Church, should take the lead in handling negotiations for the release. Both he and the Crisis Committee were aware that very few people knew of the situation in the Mandela house and that unless a much wider cross section of community leaders was informed about what was happening, any action that the church might take to obtain the release of the youths could be open to misunderstanding and could damage the church's standing not only in the community, but throughout the country.

At the same time, the general consensus was that any hasty or precipitate action might result in another 'disappearance'. So the Crisis Committee decided to call a community meeting. While it was being organised, Fink Haysom told Ayob to notify Winnie that the church was monitoring the safety of the young people, and any harm done to them would result in immediate repercussions. Later Haysom travelled to Lusaka to brief Tambo on what had happened. He gave Tambo the details of the Methodist Church abduction and assault and also described the battery acid case. As he listened to the details, Tambo threw up his hands and covered his face. 'What must I do?' he exclaimed. 'We can't control her. The ANC can't control her. We tried to control her, that's why we formed the Crisis Committee. You must tell the Crisis Committee that they must do more.'[18]

Ismail Ayob continued to frequent the Mandela house, relaying messages, checking on the safety of Mono and Mekgwe, and pleading for their release. On Friday 13 January he told Winnie that he was going to visit Mandela in prison and would brief him on what she was doing. Winnie repeated the allegations against Verryn. Ayob, who would later state that he never once throughout this whole period heard the allegations directly from the complainants, said if the allegations were true, why didn't she let him take the children to the Bishop so they could tell him. Winnie agreed. Then she called in

Xoliswa Falati and instructed Falati to accompany them to Storey. Then she changed her mind again. The children were not to leave, she said. But Storey could come to her house at 11.30 the following morning.

Storey got the message at 10.00 on Saturday morning. Ayob was already *en route* to Mandela in Cape Town and Storey could not contact any member of the Crisis Committee to tell them of this latest development. Eventually he decided that a visit to the Mandela house, where Mono and Mekgwe would not be free to tell him the truth, would be self-defeating. He was also unwilling to make such a visit without the knowledge of at least one community leader. He tried to contact Winnie throughout that Saturday to tell her he would not be coming, but was unable to reach her. Late on Saturday night Ayob returned from Cape Town. He had received instructions from Mandela that a release should be effected that night. He conveyed a message to the Methodist Church asking that accommodation be prepared. Much later that night he called again. Winnie had refused to let the youths go.

On Sunday, Dr Motlana went to the Mandela house and spoke very strongly to Winnie, urging a release. Ayob also went back on a separate visit. Neither had success. Also on Sunday, Storey got his strongest message yet that Paul Verryn's life was definitely in danger. His source of information was someone he trusted sufficiently to take action. So he finally did what he had been reluctant to do all along. He instructed Verryn to leave Soweto. Both men were fully aware of the signals that Verryn's leaving Soweto would send out, in the light of the allegations against him, but if his life really was in danger, there was no choice. Verryn officially went on leave.

Later in the day, Fink Haysom called Bishop Storey. Ayob had just called him: they were 'coming out'. And they did come out that evening. Accompanied by Richardson and Xoliswa Falati, Mono, Mekgwe and Chebekhulu went to Ayob's office. But Richardson and Falati said they had conditions for the release and refused to leave the youths behind. Ayob told them that as far as he knew the release was to be unconditional, so Richardson and Falati took the boys away again.

On Monday 16 January the boys were finally released. But between Sunday night and Monday morning a change in lawyers had occurred. Where on the Sunday, Ayob had represented Winnie and the youths had been taken to him, by Monday morning, Krish Naidoo – a local lawyer with ties to the ANC – had replaced him on the case. Rumour had it that Ayob had taken just about as much as he could of the situation, and although he was prepared to continue representing Nelson Mandela, he would no longer act for his wife. And Naidoo was quick to step into the breach. Although Winnie would later deny that Naidoo had ever been a 'family lawyer', claiming she had no need of his services, it was the understanding of community leaders on that Monday that Naidoo was representing the Mandela family, in particular Mrs Mandela.[19]

Considering the massive amount of effort that had gone into effecting the release of the youths, their initial reception was surprisingly casual. Some time on Monday morning Richardson took the three to Dr Motlana's house in Soweto. On their arrival, they were met by Motlana, who was just leaving for work. He asked the group to return at 1.00 p.m. When they went back to him at lunchtime he drove them to Verryn's manse, but the church and the house were locked up. Motlana then drove the group to Krish Naidoo's office in town. Naidoo wasn't there, but Motlana dropped the four off – Richardson was still present – and drove away. Richardson and his three charges waited for Naidoo, who, as soon as he got to his office and saw the group waiting for him, called Storey. Storey immediately contacted two other community leaders and asked them to meet him at Naidoo's office to monitor the hand-over, and then went straight to Naidoo's office.

He was surprised to find four young people waiting for him there, not recognising Richardson, who gave a false name. Richardson was aggressively unco-operative and impatient. Storey was told that those present had come to lay allegations about Paul Verryn. He agreed to listen to what they had to say, but said that he had some questions of his own which needed answering.[20]

Coincidentally, that Monday night was the same night on which the community meeting to discuss the kidnappings and assaults was due to be held. Storey wanted to take Mono, Mekgwe and Chebekhulu with him to the meeting in Dobsonville. Mono and Mekgwe were keen to go to Verryn's house and collect some clean clothes, but Chebekhulu said he didn't want to go into Soweto at all, he was too frightened. When Storey told the three about the meeting, Chebekhulu said he wouldn't go. Eventually Storey, Mono, Mekgwe and Richardson left Naidoo's office. Richardson went off on his own and Chebekhulu stayed with Naidoo, on the understanding that they would try to come along to the meeting later.

The evening meeting was cloaked in extraordinary secrecy. Those attending were sent from one location to another, before finally arriving at the community hall in Dobsonville. At each destination someone would be waiting to give instructions where to go next. The clandestine journey gave the meeting a sense of drama before it even began. The list of partcipants gave it a sense of importance. There were roughly one hundred and fifty people present. As well as Storey, Mono, Mekgwe and Kgase, Paul Verryn was there. Representatives from Fedtraw, Soyco and COSATU, and members of the Catholic and Anglican Churches had come. The whole Crisis Committee was there. Civic organisations from Soweto sent representatives, and representatives from Stompie's home town of Tumahole had driven in to attend. Every community organisation was represented.

The meeting began at about 6.30 with a prayer. Then a written statement, prepared by a number of those from Verryn's house who had witnessed the abduction, was read out by their representative. The statement described how the youths had been taken against their will. The spokesman who read it out – Sello – described how he himself had been assaulted by members of the football team while they were in Verryn's house on 29 December. There had been a debate as to whether he too should be taken along, Sello told the meeting, but he was allowed to stay behind when it was decided he was 'politically reliable'. Then Mono and Mekgwe told the meeting how they were abducted, taken to Winnie's house, beaten first by her and then by the football team.

At this point Krish Naidoo arrived, accompanied by Katiza Chebekhulu. But they were not alone. They had brought a member of Mandela United with them. The discovery that a soccer team player was actually present at this secret meeting had an immediate impact. People were terrified that the rest of Mandela United were on their way to wreak havoc. Chebekhulu and the footballer were made to wait outside, while Naidoo was confronted by an angry, frightened community. Why had he brought along a member of the soccer team? Naidoo had gone to Winnie's house to try and persuade her to come along to the meeting herself. (She would later deny receiving any invitation from anybody to attend.) She had refused to go with him, Naidoo said, but the footballer had tagged along instead.[21]

The meeting was now extremely heated. Many who were there had never heard details of Mandela United's practices before and they were horrified. Others had had experiences with the football team; their anger lay in frustration that the situation had been allowed to get so desperate. One woman refused to use the name Mandela in connection with Winnie and kept referring to her by her maiden name. Others said the soccer club was unfit to carry the name of the leader of the African National Congress and was no longer to be called Mandela United. A decision was taken that the community and the progressive movement should formally distance themselves from Winnie and her football team. There had been a plan to march on her house, but it was rejected.

When Katiza Chebekhulu addressed the meeting, it finally became clear that Stompie had been killed. At one point during his story Chebekhulu was asked outright if Stompie was dead, to which he replied, 'Yes.' Chebekhulu admitted participating in the beating of Mono, Mekgwe and Kgase, but when asked why became confused. 'They were just being beaten,' he said. 'And I felt like beating up.' He was asked for an exact description of Stompie's injuries. Stompie was soft on one side of his head, Chebekhulu said. He had been beaten so that he couldn't see out of his eyes. And he had been picked up and dropped up on the floor. Although he stated that Stompie was dead, he said he didn't know how Stompie had left the house. 'When I came back to the house, Stompie was missing.' Later Chebekhulu would tell his lawyer, Kathy Satchwell, that he had watched as Stompie's limp body was loaded into the boot of a car. In one of his versions, he would describe how Stompie's throat had already been cut.[22]

After the horrific and gruesome tale of what had been done to Stompie, the meeting turned its attention to Paul Verryn. What exactly had he done – if anything – that might have caused these allegations against him? Chebekhulu said that Verryn had approached him sexually. The Crisis Committee announced Mono had also made such an allegation when the Committee was at the Mandela house. Mono was asked if he stood by what he had said. 'I withdraw it unconditionally,' said Mono. 'I was forced to say it.'

Storey then addressed the meeting. He said that if anyone had any fresh evidence against Verryn he would like to hear it. This kind of allegation was very, very serious, he said. The Methodist Church was not prepared to have one of its ministers behaving in such a way. He specifically invited the residents of the manse who were present – about twelve in all – to mention anything that might be relevant to the charges, or evidence of any conduct by Verryn which they considered unbecoming to a Christian minister. There was nothing. Finally one youngster stood up. He had lived in the house since 1987, he said, and because of crowding, they had often slept in close proximity, but there had never been any complaints of misconduct. The rest of the group were then asked if they agreed with that statement and they did.

Storey then asked the meeting at large if anyone knew of anything negative about the conduct of Paul Verryn. But the only response he got was anger that Verryn had been put in such a position. Storey said that in measuring one statement accusing Verryn made by a person who had participated in an assault on three people present – who, therefore, might not be the most reliable of witnesses – against a lot of evidence to the contrary, he was satisfied that his own assessment of Verryn had been affirmed. No-one contradicted him.

It was now late, but there was one more case to deal with – the attempted murder of Lerotodi Ikaneng. When Ikaneng came in, with the gaping wound across his throat still fresh, there was an understandable shudder of alarm throughout the hall. Not least did Ikaneng's presence affect Mono and Mekgwe, who immediately recognised him as the man they had been forced to try to kill. Fear of repercussions for what they had done to Ikaneng would cause Mono, Mekgwe and Kgase to be initially reluctant to tell their story to the police. They were terrified that they would be charged with attempted murder. They had to weigh that fear against their fear for their own lives.

(One month later, Major-General Jaap Joubert, who co-ordinated serious investigations at the Soweto Murder and Robbery unit and liaised with the security branch, made sure they knew they would not be arrested in connection with the Ikaneng case. He also allowed Geoff Budlender and Peter Storey to be present when they made their statements to the police. It was in his interest for the youths to have their own representatives present. The police – like every other association involved in the case – did not want to be accused of putting words into anyone's mouth when they were talking about anything to do with Winnie.)

But now Ikaneng was talking, telling the meeting about his attack earlier that month. When he finished, the decision to arrange an urgent meeting between Mrs Mandela and a delegation from the community for the following day – or later that same day: it was now after midnight – was unanimously agreed and the meeting finally broke up.

Chapter Eleven

About halfway through January 1989 – at the same time as Mono and Mekgwe were being released, Dr Abu-Baker Asvat's wife, Zhora, began to realise that something was bothering her husband. Something was eating away at him, worrying him so much that she became anxious. He didn't seem to want to tell her what was troubling him and she didn't push him, knowing he would confide in her if and when he wanted to. Asvat didn't confide in his wife, instead he did something highly unusual that he had never done before. He told her he had some money for her and handed over a wad of cash. It was in case something happened to him, he said, and told Zhora to keep it. She said she didn't need it. Just hold on to it anyway, he said, in case you do.

On Thursday 26 January 1989, ten days after the community meeting in Dobsonville, Asvat was visited by a new patient. Jerry Richardson complained of an abscess and said he had been referred by Winnie Mandela. Asvat made a note in red on Richardson's patient card: 'Sent by Winnie.' He then examined Richardson, didn't find much wrong with him, but told him to return the next morning for a penicillin injection, which Richardson did. It was never established whether the two men discussed anything beyond Richardson's medical condition in either of these visits.

On the evening of that same Thursday, Asvat went to a local cricket meeting. He was used to driving around his Indian township of Lenasia at night. Indeed he was also used to driving in Soweto where he practised. Others might be afraid of street life in Soweto, but not him, he would tell Zhora. He could walk where he wanted day or night, without getting hurt. Everyone knew and respected him. But that night, while driving home from the cricket meeting in the dark, Asvat had a puncture and had to pull off the road. By the time he finally got home he was terrified. He told Zhora about the puncture and how he had been too frightened to want to stop. He thought it was a set-up and that 'they' had come to get him. But he still didn't say who or what it was that was frightening him so much.[1]

The following morning, Asvat got a call from Priscilla Jana. She had a regular prescription with him and needed a refill. Unusually, Asvat said he would bring the medicine over himself – there was something he needed to talk to her about. He sounded extremely distraught.

When he got to her office, Jana, who was late for a flight to Durban, told Asvat she didn't have time to speak to him, though she could see he was bothered by something. She said he should come to see her the following week when she returned. Appearing to be in considerable distress, Asvat stood and silently hugged her daughter. Then he left.[2]

He drove from Jana's office in town to the office of another lawyer, his good friend Yunus Mayet, in the Indian section of Lenasia. Mayet took care of all Asvat's legal affairs. He had been badgering him to make a will for some time. The two men already had an appointment for the coming Monday, when Asvat was finally scheduled to put his affairs in order. There was nothing sinister about the appointment, it was a long-standing arrangement.

Even though there was already a meeting set for Monday, none of the staff was particularly surprised when Asvat suddenly arrived on that Friday: he often dropped into Mayet's office unannounced. What was striking, however, was his manner. Usually he would stand and joke with the women who worked on the desk while waiting to see Mayet, but not this time. He paced up and down in silence, seeming tense and withdrawn. Mayet was already in a meeting when Asvat arrived, but didn't think he would be tied up for long. When told Asvat was there he stuck his head out of the office and told his friend to wait – he would only be a few minutes. Even then he noticed Asvat's distress.

Mayet's meeting took much longer than he had anticipated, and Asvat ended up waiting for more than an hour, until he finally left Mayet's office without telling him the cause of his anxiety. By the time he returned home he was two hours late for the family's weekly Hindu prayers and was so distracted he couldn't follow the set ritual. He then left for his surgery.[3]

At lunchtime on Friday 27 January, Asvat's brother Ebrahim, also a doctor, was sitting in his surgery reading the new edition of the *Weekly Mail*. The front-page story that had grabbed his attention was headlined 'Soweto anger at Winnie "team"'. It described a community meeting in Dobsonville the previous week. The 'anger' had been expressed over the abduction of four unnamed youths from a local church, one of whom was still missing and – the paper claimed – had last been seen in the hands of the football team. The 'Stompie story' had finally broken.

The *Weekly Mail*'s decision to run the piece had not been an easy one. When the story did finally break (simultaneously in the *Weekly Mail* and in the *Guardian*) *Weekly Mail* editors were so wary of its ramifications that they put it on the front page but chose not to make it the lead. Rumours about Winnie and her football team had been coming into the newsroom for several months, but the paper had been reluctant to publish them. At first it had been perfectly conceivable that they were part of a State-concocted campaign aimed at discrediting Winnie. Stories about anti-apartheid leaders had been fabricated and circulated by agents of the system for years, and the paper wanted to be sure that these were not more of the same. There was another, more pragmatic reason for caution. The *Weekly Mail* (which had been formed by former staff of the *Rand Daily Mail*, following the closure of that paper) was only six months old. It was designed to be independent, insofar as independence meant providing a much-needed voice for the anti-apartheid movement. To publish a story alleging that the wife of the ANC's leader was involved in the abduction of four youths was to risk losing the goodwill of the movement. So reporters nervously watched the story until it was clear that Winnie was indeed a real problem. When reporter Thandeka Gqubule started asking questions in Soweto, she found it hard to obtain answers. No-one would talk to her about this dangerous subject, let alone go on the record.[4]

The Dobsonville community meeting provided an ideal opportunity for the newspaper to publish what it knew. It meant that the paper was reporting an actual event, rather than taking the responsibility of running with rumours. And it also meant that when Gqubule called Winnie for comment, it would be for comment on a meeting rather than on anonymously sourced allegations – a much safer prospect, staff at the paper felt. Gqubule spoke to Winnie on the evening of 26 January. She didn't receive much of a quote, but Winnie did repeat the earlier allegations of sexual misconduct at the church manse. Earlier in the day, David Beresford from the *Guardian* had faxed a copy of his story to Krish Naidoo for a comment. He never received a response.

As a result of Beresford's fax and Gqubule's phone call, it was clear to Winnie on Thursday that the story was about to break, both domestically and overseas the next morning. Very late on Thursday evening Katiza Chebekhulu was taken down to the police station in Orlando West to lay a complaint accusing Paul Verryn of sexual assault. His complaint established an bona fide motive for the removal of the youths from Verryn's house. It was the opening of a docket against Verryn which finally caused the police to become officially involved in the case.

Ebrahim Asvat was intrigued as he sat reading about Winnie and her football team in his surgery that Friday lunchtime. He had met Winnie several times over the years through his brother, but had never liked her, finding her arrogant. He disapproved of her drunkenness. He knew that Abu put himself out for her and thought that she took advantage of his kindness. It worried Ebrahim that Abu seemed to be so much at Winnie's beck and call. Abu had never confided in Ebrahim about his relationship with Winnie because he knew Ebrahim disliked and disapproved of her. But still, Ebrahim was so interested in the story that he read it three times before resuming his work. Four hours later he received an urgent phone call – Abu had been murdered.

At about four o'clock that afternoon, two youths, Cyril Mbatha and Nicholas Dlamini, had gone into Abu's surgery in Soweto. Mbatha said that he needed to see the doctor and – like Jerry Richardson the night before – filled out a patient card. But Mbatha gave a false name, Mandla Ekwanyana. Asvat's nurse and receptionist – Albertina Sisulu – took down the details. Mbatha then went and sat in the waiting room.

A door led directly from the waiting room to the consulting room. It could either be opened electronically from inside the consulting room by pressing a button behind the doctor's chair or unlocked from the outside with a key, copies of which were held by Asvat and Albertina. Once inside the consulting room a patient could only leave when Asvat pressed the button releasing the door. It was an arrangement primarily designed to protect the privacy rather than the safety of those who went to see the doctor. Only someone who had visited Asvat or been told would know about this controlled access to his office.

Mbatha sat and waited outside the consulting room while other patients saw the doctor. When Abu finally called him there was no sign of Mbatha. Asvat carried on seeing other patients and then went to get some air in the garden. Working in the adjacent dispensary, Albertina Sisulu heard him come back into the surgery and ask a patient, 'Are you Mandla?' When she heard the patient say yes, she called to ask him where he had been. He called back that he had gone to get some money from his sister. She then heard the door to the consulting room click shut. What she didn't see was that not one but two youths followed the doctor into his room.

The next thing she heard was a gunshot, followed by Asvat's

scream. Startled, she shouted out, but there was no response. Screaming for help, she then ran through the back door and into the street, and as she ran around the house she saw two men running towards the gate. There was an ambulance waiting at the gate to take a patient to hospital, which set off after the two men, but was unable to catch them. Albertina Sisulu then returned to the surgery where she found Asvat lying in a pool of blood. He was dead. R135.00 had been stolen from his desk.[5]

As soon as he received the call, Ebrahim Asvat rushed to his brother's surgery, where he met Albertina. Once it was established that Abu was actually dead, there was not much for Ebrahim to do, so he went to Zhora's house to be with her and Abu's children. At about ten o'clock that night the family had a call from Winnie. She had just heard the news, she told them, and was on her way over. But she didn't turn up for another two hours, and when she did her behaviour was strange. Accompanied by Zinzi, Richardson and Krish Naidoo, she went straight up to Zhora. 'Who do you think did this?' she asked, and looked down. Then she sat on her heels at Zhora's feet and stared at the floor without speaking. She didn't cry at the death of one of her closest friends, but just sat silently on the floor. Richardson was silent, too. He never spoke. Not even to say that he had been in the surgery and seen Abu twice in the past twenty-four hours. Asvat was buried the next day. Winnie attended the funeral accompanied by about twenty members of Mandela United.

Initially the Asvat family thought that Abu had been murdered by right-wing forces. As an active member first of the Black Consciousness movement and then of AZAPO (he was secretary-general of the militant Azanian People's Organisation), it made sense to them that if anyone had wanted to kill the soft-spoken doctor it would have been an activist from the right.

But on the Sunday following Abu's death the South African *Sunday Times* ran an article about his killing quoting Winnie. She said Asvat had been killed – she did not say by whom – because he was going to be an expert witness in the case of sexual misconduct against Verryn. Implying that the Methodist Church had in some way caused the death of Asvat, it was Winnie who first drew public attention to a possible connection between the kidnapping from the Methodist manse and the murder of Abu-Baker Asvat.

On that same Sunday, Ebrahim Asvat and Albertina Sisulu went to open up Abu's consulting rooms for the police. They waited at the offices until the police had finished the forensic examination before starting to clean up Abu's blood. At one point as they scrubbed at the stains, Ebrahim burst into tears. He collapsed into a chair, and wept. And as he cried he kept asking, 'Why did this have to happen to him? Who would have done this?' Albertina sat and cried with Ebrahim, and the two spoke of their sorrow and fear.

Within a couple of weeks the Asvat family began getting calls from journalists asking about the possibility of a connection between Abu's murder and Winnie. The questions focused on Abu's visit to Winnie's house when he had allegedly examined Stompie, and diagnosed him as being permanently seriously brain-damaged as a result of his beating. As the press looked for a motive behind Asvat's murder, journalists kept coming back to this visit. A key witness to the condition of the missing youth had been eradicated.

Another phone call after the murder was to lead the Asvat family to hope they might learn more of what lay behind Abu's death. Priscilla Jana called Zhora Asvat from Durban, and told her she knew the truth of what had happened. She told Zhora that when she returned from Durban she would come and tell her what Abu had said to her on the morning of his death. The visit never took place. (Jana later denied saying this. She claimed only to have called Zhora Asvat to tell her she had seen Abu on the day he died and had arranged to see him properly when she got back to Johannesburg.)

Winnie's comment that Asvat's death might be in some way linked to the Methodist church resulted in another urgent meeting between church and community leaders. One leader said he would warn Winnie of the consequences of making this kind of statement. Bishop Storey announced that, in the light of what Winnie had said, he felt he would have to make public details of the abduction and assault.

The Crisis Committee and the Methodist Church were still aware of the pressing need to discover what had happened to Stompie, who was now widely believed to be dead. At the same time, dealing with the mounting allegations against Verryn remained extremely important. On the whole, Winnie remained unavailable to reporters during this period, but then she gave an interview to NBC News, with a long and detailed account of what she said had really happened.

The tragedy is that the Reverend Paul Verryn has a medical problem which needs to be addressed by responsible leaders. It's a psychological problem. I don't understand how a man of his standing continues to sodomise black children. There is clear evidence that he has fallen victim to a medical problem which should be addressed quietly with his doctors. He brutalises these youths who are with him because one youth would not give into his sexual advances. This is how it arose. It is well known in church circles and those who have been working with him. He is supposed to have been transferred from Roodeport because of this problem. He is continuing with these activities with the full knowledge of some of the top members of the church. My responsibility as a mother is to draw attention to this problem.

The youths in my premises did not abduct any children. It came about when a woman who was staying with Paul Verryn told me about this child and he was later fetched. There is a gigantic cover-up by the church. Xoliswa brought the boys – especially the traumatised child – because she panicked when he said the only way to deal with this white man is to kill him. The focus should have been on Paul Verryn and the SACC.

The SACC are worried about their image because when people discover that Paul Verryn is not very well their overseas funding may be affected. This is a problem of the church rather than the football team. We thought we were assisting the church in a problem and their only interest is covering their image.[6]

In an interview with Hennie Serfontein of Netherlands television, she said:

I feel a total betrayal by everyone who has engaged in this sordid affair. I regard it as sordid and I am very hurt that loyalties could switch over at just the snap of a finger. I am astounded that political loyalties could not stand a simple test of this nature.[7]

Although she made a number of statements to the press, denying involvement in the kidnapping and assault, she never claimed to have been away from Soweto at the time. Nor did she give the police investigating the case an alibi for 29 December. Other than blaming Verryn for what happened and expressing her outrage that she could be accused of these crimes, she remained tight-lipped. It would be more than two years before she personally swore she had been absent on the night in question.[8]

Winnie's version was that she had left for Brandfort in the early evening of 29 December to attend a meeting scheduled for the next morning. The meeting, involving various members of the community, would discuss the failure of the various projects she had initiated in the township with a view to reinvigorating them. Brandfort was too far away to contemplate driving down on the same morning as the meeting, so Winnie had arranged to stay overnight with an old friend, the school teacher Norah Moahloli.

On the afternoon of 29 December, shortly before she was due to depart for Brandfort, Winnie received a visit from Xoliswa Falati, who told her that one of the youths staying at the Methodist church house had been raped by Verryn. Falati asked for Winnie's help, so Winnie instructed her to bring the youth – Katiza Chebekhulu – to her so she could see for herself what the problem was. When Winnie saw Chebekhulu she noticed that he seemed to be in a state of shock – he was unable to speak. 'It was quite a while before I established sufficient rapport for him to have an emotional catharsis to enable him to open up to me.' Chebekhulu did not say he had been raped by Verryn, he said that Verryn had made sexual advances to him and had *tried* to rape him.

Winnie decided to take Chebekhulu to Dr Asvat. Some time after 3 p.m. she and Falati took the boy to Asvat's office, where he was exammined behind a screen. Asvat assured him in front of Winnie that even though Verryn may have made advances, there had been no anal penetration. He recommended that Chebekhulu should seek a pyschiatrist, and also recommended that Verryn – who was not his patient and whom he had never met – should be seen by a mental health expert. Asvat told Winnie that he would make the necessary appointment for Chebekhulu but because it was Christmas week it might be difficult to arrange something immediately. He said he would call her as soon as he could find an available doctor, suggesting that if she hadn't heard from him in about ten days, she call back. Winnie, Falati and Chebekhulu then left.

There was a medical record of their visit: a card in Asvat's files, made out in Katiza Chebekhulu's name, described him as being mentally confused, occasionally crying, occasionally hysterical and suffering from insomnia. The cause of his anxiety was not recorded but the prescription for ten mild tranquilisers and two paracetamol tablets was. The date of the visit stamped on the card was not 29 December, but the following day – the day after the kidnapping and assaults when Chebekhulu had 'felt like beating up'. Chebekhulu's symptoms and prescription were written in Asvat's handwriting. His name, address and age had been filled in by Albertina Sisulu.[9]

Following the visit to Asvat, Winnie's version continued, she prepared to leave for Brandfort in her combie, driven by the son of a neighbour, Thabo Motau. She left some time between 6.30 and 7.00 p.m. and did not return to Soweto until New Year's Eve. John Morgan contradicted that account. In a sworn statement to the police, on 22 February 1989, John Morgan said that he used that combie to take Falati and her daughter back to the church manse after the abductions of 29 December 1988. He left it parked on the street close to the manse overnight and collected it the next day. When he had driven it back to Winnie's house he washed it. Winnie – who was at home that day – then told him to drive her to her office in Commerce House. Zinzi went with her.

In Winnie's version, she and Thabo Motau arrived in Brandfort sometime after 10 p.m. on 29 December. She stayed with Nora Moahloli; Thabo stayed with friends. The next day she went to visit local pensioners and their families before the community meeting. Her two days in Brandfort were spent at meetings, visiting the day care centre, and attending to problems related to various scholarship projects. She arrived back in Johannesburg between 6.30 and 7.00 p.m. on New Years's Eve, to find Xoliswa Falati waiting to see her. Falati rushed towards Winnie the moment she saw her saying she was sorry she had brought the children and hoped Winnie wouldn't mind. Winnie didn't know what she was talking about, she was tired, and she was somewhat impatient. She vaguely listened as Falati rattled on about something to do with bringing similar victims of Paul Verryn for Jerry Richardson to look after, and decided it was nothing she need concern herself with, dismissed Falati and went into her bedroom.

Instead of telling anyone this story, Winnie continued to make and break appointments with various representatives of the community. There was a growing feeling that perhaps some kind of medical care should be arranged for her. Nelson Mandela was also considering the best course of action for his wife. At one point he mentioned to a church leader the possibility of her holding a press conference. She could admit that she had done wrong, apologise, ask for forgiveness and speak of making a fresh start. But Winnie was not an apologiser and was not about to admit wrong. The press conference never took place. Instead, Mandela decided the community and the church should stand behind his wife – not just from a commitment to the movement, but because of a personal loyalty to him and the Mandela name.

But such solidarity was becoming increasingly difficult to maintain in the light of what continued to emerge. On Sunday 12 February, the Johannesburg *Sunday Star* ran an un-bylined article, headlined: 'Winnie Mandela linked to beating of activist. Stompie's story of horror.' The story, quoting 'sources', included details of the night of 29 December, such as 'the boys were ordered out of the combi and into the house, and they found Mrs Mandela in the doorway. She had a glass in one hand and was very unfriendly to Stompie and his friends'. The article had a number of inconsistencies, mainly concerning dates. It became a major piece of evidence when Winnie and her lawyers later claimed that she was swiftly tried and found guilty by the media.

The *Sunday Star*'s information is that when the delegation arrived back at the Methodist Church it was decided that someone more used to Mrs Mandela be sent to her house to check on the youths. Dr Asvat was called to the church and told of the situation. Dr Asvat apparently said he was used to Mrs Mandela and she to him and if there was any truth in what the escaper [Kenneth Kgase] alleged, he would find it. Dr Asvat then drove to Mrs Mandela's home and found the escaper's story to be true. When he arrived at Mrs Mandela's home he apparently noticed that she appeared to be very worried. She allowed him to see the boys who had been assaulted, and apparently Stompie was fading fast. According to the sources Dr Asvat was very shocked at what he saw when he examined Stompie and warned that Stompie had been so badly assaulted he would not live. He treated the others. It is widely believed that Dr Asvat left Diepkloof Extension and headed straight back to Orlando West. There, in a state of shock, he related what he had seen to the group representing the various organisations. The next day Dr Asvat was shot dead inside his surgery by two young men, one of whom pretended to be a patient.[10]

Winnie had told the Crisis Committee that Mandela United had long been disbanded. This was not true. In fact, the team was entering its most active period. On Saturday 11 February, a member of the football team known as Dodo came to see Dudu Chili. He told her that Winnie and Zinzi Mandela had just finished chairing a meeting at which it had been decided that Dudu's son, Sibusiso Chili, and Lerotodi Ikaneng must be eliminated. 'They have become too problematic', were Winnie's words, according to Dodo. Dudu believed Dodo, and with reason. Her house was surrounded by strange youths carrying heavy objects, with scarves tied round their heads and faces to avoid recognition. When she went outside, the youths would turn, so that she could only see their backs, then one would give an order and the others would start to walk away. Neighbours started phoning her, warning her that her house was under surveillance and cautioning her to take care. As she watched the silent vigil of youths waiting for her son it wasn't just Sibusiso she was frightened for, but herself and the rest of her family. She felt they were all at risk.

On Monday afternoon the event she had been so afraid of finally occurred. It began with a local girl tearing up the street, screaming, 'Mama, they have caught up with Sibusiso! They are going to kill Sibusiso!' He had been intercepted on his way to the shops by Mandela United members Killer and Maxwell Modondo. Killer had a gun. Dudu immediately sent for her other sons, Mbuso and Cigar. The Chili brothers and a group of their friends rushed to the scene, swiftly outnumbering Killer and Maxwell Modondo, Killer managed to run away, but Maxwell Modondo was not so lucky. Alone and unarmed, he was quickly surrounded and attacked. First he was hit with a stick on his chest and fell on to his back. The group then beat him with whips, bars and sticks. Then he was lifted, carried across the street and laid down in the long grass. To finish him off, Sibusiso picked up a large brick and hurled it down on to his face. He picked it up again and smashed it on to his chest. Another youth repeatedly flung pieces of broken brick down on to Modondo's body. The stoning continued until the body was still and lifeless.[11]

At some stage during the murder, Lerotodi Ikaneng turned up. He had been working at a shebeen when word reached him of what was happening. Witnesses later implicated him as a participant in the attack, but he denied this, saying he arrived when it was all but over and merely stood watching the end. He would be one of those arrested but would not be convicted.

When the case came to court, an identified witness placed Winnie at the scene of the crime. She had allegedly received word that Modondo was in trouble and had driven over to see what was going on. The witness said that she did not stay long. She allegedly pulled up in her car, sat taking in the scene, and then in silence drove off. Overall, this witness was found by the judge to be unconvincing.

Meanwhile, the search for Stompie continued. On the morning of 14 February 1989, forensic pathologists Patricia Klepp and J.C.W. Cook sat having coffee and discussing the contents of newspaper articles about the missing boy. Cook – who was new to his job – mentioned he had done an autopsy on a decomposing youth a few weeks earlier. Could that boy have been Stompie? Klepp phoned the mortuary in Diepkloof and inquired if the body was still there. It was, and the two pathologists set off to re-examine the corpse. But it had been kept in the deep freeze and was frozen solid, so they had to leave it for twenty-four hours and return the next day. Only when the remains of corpse number DK 48/89 had finally defrosted were Klepp and Cook able to remove sections from the fingers for fingerprint identification. Stompie had finally been found.[12]

Once Stompie's body had been identified, the police started to move quickly, identifying and rounding up suspects. Lieutenant Frederik Dempsey had actually been on the case since 9 February, tasked with investigating press reports about Stompie and the three others. He had begun by contacting Storey, had been referred to Fink Haysom and on again to Geoff Budlender. He finally arranged with Budlender that Kgase, Mono and Mekgwe should be interviewed by him at Sandton police station with Budlender and Storey present.

All this had taken time to set up, and the interviews didn't take place until Friday 17 February. Two days later, when the Mandela house was raided, Jerry Richardson and Jabu Sithole were arrested and Winnie was questioned about the sjamboks found on her premises. She denied knowledge of any. She was not arrested, even though the statements of the three complainants implicated her just as much as they did Richardson and Sithole (one of the soccer team alleged to have participated in the kidnapping and assault). Nor was any statement taken from her – either in connection with Stompie's death, or in connection with the killing of Dr Asvat. The lack of questioning was even more strange considering that two youths who had been detained had given statements about Asvat's murder on Friday 17 February – and one of the statements specifically referred to Winnie's involvement. Both statements were given in Afrikaans; Nicholas Dlamini's translated as follows:

It was Thursday, 12 o'clock in January 1989. On that date Johannes Ndlovu came to me at 273 Marafi Hostel. Johannes said we must go to Rockville together. He said we are going to Dr Asvat's surgery together. Then I went with him. We took a taxi from Marafi Hostel to Rockville and then walked. We got out at Rockville and then walked to Dr Asvat's consulting rooms. There, Johannes told me the story. 'Look, I've been bought by Winnie Mandela and I must go and shoot Dr Asvat dead.' He showed me the weapon – a 9 mm 'short' [pistol]. He then took out the magazine and I counted 6 live rounds. He said he would first give his name to the nurse so that he could get to see the doctor in his surgery. He went in and I went in with him. He gave his name to the nurse and told the nurse he is Mandla Ekwanyana and stays at Nicefield Hostel. After that he sat down on a chair. After a while he was called by the doctor into his consulting rooms. The doctor closed the door and the door was now locked. I then heard the shots in the consulting rooms. There were two shots. Mandla then came out and he had the firearm in his hand. He said, 'Let's go.' We then left and he said he had done the job. We ran to the side of Rockville clinic. We then went to drink at number 14 shebeen. We then walked to Johannes' girlfriend at Kliptown. We sat there and Johannes changed his clothes. I then went back to Marafi Hostel by taxi. Later I saw photographs of myself and Johannes in a newspaper. Johannes and I then went to hide in Sebokeng. I came back on Wednesday and on Thursday I was caught. When we came back on Wednesday, Johannes said he must go and fetch the money from Winnie Mandela on Friday. The money was R20,000. Then I was arrested on Thursday.[13]

Cyril Mbatha also made a statement 'willingly and without compulsion' to the police, telling a completely different story.

During December 1988 at Kliptown, I met a man named Johannes for the first time. The man came with an idea that we should make a plan to get money. I asked the man what we could do to make money. He said he was going to give me equipment to get money according to his plan. From that time on we saw each other now and then.

On January 25th, 1989, he took me to Rockville. He took me to the consulting rooms of Dr A. B. Asvat. We stood in the street and he showed me with his eyes where the Doctor's consulting room was. Just before 1.00, the doctor drove in there with the Cressida. We saw he had a briefcase in his hand. I'm not sure if it was a brown or a black case. He said the case was full of money. He returned there again the following day. It was the 27th, Friday.

He said I must go inside. I must tell the doctor I am seriously ill. Johannes and I went inside and sat together on a sofa in the consulting room. You must first sit and then write in your details and then sit again until they call you. I gave the details and the nurse

wrote them on a white card with green lines. I put my thumb print
on the card. After I gave all my details, I went to sit again. After
that, Johannes said we must go and find food at the shop. At the
shop, Johannes told me that with the card they would allow me
through. We stayed at the consulting rooms, where the nurse told
us the doctor had been looking for us. When we got to the
consulting rooms, Johannes had already given me his firearm. The
doctor called me in and I went into the doctor's room after he
opened the door. I went to sit on a sofa. The doctor closed the
curtain, and he was standing with his back to me. I stood up and
moved towards the door. When the doctor turned around I already
had the firearm pointed at him. When the doctor saw the gun, he
screamed a lot. I told him I wanted money. The doctor jumped at
me and grabbed my right wrist. The gun was in my right hand and I
fired one shot at the doctor's thighs. Then I saw someone trying to
open the door, it was my friend, he could not get in and I thought I
must do the shooting myself. When the doctor saw that Johannes
was trying to get in, he jumped up and wanted to grab me again. I
shot him once in the chest. The door had now opened and my friend
had come in, kicked the doctor and said to him, 'Where is the
money?' The doctor went to lie on one side and my friend took
something out of the drawer. I don't know if there was money
inside. He opened another drawer and took out something else.
Loose money fell out. I then tried to open the door but could not
open the door. I said to Johannes that he had brought me and if he
did not open the door I was going to shoot him. I tried again to open
the door, whereupon I saw the nurse through the bars [grille]. I
pointed the gun at her and said that if she moved I would shoot her.
Suddenly the door opened, whereupon I called my friend.

We then ran away. After that we walked to Mafalo Lwo Rooms.
We went to sit there in the veld. I gave the firearm to Johannes. He
threw the loose money on the ground. There was R135.00
altogether. He then gave me R60.00 and took R60.00 for himself.
He said he was going to buy more bullets with the remaining
R15.00.[14]

At first reading the two statements made little sense and almost
entirely contradicted each other. 'Johannes' seemed to be a generic
name designed to confuse the interrogator. Anyone besides the
confessor who might possibly be implicated in the murder was called
Johannes. In Dlamini's statement, Johannes was Cyril Mbatha.

213

Mbatha's statement only dovetailed into Dlamini's if the name 'Johannes' was changed twice, first to Jerry Richardson and then to Dlamini.

Other discrepancies existed between these statements and the evidence of other witnesses. Neither of the youth's statements describes their entering the consulting room together, which eye-witnesses saw. Albertina Sisulu testified at their trial that she heard nothing inside the consulting room, between the time of entry and shots ringing out. Money was taken and it was R135. But there was more money than that in the consulting-room, in Asvat's desk. Asvat was not shot in the thigh, but twice in the chest area – one bullet entering under his left collar bone, the second by his right armpit. The pathologist, Vernon Kemp, testified it appeared as if he was bending over at the time he was shot and would have died either immediately or within minutes.[15]

The statement implicating Winnie was never produced in court, although Mbatha's statement, which had no reference to her, was. No effort was made to identify Johannes. The official motive for the murder, on the basis of Mbatha's statement – which he testified in court had been tortured out of him – was robbery. The two youths were both found guilty and sentenced to death, They are still in prison. On appeal Dlamini's sentence was reduced to life imprisonment, Mbatha remained on death row.

John Morgan was arrested on 21 February, Nompumelelo Falati on 22 February, and her mother Xoliswa on the 27th. The Falatis denied any criminal conduct. Xoliswa gave a statement to Lieutenant-Colonel C.R. Oosthuizen where she admitted that the four youths had been 'invited' to go with them to Jerry's room at the Mandela house to answer questions about the sexual misconduct of Verryn. Winnie was not there, said Falati, who also told Oosthuizen that earlier that same day she and Winnie had taken Katiza Chebekhulu to be examined by Dr Asvat, following Chebekhulu's allegations that he had been assaulted by Verryn. But Chebekhulu had already given a statement to the police, placing Winnie at the scene of the crime. So had Jabu Sithole and so had John Morgan. The police now had six statements implicating Winnie in the kidnapping and assault of Kgase, Mono, Mekgwe and Stompie, and one connecting her to the death of Asvat, but still they did nothing.

Stompie Seipei was buried in Tumahole township on 25 February. Bishop Storey gave the funeral address, describing Stompie's 'terrible and violent death' as an 'unspeakable crime'.

These past few weeks, as the facts of his dying have emerged, will be remembered as weeks of shame and of profound tragedy. These weeks have probed below the surface of South Africa's shame and exposed the deeper, hidden wounds these years have carved into a people's soul. The erosion of conscience, the devaluing of human life, the evasion of truth and the reckless resort to violence. There is a choice to be made today about these wounds. Either we will open them wider or we will seek, for Stompie's sake and hundreds more like him, to heal them.

But even as Storey spoke, a rippled murmur was spreading through the vast crowd. The body in the coffin wasn't Stompie's. Stompie wasn't dead. It was all a plot to discredit the ANC. Stompie was alive in a camp in Swaziland. The rumours – perpetrated by the ANC in a late attempt to exercise some kind of damage control – threatened to disrupt the proceedings as some of those who heard them became keen to open up his coffin and see the 'truth' for themselves.

The Mandelas' official historian, Fatima Meer, who received a letter from Nelson Mandela written on 28 February urging her to 'be as supportive as you always have been', wrote the following account of Stompie's death.

'Following the allegations of sexual abuse by Katiza Chebekhulu and his examination by Dr Asvat, [Xoliswa], with the help of Winnie's former football coach, a man in his forties, removed four other boys from the Home. She claimed that the boys had become abusers themselves. These boys were accommodated several meters away from Winnie's house where they were questioned and reprimanded. There were allegations of far more serious assault. Four of the boys ran away, one of whom, Stompie Moeketsi Seipei, was never seen again. A body was found and identified as his, though many close to Stompie doubted the identity.'[16]

The question raised by the ANC of whether the State may have been behind the anarchy caused by the football team continued to haunt the community: Since Winnie persisted in surrounding herself with those who reinforced her image of herself and did not challenge her, the thinking went, a strategy of winning her trust and then abusing it could be relatively straightforward. If Jerry Richardson was an informer couldn't there be others?

Suspicion centred on two other men at this time. The first, Peter Mokaba, was the charismatic leader of the South African Youth Congress. Mokaba was said to have been held in an ANC camp, suspected of being a spy for the system. Upon his release, he went to the Mandela house and – with the aid of youth league members – began to control access to Winnie. Mokaba – whose political activism began with the 1976 student uprising – had been detained on numerous occasions in connection with unlawful ANC activities, but he could not shake the shadow of mistrust that some in the movement felt for him. Or the sense of unease that matters surrounding Winnie might, through Mokaba, still be monitored, even manipulated, by the State. When confronted, Mokaba denied working for the State. 'How could I work for people who have persecuted my sister, detained my mother, broken my family and generally harassed my people?' he asked.

The Frenchman Alain Guenon was automatically distrusted. He was from a foreign country, he had a lot of money which he spent freely, and he was always going on trips. He may have been an agent or he may have been France's version of Robert J. Brown – an operator who liked to make a deal, knew the value of being well-connected, and was prepared to invest in the Mandelas. Whatever his agenda, he was viewed with unease.

Back in 1988, Guenon had requested that the French cultural attaché, Gilbert Eruart, arrange a lunch where he could meet Winnie. His reasons, he said, were that he wanted to make documentaries, one about her and a second about the ANC. The lunch took place, the introductions were made, and Guenon subsequently became very friendly with Mrs Mandela. He was known around her house as a kind of Mr Fix-It, involved in the affairs of the family and possessing useful amounts of cash. But it was unclear who he was working for. In 1989 the story was that he had befriended Mrs Mandela in a bid to control media access to her husband on his release from prison.

Winnie's associations with those much younger than herself continued. Twenty-five-year old Dali Mpofu worked as an articled clerk for Kathy Satchwell, the lawyer who represented most of Mandela United. He was bright, hard-working and good company. He also had a girlfriend. His girlfriend – Terry Oakley-Smith, a lecturer in educational psychology at Wits University – was ten years older than him. She was British, white, and pregnant with his child. One of the less kind stories circulating about Oakley-Smith said that, although she knew Mpofu did not want to have a child with her, she had deliberately become pregnant because she was insecure about their relationship and needed a commitment of some kind. If that was the case, her decision must have caused her untold anguish. For

Mpofu and Winnie became lovers, and Terry Oakley-Smith found herself in the third corner of an intensely bitter and acrimonious love triangle.

Winnie began buying expensive designer clothes for Dali Mpofu. Oakley-Smith would find the receipts and keep them. Winnie would write letters to Mpofu, Oakley-Smith would find them, read them and keep them. Winnie would go to Mpofu's apartment late at night, sometimes Oakley-Smith would go there too – on the same night. The two women would then compete as to who would get to stay Oakley-Smith had the child, but Winnie had the power, and eventually, as Mpofu began spending all his time with her rival, Oakley-Smith grew increasingly desperate. It wasn't just that Mpofu seemed mesmerised by this woman, caught up in some kind of spell, but more bewitched than entranced. It wasn't just that he now seemed unable to do anything that wasn't ordered by Winnie, or that he was uninterested in his old life, while obsessed with his new. Oakley-Smith could possibly have coped with that pain and humiliation, even with the additional strain of dealing with a new-born son. What made her life totally impossible, however, were the death threats.

They came late at night usually. Sometimes Oakley-Smith would be woken up by the phone ringing. She could hear Winnie's voice down the other end, drunk, slurring her words, telling her to stay away from Dali.

Two days after Stompie's post mortem the UDF (now renamed as the Mass Democratic Movement) publicly distanced itself from Winnie and her soccer team. At a press conference, the publicity secretary, Murphy Morobe, read out a statement. Winnie had 'abused the trust and confidence which she had enjoyed over the years,' he said. And the movement now had 'no option but to speak out . . . In particular we are outraged by the reign of terror that the [football] team has been associated with. Not only is Mrs Mandela associated with the team, in fact it is her own creation.' Morobe then directly linked Winnie to Stompie's death. 'We are outraged at Mrs Mandela's obvious complicity in the recent abductions. Had Stompie and his colleagues not been abducted by Mrs Mandela's "football team", he would have been alive today,' he read from the statement. Because of her behaviour, the MDM called on the people, in particular the Soweto community, to distance themselves from her in a dignified manner.

Morobe read the statement out flanked by UDF president, Archie Gumede, and the trade unions' president, Elijah Barayi. Following the press conference, Winnie refused to speak to reporters. Two years later she finally commented on it:

> The statement literally found us guilty of murder. It claimed that the Mass Democratic Movements must distance themselves from me because of my association in the murder of Stompie and the severe assaults of the other boys . . . I was tried by these so-called leaders and they called a press conference purporting to speak on behalf of the country. Most of the real leaders of the people were behind bars.[17]

But the statement, which Winnie described as only having the backing of 'a handful' of so-called leaders, was formally ratified by the MDM at a full meeting of the national executive, a number of whose members were also members of the Crisis Committee. It was issued at a point where the Crisis Committee acknowledged that it had failed in dealing with Mrs Mandela and could do no more. The MDM had not taken the decision to banish Winnie lightly. Politically, Winnie was now felt to be such a liability that she could damage the entire anti-apartheid movement. After the statement was issued, two things did not happen. The ANC did not formally ask the MDM for a retraction, and no member of the Crisis Committee publicly disassociated him or herself from it.

Although the MDM made a point during the press conference of '[reaffirming] its unqualified support for our leader, Comrade Nelson Mandela, and [calling] for his immediate release,' there can be no doubt that Mandela felt personally damaged by the attempted marginalisation of his wife, and the fact that he had not been told exactly what was planned. He sent messages from prison which made it clear that he was unable to see quite why the MDM should have issued a statement of this kind to the press. He felt that this whole matter should have been dealt with internally. Winnie could have been privately disciplined, not publicly humiliated. In prison miles away, Mandela couldn't understand the extent of his wife's problem.

It was with a sense of urgency, in response to the discovery of Stompie's body, that the press conference had been given. Only those in Johannesburg and Soweto who had been kept abreast of what was happening were initially involved. In Cape Town, for example, the first that UDF leader Reverend Dr Allan Boesak knew of any statement was when a reporter stuck a microphone in his face for a comment on it as he came out of church to attend a march. When he learnt what its contents were, he privately felt it had gone too far.

Boesak thought Winnie could have been criticised, even publicly censured, he was prepared to allow, without actually being thrown to the wolves and marginalised.

But many disagreed with him. Organisations throughout the country listened to what they were called on to do by their leaders in Johannesburg and complied. In Cape Town, Farieda Omar was contacted by members of the United Women's Congress, who came to see her about her friendship with Winnie. Farieda was an old friend of Winnie who often picked her up from the airport and took her to prison when she came down to see Mandela. In the circumstances, the women said, they felt it best if she refrained from associating with her. Farieda refused. 'I will never do that,' she told the women. 'Because her husband and she have gone through so much, and I will never break my friendship with her. If she asks me tomorrow to go and fetch her, I'll go and fetch her again.'

Coincidentally, she was asked by Winnie to go and fetch her again the following day. Winnie was on her way to visit Mandela and Farieda went to collect her from the airport. When she arrived there was a mob of reporters shouting questions at Winnie about Stompie. In the midst of the confusion, Winnie and Farieda greeted each other, hugging and kissing while photographers snapped away. Then they walked arm in arm out of the airport and drove to the prison. Three days later, Farieda's husband, Dulla Omar, came back from consulting with Mandela. The photograph of Farieda and Winnie hugging at the airport, which had run in the Cape Times, had been stuck up on Nelson's prison wall – visual proof that his wife retained some support.

The discovery of Stompie's body had finally caused the police to open a murder docket. Investigations into the murder of Maxwell Modondo were already under way – Lerotodi Ikaneng was the first to be locked up – but it was in the process of the investigation into Stompie's death that the police uncovered what would be a key piece of evidence in the Maxwell Modondo murder case. On 20 February, Winnie's house was raided by police from Orlando Murder and Robbery squad. In the course of the search, one of the policemen found a piece of paper in one of Winnie's rooms. It was a handwritten hit list. There were eleven names on the list, including two of Albertina Sisulu's boys, three Chili brothers and Lerotodi Ikaneng. The hit list formed a major part of the defence in the Maxwell Modondo murder trial the following year, but it would never be used against Winnie.

When combing through Winnie's premises that day, police found her charming and helpful. She even showed a sense of humour as she co-operated with the raid. But later the same day two members of Mandela United, Sonwabu and Gybon, went to collect Charles Zwane – who was still free after receiving a suspended sentence for his role in the killing of Xola Mokhaula. As they drove along Sonwabu and Gybon told Zwane that their task was to find and kill policemen, then steal their weapons. Outside a municipal shopping centre three policemen were walking down the street together. Twenty-six shots were fired from Sonwabu's car, killing two of the policeman and one passerby. The third policeman was injured. No weapons were stolen, however. That was Zwane's task and he lost his nerve.

The three teamed up again a couple of days later on the evening of 22 February to exact Mandela United's revenge on the Chilis for the murder of Maxwell Modondo. The plan was to attack and obliterate Dudu's home. Both Dudu and Sibusiso Chili were being detained overnight by the police for questioning in connection with the Modondo murder. The house was not empty, however. Dudu's sister, Barbara Chili, was there, watching television with her nieces, twelve-year-old Judith and eleven-year-old Finkie.

Barbara heard a click at the gate. When she went outside to look, she saw nothing unusual, except that the gate had been opened. She called to her dog, Sizwe, who was nosing around in the garden. Closing the gate, she stood for a moment in the dark, but could see nothing. All was still. She went back into the house. A few moments later, she heard another noise – a metallic scraping, as though somebody was trying to open the gate without being heard. She called Sizwe again, but this time there was silence. She went outside and stood on the verandah in the dark and as she listened she became aware of Sizwe whimpering. Looking over to where the sounds came from, she suddenly saw a tall man standing silently in the shadows with a balaclava on his face and a gun pointing straight at her. As she caught sight of him, he fired.

Barbara raced back into the house, gathered up the girls and pushed them into Dudu's bedroom. She grabbed the phone and called a friend for help. As she stood opposite the window shouting into the receiver there was a crash of glass and a blinding flare. A firebomb had been thrown into the house. The bomb landed on Barbara's thighs and her clothes caught fire. Finkie – who had been standing next to the window – was thrown across the room by the impact of the bomb. She had also been shot in the head. Barbara tried to drag Finkie out into the passage, but she couldn't – there was too much fire. Judith was outside the bedroom in the passage and she helped get water to put out Barbara's clothes, then she ran into the bedroom and tried to drag Finkie, but she didn't have the strength to move her.

By now the whole house was on fire. Another firebomb had been thrown through the dining-room window, setting it ablaze. Leaving Finkie burning in Dudu's bedroom, Barbara and Judith ran outside and hid in the chicken coop. When they thought it was safe enough, they left the coop, jumped over the fence into the adjacent yard, where they found Judith's father. They were then rushed to hospital.

Zwane, Gybon and Sonwabu had carried out their mission successfully. It had been Sonwabu whom Barbara had seen standing in the shadows. He had fired repeatedly with an AK-47 through the windows of the house. The earlier click Barbara had heard was Zwane creeping through the gate and up to the house to pour petrol under the closed doors. He and Gybon had then thrown petrol bombs though the windows. In a matter of minutes the Chili house had been completely destroyed. Finkie's body was burnt to a cinder. Later, witnesses would tell Dudu Chili that they had seen the three youths arrive by car, and again there would be accounts of someone else sitting silently watching as the house went up in flames. Neighbours would say they had seen Winnie parked in the next street. They described her arriving before the first shot was fired, and waiting in her car, not leaving until the entire attack was over.

Dudu Chili learnt about the bombing of her house and the death of Finkie while in custody. She and six others, including Lerotodo Ikaneng and her two sons Sibusiso and Sandile Chili, had now been arrested and charged with the murder of Maxwell Modondo. In a bail application hearing at the magistrates' court nine days after the fire, the prosecutor, Van Zyl, mentioned the hit list found at Winnie's house and told the magistrate that the names of three of the accused (Ikaneng and the Chili brothers) were included on it. Opposing bail for the defendants, Van Zyl said, 'For their own sake, so that they won't be murdered and prevented from standing trial, I ask that bail is not granted.' It was clear that attempts had been made against the accused, he said. He also said that members of the soccer team must be sought out.

The magistrate, Du Plessis, agreed not to grant bail. 'It is known all over in all forms of the media that the Mandela Soccer Club members are conducting a reign of terror and they don't hesitate to try to eliminate people who don't obey their demands,' he said. 'Three people have already died. People are murdered in counter attacks and it strongly indicates that people – possible witnesses – are being eliminated by these different gangs . . . it is very clear to me that all four of the accused to a great extent are living with a fear of their own life.'

Refusing bail in order to protect the accused for their own safety, he concluded 'If [the accused] are found by these people who are hunting for them and they are maimed or murdered, it would lead to a defeat of the ends of justice.'

Following the MDM's press conference, newspapers began running pieces attacking Winnie. The *Weekly Mail* ran a piece describing the ostracism of the Mother of the Nation, headlined: 'The higher the pedestal, the longer the fall'. It said:

There will be endless speculation on what led to the fall of this particular idol. Was it the tragic result of decades of suffering, or the simple tale of a woman being elevated to a divine position she could not cope with? Whatever the cause, it has been apparent for some time that Winnie has been acting and speaking alone, without consulting her colleagues or contrary to their advice. She has gradually become isolated from mainstream politics because of her refusal to tow anyone's line. It is now well known that her break up with her husband's attorney, Ismail Ayob, came about because she often refused his advice. And this week she was unceremoniously dropped by the lawyer she had appointed to replace Ayob, Krish Naidoo.

In March 1989 Nomavenda Mathiane wrote another piece in *Frontline*, this time denouncing the 'hypocrisy in the treatment of Winnie'.

Headlines like 'Fallen Idol' create the impression that blacks had revered the 'Mother of the Nation'. The fact is that this title is a mystery, and many black people have never known where it came from . . . The title was made popular in the eyes of the outside world, which shows that if a small group of people set out with a determination to create a lie they can succeed.

Currently the fashion is to load everything on to Winnie's head and to take all she says as evidence that she is out of touch with reality. When it is all over, I do not think it will be that easy.

But by the middle of the year, attention had shifted away from Winnie and on to Nelson Mandela when it was announced that a forty-five minute meeting over tea had taken place between Mandela and the State President, P. W. Botha, at the presidential residence. The possibility of a Mandela release had finally become real when Botha suffered a stroke on 18 January, permanently altering the balance of power in his own party and ultimately throughout the country. Botha's stroke signalled the end of his presidency. By April, the leader of the Transvaal branch, F. W. de Klerk, had taken over the reins of the National Party. Botha was not prepared to give up his position without a struggle, and part of his attempt to retain control was to step up talks with Mandela. Mandela was ready for the conversation. At the beginning of July he sent a lengthy statement to Botha, re-emphasising the need for a negotiated political settlement. The statement formed the basis for the 'tea party', as it came to be known, which once again fuelled speculation that Mandela would shortly be released. In July 1989, when Mandela celebrated his seventy-first birthday, he was allowed a visit from his whole family to his bungalow in the grounds of Victor Verster Prison. Winnie, Zinzi, his eldest daughter Makaziwe and several grandchildren went for the day, and for a short time they were able to forget their problems and try to be a family as they ate lunch before putting on a video – *Aliens* – for the children to watch.

One month after the tea party, Botha resigned and F. W. de Klerk became South Africa's new State President. The much younger de Klerk immediately reached out – to others in his party, to the international community, to MDM leaders and to the ANC – to create a new, more open political climate in South Africa. Within weeks Walter Sisulu and seven other political prisoners, including the remaining Rivonia trialists, had been released without restriction – even allowed to preside over a rally of 70,000 supporters in Soweto. This was a phenomenal event, especially considering that the ANC was still technically banned. Mandela had taken part in the negotiations leading to the release of his fellow prisoners. He was now regularly meeting with MDM leaders, union officials and cabinet members. On December he requested and was granted a meeting with F. W. de Klerk in de Klerk's Cape Town office. The government understood that to release Mandela would be to start immediate 'talks about talks', which it could not do if the ANC was still banned. And so, on 2 February 1990, in his opening address to Parliament, President de Klerk announced the lifting of bans on the ANC, the

SACP and the PAC and the unconditional release of Mandela. On the afternoon of Saturday 11 February watched by millions of viewers all over the world, Nelson Mandela took his wife's hand and walked through the gates of Victor Verster Prison. After twenty-seven years he was a free man.

Dressed in a black suit, Winnie was 'Ecstatic!' as she arrived by charter flight at DF Malan airport in Cape Town, shortly before 2.00 p.m. Apart from family members, others in the delegation of the National Reception Committee included Crisis Committee members Frank Chikane and Cyril Ramaphosa – attending in their official capacity as leaders of the SACC and the NUM respectively. Murphy Morobe was also there, as were Albertina and Walter Sisulu.

Winnie's influence was at its greatest in the days immediately before and after her husband's release. Those who had been loyal to her were rewarded. The Mandela household referred press queries to Peter Mokaba's SAYCO rather than the MDM. Reports also circulated that Alain Guenon was handling publicity arrangements on behalf of Mrs Mandela, and that she was clashing with the NRC over the role he was playing. Among other ventures, Guenon was said to be trying to open a press centre which would control all coverage of Mandela's release.

The disloyal were prevented from having access to her husband. Azhur Cachalia, who had helped draft the MDM statement and was a member of NRC, stood close to Mandela at a press conference Mandela gave soon after his arrival in Johannesburg. Later he had a phone call from Winnie. 'Stay away from Mandela,' she threatened Cachalia. 'If you don't you'll see what will happen.' He reported the call to leaders in the ANC, but nothing was ever done about it.

Mandela had been hidden away from public scrutiny for so many years that his legend might easily have diminished on his return to freedom. But he was such a compassionate figure in the early days that, as he grew more real, he became increasingly sympathetic. Stories were told of how he hugged tightly goodbye a white prison officer known as Gregory, who had been his principal jailer for twenty-two years. Of how, in the final stress of leaving prison, he left his spectacles and prepared speech behind, and had to speak at the evening rally from memory. Of how he flinched back when a long microphone was thrust in his face – thinking it might be a weapon. Of how he made time to see his friends, in the midst of the thousands of interview requests that were coming in. And of how in those interviews, he spoke not of bitterness at his long incarceration, but about opportunities for the future of the country.

In the newly re-established marriage of Nelson and Winnie, it soon became clear that, as well as controlling access to her husband, Winnie would not be taking a back seat to him. At the beginning of March, the couple went to Lusaka. Winnie had excluded Murphy Morobe from the delegation, thus ostracising yet another leader who had publicly objected to her behaviour. In Lusaka Mandela spoke to students at the University of Zambia about a need for discipline. They must have self control if they hoped to be future leaders, he said. After his speech, Winnie took the microphone to cheers from the crowd. 'I don't know if I agree totally with the remarks by Deputy President Nelson Mandela,' she said, smiling. 'We shall subject ourselves to discipline as much as possible – for as long as the authorities listen to us.'

Initially, however, the Mandelas had to concentrate more on where they were to start living as a family again than how. Nelson's first night of freedom was spent in Cape Town at Desmond Tutu's house. In Soweto the Mandela's base was 8115 Orlando West. The two-bedroomed house had been rebuilt since the fire, and was now modernised, freshly painted and surrounded by a concrete wall, topped with rolls of razor wire. A green, black and gold ANC flag flew from the roof. In the early days and nights of his release, 8115 Orlando West was surrounded by hundreds of members of the press as well as by ululating and toyi-toyi-ing supporters – making sleep a virtual impossibility. Many old friends were surprised and touched to be telephoned by Nelson in these early days, and asked to come and see him at the house. He was said to have spurned both the mansion now known as 'Winnie's Palace', or the 'Soweto Sun', and the house in Diepkloof-Extension as too elaborate for his needs and too ostentatious in a community as poor as Soweto. It soon became clear, though, that the four-roomed house on Vilakasi Street was no longer big enough for the Mandela family's public and private purposes. Despite Nelson Mandela's reservations, within a couple of months they had moved to the 'palace' round the corner.

Chapter Twelve

Two days before Mandela's release, Winnie had attended a funeral in Dobsonville – the same place where the community meeting to discuss the kidnapping and assault had been held a year earlier. The funeral was attended by hundreds of youths, dressed in the colours of the now unbanned ANC. Accompanied by Zinzi, Winnie herself wore khaki fatigues trimmed in ANC colours. The funeral was marked by the absence of police. This may have been a sign of the new tolerance towards organised ANC activities. It was more likely, however, that the police decided to stay away in a deliberate attempt to distance themselves from the death of the youth. For Clayton Sizwe Sithole, an Umkhonto we Sizwe soldier and boyfriend of Zinzi Mandela – father to her three-month-old son Bambi – had been found hanged in police custody on 30th January 1990.

The circumstances surrounding Sithole's death were extremely suspicious. He was said to have committed suicide four days after his arrest in White City, Soweto. Many deaths allegedly caused by hanging while in detention were often found to have occurred when strangulation techniques used in interrogation had been taken too far. Justice R.J. Goldstone was appointed to a Commission of Inquiry into Sithole's death. He began the inquest on 2nd February and issued his official finding – that Sithole had indeed committed suicide – on 20th February, having held five days of hearings on Johannesburg City Hall. In his report he gave the following official version of Sithole's death:

At the time of Sithole's arrest, 11.45 on Friday 26 January, the police searched his premises, finding a loaded .38 Special, an AK-47, 2 magazines and 27 bullets. Sithole admitted (in front of the owner of the house) that the weapons were his and told the police he had obtained them from a man who lived across the street. The house-owner and the alleged arms dealer were also arrested. Sithole was taken to Protea police station in Soweto where his initial interrogation began ten minutes after his arrival and lasted for about three-quarters of an hour. He was co-operative with the police from the start, confessing straight out to three crimes committed in 1988, one hand grenade attack, one shooting of a State witness and an attack on the home of a policeman. After his forty-five-minute confession, he said he wished to make a statement before a magistrate and at around 2.15 he was taken to the Johannesburg Magistrates' Court where – after being appropriately warned – he made a statement about the three crimes, which he then signed.

Sithole got back to Protea police station at about four o'clock. More interrogation followed. In the evening he was taken to Cell No. 231 at John Vorster Square where – apart from being taken out for further interrogation sessions – he was to remain for the rest of his life. The police officer who admitted Sithole to John Vorster Square testified that Sithole was searched on his arrival and found to have neither shoe laces, nor belt. It subsequently emerged that both his belt and some arm bands he had been wearing round his upper arms had been removed from him in the course of the journey from White City to Protea police station. But no evidence was ever given as to whether his shoe laces had been removed or when or where.

Sithole spent the next day from 6.20 in the morning to 1.15 with the police. For the first three hours he was back at Protea police station answering questions. He then took the police to his home at 43 Mofolo South in Soweto, where more guns and ammunition were seized. Two more hours of interrogation followed before he was returned to his cell for the rest of the day.

On the Sunday, Sithole took two policemen to the scenes of the three crimes he had confessed to. Photographs taken at the scenes clearly showed Sithole wearing shoe laces, although it was unclear whether he was wearing a belt. When he was returned to John Vorster Square he was not searched. He had a routine medical examination the next day, during which the Chief District Surgeon of Johannesburg, Dr E. Krausey, found nothing wrong with him except that his blood pressure level needed to be watched – an apparently common condition on newly arrested detainees.

At 9.46 on Tuesday morning in Protea police station, Sithole made a further confession. He told the police that Winnie and Zinzi Mandela were both guilty of serious criminal conduct. He described the particulars of their criminal conduct until 12.30 p.m., and continued for another hour in the afternoon. The session ended just after two o'clock, and Sithole was told it would resume the next day. Three hours later he was found dead.

At the inquest it was common cause that the death was a suicide. Chris Loxton, the counsel representing the Sithole family under instruction from Kathy Satchwell did not dispute that Sithole had taken his own life. There was no evidence to the contrary, he

227

conceded. No-one disputed the testimony of Constable Powrie, who said that at four o'clock he had taken Sithole to shower room 5 in John Vorster Square for exercise and showering, locked him into the room and returned an hour later to find one shower running and in the adjoining cubicle, Sithole hanging by a belt and shoe laces from a water pipe. The shoe laces were tied so tightly round his neck that two officers could not undo them.

Sithole's confession about Winnie and Zinzi Mandela was made to Sergeant Jan Augustyn, who testified at the inquest that he had not discussed the allegations with anyone because he 'did not think it necessary'. During his sessions with Sithole Augustyn took extensive notes which were never made public. In fact, the police were extremely anxious to keep Winnie's name out of the whole affair. When Loxton applied for Sithole's police docket, the police objected on the grounds that it contained information about police investigations into unnamed 'others'. The only way Loxton and Satchwell could eventually get the docket was to agree to its being given to Justice Goldstone. Goldstone would then decide which of its contents were relevant to the scope of the inquest and pass only those documents on to the Sithole lawyers.

Goldstone decided that Augustyn's notes were relevant and that Satchwell and Loxton could have them. But in his ruling he added, 'I do not consider that it is relevant or in the interests of fairness and justice for the details of these untested allegations to be made public'. Both the police lawyers and the lawyers for the Sitholes agreed to keep Augustyn's notes secret. Sithole's accusations made against Winnie and Zinzi Mandela in the final hours of his life would not be read aloud. The notes were never released.

Another witness testified before the Commission. Phillemon Menziwa – the man who Sithole had said provided his weapons, now also in detention – testified that he saw Sithole just before Sithole was returned to his cell on the afternoon of his death. The two men exchanged a few words and Sithole told Menziwa he had been falsely accused by 'certain people'. Sithole had apparently made a similar comment in the police car returning to John Vorster. 'The people of Orlando West' had given false information about him, he said.

The presence of Sithole's belt and shoe laces in the shower room was never explained. Confusion surrounded their ever being at John Vorster Square police station. But for Sithole to have committed suicide he had to have had the means. He also had to have had a motive. Goldstone came to three conclusions as to why Sithole chose to kill himself. The first was 'his anger and upset that certain people from Orlando West had provided the police with fake information against him'. Sithole felt he had been set up as a scapegoat – for whatever reason – by those he was close to. He felt he had been abandoned by the Mandelas, who had left him to his fate once he had been arrested. The second reason was Sithole's fear of being detained under section 29 of the Internal Security Act 'for a long time', supposedly indefinitely. Goldstone's final reason – that Sithole killed himself because of 'his having implicated people very close to him in criminal conduct, i.e. Winnie and Zinzi Mandela' – was the most intriguing. If Clayton Sithole really did commit suicide, was it due to remorse – or fear?

Jerry Richardson's trial had originally been scheduled for February 1990, when it would have caused considerable political embarrassment by coinciding with the unbanning of the ANC and Nelson Mandela's walk to freedom. The Attorney-General's staff had received the police docket in July 1989 and decided to try Richardson alone and first of all the accused because of the number and severity of the charges against him. He was the only one to be tried for the murder of Stompie and the attempted murder of Lerotodi Ikaneng. In addition, he was charged with four counts of kidnapping and four counts of assault with intent to cause grievous bodily harm, as were Xoliswa Falati and her daughter, Nompumelelo, John Morgan, Jabu Sithole and two other Mandela United members, Mpho Mabelane and Brian Mabuza.

Richardson's trial was moved from the regional court to the Rand Supreme Court – not unusual for a murder trial. Publicly the postponement from February to May 1990 was justified by the change of location rather than any political consideration. Prosecutors did have a political reason for trying Richardson first. They wanted to see how their key witnesses, Kgase, Mono and Mekgwe – the three complainants – would stand up in court. If their testimony was credible enough to get a conviction against Richardson, then charges brought against Winnie, using the same State witnesses in a trial, would presumably result in a conviction too. In a sense, Richardson's trial was a trial run. If successful, a prosecution against Winnie Mandela would be mounted. If not, then the government and the ANC would be spared the scandal of a having Mandela's wife on trial in the early days of negotiating a political settlement.

When the three complainants did testify, their evidence incriminated both Richardson and Winnie in the kidnappings and assaults. Their evidence included details of Winnie telling them they were not fit to be alive, accusing them of sleeping with Paul Verryn, and charging Stompie with being a sell-out. They said that she beat them first, using fists and whips, and that the football team joined in afterwards. Dr Martin Connell gave evidence as to the extent of their injuries and Dr Patricia Klepp testified about the condition of Stompie's body. Stompie's mother, who sat in the public gallery throughout the trial, told the court she had identified her son primarily by recognising his left foot, which turned out slightly and had a birthmark on the sole.

The Reverend Paul Verryn denied sexually abusing those seeking refuge in his house. He spoke of the events of 28 December, when on returning home briefly he was told that Xoliswa Falati had threatened to bring the football team in to discipline the youths in his house. In earlier testimony, Kgase had also described Xoliswa's threats of discipline. In addition, Verryn spoke of the tremendous lengths to which the church and community had gone to get Mono and Mekgwe released from the Mandela house, as did Bishop Storey when he took the stand.

Richardson's trial was not just a rehearsal for the prosecution, it became a rehearsal for the defence – Winnie's defence. Though not on trial, her presence hovered over the court, invisible yet influential. The case was as much about her as about Richardson, sometimes more so. Her name came up again and again, as Richardson's lawyers appeared to be defending her as well as their client. As part of his cross-examination of Kgase, Richardson's counsel, Henti Joubert, made a point of repeating, 'As far as [Richardson] can remember, Mrs Mandela went away that morning of the 29th December and as far as he can remember she only returned the next Monday which was 2nd January.' When Bishop Storey testified, Joubert only asked him two questions. Why hadn't Storey called the police? It was a sensitive matter, Storey replied. 'I presume you are saying it was sensitive because it involved Mrs Mandela?' asked Joubert. 'Yes,' responded Storey. An attempt by Kathy Satchwell to get Winnie to actually come to court to testify on behalf of Richardson resulted in Satchwell taking the stand herself.

On Friday afternoon at the end of the first week of the trial, that is Friday May 4th, I did two things. The first was that in the course of the morning, just before – I think – the tea break, I sent one of my articled clerks to contact Mrs Mandela, to pass the message on that we would want to consult with her and that we would be making a formal approach to her in this regard. Mrs Mandela gave my clerk to understand that her availability was not decided one way or the other, but she was obviously aware of the evidence that had been led in court during that week and she indicated to my clerk a witness whom we could contact and possibly bring to court as a defence witness. The second thing was to phone Ismail Ayob after court on Friday afternoon. Ayob said he would be seeing both Mr and Mrs Mandela on Sunday evening and would discuss it with them. We exchanged home numbers.

But to no avail. Satchwell then wrote to Ayob on 9 May, saying 'it is absolutely essential for preparing and presenting the defence of Mr Richardson that we have the opportunity to consult with Mrs Mandela timeously [sic] with regard to various of these allegations'. In response to her letter, Ayob wrote back, 'We have consulted with Mrs Mandela and had advised her not to make herself available to give evidence in this matter. She has accepted our advice.' Neither the State nor the defence exercised the option to subpoena Mrs Mandela.

The articled clerk sent by Kathy Satchwell to see Winnie was Dali Mpofu, with whom Winnie continued to be heavily involved. At Winnie's suggestion, Mpofu went and found the witness for the defence, and Norah Moahloli, the school teacher from Brandfort, duly came to court. She testified that Winnie had come to stay with her in Brandfort, arriving on the evening of 29 December 1988, staying for a couple of days, visiting the elderly, attending township meetings, discussing how best to revive some of the social work projects which in recent years had lapsed, before returning to Soweto on New Year's Eve. Her testimony had nothing at all to do with Jerry Richardson. It mapped a strategy for a future Mandela defence. For the first time in the seventeen months since the abduction, an alibi had been mentioned.

At this stage, details of the alibi were still confusing. Moahloli's time of Winnie's arrival in Brandfort contradicted Falati's time of her departure from Soweto. (There were hisses from the public gallery as Falati gave evidence about the assaults.) When Richardson testified he made a point of stating categorically that Winnie was indeed absent from her house on 29 December. But he had her absent from Soweto for four days, not two. She left on 29 December, he said, not returning until the day after Stompie's disappearance, Monday 2 January. Henti Joubert emphasised Winnie's alibi by twice asking Richardson if she was away during this time. She was, Richardson said. Joubert also asked Richardson about State evidence that Kgase, Mono and Mekgwe had been viciously assaulted by Winnie, to which Richardson again replied, 'Mrs Mandela was absent the day when I went to fetch them, the 29th.'

Falati told the court that Asvat had been murdered to destroy evidence of sexual molestation against Verryn which she and Mrs Mandela had gathered. When prosecutor Chris Van Vuuren suggested that Asvat had been shot dead in a robbery, Falati said that 'was a vivid lie', adding that Asvat had telephoned Mrs Mandela at 3 o'clock on the day of his murder to discuss the assaults – half an hour before he was gunned down. Under cross-examination, she was also questioned about discrepancies between her version of when the visit to Asvat had taken place and the medical card from Asvat's surgery recording Katiza's visit. Falati's response was that the date on the card had been changed, 'to destroy evidence'. She was sure the visit had taken place on the 29th as Mrs Mandela was not at home on 30 or 31 December.

Speaking through an interpreter Richardson said that Xoliswa had come to tell him that small boys were sleeping with a white man. She needed assistance in dealing with the problem. Richardson had agreed that the boys in question should be fetched and, with John Morgan driving the mini bus, Xoliswa, Nompumelelo, Katiza, Jerry and Mandela United members Slash and Amos went to the house:

Xoliswa is the person who knocked at the door and the door was opened. We entered the house. We found some boys standing next to the stove . . . I did greet them. They responded and I introduced myself to them as Jerry. Xoliswa started by pointing out the people we came to. It was Kenny, Stompie, Thabiso and Pelo. I then told them I was going to leave the place with them, if they do agree. They agreed, they said yes and I said to them we cannot discuss the issue at that place. I told them that the discussion will take place at Mrs Mandela's place and we left . . . We went to the bus and entered into the bus. We started chatting, singing in the bus until at the time of our arrival at the rooms. I told Slash we were going to separate these boys and see whether we can get at the truth. We did separate them. I went along with Kenny . . . I discussed the matter with Kenneth. Kenneth did agree, he told me the allegations were the truth. He said that Paul Verryn sometimes touches his feet in the morning when he wakes up.
Q. His feet?

A. Upper leg, yes. Kenneth was laughing with me. I told him that this is a serious matter. We finished this issues with Kenneth and Slash and the others did also finish their discussion, then we once more rejoined, we came together again . . . I clapped Kenny and hit him with a fist.

Q. Why?

A. Because we were discussing a serious issue and he was laughing. Slash and Moss told me that the other people also agree that this did occur and I was also told that Stompie also agreed that is occurred. Food was brought. We then closed the topic, started eating, our attention was now on the food. Everybody was eating. We finished our plates. I told them, I said to them, gents, we are all going to sleep here. They agreed. We took blankets and put blankets on the floor, then slept.

Later in his testimony, Richardson said that he had in fact punched and slapped all four youths. He was not asked why. Apart from that admission, he denied using violence against any of the four. He testified that Ismail Ayob had come to the Mandela house – again at a time when Winnie was absent – with a message from Nelson Mandela that all the boys on the premises should leave 'his place'. He agreed he had taken Katiza, Pelo and Thabiso to Ayob's office but maintained that on the way they told him they wouldn't stay there, which was why he took them back to Mrs Mandela's. He claimed that when he finally took the boys to Dr Motlana's, it was on the instruction of Mrs Mandela.

Anything that could possibly be interpreted as being harmful to Winnie was denied by Richardson. When questioned about Kgase's escape he said:

A. I woke up in the morning and Kenny had disappeared. We asked each other, that is myself and the boys, we wanted to know where Kenny was. Now we said but Stompie has left and it is Kenny that is leaving. And I said to them, gents, this is amazing me. I am amazed as to what is happening.

Q. Now, Kenny said that he was actually on duty when he ran away?

A. I do not know the duty he was referring to.

Q. He said he was guarding the house?

A. There are no such duties at Mrs Mandela's place.

At one point Joubert asked, 'How do you feel about Mrs Mandela, Mr Richardson?' which prompted the following exchange:

A. I pity her because we talk about her all over.
Q. Why do you pity her?
A. It is like God when we pray.
Q. I do not understand?
A. Whenever one opens a paper, you read about Mrs Mandela. There are allegations. It is being said what she said, whereas it is not the case.
Q. Do you think these things are untrue?
A. Yes, because they must be proved.
Q. I asked you a question and you answered, 'It is like God when we pray.' What do you mean?
A. I wanted to explain when I said about God. The position is we have got to pray for God, but we do not know him.
Q. How is that relevant to Mrs Mandela?
A. The position is, if I do not know her I must not talk about her.
Q. Well, do you know her?
A. I know her presently.
Q. Has she been good to you?
A. Yes.

During the course of his testimony Richardson repeatedly implicated himself, and told a series of evasive and contradictory lies. He categorically denied killing Stompie. He admitted stabbing Ikaneng in the neck – on the spur of the moment to prevent him from drawing attention to the football team. This happened, he said, when members of Mandela United had caught Ikaneng to take him to task for stealing football jerseys from Mrs Mandela's house. Lerotodi Ikaneng had already testified for the State, with his scarred neck still visible, and had corroborated the three complainants' version of what had been done to him in early January 1989. But Richardson maintained that anyone who told a different story from his was not telling the truth. When asked why Kgase, Mono and Mekgwe would tell numerous lies against him, he suggested it might be because he had assaulted them and removed them from the church.

When Joubert came to sum up for Richardson, he admitted his client had lied to protect Mrs Mandela and to prevent her being involved in the matter. 'He is protecting himself, protecting others and protecting himself from others,' Joubert said. 'He is protecting himself from others because if he mentions their names his life won't be worth much.' Joubert told the judge that the three complainants had lied, exaggerating Winnie's presence. Her involvement could not be left out, he said, because the State's whole case fell down if the court found that Winnie had been lied about. Therefore, the court's finding on whether or not she had been present was very important. There could be very serious consequences if she had been there, he added, causing Justice O'Donovan to point out that this trial, 'was not about Mrs Mandela'.

Summing up for the State, Van Vuuren also emphasised the evidence about Winnie. The three 'honest and truthful' State witnesses had no reason to lie about her involvement, he said. 'They testified in court that they feared for their lives, so why would they lie about Mrs Mandela's involvement and by doing so enhance the danger to themselves?' Nothing prevented the Attorney-General from indicting Mrs Mandela with the alleged crimes in the future, he said. No inference should be drawn from the fact that she was as yet uncharged.

On Friday, 24 May a packed Rand Supreme Court heard Justice O'Donovan, flanked by two assessors, pass judgment. In reading a summary of the trial before coming to his verdict, O'Donovan made specific reference to Winnie, commenting on her presence during the beatings and her absence during the trial. 'Mrs Mandela herself, acting on legal advice, declined to testify,' he said. 'This is a matter which was canvassed extensively by both the State and the defence and on which both asked the court to make a finding as to whether Mrs Mandela was present at any time during the assaults. The court finding on this issue is that Mrs Mandela was present on December 29 for at least part of the time.'

O'Donovan accepted the testimony of Kgase, Mono and Mekgwe as credible. Any inconsistencies in their evidence, which the defence had tried to exploit, could be explained by the amount of time between the crime and the trial, the almost kaleidoscopic nature of the scene, and the fact that different witnesses observe different facets of a situation, he said. Richardson, on the other hand, gave evidence containing 'manifest absurdities'. 'The general impression the court gained of the accused in the witness box was unfavourable,' stated O'Donovan before convicting Richardson of four counts of kidnapping, four of assault with intent to cause grievous bodily harm, one count of attempted murder and one count of murder. Sentence was to be passed in early August. The stage had been set.

O'Donovan's finding put considerable pressure on the Attorney-

General's office to indict Winnie on kidnapping and assault charges. Set against this, however, was the overwhelming political pressure to let the whole thing slide. Charging Winnie could be construed as indicting the entire African National Congress in an attempt to weaken the recently unbanned organisation. Nelson Mandela might be a less effective negotiating partner if his wife were on trial for criminal conduct. It might appear strange if Winnie was sent to prison just months after Nelson Mandela's release. There was also the consideration that if Winnie was out of control, and a dangerous law unto herself, the government of South Africa could well be accused of having caused her ruin. 1990 was supposed to have begun a period of conciliation, of optimism about the future. It was not the right time to air voluminous amounts of dirty laundry.

To buy time, State Attorney-General Klaus Von Lieres decided to take advantage of the two-month delay between Richardson's trial and sentencing before taking action. In a statement reacting to O'Donovan's finding he said, 'We will consider the position in the light of the totality of the evidence available. The normal role is that the findings in one case do not carry any weight in a different case.'[1]

Chapter Thirteen

While State prosecutors deliberated how best to proceed in their case against Winnie, and the trial of Jerry Richardson recessed before his sentencing in August, the Mandelas made their first major foreign trip together. In June 1990, after a brief stop in Canada, they began a ten day eight-city tour of the United States.

The Mandelas had resumed married life with difficulty after their twenty-eight years apart. The young woman Nelson Mandela had left was not the middle-aged woman to whom he returned. And she, accustomed to the company of men in their teens and twenties, was uncomfortable around the old man who came back into her life. Although they posed at home for a photographic lay-out in *Drum* magazine – 'Winnie seems to be relishing in the delights of being an ordinary mother and housewife' – they spent little time together.[1] Mandela's schedule of re-establishing the ANC and conducting talks with the government meant he was not often at home. Nor was his wife. In that regard their life together was just as it had been early on in their marriage. It took second place to everything else.

On the first few days of their tour, 750,000 people turned out to see Nelson and Winnie in New York. The Mandelas' American visit drew record crowds and raised unprecedented sums for the African National Congress. Winnie got a warm and enthusiastic welcome, despite recent coverage in the United States of the trial of Jerry Richardson, but it was Mandela who was the real hero of the trip. Whether he was putting on a baseball cap and jacket at Harlem's Yankee stadium before declaring 'I am a Yankee!', addressing a joint session of Congress or speaking to the United Nations General Assembly about the need for continued economic sanctions against the South African government, he drew lengthy cheers and roars of approval.[2]

The couple shared the same itinerary but showed very different public styles. Dressed impeccably in well-cut Western suits, Mandela waved cheerfully and continually, but at times he seemed exhausted and his face, when not wreathed in smiles, looked sombre and weary. His fatigue caused him to call off all engagements on his first night in New York, and to cancel several more appointments as the trip continued. His exhaustion was not surprising: he had left

Johannesburg the day after his discharge from the Park Lane clinic following surgery to remove an inflammatory cyst from his bladder. Winnie, on the other hand, who mainly wore African dress throughout the visit, never seemed tired, though sometimes she looked a little bored at the number and length of the speeches. She rarely waved. Instead, smiling radiantly, especially when called for by name, she raised her clenched fist at the crowd, prefacing and ending her remarks with the call of 'Amandla!' She carried out a few engagements of her own, speaking at a church in Washington D.C. and at the Brooklyn Academy of Music in New York. When she did speak, she kept her remarks brief, thanking the American people for their support and making it possible for South Africans to go the 'last mile towards liberation'.

Her speeches were those of South Africa's Mother of the Nation, heavily interspersed with references to family and children. In New York, she specifically gave thanks that the Americans had not forgotten South African children, and in Atlanta she said, 'We are here, because like every parent . . . since we are walking the last mile towards our freedom, at the end of the day we collect our families and we go back home.' Only once did she raise eyebrows. At a tree-planting ceremony in Harlem, when Mandela planted a tree with soil brought from Soweto, Winnie described the district as the Soweto of America.

Rarely, if ever, was her role as the founder and manager of Mandela United referred to. Her close friend Julie Belafonte, wife of the entertainer and activist Harry Belafonte, summed up the attitude of Americans when she said that no-one attending the tributes in Mrs Mandela's honour ever mentioned her 'troubles' back home. 'We don't know what happened over there,' she said. 'And in any case it's irrelevant in relation to the positive power she has displayed and the pressure she has been under. She's a wonderful role model for women.'[3]

Mrs Belafonte's sentiments were echoed by members of a studio audience when Winnie appeared on the Phil Donahue talk-show in New York. Without exception, those who stood to speak praised her. 'We applaud your visit and we salute your husband. Amandla into the twenty-first century. Free out the people. Free out the world!' said one person. 'You, as a black woman, you have been blessed by God to go through what you have went through,' said another. 'You are really a powerful example to black women, to African American women. really.' 'When I took in you eyes I see pride and love . . . and I thank God for you and I thank God for your husband.'

It was Donahue who, virtually alone among journalists, asked Winnie about the Stompie affair. He led up to the subject by playing an extract of an interview he had conducted with Mandela shortly after his release.

Donahue. Mr Mandela, do you see the upcoming trial of the head of the Winnie Mandela soccer team, following the death of the young adolescent as another government set up?

Nelson Mandela. Well I have no doubt that it is. The way the South African police have conducted themselves in the investigation of the so-called offence has been totally disgraceful. And it is clear that their intention was not to investigate the commission of any crime, but it was partly to destroy the image of the family.

'Do you wish to add anything to that?' Donahue asked Winnie.

'Unfortunately, in terms of the law in South Africa, the case is still going on and I cannot personally comment on it,' she said. 'But as you well know, it was never really a trial of Mr Richardson. The trial itself was conducted by the press, and it was the family that was on trial. If I had been part of that, the natural thing for the government would have been to charge us. I was not given that opportunity to be charged and to clear myself in a court of law.'

'You were not only not charged, you were not called as a witness,' commented Donahue.

'I am not called as a witness, I still look forward to one of those. That's the only way I can explain myself to the public,' replied Winnie.

'No-one remotely suggests that you supported or co-operated in this murder,'

'The South African press did.'

'Well all right. Okay they did,' conceded Donahue.[4]

Cheques written to the African National Congress were tax-deductible, and the Mandelas were able to attract thousands of supporters to a number of fund-raising receptions and dinners in the course of their tour. In New York, the price of eating with Nelson and Winnie was $2,500. In Boston it went up to $5,000. The *New York Times* reported that Eddie Murphy had given $20,000 to the ANC, and Oprah Winfrey $10,000. Other celebrities who were reported to have given money were Spike Lee, Paul Newman, Richard Gere, Robert de Niro and Madonna. A $5,000-a-plate fund-raising event in Los Angeles raised over $1 million. In Florida, where Mandela addressed 6,000 members of the American Federation of State, County and Municipal Employees, union officials announced they had raised almost $300,000 for the ANC. Winnie went shopping at the Victoria Royal showroom on 7th Avenue in New York to buy western-style evening dresses to wear to some of these events. Picking one cocktail suit – black crepe with beaded trim – and two ball gowns, one purple satin, one green satin (price tags $600–$1,000), she so won over the store's president, Alan Sealove, that he pronounced all three gowns a gift.

From the United States the Mandelas went on to Ireland, and then to London for a two-day official visit. The attitude of the British government to Mandela was far less effusive than that of the US Congress – who had given him a lengthy standing ovation – or even the White House, where George Bush had been at pains to praise both Mandela and de Klerk for progress towards a political settlement in South Africa. Mandela arrived in England to outrage over remarks he had made in Dublin about the relationship between the IRA and Westminster. One of his answers at a news conference was interpreted as suggesting that the government should open immediate and unconditional talks with the IRA. While in London, Mandela had to explain his Irish remarks, lay to rest British fears about the ANC's use of violence, and reassure potential government and corporate investors that an investment in South Africa would not be swallowed up by a nationalising ANC. From the point of view of the ANC, the huge front-page story about Mandela's wife that appeared in the review section of the *Sunday Telegraph* just two weeks after his attempts to cultivate the British could not have come at a worse time.

Kenneth Kgase had broken the cardinal rule of a trial witness – he had sold his story. Kgase was a very different character from his fellow complainants. Unlike them, he was not an activist, he had not spent a large part of his life on the run from the police, and he felt no particular allegiance to the ANC. He was a dreamer who wanted to be something more than he was, from somewhere more glamorous than Pretoria. Often, in conversations with friends, he would pretend to be an American, and occasionally spoke in a false American accent. Though unemployed for extended periods, he took a great interest in his personal appearance, and dressed fashionably with a flat-top hair cut. He loved to write and although he had never been published, he continued to produce long, sometimes incoherent pieces of prose. He had, in fact, moved into Paul Verryn's house with the intention of collaborating with Verryn on a gospel play to be performed by the church. Throughout the course of his experience following his kidnapping, he wrote many letters, experimenting with a flowery – sometimes confused – use of English. One of the earliest – dated 23 January 1989 – was to thank Bishop Storey for his intervention in the crisis at Winnie Mandela's house.

> I was very overjoyed to hear that you took it upon yourself, on humanitarian grounds, personal responsibility and saw fit that without the church's bold intervention on issues amongst the many communities involved gradually creating a battlefield, there wont be the right time within a crossfire. Your timing Sir was absolutely perfect, and the boys and I feel so proud of you and everyone in the church for that. You took bravery to advance a wayward person who believes in a person's skin color to determine what ever she may be involved with, that she's a tigress and will never give a second thought to what she may do. You have tamed her. We are prou of you, and so many who were involved.

Kgase was astute enough to realise that he had a hot story to tell, or sell, but feared for his life if his story were to be told or sold in South Africa. With a certain naïveté, he thought that one way of avoiding ramifications at home would be to publish overseas. Overseas publication might bring the added bonus of travel, something for which Kgase longed. He decided that, now the verdict in the Richardson trial was in, and no charges had been brought against Winnie, the time had come for him to talk – or rather write. He had actually been writing for several months, recently completing a vast manuscript of his experiences in the Mandela house.

When he turned up at the office of London *Sunday Telegraph* correspondent Peter Taylor clutching his 500 pages he did not – as Taylor later testified – march in shouting, 'Hey, have I got a story for you!' He was not interested in Taylor's newspaper.[5] Instead he had come to get Taylor's advice on getting his book published in the United Kingdom, having been told by a mutual friend that Taylor had some good British publishing contacts. Taylor had never met Kgase before, and did not immediately realise who he was, when Kgase walked in off the street. But once Kgase began talking, Taylor became interested in what he might have written and asked if he could take the manuscript home to read. Kgase agreed.

As he worked his way through the substantial text, Taylor realised that, muddled in with several streams of consciousness, confused philosophising and political theory, was an incredible story. At his next meeting with Kgase, Taylor said he could get the manuscript published – in his own newspaper. He would edit it heavily and it would appear as a front-page story in the review section of the Sunday edition. Kgase never asked for money. He did, however, get paid for his story at the *Telegraph*'s going freelance rate of £200 per thousand words, receiving just under R6,000 (£1,200) for more than five thousand words. By South African standards it was an astronomical amount – roughly what a staff writer at a major newspaper would take home for two months' work. This would later be used against Kgase.

Taylor later testified that his role as Kgase's editor was to 'tighten his grammar up a bit', while trying to keep the original style. This was no mean feat. Kgase's style was inherently long-winded – English was his second language, Tswana was his first – and he was by no means fluent. He would later be mocked in court for having literary aspirations which transcended his prowess, but in July 1990, with no knowledge of what repercussions lay ahead, Kgase and Taylor worked closely together honing down the text. The final story began with a description of Stompie's life in Paul Verryn's house, continued with an account of the kidnapping and assault, recounted Stompie's sinister disappearance as well as the attack on Ikaneng, and ended with Kgase's escape. It appeared in the 22 July 1990 edition of the *Sunday Telegraph* under Kgase's byline. It was an absolutely sensational article, and it effectively served to demolish Kgase as a witness against Winnie. From then on he could be (and was) portrayed as a self-promoting opportunist. There were a growing number of versions of Kgase's experience in Winnie's house. As well as his evidence in the Richardson trial and his *Sunday Telegraph* story, Kgase gave on-the-record interviews to the Johannesburg *Star*, and *Vanity Fair*. All the articles in which Kgase was quoted later became defence exhibits.

In his *Sunday Telegraph* article Kgase essentially stuck to his testimony from the Richardson trial, though there were descriptive embellishments. 'Mrs Mandela came into the crowded room. Her movements seemed slow and weary, but she seemed to tower over everyone. She had the confidence that comes from power . . .' 'She talked in haughty Zulu.' 'I wondered again about Winnie Mandela, about those savage eyes of hers as she struck you. Being struck by a woman was bad enough, but by Nelson Mandela's wife!'

He also showed some insight as to how his story would be received. 'I knew these things would seem like fiction if told about a woman whom the outside world admired so much.'

Inside South Africa, a copy of the *Sunday Telegraph* story had been faxed to the newsroom of the Johannesburg *Star*. 'When editors read it, their initial intention was to reproduce the article verbatim, but, not wanting to risk infringing *Sunday Telegraph* copyright, they asked the journalist Pat Devereux to interview Kgase, get verification that the information was correct, then write her own version. When Devereux contacted Kgase he was extremely unwilling to co-operate. He feared for his life were his story to appear in South Africa, he told her. He finally and reluctantly agreed to talk when he realised the story would be printed with or without his consent. The *Star*'s article did not differ noticeably from the *Sunday Telegraph*'s, though Kgase was quoted in inverted commas, rather than telling a first person version. Publication of this story in South Africa carried with it the risk of the *Star* being prosecuted for contempt of court. Not only was the Richardson trial technically unfinished pending his sentencing, but seven others had been arrested and awaited trial for the crimes detailed in the article. And even though Winnie might remain unindicted, there was at this time a well-publicised debate going on in the country about prosecuting her, bearing the real possibility she would be charged. No action was taken against the *Star*.

Throughout 1990, the ANC had many more pressing problems to deal with than the legacy of Mandela United. The Congress had to transform itself overnight from an underground and exiled liberation movement into an opposition party – an enormous task after decades of banishment. There were departments to set up, exiled leaders to be repatriated, housed and put to work. A bureaucracy was needed, to be created from scratch. Office space was rented, phones installed, desks and chairs bought, secretaries and administrative assistants hired. Unskilled volunteers would eventually need training and pay. Regional organisations had to be communicated with and enlarged, a massive undertaking as ANC branches in poverty stricken rural areas had no resources. In many cases these local groups, with their own power structures and problems, were in no position to pay heed to the intermittent, distant resolutions which would come their way from Johannesburg. Turf battles were fought between activists who had remained inside the country and those who had been powerful in exile or prison.

At the head and the heart of the ANC was the 35-strong National Executive Committee, with Oliver Tambo as President-General. But the ailing Tambo, who had never fully recovered from a stroke some years earlier, was President in name only. From the time of his release, Mandela, acting as Deputy President, actively ran the ANC. Working down to grassroots levels from the National Executive were regional and branch executives.

Women in the ANC were conscious that although the Congress may have been committed to their right to democratic participation in all decision making (the ANC's constitutional guidelines included a pledge that 'women shall have equal rights in all spheres of public and private life'), the commitment was more one of principle than practice. Early complaints of ANC women members during this period of reconstruction were not unlike the universal grievances of working women. Senior positions existed for women at a functionary level only; women workers were given the 'women's work' of back-up staff, telephoning, typing and making appointments for men. If allowed to be decision makers they were given 'women's issues' such as health, safety, education, housing and sexual harassment, which were regarded as being of secondary importance. At a time when the ANC had so much to organise, any issue less than pressing was completely ignored, or at best given scant resources. Some women who wanted to be part of the mainstream refused to join the women's associations, others refused to learn administrative skills. Those in the Women's League tried hard with what limited assets they had – working at home, using their own money to subsidise their efforts, engaging unpaid volunteers – to build the movement into an influential component of the ANC.

Winnie did not have these problems. In August 1990 she was awarded the powerful portfolio of the ANC's Head of Social Welfare, with the initial task of controlling the return of thousands of exiles. Nominated by her friend and supporter ANC Secretary-General Alfred Nzo, her extremely controversial appointment was ratified by a meeting of the NEC.

Her well-publicised role as the head of Mandela United and her lack of experience led many to feel strongly that she was not the right choice. Though a trained social worker who had in recent years devoted a certain amount of time to providing some members of her community with housing and education when needed, her social work mirrored her activism: she either ignored existing institutions or worked in opposition to them. Operating from the outside, she lacked the requisite knowledge of the structure and dynamics of the welfare sector. She knew little, if anything, of current welfare policy. She had not been involved in recent welfare debates, nor had she been engaged in addressing the needs of the people. The kindest criticism that could be made of her was that she lacked credibility.

In the social welfare sector the offence caused by the appointment was so great that on 28 August 1990 an eight-strong delegation of social workers, psychologists, teachers and administrators went to the NEC to complain. At a meeting with six NEC members, including Alfred Nzo and Walter Sisulu, the social welfare delegation presented a memorandum outlining their 'considerable regret' at the appointment of Winnie. Minutes of this meeting recorded that the delegates desired to understand the process and criterion used in Winnie Mandela's appointment, wished to share their vision of the kind of welfare leader needed, and were there 'to request the NEC to review and rescind their appointment'. The minutes explained the 'notable absence' of blacks in the delegation.

'In essence there is much fear amongst social workers to be present in such a delegation, particularly fear of retribution.' Or as one delegate put it more bluntly later in the meeting: 'We still sit with the fear. Our African colleagues would not come as they fear for their positions and their lives.'[7]

When Nzo came to describe how Winnie had been chosen as head of social welfare, it was clear that the NEC's decision had been less a case of what to do with social welfare than of what to do with Winnie. The irony of putting the needs of a poorly qualified department head over those who would need to use the resources of the department was not lost on the delegation. They were as appalled by the justification as they had been by the appointment.

Nzo conceded that the ANC should in future be more sensitive in recognising the implications of its appointments. With the ANC in such a state of flux, every appointment should be considered as temporary. This prompted one delegate to ask whether the meeting could then issue a joint statement as to the temporary nature of this particular appointment. It could not. There was a need for further consultation. 'As loyal members of the ANC, what position must we take?' asked a social work delegate in exasperation. 'Are we expected to defend something which is indefensible?'

The social work delegation waited for a month before writing a letter asking whether any action had been taken to address their concerns. There was no reply. The concern that welfare would continue to be abused and manipulated under the stewardship of Winnie proved to be well founded when, eight months after her own appointment, she named a deputy with no social work experience whatsoever – Dali Mpofu.

Winnie's appointment as head of Social Welfare sent a message to the government that the ANC held her in high esteem and would protect her. Bringing her into the mainstream and promoting her to a conspicuous leadership position indicated that, now she was a bona fide ANC leader, a charge against her could only be construed as a charge against the entire Congress. Prosecuting her would be interpreted as a political action and would be reacted to as such.

This form of damage control came from Nelson Mandela himself, who personally continued the strategy of depicting the criminal charges against his wife as political. Other ANC leaders and related support groups also took the offensive, assailing the government for its persecution of Mrs Mandela, berating the media for continuing to try to convict her, and insisting that an attack on her was an attack on their leader and their organisation. But no offence could be more than an aggressive defence, as the Mandelas and the ANC remained in the uncomfortable position of having to react to events they could not control.

Jerry Richardson's sentencing had taken place on 8 August, with Winnie featuring as heavily in the evidence submitted in mitigation as she had done in the actual trial. Arguing that extenuating circumstances existed in Richardson's crimes, Henti Joubert called to the stand Midge Doepel, a clinical psychologist who had evaluated Richardson for the defence. She described his dependence on Winnie and testified that his repeated lying in the face of damning evidence could have arisen from his need to protect Mrs Mandela as the source of his self-worth. He seemed to take his cue from her, Doepel added. Prosecutor Chris Van Vuuren took her theory one step further, asking whether Richardson had murdered Stompie to gain Mrs Mandela's approval. Doepel denied this. 'I can't make those jumps,' she said.

Joubert used Doepel's testimony as the basis of his final argument. There was no longer any question of protecting Winnie. Pleading for leniency on behalf of his client, Joubert said that Richardson was a product of his environment, who had had little contact with his parents. He was poorly educated and mildly retarded. In fact the only area where he showed any aptitude was soccer. 'Unfortunately, soccer led him straight to Mrs Mandela's home and the circumstances under which those crimes were committed,' said Joubert. The soccer club, the struggle, Mrs Mandela – these were the things that gave Richardson's life meaning. In such a situation, his client's 'terrible qualities' were 'easily exploited by people involved in the struggle, people like Mrs Mandela', said Joubert, pointing out there was no doubt that Mrs Mandela herself had been involved in the assaults, and had in fact started the whole thing.

Van Vuuren dismissed Joubert's argument, contending that Richardson was a ruthless and merciless killer who, rather than being dependent on Winnie, had shown leadership qualities of his own. Justice O'Donovan believed Van Vuuren and gave Jerry Richardson five years for the four kidnappings, and three for the assaults – with an additional two years for the further assault on Stompie on 31st December. For the attempted murder of Ikaneng, Richardson was sentenced to eight years' imprisonment, and for the murder of Stompie he was sentenced to death.

Also in August, Mandela United member Charles Zwane came to trial, charged with nine counts of murder, eight counts of attempted murder, one count of arson and the unlawful possession of firearms. The charges arose from the firebomb attack on the Chili house, the shooting of the three policeman, and the shebeen massacre. Like Richardson, the twenty-one-year-old Zwane was found guilty on all counts against him and sentenced to death. His counsel, S. Jacobs, argued, as Henti Joubert had, that there were mitigating circumstances surrounding these crimes, notably that Zwane was influenced by the dominant personality of Mrs Mandela. Another similarity between the Zwane and Richardson defences lay in their unsuccessful attempts to consult with reluctant witnesses. In response to allegations that Zwane was a member of the football team, Jacobs had wanted to call Jerry Richardson to testify about Mandela United. He ended up addressing the court about his efforts, just as Kathy Satchwell had before him.

'I have been in touch with [Richardson's] attorney, who is Mr Mpofu of the firm Kathy Satchwell,' he said. 'Mr Mpofu indicated that at the first opportunity he would come and consult with Mr Richardson in the cells at the Supreme Court . . . Mr Mpofu kindly took time off from his work today to consult with him and he told me in chambers today that Mr Richardson does not wish to speak for various reasons, and I certainly don't wish to apply pressure in calling a witness who may be hostile.' The upshot was, Jacobs told the court, that Richardson would not be making an appearance.

It had been Dudu Chili who testified that Zwane was a member of Mandela United. Jacobs questioned her about Winnie's influence:

Q. Did Winnie Mandela really have the power of life and death over these people? If she made a decision to kill, would the people kill?

A. I believe so.

Q. Say, for example, she took a decision that Mr X should be killed – a notional person – and she ordered Mr Y to do it, if Mr Y did not carry out his orders did you think Mr Y would be in danger himself?

A. I should think so because they seem to fear her so much.[8]

On Monday 17 September Charles Zwane was sentenced to death nine times for the nine murders. The next day, Attorney-General Klaus Von Lieres announced that Winnie would be prosecuted on four charges of kidnapping and four charges of assault with intent to cause grievous bodily harm. The decision had finally been made, he said to a group of reporters gathered at an early morning press conference in his chambers, after a careful consideration of all the relevant facts – including, he added, possible implications beyond normal legal ones. Claims and statements in the press had not been an issue, he said, and had not interfered with his duty as Attorney-General to uphold and apply the law to all alike.

Von Lieres pointed out that, while she was in the United States, Mrs Mandela had said she would welcome being charged in the murder of Stompie so that she could defend herself. Referring to her comments on the Phil Donahue show, he told reporters she had complained of being unjustly victimised without having the opportunity to defend herself. Now she could have her day in court, joining the seven other accused already awaiting trial on the same charges. Her name would be added to the court roster as accused number eight.

Adding an eighth name meant that the seven other accused – most of whom had been charged nineteen months earlier – would have to wait a few more months for their day in court. A hearing in the case was scheduled for 24 September in Soweto's Protea Regional Court – less than a week after Winnie's indictment. At the hearing, the eight defendants were told their trial would be remanded to the Rand Supreme Court and postponed until November. There was no question of taking Winnie into custody while she awaited trial, and so all eight accused were granted bail, even though most of the others had previously been held on remand. They would never appear collectively again. In November the Mandela defence asked for more time to prepare. All sides then agreed to the final trial date of 4 February 1991. At his press conference Von Lieres had made a point of stressing that anyone who attempted in any way to interfere with any of his witnesses – either directly or indirectly – would face massive legal consequences. His warning went unheeded. By the following February four of the defendants had disappeared.

Winnie, the two Falatis, Jabu Sithole, Brian Mabuza, Mpho Mabelane and Katiza Chebekhulu, whose name had also been added to the list of accused, were at the Regional Court in Soweto on that day in September. So was an extremely disgruntled John Morgan. Morgan had never been able to understand why he had been charged at all. He complained about the unfairness to the foreign journalist who gave him a lift back into Johannesburg. He shouldn't have been an accused, he was a witness. He felt he had been arrested for what he had seen rather than what he had done.

Alfred Nzo who had become the ANC's spokesman on Winnie, issued a reaction to her indictment, stressing media involvement in creating the public impression that she was guilty. Other than that he was restrained. 'The matter is now in the hands of the courts and as such it would be improper for the ANC to make any comment on the pending judicial process,' he said.[10] Continuing the strategy of presenting Winnie as part of a greater whole, Nzo expressed the unequivocal support of the NEC for its Deputy President Nelson Mandela and his family in their time of stress.

In the weeks following her indictment, Winnie carried on with business as usual, travelling round the country and speaking to enthusiastic supporters as more branches of the ANC were established. Her speeches remained militant, received as well as they had ever been by the youths in the townships. She was still adored by the youth across the country, and had a significant power base among them. It was her militancy – which caused so many of the older leaders in the organisation to shudder – which was her attraction. Her message remained one of confrontation rather than negotiation. In the townships where the only change in black lifestyle since the unbanning of the ANC had been a deterioration, she spoke the right language.

Business as usual included amassing personal support. It was no coincidence that when her case came to court sizable crowds from a number of townships had been bussed in to show solidarity for the Mother of the Nation. Nor did the Winnie Mandela Support Adhoc Committee – whose members included friends, ANC and church members – spring from nowhere. And the ANC Women's League regional branch which Winnie chaired was gearing up to condemn the treatment of their leader. Politically, it was as important to control what would happen outside the court as it was to prepare for the trial itself.

Shortly after the indictment Von Lieres spoke to reporters again to announce that Winnie would not be indicted on any other charges. He referred to the number of general allegations against her and specifically spoke of evidence from two trials held earlier that year. In Sibusiso Chili's trial for the murder of Maxwell Modondo, the court had heard that Winnie Mandela had ordered the murders of Chili and Lerotodi Ikaneng. And in the Seheri case the court had heard that Seheri's Scorpion machine pistol had been stored at Winnie's house. But, von Lieres said, although Winnie's name had come up several times in a number of cases, each time his staff had investigated the allegations they could find nothing. But at the outset of Winnie's trial, Deputy Attorney-General Jan Swanepoel outlined the State's intention of presenting two other kidnapping and assault cases as similar fact evidence against her.[9] Both cases which Swanepoel said would establish her pattern of behaviour – had taken place prior to the Stompie case in 1988 and the police had immediately been informed about them.

The first had occurred in the early hours of 26 September 1988. According to Swanepoel's summary: 'Two persons were taken out of their homes by a group of men. They were taken to 585 Diepkloof in a minibus, in which accused number 8 [Winnie] was a passenger. They were kept in one of the premises, where they were assaulted, inter alia by being lifted up and dropped, and by having a plastic bag pulled over their heads. Accused number 8 was present at some stage during the assaults. They were released the next day.'[11]

The second case was much more serious. On 13 November, four days after the attack on Jerry Richardson's house in which the two Umkhonto we Sizwe terrorists had died, a Sowetan youth called Lolo Sono disappeared. Sono had been friendly with the terrorists, and when they were killed, it was he rather than Richardson who came under suspicion.

On the day his son disappeared, Sono's father was at home. A minibus containing Winnie and members of Mandela United drove up and Winnie got out to speak to him. She told Sono's father that she didn't trust his son any more – that he was a sell-out. Sono's father denied this. His son hadn't had anything to do with what had happened at Jerry Richardson's house, he said. He asked Winnie where Lolo was and she told him he was in the back of the minibus. Lolo Sono was there, badly beaten up, with his eyes already swollen.

He tried to speak to his father, but Winnie told him to shut up. Once Sono's father saw the state he was in, he began pleading with Winnie to let his son go. She refused, saying she would take him with her and the movement could decide what to do. The group then returned to her house where Sono continued to be beaten up. He was not seen again.

It was unclear why Von Lieres chose to say that nothing had been found in other investigations when the State had these two open cases on their books. It was also unclear why the State chose to present these two cases as similar fact evidence, rather than prosecuting them in their own right.[12] It was true that the witnesses in these cases were terrified of retribution if they gave evidence against Winnie and had expressed that fear to the police from the start, saying it was too dangerous to take the stand. This was the reason no charges had been brought in either case. But presenting a case as similar fact meant the witnesses would have to take the stand – just as they would in an ordinary trial.

Knowing that similar fact evidence was very rarely admitted in court. It was also unclear whether Swanepoel ever expected his application to be successful. It may have been that he thought it was more likely to be dismissed at the outset. In fact his application was successful, but for whatever reason he chose not to proceed with presenting the evidence of these two cases.

Chapter Fourteen

Chaos ruled on the steps of the Rand Supreme Court and in the surrounding streets on the morning of 4 February 1991. The crowds had gathered early. Chanting ANC supporters, dressed in black, green and gold, mingled among the light blue and black uniforms of the police. Reporters elbowed their way through, pushing into the courthouse or clambering up step ladders with their cameras. Guard dogs strained at leashes.

Up on the 4th floor, outside courtroom 4E where Winnie would spend most of the next four months, the chaos had subsided into a muted buzz. Members of the State Bureau of Information had taken control of media access to the courtroom, handing out passes to the few accredited journalists. ANC marshals controlled the court space allocated to family and friends, but insisted on inspecting journalists' passes too – much to the annoyance of the police on the door.

Inside court the atmosphere was almost festive, as gathering defendants, lawyers, supporters and journalists chatted and laughed in little groups waiting for the trial to start. In the press benches bets were being taken as to whether the trial would even proceed. But beneath the jollity there was no small measure of unease. Some reporters who were covering the trial had been friendly both with the Mandelas and their lawyers for many years. Some had spent most of their careers supporting the ANC and taking on the State. Now they realised they had somehow changed sides.

Defence lawyers seemed to recognise this. Winnie's senior counsel, George Bizos, who as henchman for the team would be its most vocal and visible member, was particularly aware of the press gallery. While those who approached him for comment were swiftly and smilingly rebutted, he enjoyed the approaches. Representing John Morgan and the Falatis, Kathy Satchwell, who had resolutely stuck to the letter of the law, invoking the *sub judice* rule or attorney client privilege when reporters called her with questions, spoke loudly and clearly to her clients before packed press benches briefing clients and journalists alike.

Behind the press the public benches were filling up. Chris Hani, Alfred Nzo, Joe Slovo, Fatima Meer and other ANC leaders and supporters squeezed in together. If the entrance of the Mandelas raised the level of tension, they were ignorant of it, greeting friends with bear hugs, kissing, smiling and joking as the minutes towards ten o'clock ticked away. Prosecutors Jan Swanepoel and Chris Van Vuuren sat quietly talking together behind a small podium to the right of the Judge's bench. In contrast to their small space, the defence team was spread over two long desks, with lawyers for the Falatis and John Morgan in the front, and Winnie's team taking up the whole of the back table. In addition to George Bizos and Ismail Ayob, Winnie had the highly respected counsel and PAC vice president, Ernest Mosaneke and his articled clerk working on her behalf. ANC lawyer Pius Langa completed her team. Dali Mpofu was in court too, as a lawyer, and sat with the defence. In the early days of the trial, he would sit at the front table with his boss, Kathy Satchwell, and her two advocates, Henti Joubert and Hendrik Kruger. Half way through he would move to the back table of the Mandela defence as his employment as Satchwell's clerk came to an abrupt end. Some would say he was fired when Satchwell became frustrated at his working full-time for a defendant who was not her client. Others claimed he quit before he could be dismissed.

At exactly ten o'clock Justice Michael Stegmann walked into the courtroom. Winnie was composed in the dock, as she placed her handbag carefully at her feet, and waited with her three co-accused as her trial finally began.

There was an immediate adjournment. The State needed until 2.00 p.m. to provide further particulars for the defence and a recess was granted. The unpredictability of proceedings which stopped the moment they started was to be a feature of this trial. Legal arguments about the contents of the charges continued for the next two days, with Stegmann eventually ruling that all the indictments would stand, providing the State elaborated on some of the counts. He gave Swanepoel a week to work on his amendments – the court would reconvene on Monday 11 February.

On the morning of the 11th, the defendants finally got a chance to plead. All pleaded not guilty to everything, with Winnie sounding confident and clear. She had prepared a statement for the court, outlining her defence, which Bizos read aloud for her. She finally claimed to have an alibi.

In essence her defence was that Xoliswa Falati had come to her with Katiza Chebekhulu, who had become mentally disturbed following his abuse by Verryn. On 29 December, the three of them went to see Dr Asvat, who recommended psychiatric treatment for both Verryn and Chebekhulu. Winnie then left for Brandfort, and was away until 31 December. On her return, Falati told her she had brought four other youths to her house to prevent Verryn from frustrating an investigation into his homosexual practices. Winnie believed they were there 'at the instance of Xoliswa Falati in whose care they had been placed'. She did not deprive them of their liberty of movement, nor did she associate with anyone else who might have done so, nor did she commit any assault, nor was any assault committed in her presence, nor did she associate herself in anyway with any assault.

Following Winnie's statement, Swanepoel spoke on behalf of the State. 'At the outset it has to be pointed out that no matter who the accused are, this is not a political trial as far as the State is concerned,' he said. 'The accused are charged with ordinary common law crimes, i.e. kidnapping and assault with intent to do grievous bodily harm.' He went to outline his case, listing his witnesses and exhibits. Then he dropped his bombshell. He would introduce the two other kidnapping cases in which Winnie took part as similar fact evidence, he said. There were gasps in the courtroom as the implications of this development sank in. If the State had other evidence it was prepared to use against Winnie, maybe it was serious about getting a conviction. If the State could prove that Winnie had a pattern of depriving individuals of their liberty, what would that do to the defence claim that in this isolated case these youths were taken without her knowledge, for their own protection?

While spectators ruminated, court adjourned for the 15-minute mid-morning break. On re-convening, Swanepoel had another bombshell – this one even more explosive. He had just been informed, he told the judge, that one of his witnesses had been kidnapped. He had yet to establish whether or not this was true, but if it were, he said it could have an effect on the willingness of other witnesses to testify.

He asked for a recess so that Frederik Dempsey (now promoted to Captain) could investigate the disappearance. Court adjourned until the next morning. Journalists swarmed around Swanepoel clamouring for more information, and he was happy to tell them what he knew. It was Swanepoel who first used the word kidnapping and it was Swanepoel who expressed the fear that the other two witnesses' lives could be in danger if they gave evidence. The witness in question was Pelo Mekgwe, he said. He had been seen being taken away against his will. Why would anyone kidnap him? He thought the answer was obvious. In this fashion, Swanepoel controlled the way Mekgwe's disappearance was reported.

Pelo Mekgwe and Thabiso Mono had gone to their home town of Potchestroom for the weekend, having arranged to meet Paul Verryn and Kenneth Kgase at the Central Methodist Church in Johannesburg at 8.00 p.m. on the Sunday evening before they were due to testify. Afterwards, Kgase, Mono and Mekgwe were to go and stay in Parktown, with Dr Martin Connell's parents. But when Kgase, Verryn and Eugene Klaaren – an American friend of Verryn – got to the Methodist church in Pritchard Street, only Mono was there. He told them he didn't know where Mekgwe was. He hadn't shown up in Potchestroom at four o'clock to come back to Johannesburg, and Mono eventually decided to come back to town without him.

The four waited for Mekgwe for a few minutes, then decided to go and get something to eat. Afterwards Verryn dropped Kgase and Mono at the Connells' house and went home. At home, Kaiser, one of the youths in the manse, was waiting to speak to Verryn. Something had happened, he said. It had begun that morning. Nono Maloi and Saliva Molapisi had come to the house and hung around outside all day asking questions.

Kaiser was talking about two other youths from Potchestroom who had lived in Verryn's house for a year in 1989. Their presence was not in itself necessarily sinister. But then, Kaiser had said, Pelo Mekgwe had turned up unexpectedly in the evening, and said he was going to spend the night at the manse. Just as everyone was getting ready for bed, Nono and Saliva had come inside and told Pelo to get dressed and bring his things. Then the three of them had got into a Mercedes and driven off.

As Kaiser was telling his story to Verryn, there was a knock at the door and Nono came in. He told Verryn they had met with Mekgwe, he had gone with them, but he would be coming back to the mission. Other youths were now swarming all over the house and one of them accused Verryn of not keeping his side of the bargain. They had been assured that testimony in the trial would not harm the ANC, he said. That no longer seemed to be the case. At that point, Verryn lost his temper. 'Fuck off out this house!' he shouted.

Once the youths had left, Verryn called Mono and Kgase, told them what had happened and said that they were in danger. It was now about 11.30 p.m., and he decided to do nothing until the next morning.

Whether Mekgwe had been kidnapped or whether he had agreed to disappear, one thing was clear: the emotional pressure brought to bear upon both Mono and Mekgwe by their friends from the

Potchestroom branch of the ANC Youth League had been intense. The general consensus was that whatever harm Winnie had done to them personally was heavily outweighed by her enormous positive contribution to the struggle. Many also felt that she had been set up by agents of the State to attack the youths, and everyone agreed that her trial would do untold damage to the movement. Mono and Mekgwe should not testify was the feeling among their ANC friends, who included Nono and Saliva. Instead, they should leave the country while they could. Mono told the comrades he couldn't – he had two small daughters who had no-one else to take care of them. Mekgwe, on the other hand, had no such commitments. He could go at any time and he did.

No-one – apart from Nono and Saliva apparently – knew that Mekgwe would be at Paul Verryn's house when he was. Mekgwe, however, aware of the plan to meet and have dinner in town, knew that Verryn would *not* be at home on that Sunday evening. The manse could therefore be used as a meeting place. Members of the Potchestroom Youth League could not get Mekgwe out of the country on their own – they needed help from Johannesburg. Reports surfaced soon after Mekgwe disappeared that Umkhonto we Sizwe commander Tokyo Sexwale had provided the help that was needed. It is an allegation he has denied, claiming in his defence that he could not have been involved as he was not released from prison until June 1990. It is true Sexwale was released in June 1990 – but this was eight months before Mekgwe left the country.

The disappearance of Mekgwe caused an absolute uproar, following as it did on the disappearance of the four defendants. When the Johannesburg *Star* ran an article alleging that a senior ANC official had been one of the men responsible for the disappearance of Mekgwe, it unleashed a stream of editorials attacking the ANC and the Mandelas for interfering with the judicial process. Most opinion pieces looked to the time when the ANC would control that process, and thought this situation boded ill. Ironically, given the preoccupation with the judicial system, the most perceptive response to Mekgwe's disappearance came from Justice Stegmann, who asked in court whether Mekgwe might have had a change of heart and disappeared in circumstances made to look like a kidnapping. The answer to his question came from Swanepoel, who said he had to accept that kidnapping was what had happened. Swanepoel also told the judge that Mono and Kgase were too frightened to testify, and that there was a real possibility the trial might be derailed. But Justice Stegmann, who was fast running out of patience at the confusion in his court, was not going to accept this. He promptly found Mono and Kgase guilty of recalcitrance and ordered them into custody.

He did so against the will of the prosecution. Rather than send them to prison, asked Swanepoel, could they not remain at large while the police searched for Mekgwe? The trial would have to be postponed in any case while that search was conducted. Could the court not wait until the search was completed to see if the witnesses had changed their minds, and then decide what to do with them?

'Your attitude is making it easy for the witnesses to adopt an attitude of recalcitrance,' commented Stegmann, none the less agreeing to postpone the prison sentences.

The trial adjourned until 6 March while the State tried to salvage its case. As court cleared for the three-week break, no-one knew that the delay would prove unnecessary. Mono and Kgase had already changed their minds and decided to testify. They had made their decision as they spent the mid-morning break down in the police cells. They could have come back to take the stand before lunch – but no-one asked them.

During the hiatus, as the police tried to find Mekgwe, one of their first steps was to subpoena journalist Patrick Laurence. It was Laurence who had written the article about a senior ANC member being involved in Mekgwe's kidnapping. When he refused to reveal his source to the police, he too was found guilty of recalcitrance and taken into immediate custody – making him an instant hero. He was released on bail pending appeal after a few hours.

As journalists continued to receive inside information about witnesses and defendants, leaked by those who were reluctant to speak to the police, the relationship between press and protagonists remained uneasy. Senior ANC members, unhappy at the role their organisation was forced to play in this drama, spoke to reporters. Mandela supporters also tried to control press coverage by holding their own press conferences and issuing their own statements. The Winnie Mandela Support Adhoc Committee held a press conference which, they announced, both Nelson and Winnie Mandela would attend. They didn't, but Helen Joseph was helped up on to the stage and a statement of support read out. Even this committee was divided about how unconditional support should be, and a clause had been inserted in the statement reflecting the ambivalence. 'We do not support her because she is involved in the present trial, we support her in spite of that fact.'

Three members of the ANC regional Women's League also held a press conference and issued a statement condemning '. . . The recent spate of specious journalism related to the Winnie Mandela trial.' No attempt to distance the support from the supported was made here. At the bottom of the statement was a list of Winnie's supporters, headed by 'Chair: Winnie Mandela'.

Joan Fubbs, Winnie's deputy on the Women's League, was one of the women who held the press conference. She was also the founder of the Winnie Mandela Support Adhoc Committee. She was asked during the press conference whether she had consulted with Mrs Mandela before holding it. She had not, she replied. Was Mrs Mandela aware it was happening then?

'No, when I say that we did consult, perhaps I should clarify this,' she said. 'I certainly didn't consult in terms of what we would say. However, she was present at our last meeting on Monday as chairperson, and prior to that meeting, members of the committee rang me and suggested it was possibly time to put out some sort of statement and I raised this at the meeting, at which people concurred that we should do something. However, it was not a consultation with Mrs Mandela in terms of consulting in terms of what we would say as an individual, but as a member of the committee per se.'

When the trial resumed and Kenneth Kgase took the stand, the defence was well prepared to wage its war on the media. Bizos had already complained about press coverage in court, saying that Mrs Mandela was being treated unfairly. At one point he asked the judge to order reporters not to report or to speculate on matters outside the court. This Stegmann did. The unfortunate Kgase – with his paper trail of interviews and articles – was the ideal weapon to use against reporters. As he handed in article after article as defence exhibits, Bizos lambasted the press as well as the witness on the stand for inaccuracies, inconsistencies and sensationalism. Doing battle with journalists was a complete turn-around for Bizos and it took its toll. He looked increasingly haggard as the trial progressed, and complained to friends of depression, insomnia and an inability to eat.

Bizos's role in this trial was controversial and sparked much legal debate, especially among his colleagues. It was his job to defend, he couldn't be criticised for his clients. Nor should he have been criticised for carrying out his client's instructions. But he was. He was condemned not only for his attacks on Kgase and Mono, but particularly for those on Paul Verryn. Kenneth Kgase and Thabiso Mono both testified that they had been taken against their will and assaulted. It was Bizos's job to undermine their credibility and suggest that they had left the manse voluntarily and were now lying for Verryn (described by Bizos as the youths' mentor and protector), who was desperate to save his reputation. With the ability and experience to mount an effective offensive, and the intelligence to realise what he was doing, it was not surprising George Bizos was depressed.

Verryn's role in this trial bore a marked similarity to Winnie's in the trial of Jerry Richardson. He was not there, he was never called as a witness, he was not charged with any crime, but his name was continually mentioned, and the trial was as much about his innocence or guilt as that of anyone in the dock. Swanepoel decided not to call him, having decided that Bizos would launch an all-out personal attack on the man's sexual history. Bizos did so anyway, successfully arguing to call male witnesses (including Maxwell Rabolou, whom Verryn had asked to leave the manse for repeatedly staying out without permission[1]) who testified that Verryn had attempted to initiate sex with them as they lay on his bed.

In the absence of an appearence by Verryn the court did not hear his explanation of why Maxwell Rabolou had left his house. Nor did it hear about the meeting at the manse the day before the abduction, when Falati's threats to call in Mandela United had been discussed. Nor did it hear that one of the people contacted for help in getting Mono and Mekgwe released was Bizos himself. The lack of this testimony made it easier for the defence to continue its allegations of abuse. The dubious logic seemed to be that if Verryn was guilty of sexual misconduct then Winnie had to be innocent of the charges against her.

Kgase's three days of cross-examination by Bizos were brutal. Over and over again he was asked about Verryn: his behaviour, his relationships with the youths in his house, his alleged homosexuality. Bizos challenged Kgase on every aspect of his story and ultimately he was able to undermine Kgase as a witness for two reasons. Kgase lied – denying receiving payment for his article in the *Sunday Telegraph* early on his cross-examination – and he had talked too much. He had said enough on the stand and in the papers for Bizos to be able to catch him on the smallest discrepancies. If one detail was missing from a particular version, he was asked why had he 'suppressed' information. If details appeared in one article and not in another he was asked why he had 'fabricated' some of his 'facts'. After three days of this Kgase was worn down. His answers had become a monotone rote of 'I have no answer' and 'I don't remember'. Yet he remained unshakeable in his version of events at the Mandela house on 29 December: the four youths were whipped by Winnie Mandela, who sang while she abused them. She punched and slapped them, while saying they were not fit to be alive. She accused them of being homosexuals and charged Stompie with being a sell-out. And finally there was an all-out prolonged assault by the entire football team.

During Bizos's cross-examination of Kgase, Winnie became actively involved in her defence. She wrote questions and notes which she sent to her lawyers via a courtroom guard, and spent recesses poring over documents and discussing evidence. Earlier she had sat stony-faced and unnervingly upright and still while Kgase gave his evidence-in-chief. She kept her eyes fixed unblinkingly on his face, occasionally re-directing her glance towards the judge's bench, while Kgase tried – not always successfully – to avoid the unrelenting pair of eyes in the dock.

Unlike Kgase, Thabiso Mono had been cautious and spoken to no-one. His testimony corroborated Kgase's in every major material aspect. Having been questioned by the police on several different occasions while in detention as a teenager, Mono was skilled in the art of evasive answering. He used his experience to block any attack from Bizos. He also exercised an option Kgase had chosen to ignore. In South African courts, black Africans were able to testify through an interpreter in their native tongue. Witnesses able to understand English who spoke through an interpreter had twice as long to consider each answer. Mono, whose English comprehension was perfectly reasonable, was thus able to hear Bizos's question in English, ponder it while it was translated, reply, and while his answer was being translated back into English, have a brief interval to collect himself before the next question. Translation also diminished the effectiveness of sarcasm, shouting and interruptions. Exchanges between lawyer and witness could be little more than literal interpretations of language.

The combination of Mono's unco-operative attitude and the delay of his translations made him a frustrating witness, particularly when Bizos tried to establish lines of questioning. When he asked Mono whether Verryn had tried to influence his story, immediately after his release from the Mandela house in early 1989, Mono made him work for each answer.

Q. How often did you see the Reverend Paul Verryn?

A. We saw him at the meeting and the morning he took us to the doctor.

Q. Didn't he visit you where you were living?

A. I don't understand.

Q. Did he visit you between the meeting and the time you went to the doctor?

A. I only remember him coming in the morning the time he took us to the doctor.

Q. Did you ask him what had happened to Kgase?

A. I did not ask him.

Q. On any of the occasions when you saw Paul Verryn before you went to the doctor, did you ask him what had happened to Kgase?

A. I did not ask him because I did not meet with him before I went to the doctor.

Q. Did you on either of the two occasions when you admit seeing him, ask him what had happened to Kgase?

A. Yes I did ask him, on the time when he took us to the doctor.

Q. Why do we have to struggle to get out such a simple answer! Are you reluctant to be completely open about discussions you had with Paul Verryn?

A. What discussions are you talking about?

Following the evidence of the two complainants (Mono had spent a total of two and a half days on the stand, less than half the time of Kgase), Bishop Storey was sworn in. The change in attitude as this new witness prepared to give evidence was remarkable. Storey was highly respected by all sides in court – the esteem in which he was held matched the deference with which he was treated. The deference was all the more marked by its previous absence from the courtroom. But the transformation provoked by Storey's appearance went beyond the manner in which he was addressed. As he stood ramrod straight, swearing his oath with authority and conviction, Storey appeared as a *deus-ex-machina*, a soldier of God, restoring sanity and order to the proceedings.

Gone was the intimidation and gone was the hectoring. As he calmly spoke of meetings and phone calls between community and church leaders, Storey dispelled much of the tension in the court. He was paternal, reassuring, resolute and entirely credible. With kidnapping legally involving the continued deprivation of liberty, Storey was crucial to the prosecution. No alibi was claimed by Winnie for the entire first half of January, and with Storey describing the enormous efforts that had been made to persuade her to let the boys go, it was clear to the court that she had known they had not been in her house voluntarily. The quality of Storey's evidence made it much harder for the defence to say Winnie had been unaware of what had transpired in her absence.

Meanwhile Winnie had to prove she had actually been absent. Witnesses had already been lined up in Brandfort to say she was there on the night in question. Anyone in Brandfort who felt she had not been there was now too afraid to come forward. Of those besides Kgase and Mono who had given statements to the police saying she was actually at her house, three were now missing – which left only John Morgan.

Morgan's statement to the police from February 1989 placed Winnie firmly at the scene. He said that before the group beating began he saw her slap Stompie, asking him, 'Such a little person, do you also sleep with Paul Verryn and let him fuck you up your arse?' His statement also quoted her as saying, 'This thing speaks shit,' when Stompie denied having sex with Verryn. Midway through the trial, however, Morgan was denying both the veracity and the admissibility of his statement. It had been tortured out of him by the police in an attempt to get Mrs Mandela, he testified, and tried to have it thrown out of court. The truth was, Morgan now said, Mrs Mandela hadn't been at home on 29 December, she was in Brandfort.

When Justice Stegmann ruled that Morgan's claims of police torture lacked credibility, that he had made his statement freely and voluntarily and that it was therefore admissible, Morgan refused to take the stand. His refusal to testify did not particularly help or hinder his own case, which was fairly cut and dried. The State already had corroborating evidence that he had been the driver of the minibus – thus his being a party to the kidnapping was easy to prove. The assault charge against him was tenuous at best. No-one had actually accused Morgan of participating in the assaults, though there was testimony that he had watched. However, Morgan's refusal to testify was of great benefit to Winnie and Xoliswa Falati. Allegations about them in his statement were effectively rendered inadmissible.

The crowds had dwindled as the defence began to present its case. ANC marshals and Bureau of Information personnel were long gone – as was Nelson Mandela. He was out of town on holiday, spending two weeks of a long-planned month hunting on safari at the Mthethomusha Game Reserve. Only a handful of reporters were present as Xoliswa Falati took the stand and even they began staying away as her rambling testimony dragged on for days. She told the court that Verryn had raped children in his house. Some had consensual sex with him, she added, others abused each other. All four of those said to have been kidnapped had admitted to having homosexual relations of some kind. Kgase, Mono and Mekgwe had each slept with Verryn, she claimed, and Mono and Mekgwe had spent one night caressing Stompie, after which Stompie slept with a knife for self protection.

Through all this bizarre activity Falati described herself as a kindly, concerned housemother. She went to see Winnie, she said, after Chebekhulu had been raped by Verryn. 'She is a social worker as well as a community leader,' Falati explained. Winnie seemed to know of Verryn's reputation already, she said, exclaiming 'How is this Reverend still doing these things?' when told of the rape. She and Winnie took Chebekhulu to see Dr Asvat who told them after examining the youth that Verryn was mentally sick and needed treatment. Winnie then left for Brandfort. It was Falati who took the four youths to the Mandela house, 'So that this issue of Paul Verryn sleeping with young kids could be attended to,' but she did not assault them.

Like some interminable supporting act before the main performance, Falati went on and on before relinquishing her moment in the spotlight. 'As I am thinking, I realise there are many things I have forgotten,' she said on her second day of testifying. And so she continued for another two, denigrating Verryn and praising her friend and leader who was waiting to take the stand. It was clear that she strongly identified with and took her cue from Winnie. In his judgment, Stegmann said, 'The issues in this trial are not directly related to the political tensions and confrontations in this country, but the political position inevitably forms a general background against which the relevant events occurred. However, Miss Falati was not prepared to leave background in the background, with some determination she created various opportunities to represent herself as a political activist of some consequence [with] a tacit implication that she has been prosecuted in these proceedings on that account.'[2]

Finally, she finished. Two and a half months into the trial Winnie was sworn in. As Bizos waited to question his client, it could have been just like the old days. Only this time she wasn't charged with violating a banning order or distributing communist literature. And this time she wasn't defiant – at least not outwardly. Instead, elegantly dressed in a cream suit, she was sedate and respectable as she sat down.

Yet, just sitting down sent its own quiet message of defiance in a court where other witnesses had been told to stand while testifying.

Bizos's initial line of questioning sent another such message. Opening with 'You are the wife of the Deputy President of the African National Congress?', he immediately established the position of the Mandela defence that this was a political trial. He asked Winnie what year Mandela was imprisoned, when he had been released, whether she herself was a member of the ANC, when and under what circumstances she had gone to Brandfort, whether she had been house-arrested there, whether she had been under heavy surveillance there, whether she had been able to form any associations with the people there.

If Bizos was trying to remind the court of the political context of this trial. Judge Stegmann remained obtuse. 'You used the term that you were exiled there in 1977,' he asked Winnie as she was talking of Brandfort. 'This was not the home from which you originally came or anything of that sort?'

'I had had no previous contact,' she replied.

Composed as she outlined her alibi, she said she had left Soweto between 6.30 and 7.00 p.m. on 29 December, arriving in Brandfort some time after ten. She spoke of her outrage when she first learned of the false allegations against her and denied any involvement in or knowledge of assaults or kidnapping. She told the court she had first been informed of the kidnapping and assault allegations against her during a visit to her house by leading members of the Soweto community – known as the Crisis Committee – after Kgase's escape. She said she was so infuriated that she told the committee that they could go to the back rooms and speak to the children themselves, or take them to a venue of their choice and speak to them there. Instead of going to see the youths herself, she kept away from the back rooms, deciding not to have anything whatsoever to do with the people staying back there. She had sent Ismail Ayob to tell her husband of the allegations and Ayob brought back a message saying that her husband fully agreed with her attitude. She did say her husband had recommended that all the youths in the back rooms should be made to leave. Even then, she said, she refused to get involved and asked Ayob to take steps to ensure the youths left.

'Details of how they were removed from the house had absolutely nothing to do with me,' she said.

Sparks flew on her second day on the witness stand when a feisty Swanepoel began an aggressive cross-examination. Why, he immediately asked, had Winnie never told anyone she was in Brandfort, two hundred kilometres away from her house, on the night of the alleged abduction until she came to court? Why hadn't she given her alibi to those who first came to her with the allegations, to the police when she was first interviewed or to the magistrate who committed her to trial?

'Surely the easiest way to clear it up would have been to say, "I was not in Johannesburg at the time so I could not have done it"?'

The allegations were so absurd she didn't need to give an alibi, said Winnie. And she was advised by her attorneys to keep a dignified silence.

'But you did not maintain that, did you – the silence I mean, not the dignity,' said Swanepoel as the court broke into laughter. 'You didn't keep silent, you spoke to various members of the media.'

So why, when giving an interview to Dutch television especially to clear her name, hadn't she mentioned she was in Brandfort?

'My answers were to his questions,' replied Winnie as she folded her arms tightly across her chest. 'It may not have arisen where I was. If he had specifically asked where we were we would have had no problem. [He] did not ask me if I was in Brandfort.'

'He could not have known.'

Moving on to Verryn, Swanepoel put it to Winnie that sexual misbehaviour had nothing to do with her defence. 'Sexual misbehaviour by Paul Verryn brought us to this court,' she said. 'If there hadn't been a problem with Paul Verryn I would not be in court.' She agreed that if the allegations of sexual misconduct were true, they did not justify assault, and admitted that she had never approached Verryn to give him a chance to put his side of the story to her.

Besides outlining her case, Winnie's three days of testimony provided a rare insight into her life and how she saw herself. She often spoke of herself autocratically and in the third person. At the same time she took pains to stress that she had arrived at her position of authority in Soweto democratically. As a community leader and social worker, many felt able to come to her with problems, she said. She preferred that people be brought to her rather than visiting them herself and often summoned individuals to her house or office, though when she did travel by car, she was usually driven – the job being shared by a number of people.

She was occasionally made angry by Swanepoel but she never lost control. Instead she became sullen and terse as he shouted. If she couldn't explain a discrepancy, she said so. When, for example, Swanepoel pointed out that her claim to have been driven to Brandfort clashed with Morgan's statement to police that he had used the minibus to drive the Falatis home on the night in question she said she 'had no idea' how to explain the contradiction.

Describing Winnie in his judgment, Stegmann said, 'Mrs Mandela is not of a shy or retiring nature. She is a mature woman, evidently experienced in the ways of the world, and very much in command of herself. Throughout the period of nearly five days that she spent in the witness box she maintained her dignity and self possession. She kept a pleasant expression on her face throughout, and generally maintained a reasonable tone of voice. She did not allow the expression on her face, or the tone of her voice, or any body language, to betray her feelings about the matters to which she testified. She was in fact poker-faced.'[3]

Swanepoel was thorough in the areas he covered, but he left many alone. He did not ask Winnie why, if she thought Paul Verryn to be such an abuser, she had continued to send youths to be housed by him. Nor did he press her on the contents of her alibi.

Winnie's alibi came to be a source of contention between the police and the Attorney-General's office. After the trial each blamed the other for a less than thorough job in investigating it. The Security Police in Bloemfontein knew that a local ANC leader in Brandfort had been contacted to arrange an alibi for Winnie. They had been told by an informer, who had also been contacted, that an alibi was being constructed. The identity of the person who contacted residents of Brandfort was known to them. To counteract it, they said they had a statement from a community leader swearing that Winnie had not been in Brandfort in December. They claimed to have a log-book of dates of community meetings which recorded no meeting for the date Winnie said she attended one. They said they passed all this information up to Johannesburg.

Few cars drove along the dusty track that led into the township and the township police were aware of each one that did. The police station was situated right at the township's entrance – every car and most people that passed it were noticed. The township police knew Winnie had not been there on 29 December. They too said they had passed their information up to Johannesburg. Whenever Winnie had come to Brandfort in the past the South African Police had been phoned ahead and alerted to her arrival by Security Police officers in Johannesburg who kept her under surveillance. They were not alerted to her arrival at the end of December 1988, because she didn't come.[4]

The Attorney-General's staff were not detectives. They received their information from the police. If they had questions, the police were instructed to find answers. They did not deal directly with the Security Police in this case, but briefed the investigating officer, Captain Dempsey, who liaised with the Security Branch as and when necessary. Whatever information Dempsey received from any branch of the police force he passed on to the prosecutors. Yet Swanepoel later maintained he was frustrated at the quality of police work, that he was not given the wherewithal to disprove Winnie's alibi effectively, that he was never presented with any evidence of Winnie definitely being in one place as opposed to the other. If he had possessed such evidence he would have used it. That was precisely the evidence he was looking for.[5]

Calling Security Police to testify that they knew Winnie was in Johannesburg rather than Brandfort because they kept her under surveillance would have added the political element the State was anxious to avoid. Calling Paul Verryn would have added an embarrassing sexual element the State claimed it was anxious for him to avoid. Calling Albertina Sisulu would have added an element of embarrassment to the ANC that the State had no reason to want to avoid. Albertina could have demolished Winnie's alibi had she testified. She could have identified Dr Asvat's handwriting on Chebekhulu's medical card.[6] She could also have identified her own handwriting in the surgery's record book, listing Katiza Chebekhulu as a patient on 30 December. She could presumably have said that Winnie was in Soweto on 30 December. But she was never called. Winnie never denied taking Chebekhulu to the surgery, she only disputed the date. Swanepoel did contact Albertina's lawyer, Priscilla Jana, to ask what her attitude to testifying was. Jana said Albertina wasn't prepared to, whereupon Swanepoel said he wouldn't pursue it – to Jana's surprise. She half expected her client to be subpoenaed, but she wasn't and Jana got the feeling Swanepoel didn't want to call her in.[6]

Swanepoel later said that the reason neither Albertina Sisulu nor any of the members of the Crisis Committee were called to appear for the State was because they would only have appeared under subpoena as hostile witnesses. That may have been the case, but the State only needed Albertina Sisulu to identify the record book and the medical card from Asvat's surgery. Two questions – then she could have been dismissed. The book and card would have been entered as exhibits, and the judge would have had two further pieces of evidence to consider when judging the veracity of Winnie's alibi. Swanpoel did produce the card at one point. When questioning Winnie, he gave her the card and asked if she recognised it. She said she did not, so he put it to one side.

Thabo Motau, a seventeen-year-old boy who lived opposite the

Mandela house in Orlando West, testified that he had driven Winnie (whom he described as his benefactor) to Brandfort on 29 December. Norah Moahloli came back up from Brandfort to testify that Winnie had indeed been with her then. Their testimony led Justice Stegmann to consider it 'reasonably possibly true' that Winnie had left her house by seven o'clock on 29 December and was therefore not at home when the assaults took place.

Stegmann found Winnie's vagueness disturbing. 'She showed herself on a number of occasions to be a calm, composed, deliberate and unblushing liar,' he said. 'She gave her evidence in a manner which impressed me with her wariness, her unwillingness to commit herself to anything clear-cut or definite, and in short, with a remarkable absence of candor.' She went to extraordinary lengths to distance herself from the soccer team bearing her name. 'It is odd to encounter a leader who went to as much trouble as Mrs Mandela to distance herself from the club which adopted her name and many of those members lived in her own backyard.

'Her suggestion that these previously disorganised youths and youngsters had only to hear the words "formalise your games" from her in order to establish a team; to find sponsors; to have their uniform tracksuits made; to find themselves a coach; and generally to show the organisational skills, determination and effectiveness that they previously lacked, seems to me to bear so little relationship to the practical realities of organising the activities of young people who have shown no inclination to organise themselves that I can only conclude that she did not wish to reveal the whole truth about it.' But he added, 'What there is about it that she chose to conceal, the evidence did not disclose conclusively.' Later he said, 'In the nature of things, less creditable motives tend to remain hidden.'

What Stegmann was able to accept as an undoubted fact, was 'the existence of a campaign to discredit Mr Verryn by the spreading of allegations of homosexual conduct on his part'. While not ruling on any factual basis for this campaign – Verryn was of course entitled to the presumption of innocence – Stegmann said he had come across more than one malicious campaign to discredit a minister of religion on pretexts put forward to conceal the true motive, and would keep his previous experience in mind when ruling on this case. It may have been that there was an ambitious person or group who wanted Verryn replaced as minister. Whether related or not, Stegmann said it was his impression that 'Youth X had been prevailed upon to allow himself to be used as a puppet in these proceedings.'

Stegmann found that Winnie had authorised the kidnapping but that she was not at home for the assault. However, by continuing to hold the four captive and to give accommodation to those who had committed the assault, she associated herself with the crime. In effect she was an accessory after the fact. Sentencing her to five years for the four counts of kidnapping and an additional year for her role as accessory in the assault, he said, 'Your position of leadership was not something which entitled you to play fast and loose with the liberties of others to serve your own purposes. You fundamentally misunderstood or ignored the responsibilities which came with your position as leader. In this case one of the worst features was your complete absence of compassion towards the victims of the assaults, suffering in your own backyard, just outside your window.'

John Morgan was found guilty of kidnapping and acquitted of assault. He received a sentence of one year's imprisonment suspended for five years. Xoliswa Falati, who was found guilty of all the charges against her, received the same sentence as Winnie. Her six years were broken down into four for kidnapping and two for assault.

Nelson Mandela was in court as the verdict was handed down against his wife. He looked drained, old and ill. Friends who saw him later in the day were concerned for him. But when asked how he was, Mandela dismissed their enquiries. He said he was fine and refused to discuss what had happened. In comparison, Winnie looked radiant and defiant as she left court with her raised fist clenched. She seemed to think she had been exonerated by the trial. Accentuating the positive as she left court, she said, 'I want you all to know that I did not assault any child. The rest I leave to my attorneys.'

Chapter Fifteen

Winnie was released on R200 (£40) bail pending her application to appeal. Bail had been paid by Dali Mpofu. She seemed to regard the entire affair as over. Immediately resuming her political activities, it was barely a week before she was arrested again. This time she was charged with blocking traffic in the middle of Johannesburg. She was arrested in the morning, charged, released on bail and re-arrested for the same offence in the afternoon. Traffic came to a standstill as, accompanied by a group of a dozen or so women, Winnie read out a statement attacking the government for reneging on its promise to release political prisoners. It wasn't long before a crowd surrounded her – mainly police. Five of them dragged her to a police vehicle as she loudly denounced their 'terrorist' attack on 'innocent women'. Her action made it clear she would remain impossible to ignore.

Continuing to portray her trial as 'the trial of the ANC; that ANC symbolised in Mandela', she gave an interview to *Tribute* – a magazine with a largely black readership. 'You can imagine the irony of it all,' she said. 'The murderers of my people, trying me for a so-called indirect murder. I had nothing to do with Stompie's death.' Her 'own people' had put her on trial too, she said, an aspect of the case that had made her 'very hurt at the beginning'. Then she spoke of Verryn.

'I could not believe that a minister of religion entrusted with children's lives would abuse them. Children who could not make any other choices but depend on him. What kind of beast is this? Who wears a collar on Sunday, and goes to preach to parents of these children, and preaches the word of God even to some of these children? At night he becomes something else.'

She still saw him as the guilty party. It was Verryn who was the abuser, who violated the trust of children; a symbol of a greater good whose reality 'stinks of such filth'. She, on the other hand, continued to provide a place of refuge for the children who came to her, some of whom 'truly have nowhere to go'. She, as a mother and as a social worker, advocated restoring society to its morality and dealing with the bread and butter issues that faced the children. She had done nothing wrong – nothing she would not do 'a hundred times more'. It was conceivable that she occasionally thought about one of those children. But in answer to the question, 'Do you ever think about

Stompie?' she said, 'Unfortunately I do not even know the child. In retrospect I would have loved to speak to the child. I would have loved to give him the warmth he seemed never to have had. I would have liked to speak to his mother; to help him.' Stompie's mother would have liked to speak to her too: setting aside any question of innocent or guilt, she said in an interview, 'If anything happens to anyone staying at my house I am bound to explain to their next-of-kin what happened. It is in that vein that I expected Mrs Mandela to come and tell me what happened to my son while he stayed at her house. As Stompie's mother I deserved to know.'

Winnie seemed to have no understanding that her past actions could have consequences. To a certain extent they didn't. Attending the ANC's national conference in Durban in July, she was elected with a respectable vote to the National Executive Committee, while her husband finally became the organisation's president. Earlier in the year, while her trial was still under way, she had canvassed heavily to be elected President of the Women's League. She was defeated, but only as a result of direct intervention by Albertina Sisulu, who was also standing. Albertina was so worried at the prospect of a Women's League headed by Winnie that she withdrew her own name from consideration and gave her votes to a third candidate, Gertrude Shope, who thus won the election.

Both Mandelas were struggling to maintain power. Nelson was facing an onslaught of criticism from the ANC, not just on account of his persistent support and promotion of his wife but also because, in the two years since his release, he had been found to have his own feet of clay. He too was autocratic. He expected his decisions to be final and respected. He listened to those who had his ear, but only a few had access to Mandela, and many were ignored. In particular he was felt to be out of touch with his wife's core constituents, those in the townships who were exasperated by the length of time it was taking to improve their standard of living.

In August, while the Mandelas were out of the country on a trip to Cuba, in Winnie was relieved of her post as head of the ANC's social welfare department. In Nelson Mandela's absence a form of coup took place which undermined his authority and set the pattern of future leadership. The Mandela intimates Thabo Mbkei and Jacob Zuma were ousted from the negotiating team, to be replaced by Cyril Ramaphosa, Joe Slovo and Mohammed Valli Moosa. Winnie was replaced by Cheryl Carolus. Mandela was outraged. On his return he insisted that Winnie be reinstated. It was more important to him that his leadership (and therefore his wife's position) be respected than his organisation's social welfare department have a competent head. He ignored the fact that Winnie's effectiveness had been undermined by her conviction. He ignored reports that the department was in chaos under her rule. He ignored the protests of many who felt she was incompetent and he asserted his own authority by giving Winnie her position back.

In fact, said a statement issued by the ANC, Winnie was not reinstated – she had never lost the job. 'It is the channel of accountability and responsibility that has been streamlined.' Winnie was the department head, Carolus carried the portfolio. As a compromise, Social Welfare was brought under the authority of the ANC's treasury department. In theory, Winnie had lost complete autonomy since she was now accountable to both Carolus – head of all ANC human resources and health departments – and Thomas Nkobi, the ANC's treasurer-general.

To make matters more complicated, stories began appearing about Winnie's relationship with her deputy head. Dali Mpofu dismissed articles which claimed he was romantically involved with his boss, but in June Terry Oakley-Smith was reported to have given lawyers a statement alleging continued harassment from Winnie and saying she had received another death threat. Then Winnie and Mpofu travelled to the United States together, apparently spending a fortune on plane tickets and hotel rooms – much to Mandela's fury. Reportedly the final straw came during a trip which Mandela didn't know about. When Winnie made another expensive trip to America accompanied by Mpofu, Mandela finally moved out.

He stayed at more than one house. Leaving Soweto for Johannesburg's northern suburbs, he kept his departure from home secret. The official line was that he had moved for secruity reasons, following a right-wing plot to kill him. No-one was fooled. Reporters were initially kept quiet by pleas from the ANC to protect Mandela's safety. It emerged in January 1992 that he was living at the home of one of South Africa's richest Afrikaaners, millionaire insurance executive Douw Steyn, and had not been at home in Soweto for nearly two months.

The fact that the Mandelas were now married in name only did not create too much of a ruckus. They had led separate lives for so long, it was hardly surprising that they chose to do so now. Conceivably they could have continued in this way indefinitely had not Winnie – whose status as Mandela's wife was considerable – attacked Xoliswa Falati shortly before Easter.

According to Falati, the trouble had begun a week earlier when Falati was summoned to the ANC offices in Johannesburg. On her arrival, Ismail Ayob told her to go to see her own lawyer, Kathy Satchwell. When Falati got to Satchwell's office, Satchwell told her that as there was no longer any money to pay for Falati's appeal; she was withdrawing as her attorney. IDAF was no longer in a position to pay Satchwell's fees and Satchwell could not afford to represent Falati for nothing. As it was, Satchwell didn't even have the money to pay for a record of the trial, let alone hire an advocate and provide transport to the Appeal Court in Bloemfontein. Therefore, unless Falati could find some alternate method of fund-raising, Satchwell told her, she would have no option but to serve her sentence. Time was running out too. Heads of argument for the appeal had to be filed by 30 April, giving Xoliswa Falati four weeks to raise R70,000 (£14,000).

This news came as a tremendous shock to Falati, who had assumed the Mandelas would automatically ensure she was adequately represented. For some reason she was also under the impression that Libya had donated one million rand to pay for the trial. It had never occurred to her that the money for her defence might become her own problem. Satchwell – who knew nothing of any Libyan money – suggested Falati contact Nelson Mandela for help, which Falati did that same day. Mandela immediately reassured her that he would take care of the problem.

The following day, Falati got an abrupt call from Winnie who told her to get out of the room she had been living in. The family needed it back, Winnie said. Falati again called Nelson Mandela for help, and again managed to speak to him directly and at short notice. She told him that Winnie had said she must move out and asked him what she should do. Ignore Winnie, was Mandela's answer, and stay put. But it wasn't to be so simple. That night Winnie came bursting into her room brandishing a gun and shouting at her to get out. As Falati fled outside in her nightdress Winnie began hurling her belongings into the street, screaming that Falati would go to prison. When Falati disclosed that she had spoken to Mandela himself and had been told by him that she could continue to stay in the room, Winnie became even more incensed. 'Who do you think you are? Who are you to speak to the President?' she demanded.[1] Locking Falati out, she stormed off.

Falati went to a neighbour's house where she made two calls. One – her third in two days – was to Mandela, and the other was to

The Sowetan newspaper. In both calls she described what had just happened. *The Sowetan* immediately sent a reporter, Ruth Bhengu, over to the house, who found a tearful Falati standing in the yard. 'I can't believe she is dumping me after all I have done for her,' cried Falati. Winnie was ungrateful and socially irresponsible for throwing her out of her house without any reason, she said.

Bhengu had brought a photographer with her. She sent Falati to have her picture taken against the house she had just been thrown out of while she waited at the neighbour's house. When some time had elapsed and the two hadn't returned, Bhengu went off to see what was happening. She found an embarrassed Nelson Mandela had arrived on the scene to arrange for a locksmith to open the door to the back room for Falati. He had also asked Falati not to talk to reporters and told the photographer not to take pictures. Bhengu was irritated at Mandela's high-handed interference, remaining unimpressed when Mandela said that although he believed in a vigorous free press he would rather Bhengu did not write this particular story. It would cause trouble, he said. Bhengu replied that it was not her responsibility to decide what was or wasn't printed, she was merely on an assignment. Mandela then changed the subject, saying that the ANC was going to start newspapers and television stations, which would need responsible black journalists who had the interests of the struggle at heart. What had Winnie throwing Falati out got to do with the interests of the struggle he asked. Bhengu replied she was not in a position to change what had happened and went back to the office.

On her arrival, she discovered that Mandela had already been on the phone to Moegsien Williams, acting editor of *The Sowetan*, who was keen to know exactly what had happened at the old Mandela house. 'Write the story,' he said when he was told. Meanwhile Mandela phoned again, asking what the paper was doing. When he called a third time, Bhengu and Williams decided to go to see him in person.

They arrived at the mansion to find Zinzi's engagement party in full swing. In a separate room Mandela got straight to the point. They shouldn't publish the story, he said. It would ruin his wife's chances for a successful appeal. The lawyers had advised that Winnie keep a low profile until her case came up before the appeal court, as she stood a good chance of getting acquitted. Falati, on the other hand, was definitely going inside. Couldn't this whole incident be played down?

Rather than being silenced by Mandela's arguments, *The Sowetan* journalists were more convinced than ever that they had a big story. The account of Winnie throwing Falati on to the street ran on Monday

30 March, when it was immediately picked up and published verbatim by the Argus group of newspapers, including the Johannesburg *Star*. Publication caused widespread concern in Soweto that Falati was in danger. But it was from a sense of that danger that Falati had spoken to *The Sowetan* in the first place, assuming that known danger meant relative safety. For if anything happened now, fingers would point straight to the Mandelas, Falati reasoned. She knew that Mandela himself had put her room under surveillance and posted ANC guards outside as protection. *The Sowetan* also had someone watching for any unexpected activity in the area. So when an unidentified white male picked Falati up a couple of days later and drove her off, there was immediate consternation. The white male turned out to be Richard Ellis of the *Sunday Times*, who gave her a lift into Johannesburg while interviewing her for a piece he was writing on the state of the Mandela marriage. The next day Falati disappeared.

Ruth Bhengu got a call on Thursday from a distraught Falati, begging her to come quickly. But by the time Bhengu got to the house Falati had gone. She had called Bhengu after she returned to her room and found herself unable to get in – the locks had been changed. Before Bhengu's arrival, a group of ANC security men had driven up to the house, picked up Falati and sped off.

Falati's disappearance caused enormous panic as it re-awakened memories of the disappearance of four defendants and a State witness a year earlier. Falati hadn't kept Mandela's involvement in her affairs secret, nor had the staff at *The Sowetan* remained quiet about his attempts to suppress their story. Why had he been so quick to tell Falati he would take care of her appeal? Why was she able to speak to him at any time? Why when she called him for help did he come immediately? Why had he been so anxious to keep her quiet? If Falati had, as she was now maintaining, committed perjury to protect his wife at her trial, was Mandela now dealing with the ramifications of a cover-up?

On 5 April, three days after Falati disappeared, the London *Sunday Times* article on the Mandela marriage came out. The story dropped several bomb shells as it described a four-hour briefing Falati had given to ANC intelligence officials at Nelson Mandela's request. The purpose of the briefing – which had obviously been given since Falati vanished – was to give the ANC an idea of what Falati knew and might tell the press about Winnie. The contents of her briefing, said the *Sunday Times*, confirmed what Mandela had already decided – he would have to separate from his wife. An announcement of the

Mandelas' separation would be made shortly, precipitating Winnie Mandela's resignation from the ANC and retirement from politics.

The article established that Mandela was virtually alone within the ANC in wanting the details of his wife's behaviour covered up, and it provoked a torrent of devastating stories. The *Guardian* ran the story of Mandela's attempts to suppress *The Sowetan's* story about Winnie, pointing out that this was the first time Mandela was seen to involve himself in a cover-up. The *Christian Science Monitor* ran the result of a five-month investigation into Winnie Mandela, exploring the possibility of another cover-up, this time surrounding Dr Asvat's murder. The *Monitor* had interviewed State prosecutor Jannie van der Merwe, and quoted him saying, 'My gut feeling all along was that there was something very strange . . . I just had the feeling that this was not an armed robbery or murder – but an assassination. But we never had any hard information.' The newspaper also quoted an interview with Katiza Chebekhulu, conducted in Lusaka Central Prison, where Chebekhulu said Mrs Mandela ordered Asvat's death after she realised he would not take responsibility for the dying Stompie.

Both the *Guardian* and the *Christian Science Monitor* quoted ANC officials. The *Monitor* quoted spokeswoman Gill Marcus as saying she did not know of Falati's whereabouts; the *Guardian* quoted the ANC as insisting it knew of no plans of a separation between the Mandelas. While the South African police said the Asvat murder docket would not be re-opened, Ramaphosa attempted damage-control by criticising the press for conducting a trial by media, suggesting that outside forces hostile to the ANC could be using the case to discredit, weaken or destroy the organisation, and appealing to the media 'not to lend itself to these mischievous purposes'.

No-one was fooled. The new spate of publicity raised speculation about the Mandelas to a fever pitch. Was a divorce announcement imminent? Was the trial to be re-opened? Was Winnie going to be charged with Stompie's murder? Or with Asvat's? Throughout that Monday, as Ismail Ayob and George Bizos were frequently sighted in ANC headquarters, rumours flew about Johannesburg – Falati was going to the police; Winnie would be re-arrested; Nelson would have to leave her; Nelson would have to resign; Winnie would have to resign; Dali would have to resign. Winnie would be sent to a mental health hospital. Winnie would never agree to resign or be treated. Nelson would never divorce Winnie.

The family's reaction to the stories came when Ismail Ayob held a press conference at 3 p.m. on Tuesday afternoon. The general expectation among those waiting to hear him was that he would have some earth-shattering news to give. He did not. Instead his statement refuted the allegations against Winnie. They were 'A rehash of the gossip that was prevalent before the trial and based mainly upon the statement of Kenneth Kgase who was well renumerated by an overseas newspaper', Ayob said, pointing out that Kgase's evidence had been rejected by the Supreme Court. He then continued, 'The evidence was clear that neither the late Dr Asvat nor any other doctors saw any of the people who were at the back of her house. Mrs Falati gave evidence under oath at two trials. Her allegations now published in the media are inconsistent with her evidence. Mrs Mandela helped Mrs Falati and her daughter before the events which led to her trial. Mrs Falati seems to feel that Mrs Mandela owed her a living for the rest of her life. She was assisted on humanitarian grounds for long enough. Her allegations came forth when the assistance ceased. Mrs Mandela's appeal is still pending. This appeal is not about to be heard as Heads of Argument are still being prepared. The *sub judice* rule is being ignored to her prejudice. Some respect has to be shown to the interest of justice by the media for this time-honoured rule. Mrs Falati's new allegations about Mrs Mandela being involved in murder and having hit lists are false. They are no doubt inspired by a desire to harm Mrs Mandela and the African National Congress. Mrs Mandela appeals to the media not to concern itself with nor speculate about her personal relationship with her husband which has endured despite 27 years of imprisonment and many years of exile.'

The statement Ayob read out was not entirely accurate. The allegations described were not a rehash of old gossip. They were either new, or had the backing of new evidence. They were not based mainly on the statement of Kenneth Kgase, but on interviews with ANC officials and black journalists as well as Xoliswa Falati, Katiza Chebekhulu and the former state prosecutor Jannie Van Der Merwe. A police statement was produced which claimed that Mrs Mandela was behind the murder of Dr Asvat. Pleas that journalists keep to the *sub judice* rule had nothing to do with the reporting of allegations surrounding Dr Asvat's death or of intended assassinations, as Mrs Mandela's appeal only covered the 29 December kidnapping and assault. It was true that Falati's allegations were inconsistent with her evidence at trial, but that was the point. Falati was now saying she had committed perjury on the witness stand. Appeals to the media not to concern itself with the Mandelas' enduring relationship were easy to ignore when members of the

ANC's inner circle were conducting off-the-record briefings to reporters, saying that as far as they were concerned it could be open season on Winnie Mandela since the ANC had had enough.

Ayob told reporters that he was not briefed to answer questions, but he still managed to respond to a couple. In answer to one, he said that the Mandelas continued to live together in the same house, and in response to another about the Asvat family calling for the investigation into Abu's murder to be re-opened, he said that that was nothing new. But it was. Ebrahim Asvat was now calling for the case to be re-opened in the light of the two allegations made by people who had been very close to Mrs Mandela. Only now was there finally justifiable cause, he said.

Elsewhere in Johannesburg, Nelson Mandela looked tired and careworn as he was repeatedly asked questions about the state of his marriage. 'If there is any necessity for me to make a statement, that will be made in due course, but for the time being I have no intention to make any statement,' he said. Winnie also refused to comment on their reported separation, saying she was not in a position to answer questions on the subject. Neither one denied the reports of a break-up.

Nelson, Winnie and their lawyers were, however, not aware of a seriously damaging article that was being prepared for publication the following Sunday. In a hotel room in Pretoria, John Morgan was telling Dawn Barkhuisen from the Johannesburg *Sunday Times* that he too had committed perjury to protect Winnie Mandela at her trial.

Barkhuisen had stumbled on Morgan by chance when she had gone into Soweto looking for Falati. As droves of journalists roamed the township, bumping into each other searching for a new angle on the Mandela story, Barkhuisen spotted Morgan in the street. Morgan recognised her from court and greeted her. Barkhuisen asked Morgan if he would give her an interview, but he was reluctant to do so, he said, for fear of his life. Barkhuisen continued to press him, though, saying she would do everything she could to keep him safe. Eventually, with the agreement of her paper, Barkhuisen arranged to pick Morgan up and take him to Pretoria. The secrecy of the interview was taken as seriously by the paper as it was by Morgan himself, and not just because it was a competitive story. Both sides agreed that Morgan's life would be in considerable danger were it to be known that he was talking to the press. Barkhuisen and her editors believed Morgan when he told them his house was now being watched by members of Unkhonto we Sizwe. Thus Barkhuisen lay on the floor of the car as she was driven up to collect Morgan, who had arranged for his suitcase to be put into the car at another point in the township.

Morgan and Barkhuisen spent eight days together in Pretoria, checking Morgan in and out of hotels. Barkhuisen went over and over Morgan's story with him, concerned not so much in finding out everything he knew as establishing whether he was consistent in the small amount she was going to use. In the evenings she took him to the cinema to try to alleviate the tension. Satisfied with his honesty, she sat down at her desk in Johannesburg on Friday 10 April (the same day that the investigative Afrikaans-language weekly *Vrye Weekblad* came out with a story alleging that Mandela had moved out of the Soweto mansion because his bodyguards believed a plot was being hatched 'close to Winnie Mandela' to assassinate their leader) and wrote that a second co-accused had admitted lying to protect Winnie. Morgan's new version substantially corroborated Kgase and Mono's evidence. And he said that the contents of his original police statement were for the most part true and not fabricated by the police as his defence had claimed. The reason he was telling the truth now, he said, was that both Winnie and Dali Mpofu had turned down his requests for funding for his appeal against his kidnapping conviction, although Winnie had provided his original bail money. Morgan seemed extremely anxious to clear his name. He had already spent the one year of his sentence in prison and would have to serve no more jail time, but the tone and content of his interview stressed both his anxiety and his anger.

'People call me a child beater. I am battling to feed my daughters and two children,' he said. 'Winnie used me and dumped me.'

As soon as Barkhuisen had finished writing, she called Morgan in Pretoria to check that he agreed with what she had written, after which she filed her story, loading it from her computer disk into the terminal of her news editor. No-one else had a copy of the article or details of its contents. It was mid-afternoon.

Early that same evening Barkhuisen got a call in the Johannesburg *Sunday Times* news room from a friend in Soweto who was also close to Winnie. Winnie had a copy of Barkhuisen's story, the friend said, and was absolutely enraged, ranting about its contents to anyone in earshot. Her friend thought Barkhuisen should know.

Barkhuisen was flabbergasted, unable to understand how her story could have travelled to Soweto in such a short time, given its extremely limited distribution. Initially she was skeptical that Winnie had a copy of the article itself, thinking at most she must have learned that Morgan had given an interview. But when her friend started quoting extracts from the copy, Barkhuisen grew alarmed. She immediately informed the news editor what had happened, who told the paper's management. Barkhuisen was forbidden to return home and armed guards were placed around her house. A bizarre postscript to this nerve-wracking episode occurred a few weeks later when Barkhuisen returned from vacation to discover that an office move which had taken place in her absence had resulted in the disappearance of every single file and notebook she possessed. She was told that her possessions – which she had left in a padlocked cupboard – had been shredded when the cupboard had been opened and no-one had claimed its contents. This happened despite the fact that Barkhuisen's name was all over her books and it was no secret that she was on holiday.

The day before she knew the Morgan story would appear, Winnie kept an appointment to address a demonstration in the farming town of Warmbaths, and took the opportunity for some fighting rhetoric proving she might be down but she was far from out. Dressed in military-style khaki fatigues, the words she shouted at the police might have been aimed at all her critics. 'We have been pushed and pushed too far!' she yelled as the crowd of 2,000 roared its approval. Back at Shell House an emergency meeting of ANC leaders convened in Nelson Mandela's absence to discuss the onslaught of damaging Winnie stories, many of which contained details leaked by those present. With advance knowledge of the next day's Johannesburg *Sunday Times* story there was no longer any doubt that Mandela had to announce that his marriage was over. Both he and the movement stood to be seriously damaged by the revelations about Winnie.

Ramaphosa and Sisulu went to see Mandela to put the case that he no longer had any choice but to make an announcement. They did not make the decision for him, but put their arguments before him and left him to decide for himself. It was an agonising choice. Mandela found it harder rather than easier to come to terms with what he saw as his own culpability, continuing to feel responsible for the woman his wife had become. But when the Johannesburg *Sunday Times* splashed the John Morgan story across its front page and Morgan gave a live interview on national television repeating his allegations, a press conference was scheduled. On Monday morning Mandela would read a statement and take no questions. His separation would finally become public.

For a man as essentially private as Mandela, who never spoke of the difficulties of his personal life, even to close friends, the ordeal of having to announce that his marriage was over to the world's press under the unrelenting glare of television lights must have been excruciating. As he sat down, flanked by Tambo, Sisulu, Ramaphosa and Thomas Nkobi, and began to speak stiffly to a packed and silent room of journalists, many were overcome with the emotion he was obviously struggling to control.

In the end, he stuck to the subject he knew best – the struggle. Reading from a prepared statement and referring to his wife throughout as Comrade Nomzamo, he described a life and a marriage set against a political backdrop.

'Comrade Nomzamo and myself contracted our marriage at a critical time in the struggle for liberation in our country,' he began. 'Owing to the pressures of our shared commitment to the ANC and the struggle to end apartheid we were unable to enjoy a normal family life.'

Though he punctuated his remarks with testimonies of his feelings for Winnie – 'Despite these pressures our love for each other and our devotion to our marriage grew and intensified'; 'Her tenacity reinforced my personal respect, love and growing affection' – those comments were brief and intermittent, a sad reflection of the couple's history together. Instead Mandela was more at ease outlining Winnie's political role in the events of the last thirty years. 'During both my trials, the first in 1962 and during the Rivonia trial of 1964, Comrade Nomzamo was a key figure in mobilising solidarity and support for myself and the other Rivonia trialists alongside other members of the ANC and its allies . . . she endured the persecutions heaped upon her by the Government with exemplary fortitude and never wavered from her commitment to the struggle for freedom.'

Saying his love for her remained undiminished, Mandela finally gave the expected news. 'In view of the tensions that have arisen owing to differences between ourselves on a number of issues in recent months,' he said, 'we have mutually agreed that a separation would be best for each of us . . . I part from my wife with no recriminations. I embrace with all the love and affection I have nursed for her inside and outside prison from the moment I first met her.'

He did not say whether there would be a divorce. In fact, the statement he read merely confirmed the rumour which preceded it, without giving any additional information. Reading it had left Mandela drained and upset, and once he had finished he got up to leave. 'Ladies and gentlemen, I hope you appreciate the pain I have gone through,' he said and walked out of the room.

Chapter Sixteen

As the months after the separation passed, those close to Mandela noticed a change in the man. He seemed happier, more light-hearted, more at ease. It was not, friends said, that he was relieved to be living without Winnie – the couple had been living under separate roofs for more than five months now. His relief came at having finally made a decision after more than four years of being urged to do so.

But it was a lonely man who settled into his new house in Houghton. Naturally gregarious, Mandela spent too many evenings alone save for the company of bodyguards and housekeeper. Certainly he had more than enough to occupy his working day as talks with the government stalled and violence escalated across the country, He was as busy as he had been thirty years earlier, with as little time to devote to a personal life. Only now there was no-one to make his house a home. In leaving Winnie, he may have walked out on an untenable domestic situation, but he was too old and had spent too many years in prison to be able to establish any real home of his own. Years of choosing politics over a personal life meant that finally Mandela had no personal life to choose.

Later in the year, when he spoke as father of the bride at Zinzi's wedding to Soweto businessman Zwelibanzi Hlongwane, he spoke of how he felt at sacrificing his private life.

'One wonders whether it was worth it,' he said. 'But when those doubts come, you nevertheless decide, for the umpteenth time, that in spite of all the problems, it was, still is, the correct decision that we should commit ourselves.'[1]

Even those who had been adamant that Nelson and Winnie should separate felt the sadness of the situation, as the myth of the marriage finally crumbled. Not that sentiment in the ANC was allowed to stand in the way of pragmatism. Two days after Mandela's announcement that his marriage was over, Winnie made her own announcement – she was resigning as the head of social welfare. 'I have taken this step', she said at a press conference, 'because I consider it to be in the best interest of the ANC.'

In fact she had taken this step because she had no choice. Immediately after Mandela's announcement, she had been urged twice by NEC leaders to resign both her position as head of social welfare and her place on the NEC, and had refused both times. It was then that Ramaphosa had given her no option. She could resign voluntarily or be publicly fired, he told her bluntly. Either way she was out of the leadership.

With her back up against the wall, Winnie resigned only as head of social welfare, refusing to allow Ramaphosa the total satisfaction of removing her from the NEC as well. She spent no time mourning the end of her marriage. With her resignation began her immediate campaign for reinstatement, as she began amassing support against Ramaphosa. As she had done earlier with Verryn, she portrayed her beleaguered situation as the result of one man's campaign against her. This time, she told friends and supporters, she was a victim of Ramaphosa's ambition and desire for self promotion. And Ramaphosa would not be content with ousting her, she emphasised, when his main aim was to replace Mandela as the movement's leader.

There was an element of truth in what Winnie said. Just as she had earlier preyed on existing suspicions about Verryn's sexuality – portraying herself as the innocent victim of her own courage in taking on this aggressive homosexual – so she now focused on Ramaphosa's ambition at a time when the young negotiator was rapidly gaining control of the ANC. A not unambitious man, Ramaphosa had initially been reluctant to run for the post of ANC Secretary-General the previous year. Once decided, however, he campaigned all-out for the position, making it clear he would accept nothing less. Having won despite an active campaign waged against him by both Mandelas, the 38-year-old Ramaphosa immediately began reorganising the day-to-day running of the ANC. His influence was everywhere. Under Ramaphosa, meetings began on time, telephones were answered, moderation began to win out over militancy, and he was soon spoken of as Mandela's natural heir. Ramaphosa was a trained lawyer, and it was his negotiating skills that were responsible for his political rise. Ten years earlier he had driven 2,000 miles a week recruiting members of the fledgling National Union of Mine workers (NUM). As Secretary-General he built the union into a major power-broking organisation – membership rose from 18,000 in 1982 to almost 300,000 a decade later. Ramaphosa then turned his attention to the consolidation of all South African unions, playing a major role in the formation of the Congress of South African Trade Unions in 1985.

With the formal alliance of COSATU and the UDF a year later, Ramaphosa gracefully took centre stage in South African politics, where he looked set to remain until Winnie's antipathy towards him forced him into the political cold. She had not forgotten that Ramaphosa had helped draft the 1989 MDM (what the UDF became after it was banned by the government) statement against her. It was the legacy of this act which affected Ramaphosa's political career for eighteen months following Mandela's release. Despite being on the Mandela Reception Committee and visiting Mandela several times at Victor Verster Prison to discuss his release, Ramaphosa was not to be an immediate member of Mandela's inner circle – thanks to Winnie's intervention.

He may have walked from prison at Mandela's side, and even held the microphone to Mandela's lips during his first speech – an act of obsequiousness which led to months of teasing from friends and colleagues – but there was to be no subsequent call for his assistance and Ramaphosa went back to his union work with hurt feelings. Refusing to capitulate – this, after all, was a man who had been known to throw tantrums in meetings with mine owners to win concessions for his men – or to suffer permanent ostracism, Ramaphosa bided his time. When he did come back to an official position in the ANC, he was finally able to deal with Winnie from a position of strength at the organisation's helm.

A small, softly spoken, highly articulate, expert strategist with a sense of humour, Ramaphosa was not shy about taking on Winnie. Nor was he under any illusions as to her feelings for him. Though she continued to be warm and affectionate to his face, constantly telling him how much she admired and respected him, he knew that behind his back she was whistling a very different tune. Reports of what she said about him and how she was organising against him were not slow in coming to Ramaphosa's attention. Occasionally he countered Winnie's compliments, telling her that he had heard fairly negative things about himself for which she was the source, but she remained adamant. She could never say anything to the detriment of Ramaphosa, a man she admired so greatly, she laughed, adding that it had to be elements hostile to the ANC who were spreading these rumours. For she too had heard unpleasant and untrue stories about herself, she said cheerfully. And, surprisingly, they had been attributed to Ramaphosa.

She wanted it to be known that Ramaphosa was acting alone, or at the head of a cabal of self-promoting accomplices, in casting her down. By articulating the ANC's response to her resignation – commending her for the courageous initiative she had taken in the best interest of her organisation – Ramaphosa showed that he was definitely the point man in dealing with Winnie, but he was far from alone. Nor did he merely have the support of a small group of friends. When the national executive of the ANC's Women's League began their own efforts to oust Winnie, they acted independently.

Although some Women's League leaders were also leaders of the main body of the ANC, the Women's League still saw itself as a separate entity with its own concerns. As it struggled to establish itself as a viable organisation, the League continued to feel resentful towards the ANC proper for a chauvinistic, cavalier attitude to what were still regarded as 'women's issues'. In the days following her departure as the head of social welfare, Winnie began to exploit this disenchantment in the Women's League. She was not only reaching out to the women. Visiting Soweto and Sharpeville, she publicly criticised the government for killing ANC members, while privately she was amassing support to challenge her forced resignation. By saying that 'MK will never be disbanded' because it was the future democratic army of the country, Winnie reminded the youth and the militants that she remained their champion.[2] She went on national television saying, 'As far as I am concerned my political career goes on as if nothing had happened.'[3] By the end of the month she had openly consolidated her power base.

Once again, concentration of her own power came as the result of dividing those around her. SACP and Umkhonto we Sizwe members vowed to support her, while her long-time ally Peter Mokaba, militant head of the Youth League, told reporters that 'We are going to confound those who are biting behind her back. She has the support of all those who support me.'[4] Moderates and militants in the ANC were polarised for the most part into pro- and anti-Winnie camps.

Organising the women required more subtlety. The ANC was unable to remove her from her democratically elected leadership positions in the regional and national Women's League, or on its own NEC, unless it held an inquiry and found her guilty of political misconduct. One inquiry was already under way into an alleged misappropriation of R400,000 (£80,000) of social welfare funds, which caused Dali Mpofu's speedy removal as deputy head of social welfare. He later challenged his dismissal in the Industrial Court. From the security of her Women's League leadership position (she was re-elected unopposed chairwoman in elections held in early May) and manipulating existing grievances, Winnie began to organise a group of disgruntled, loyal or frightened women into the 'Social Welfare Support Committee'.

The committee acted a month after its formation. Action would have been quicker, but Winnie suddenly checked into the Lesedi clinic in Soweto for what was officially described as an 'undisclosed illness' or 'an infection', leading to a rumour that she was hospitalised to control her drinking, but her stay in hospital was only a week long and on her release she continued to rally support as if there had been no interruption.

Assembling in the regional offices of the Women's League to march on Shell House on 21 May, many of the women bussed in from squatter camps thought they would be protesting a range of different issues.[5] Some thought they were marching against the government, others thought they were criticising press coverage of the ANC, a few, but by no means all, knew they were calling for the reinstatement of Winnie Mandela as the head of social welfare.

Winnie wasn't with them. She was at home, seemingly ignorant of this spontaneous show of support for herself. Nor was she aware of a petition signed by the committee which claimed both she and Mpofu were an asset to Social Welfare, called for their reinstatement as head and deputy head of the department, and echoed a grievance close to her heart.

The Department of Social Welfare is constantly being used as a political football to settle old scores and to play power games. We believe that Comrade Winnie Mandela was a wise choice of the previous national executive committee to head the department.

For too long now there has been talk of a secret cabal operating within the leadership of the ANC. These allegations have either been denied, downplayed or said to be 'investigated'. What action has been taken? Every day we read about a senior source within the leadership who wishes not to be named. Who are these people? THEY MUST BE EXPOSED!

The march never made it to Shell House. Security personnel at ANC headquarters had got wind that a protest was planned three or four days earlier and were ready to send intermediaries down to talk to the women at the regional offices. The two men who arrived, Steve Tshwete – head of mass action at the ANC – and Peter Mokaba, came and persuaded the majority of the women to disband, with a few token representatives going to Shell House to hand the petition over to Ramaphosa personally.

The sit-in – as it came to be known – did an enormous amount of damage to the Women's League. With a number of leading women from the regional branch marching in support of Winnie, the regional executive of the Women's League mirrored the sentiment in the main body of the ANC – polarised into pro- and anti-Winnie camps. The split was almost straight down the line, with the regional anti-Winnie faction of women just squeaking a majority of eleven to nine. So intent was this majority in ousting Winnie, that they voted to suspend the entire regional leadership in order to abolish her position of chairwoman. In doing away with all leadership positions they effectively threw the baby out with the bath water, voting themselves out of office too, but it was a measure of the intensity of their feelings that they were prepared to take this drastic step. Their chairwoman did not attend the vote. She was said to be convening other meetings, urging women to challenge the suspension, and seeing lawyers to establish whether it was legal.⁶ She then released a statement. 'It would seem that my resignation as head of the department of social welfare was not enough for my detractors,' she said. 'This must be seen as yet another attempt to split the ANC.'

A week later, the national executive of the Women's League met. Again feelings ran high, and again the vote went against Winnie. She was removed from the board.

Technically, this was unconstitutional behaviour and Winnie knew it. A democratically elected official could not be removed from a leadership position until an internal inquiry had proved professional misconduct. As yet no proof had been established. With Winnie investigating whether she might have legal recourse against the ANC, Ramaphosa convened a commission of inquiry to deal with the matter promptly yet properly. He personally approached two outside lawyers for the task, Linda Zama – a prominent Durban lawyer – and Dennis Davis of Wits University Law School, and gave them two or three days to come up with a legal, not a political, report.

In the short time given, the lawyers told him they could do no more than establish whether Winnie had been improperly suspended, and whether there should be a disciplinary inquiry into her alleged organisation of the march. Telling Davis that Mandela wanted to see a report as soon as possible, Ramaphosa left him to get on with it.

Hearings were held in Shell House. Winnie did not testify, and the women who did were divided into two camps. There were the embittered, roughly ten people who felt they had been used and deceived, organised by Winnie into a march for her own purposes. They told the commission that Winnie had personally informed people of the need to protest against the way the press was handling the ANC, that the final meeting before the march had taken place in her house, and that she had personally made some of the placards carried by the women. The evidence of these witnesses was given with much trepidation. They came to the hearing room reluctantly, frightened at the potential consequences of their testimony.

Then there were the loyalists, those who maintained that Winnie – who could do no wrong – had had absolutely nothing to do with the march, which had been nothing more than a huge spontaneous gesture of support for her. They came to the hearing with prepared statements which didn't just stick to the particulars of the protest but expressed support for Winnie and said she had been victimised by a cabal within the ANC. These people were organised to the last. But their statements did not pre-empt questioning, and when examined they began to contradict each other. fifteen witnesses produced fifteen stories, none of them matching. Lawyers did not take evidence from Winnie at that stage.

The two lawyers found that Winnie had been the guiding light behind the march and, with a small number of supporters, had manipulated the majority of the marchers. These were grounds for a further disciplinary inquiry, they said. But they also found in Winnie's favour, concluding that her suspension from the national executive of the Women's League had been improper. Legally, suspension couldn't be used punitively, but was a temporary measure pending other action.

The report was sent to the national executive of the ANC – of which Winnie was still a member – and several hours were spent debating it. At a meeting in early June, the majority of the committee insisted that Winnie be suspended from all her leadership positions, but as such a suspension had already been found to be improper, it was decided instead to submit the report to the smaller, more powerful National Working Committee – of which Winnie was not a member – for disciplinary action. Meanwhile, Winnie would be forbidden to appear publicly on behalf of the ANC or to work at any level within ANC structures.[7]

And there the matter stalled. As weeks dragged into months without a resolution, Winnie continued to appear publicly, and to use her Women's League regional office, changing the locks when she was locked out.[8] By late August she had contacted Dennis Davis and asked to testify before his commission in an attempt to prove to him that his finding against her had been wrong. The ANC insisted that Winnie be allowed to testify and hearings reconvened. When questioned about events leading up to the march at new hearings, she said she was unable to respond as she had known nothing about the march – it was a spontaneous uprising. She also claimed to know nothing of Davis's report, denying she had ever seen it, even when quoting verbatim from it. When Davis commented that she had a remarkably good memory, she looked at him and laughed. An addition to the original report, written after Winnie's testimony, confirmed the original finding and went further, saying that if anything there were even stronger grounds on the basis of Winnie's evidence to proceed with a disciplinary hearing.

Other wheels were grinding while the infighting in Johannesburg continued. At the beginning of September there was the Appeal Court's judgement in Jerry Richardson's case. Substituting life imprisonment for the death sentence, the court found that the influence of Winnie Mandela on Richardson had to be seen as a mitigating factor in his crimes. A reasonable possibility existed, and the evidence as a whole had tended to confirm, that Richardson had acted, if not on the express orders, then at least under the influence, of Mrs Mandela. It was significant, said Justice Hefer, that Mrs Mandela had declined to testify when invited to do so by the defence. The day after this ruling, Winnie resigned from all her ANC posts.

Her resignation actually had nothing to do with the Richardson verdict, but followed a weekend publication in the Johannesburg *Star* and *Sunday Times* of a letter Winnie had written to Dali Mpofu in March.

'Dali,' the four-page letter written on ruled paper began:

I suggest you read the contents of the two letters I referred to last night at 12.30 a.m. and remind yourself I am not another Terreza [Terry Oakley-Smith] you used when it suited you and dumped when it suited you. I will never be used by you for ukufeba kwakho [promiscuity] and you use our things we acquired together for running around fucking at the slightest emotional excuse. I can understand the bleeper because I realize the last thing you've ever had after reading Terreza's letter when she gave you up is a conscience, just like Fatima said.

I suppose you do remember that inter-alia you were supposed to be using me for material things according to Terreza and you asked her to bear with you when she said but she was providing you with those material things.

Thinking back I'm horrified at your dishonesty, Dali, you were prepared to go along with Terreza's *City Press* report to the effect that you separated with her because of me when it is quite clear she had given you up in February of 1991 when she found you sleeping with Nonxolisi that Saturday morning. Do you remember how in love we were then? You were able to come to me my love with a straight face as if nothing had happened and in fact on most occasions I was responsible for your quarrels with Terreza, even when she telephoned Pumla to tell her all that rubbish about how you didn't marry her because of me, you protected her and sided with her. It was your Terreza who introduced Pumla to this whole thing and today you insult me and say I did? Ndoze ndibe sisibanxwa sakho mina [I won't be your bloody fool] Dali, before I'm through with you you are going to learn a bit of honesty and sincerity and know what betrayal of one's trust means to a woman!

You lie to me and suggest that in order to preserve our relationship you have to have a relationship as a cover to defuse our problem? I understand and know how difficult it was for me to accept that reality but it eventually dawned on me that because I love you so much I had to agree with you even though I still shuddered at the thought of you lying and pretending to love this other woman and as you said 'You were just involved with Imogen' and you never said you loved her.

Your shabby treatment of me of last night has compelled me once more to show you I can do exactly the same Dali, I beg nothing from you and you are not going to make me another Terreza, you need to read her last paragraph of the letter to Nonxolisi to know how much of a compulsive sophisticated liar you are. What you must know is that whilst I agree to the 'policy' I will never let you undermine me to this extent again. You knew that you had been 'emptied up' last week – and so in order to overcome your physical problem you pick out a quarrel over Nonxolisi. You think you can just wish away certain things Dali, not with me. I tell you I'm in trouble with the Simmons Street A/c which reflects over R160,000 drawn over a period for you. You don't even bother to check how we can overcome this. I tell you Ayob has been sent by tata [Mandela] to get an accountant to investigate my A/c! I tell you Ntombi is gossiping about the cheques we used to ask her to cash for in the name of the Dpt and how I gave you all that money and you and I are now being investigated, instead you chose not to talk to Ntombi's sister because she is talking about a friend of the woman you were sleeping with on the 21st floor. The only time you have time to talk to me in about women ofeba nabo (you have sek with) as you are doing right now. You are supposed to care so much for me that the fact that I haven't been speaking to tata for five months now over you is no longer your concern. I keep telling you the situation is deteriorating at home, you are not bothered because you are satisfying yourself every night with a woman you are 'involved' with and you are not in love with her.

How did you think I will buy this? I've written this letter because clearly it has become impossible for us to have any healthy discussion in the present atmosphere. There are certain things I'm finding difficult to resist doing for you to remember always how much you have hurt and humiliated me as a woman. By the way I spoke to the person you are not interested in, the person who was present with one of you as you spoke to each other with Nonxolisi and the person who phoned Nonxolisi to tell her you were no longer coming to east London. The person is prepared to speak to you and reveal himself/herself to you personally and tell you why that was done. In the light of your behaviour last night over this issue, I'll do something better than that so that we are through with lying once and for all.

I'm going to University for the tut. I was preparing for and I'll go and deliver the copy of those letters. I have discovered that what you have got used to from your white hag since we seem unable to communicate.

It's me

PS/ I'm making things easier for you since you gave my last letter to Terreza and she wrote Nonxolisi name and some boer name on it. You must have been trying to convince her that 'that's what you had been telling her all along'! There was never any affair, in the process you sell me out like that? You give her my letter?

Envelopes containing copies of the letter had been dropped off at the offices of the *Sunday Star* and the Johannesburg and London *Sunday Times* a week earlier. It had taken the papers that long to establish that the letter had been written by Winnie. After consulting a handwriting expert, the Johannesburg *Sunday Times* and the London *Sunday Times* – working together – had finally felt confident to run it, when a member of the Mandela family legal team had confirmed off the record that the letter had indeed been written by Ms Mandela. On the record it was pointed out that the Simmons Street account referred to was a personal bank account and not a Social Welfare one.

Aside from any insight the letter shed into Winnie's character, her relationship with Dali, its effect on her relationship with Mandela and her attitude to the other women in Dali's life, the letter forced her resignation because of the financial references. Even if the bank account referred to was a personal account, the anxiety expressed by Winnie at gossip over cheques cashed 'in the name of the Dpt' gave credence to previous reports of massive misappropriation of funds at the social welfare department under her rule.

Two years earlier lawyers for The First National Bank had been forced to act in a case brought against the bank by a woman's group known as the Malibongwe Women's Project, which sewed and did other work on behalf of prisoners and former prisoners. The project had two accounts. At the end of 1989 one account had R60,000 (£12,000) in it, the other just under R23,000 (£4,500). The first indication that something was wrong came in January 1990, when four members of Malibongwe's executive committee wrote a letter to their bank manager at First National asking that the operation of the second account be suspended while 'the identities and status of those that have been entrusted to administer our funds . . . is under discussion.'[9]

One month later the bank received a letter from lawyers for the Malibongwe project asking that it advise them who and on what basis it recognised as signatories on this account, and from what date those signatories had been operating.[10] It subsequently emerged that R14,652.50 (about £3,000) had been signed out of the second account without authority. The money had been withdrawn on four cheques. Three of those cheques – totalling R10,652.50 – had been signed by Winnie.

By October 1990 the money in both accounts was frozen and nothing had been resolved. Somewhat impatiently, the Malibongwe project's lawyers wrote to the lawyers for First National.

We are under extreme pressure from our clients to obtain a speedy resolution of this matter, failing which our instructions are to proceed to Court.

No doubt you will appreciate that we have attempted to resolve this matter for several months now. Our clients are therefore not willing to grant either your client or attorneys Soman,

Kamdar and Partners further unnecessary and lengthy extension of time either to discuss the matter between yourselves or to attempt to secure an appointment with Mrs Winnie Mandela in this regard.[11]

Still nothing happened. In February 1991 lawyers for the bank got a letter from Soman, Kamdar who were representing Winnie in the case. 'We have been trying to communicate with Mrs Winnie Mandela so that we may obtain further instructions therein. Unfortunately we have a slight problem in that Mrs Mandela has been busy with preparations for her defence in the forthcoming trial. However we hope to see her over the weekend and it would be appreciated if you could grant us an extension until 15 February 1991.'[12]

Finally, in April, the bank sent the women's project a cheque for R82,346.82 – the contents of both accounts before the unauthourised withdrawals.[13]

Of the three cheques written by Winnie, one for R10,000 was made out to a Mr Piccoli and cashed in Yeoville. Another was to an Autorama in Kroonstaad for R107.50, and the third for R545.00 was to Empire Fish and Chips. All three cheques were written in the first two weeks of December 1989. The Empire Fish and Chips Store was a fast food outlet in Soweto – owned by Winnie. It had already been a source of controversy in November 1990 when Winnie was taken to court and fined for failing to pay social security benefits for the shop's four employees. After her conviction a reporter visited the store. He found no fish, virtually empty fridges, sparsely stocked shelves and the gas stove on the blink. 'Sometimes it takes months before we get stock,' said an employee, adding that the last time Winnie had visited the store was four months earlier.[14]

When the letter implying that social welfare funds had been misused was published, Winnie never denied that it was hers. Mpofu did though (but then Mpofu was in the process of suing the ANC for wrongful dismissal.)[15] Mpofu announced that the ANC was becoming 'a monster that abuses human rights' and described rumours of a romantic association between Winnie and himself as 'rather a sick joke'.[16] Rumours that all was not well in their romantic association had been circulating for months. Reports of their fights were numerous, one scuffle in the ANC's underground car park had reportedly been watched by security guards who saw Winnie's wig being knocked off on closed circuit television.

Who leaked the letter? Copies of it had circulated throughout Shell

House before making it to newspapers, and ANC sources reported that Mandela himself had read it. Someone or some people in the ANC knew that publication of this letter was an effective way of finally resolving the Winnie problem.

Resigning 'in the interest of my dear husband and my beloved family', Winnie said in a statement addressed to 'all my people in South Africa' that she would remain a 'convinced member of the ANC'. She continued: 'Those who have rejoiced in reading about our problems and those who for selfish political and personal reasons have waged a vicious and malicious campaign against me and, through me, the leadership of my husband and our organisation, have unfortunately partly succeeded in their aims.'

Winnie laid low for several months after her resignation. According to the general consensus, her political life was finally over. Her next major public appearence wasn't until the October wedding of her daughter. With a Christian service in Johannesburg – coincidentally at the Central Methodist Church where the Reverend Paul Verryn worked – and a traditional ceremony in Soweto, Zinzi was able to have the full wedding her mother never had. Standing next to her estranged husband, dressed in glittering green and purple, with green ribbons glimmering elaborately through her hair, Winnie was beautiful. She had lost weight and looked rested. But one senior ANC official who was present at the wedding noticed that her eyes werè bloodshot. He said that she sat as if tranquillised, smiling blankly and saying nothing. None the less, as she shimmered and smiled, surrounded by dignitaries, she was impossible to ignore.

Epilogue

Two years after Dr Klepp took the stand, there was a reunion of sorts among the particpants of Case Number 644/91. Lawyers and journalists involved in the trial boarded a plane together and travelled to Bloemfontein – just half an hour from Brandfort – for the appeal of John Morgan, Xoliswa Falati and Winnie Mandela. The following day, in a beautiful wood-panelled courtroom, beneath high arched windows, before five judges of the Apellate Division, the highest court in South Africa, Jan Swanepoel and George Bizos faced each other for the last time. Their lives had changed considerably in the intervening two years. Bizos had retired from the bar and now worked part-time for the Legal Resources Centre – the same organisation which had represented Kgase, Mono and Mekgwe in Winnie Mandela's trial. He had come out of retirement to argue this appeal. Instructing him was Ismail Ayob. Though Ayob continued to represent Nelson Mandela, this would be his last piece of work for his client's estranged wife.

Swanepoel and his deputy, Chris Van Vuuren, had been promoted. Now they ran the government's Office for Serious Economic Offences in Pretoria. Behind them sat Frederik Dempsey, who had become a Major in the South African police force. His investigation into the allegations raised in the previous year was complete, having uncovered no significant new evidence.

Indeed, no new evidence would be introduced before this court. Though the original case had long been overtaken by events, the original testimony of the witnesses would be taken at face value. Neither Xoliswa Falati, nor John Morgan, nor Thabo Motau would appear to claim they had been bribed to lie for Winnie. Pelo Mekgwe, now back in South Africa, would not come to give his version of the kidnapping and assault. No surprise witness would be called. This hearing was solely on the facts presented in the earlier trial and the merits of Justice Stegmann's ruling. So none of the apellants was in Bloemfontein. Winnie hadn't come, but the Brandfort branch of the ANC filled the three small benches of the public gallery: having lived in Brandfort for nine years, Winnie was considered a local and deserved some support. They weren't dressed in ANC colours, though, and there was no chanting or toyi-toyi-ing outside the court.

Most of them sat dozing through the proceedings and left at the end of the morning. Except for one wire reporter, the international press was absent. The intense interest in this case would be briefly and finally revived later, when judgement was issued.

It was in this intimate and rarefied atmosphere that the events of 29 December 1988 were judged for the last time. The hysteria and political rhetoric which had surrounded the case from the start had gone. This court had long had a reputation for being just and above politics, and the five legal minds on the bench were reputed to be brilliant. As Bizos and Swanepoel argued the merits of their respective cases the Justices interrupted them politely and gently, but persistently. Should they accept Winnie's alibi? What must they conclude then about her involvement? What must they conclude if they rejected it? Leaving Bizos with little to fall back on, they repeatedly attacked the screen he had raised in the absence of his client's having any real defence. What was the relevance, they asked again and again, of the case against the Reverend Paul Verryn? What did it have to do with the manner in which the youths were taken in her bus to her house?

Outside the courtroom there was little interest in the proceedings. Winnie kept in touch by phone and was interested enough in her own case to travel to Pretoria on the last day of the appeal to have dinner with her junior counsel. Bizos couldn't brief her personally. He went from Bloemfontein to Cape Town for a meeting of the ANC's legal and constitutional committee, of which he was a member.

Elsewhere the protagonists were getting on with their lives. Nelson Mandela was in Johannesburg working on his memoirs. His health had not been good and he was about to cut his schedule down to half days. Winnie was also in Johannesburg, where she had opened her own social welfare office in town. She had begun writing articles and making speeches criticising the ANC for being out of touch with the people. Recent news reports had told of Nelson Mandela's refusal to pay her R19,000 (£4,000) telephone bill at the house in Diepkloof Extension. Dali Mpofu, who had begun training at the bar as an advocate had just appeared in magistrate's court charged with cheque fraud. Charges against him were subsequently withdrawn. In Soweto, dressed in her nightgown, Xoliswa Falati had received Communion from the Reverend Paul Verryn at a prayer meeting. She had interpreted the reading he had inadvertently prepared from St Paul to the Romans 'Who shall attack God's servant?' as a prayer for the downfall of Winnie Mandela.

In Pretoria Central Prison, serving life without parole, Jerry

Richardson, who had become something of a kingpin in jail, continued to speak endlessly about how 'Mommy' was going to save him. Nicholas Dlamini and Cyril Mbatha were also in Pretoria Central. Mbatha remained on death row for the murder of Dr Asvat, but Dlamini's sentence, like Richardson's, had been commuted to life without parole. The two had been re-interviewed by Captain Dempsey in late 1992 and had remained adamant that the killing of Dr Asvat was an accident in the execution of a straightforward robbery. They had also begged Dempsey not to let Richardson find out they had spoken to him.

Kenneth Kgase had disappeared. No one had heard from him for nearly two years. After the trial he had been found a job in a diamond mine, where he had worked for a couple of months. In July 1991 he left for a technical college in Bophutaswana. After that there was silence. Pelo Mekgwe was back in his home town of Potchestroom, unemployed but politically active. Thabiso Mono had suffered from intense depression after the trial. In recent months he seemed more cheerful, however. He had a job cleaning machines for a food company and was looking after his sisters. Paul Verryn continued his work in the Methodist Church. He was busier than ever. Continued violence had caused a massive rise in his congregation. He rarely stayed the night in Soweto any more, preferring to stay with friends in the white working-class suburb of Brixton.

Three weeks after the hearing, Winnie's close friend and fellow militant, Chris Hani, was assassinated as a result of a right-wing plot. With her own future hanging in the balance, Winnie rushed over to the Hani house and that evening appeared sobbing on newscasts around the world. Although Mandela and other ANC leaders pleaded for calm, the following weeks saw some of the worst rioting in South African history. Youths took to the streets of both black and white neighbourhoods, breaking windows, tearing down walls, setting buildings and humans on fire.

'Chris Hani believed in peace,' said Winnie addressing a rally in Cape Town dressed in full combat military dress. 'But peace after the revolution. We will not tolerate a misinterpretation of Chris's mission.'

Chris Hani and countless others, she said, did not pay the supreme price 'In order that our freedom be allowed to disappear into the sunset of political oblivion.'

Winnie's freedom, it soon became clear, was not about to disappear anywhere. When the judgement of the Appeal Court was handed down on 2 June 1993 her kidnapping conviction remained, but she was found not to have been an accessory to the assaults. And it turned out that she would not have to serve the five years imposed by the lower court, or any time at all for that matter. In the Appeal Court's words: 'In appropriate cases the Court should always consider the possibility of alternative sentences to imprisonment.' After 'careful and anxious' consideration, the court had come to the conclusion that Winnie's was such a case.

Winnie was given a two years' suspended sentence and ordered to pay a fine of R15,000 (£3,000). In addition she had to pay the three surviving complainants compensation of R5,000 (£1,000 each) – R1,000 less than Kenneth Kgase got for selling his story to the *Sunday Telegraph*.

Apart from its consideration of Winnie, the 200-page judgement from the Appeal Court seemed neither especially careful nor anxious. In fact, the references to the four victims seemed almost cavalier. An early reference to the deceased Stompie stated: 'Although Seipei was murdered shortly after the kidnapping, I shall for convenience refer to all four victims as "the complainants".' And 'Apart from the initial assaults, and leaving aside the case of Seipei, and apart from being confined, the complainants do not appear to have been maltreated in any way at number 585.'

It was, however, in comparison with Xoliswa Falati that Winnie seemed to have got off lightly. Falati's convictions stood. Like Winnie's, her sentence was reduced by the Appeal Court. But, unlike Winnie, there was no mention of a careful or anxious consideration of her case. As a convicted felon Falati got four years' imprisonment, two of which were suspended. Unlike the estranged wife of the President of the ANC, Mrs Falati served time for her crimes.

On December 8th, 1993, Winnie achieved the impossible. She made a comeback. At the annual women's conference in Durban she was re-elected President of the Women's League, soundly defeating her opponent, Albertina Sisulu. All the hours she had spent painstakingly re-establishing her credibility among the women had paid off. The final tally was 392 to Mrs Mandela, 168 for Mrs Sisulu.

Her re-election took her back into the heart of the ANC's leadership, giving her an ex-officio place on the National Executive Committee. It would grant her an automatic right to speak at public meetings and on political platforms during the run-up to the April elections. It would bring her into far greater contact with her estranged husband than she had enjoyed in recent months. Once again he was the ANC's premier man and she its woman. And she had done it without him and without the advantage of his support.

In late January 1994, overriding some internal objections, the ANC waived its internal rules and put Winnie on its list of nominees to stand for Parliament. Having been convicted of a nonpolitical crime she was technically ineligible, but after her strong showing among delegates the congress decided it was in the best interest of democracy for the 1988 kidnapping to be ruled political. If, said Mandela, the masses decided that in spite of a 'so-called criminal record' she should be elected, then the ANC had to accept that. As she increased her power base and positioned herself for the future, Winnie had one indisputable advantage over her seventy five year old husband.

She was nearly twenty years younger than him.

Abbreviations

ANC	African National Congress
ANCYL	African National Congress Youth League
AZAPO	Azanian People's Organisation
BPC	Black People's Convention
BPA	Black Parents Association
COSATU	Congress of South African Trade Unions
FEDTRAW	Federation of Transvaal Women
IDAF	International Defence and Aid Fund
MDM	Mass Democratic Movement
NRC	National Reception Committee
NUM	National Union of Mineworkers
PAC	Pan African Congress
SACC	South African Council of Churches
SACP	South African Communist Party
SADF	South African Defence Force
SASM	South African Student Movement
SASO	South African Student Organisation
SAYCO	South African Youth Congress
SOYCO	Soweto Youth Congress
UBC	Urban Bantu Council
UDF	United Democratic Front
UNISA	University of Southern Africa

Notes

Chapter One

1 Interview with Hilda and Sylvia Madikizela, March 1993
2 Ibid.
3 *Part of My Soul* by Winnie Mandela, edited by Anne Benjamin and adapted by Mary Benson, Penguin Books, 1985, pp. 46–7.
4 In his book *Frontiers: The Epic of South Africa's Creation and the Tragedy of the Xhosa People* (Jonathan Cape, 1992) Noël Mostert writes: 'The earliest discernible possibility of a Bantu presence in the area associated with the Xhosa is around the seventh or eighth centuries A.D. At the mouth of the Chalumna river, near the modern port of East London, an archaeological site has yielded fragments of pottery associated with the early Iron Age of the Bantu speakers. Whether the pottery in fact was borne there by Bantu speakers or by people who obtained it from them cannot of course be certain, but the early occurrence of this domestic pottery in other coastal sites as far as Chalumna and its association with similar pottery sites in Natal and the Transvaal would seem to suggest an early Iron Age Bantu origin.'
5 Interview with Winnie's brother Msuthu Madikizela, July 1992
6 Interview with Msuthu and Princess Madikizela, August 1991.
7 Xhosa poet Sandile Dikheni says that the Xhosa prophet Ntsikane is supposed to have warned that people with hair whose texture was like algae would come bearing a button which did not have holes – meaning money. He warned that people should not take the button. 'Buttons' in this legend would have been referred to (in Xhosa) as *iQosha*.
8 *Winnie Mandela: Mother of a Nation* by Nancy Harrison, Victor Gollancz, 1985.
9 African owned trading posts were extremely rare. In response to a question tabled in Parliament in 1944, it was reported that there were only four African-owned trading posts in the Transkei.
10 Interview with Headman Themba Madikizela, March 1993.
11 Figures quoted by Frank Molteno in 'The Historical Foundations of the Education of Black South Africans' in *Apartheid and Educations: The Education of Black South Africans*, Ravan Press JHB, 1984 (ed. Peter Kellaway) concerning the situations in black education in 1940 attest to the meagreness of African education. In 1940, fewer than one quarter of black children aged between six and sixteen in South Africa were enrolled in school. For more than half those attending school, education would end in the sub-standards, and most of the remaining 40 per cent would only reach Class 2. Only 0.5 per cent of black children attending school reached the 6th class.
12 *Lives of Courage: Women for a New South Africa* by Diana E. H. Russell, Basic Books, Inc., New York, 1989.
13 *In Her Own Time: Winnie Mandela* by Sharon Goulds, Hamish Hamilton Children's Books, 1988.
14 *Higher than Hope* by Fatima Meer, Madiba Publishers, 1990.

15 Fatima Meer says the fight was with Winnie's elder sister Nancy. When interviewed for this book, Msuthu said the fight was with the younger sister Beauty. The details of the fight – apart from the identity of the victim – are strikingly similar.

16 *Part of My Soul*.

17 "From the Welsh name Gwenfrewi, meaning 'blessed reconciliation', influenced by the masculine name Winifred. St Winifred, one of the earliest known bearers of that name, is traditionally believed to have been beheaded and restored to life in the seventh century; the Welsh town of Holywell is named after the spring of healing water that is said to mark the spot where her head fell . . . ' (*A Dictionary of First Names* by Rosalind Fergusson, Market House Books, 1987).

18 "Fathers also are devoted to their children and make much of them small, carrying them about in their arms, fondling them, playing with them, teaching them to dance. Often one sees a child of three or four climbing over his father, and mauling him with impunity. Parents have fierce arguments as to whether a child's first word was 'mama' (mummy) or 'tata' (daddy)." 'Pondoland: Family Life' in *Oxford History of South Africa* by Monica Wilson.

19 *Part of My Soul*.

20 *Higher than Hope*, p. 126.

21 *Part of My Soul*, p. 47.

22 Using Msuthu's birth to date precisely his mother's death has been little help. In interviews with a group of the Madikizela family, including Msuthu, the date of his birth was given as 1952 – at least six years after the death of his mother. Princess Madikizela also gave a birth date after the death of her mother – she was born in 1948, she said. She has been consistent on that date. Giving evidence in a trial in December 1969 she said she was twenty-one years old. The four-year age difference between Gertrude's two youngest children is, however, probably accurate.

23 *Higher Than Hope*.

24 *Part of My Soul*.

25 Interview, July 1991.

26 Speech of the Minister for Native Affairs on 17 September 1953 moving the second reading of the Bantu Education Act in the House of Assembly.

27 Mark schedule for Standard 9, May and December 1951, Shawbury High School, Qumbu.

28 *Part of My Soul*.

29 Debate on Bantu Education Bill, in *Apartheid and Educations*.

30 Reports by Inspector of Schools on visits to Shawbury School 1947–50, S. A. Archive.

31 In other regions of the country measures had been harsher. Free State Indians were only permitted to work as manual labourers, while Transvaal Indians, who had lost the right to vote in 1885, were not allowed out after 9.00 p.m. at night without a permit and were forbidden to walk on public footpaths.

32 Autobiography: *The Story of My Experiments with the Truth* by Mahatma Gandhi, Dover Publications, New York, p. 117.

33 From 1906 to 1913, *Satyagraha* led to imprisonment with hard labour for Gandhi and his followers and a severe strain in relations between South Africa and India. Eventually, however, there would be success when many discriminatory laws

challenged by Gandhi were repealed, proving that *Satyagraha* could be a way of avoiding both compromise and violence.

34 *Part Of My Soul.*

35 *Lives of Courage: Women For A New South Africa,* p. 100.

Chapter Two

1 *Higher Than Hope* by Fatima Meer, Madiba Publishers, 1990.

2 Speech at treason trial: 7 November 1962.

3 There is more than one date given for Henry Mandela's death. Nelson Mandela has said he was barely ten when his father died. Mary Benson, Mandela's biographer has said Henry Mandela grew ill in 1930 – when Nelson was twelve years old.

4 This incident is related on page 9 of *Higher than Hope.* Mandela's eldest daughter, Makaziwe, says that her father stole one of Jogintaba's cows. On the following page Mandela corrects his daughter's downplaying of the incident, pointing out that in fact he stole two oxen.

5 *Mandela, Tambo, and the African National Congress: The struggle against apartheid, 1948–1990: a documentary survey,* eds Sheridan Johns, R. Hunt Davis, Jr., Oxford University Press, 1991.

6 *Time Longer Than Rope: The Black Man's Struggle For Freedom in South Africa* by Edward Roux, University of Wisconsin Press, 1948, 1964.

7 *The World That Was Ours: The Story of the Rivonia Trial* by Hilda Bernstein, S. A. Writers, London, 1989, p. 21.

8 *Higher than Hope,* pp. 95–6.

9 *In Her Own Time: Winnie Mandela* by Sharon Goulds, Hamish Hamilton Children's Books, 1988.

10 *1949 Handbook on Race Relations in South Africa,* eds Ellen Hellman and Leah Abrahams, Oxford University Press, Cape Town, 1949.

11 Interview with Princess Madikizela, October 1992.

12 *Part of My Soul* by Winnie Mandela, edited by Anne Benjamin and adapted by Mary Benson, Penguin Books, 1985, p. 57.

13 Interview on Carte Blanche (M–Net), Sunday 26 April 1992.

14 *No Easy Walk to Freedom,* Nelson Mandela, ed. Ruth First, Heinemann, 1965, p. xiii.

15 *The World that Was Ours,* p. 20.

16 *Part of My Soul,* p. 58.

Chapter Three

1 *Golden City Post,* 1 June 1958.

2 *Part of My Soul,* by Winnie Mandela, edited by Anne Benjamin and adapted by Mary Benson, Penguin Books, 1985.

3 *Winnie Mandela: Mother of a Nation* by Nancy Harrison, Victor Gollancz, 1985.

4 *Let My People Go: An Autobiography,* Albert Luthuli, Collins, 1962.

5 By 1970, when journalist Anthony Sampson visited Sobukwe living under house arrest and in isolation in Kimberly, his decade of defiance had taken its toll. Still under constant surveillance, Sobukwe had become paranoid, and was convinced the police had inserted a listening device into his body. He died in 1978, having

considerably modified his extremist views. (*Black and Gold: Tycoons, Revolutionaries and Apartheid* by Anthony Sampson, Pantheon, 1987.)

6 In *Black Politics in South Africa Since 1945* (Ravan Press, Johannesburg 1983), Tom Lodge writes that at the start of the shooting, 300 police faced a crowd of 5,000. In *Time Longer than Rope* (University of Wisconsin Press, 1948, 1964) Roux doubles the estimate and says that 10,000 men, women and children surrounded the police station.

7 *Africa Today*, May 1960.

8 *In Her Own Time: Winne Mandela* by Sharon Goulds, Hamish Hamilton Children's Books, 1988.

9 *Higher than Hope* by Fatima Meer, Madiba Publishers, 1990.

10 *In Her Own Time.*

11 'Winnie Mandela', documentary by Peter Davies, PBS network, USA, 1986.

12 Interview with Harold Wolpe, November 1992.

13 Interview with Amy Thornton neé Reitstein, November 1992.

14 The chief suspect was for a long time said to be the CIA's South African station chief, Millard Shirley. But in 1986, the *Johannesburg Star* produced another suspect, one with no name. Under the headline, "Mandela's arrest: A Tale of Betrayal", the newspaper quoted a retired senior police officer who had attended a 1960s farewell party for an American diplomat, who was in fact the CIA operative for the region. According to the police officer, the "highly personable" individual in his late thirties got drunk and started boasting of the role he had played in the arrest of Mandela. This was apparently in response to his being teased by other guests that his four-year tenure in Durban had been little more than a holiday.

The young American was said to have claimed that the ANC – feeling him to be sufficiently trustworthy – had arranged a rendezvous with Mandela for him. He had then traded details of the date, time and place with the head of the Natal police in return for information about the status of the government's plans for the homelands. Mandela was driving on the Natal road to keep a meeting with this American when he was stopped.

The diplomat's story was made more credible by its epilogue. Someone at the party reported his boasting — either to US or to South African officials — whereupon he was immediately summoned to Pretoria, extensively debriefed and flown out of the country on the next plane. Other party guests who were also subsequently debriefed were warned against discussing the matter. (*Star* newspaper report, 14 July 1986.)

Following publication of the *Star*'s story, CBS News ran a report in which they named Don Rickard, the consular officer of the period, as a CIA operative. Rickard refused to talk to the network and the best CBS could do was run an off-camera quote where he said, "If it were totally baseless, completely made up and malevolent, if you will, just intended to create trouble, even if that were the case, I still wouldn't comment."

The *National Reporter*, a left-wing monitor of US covert action, formerly known as *Counterspy*, then confirmed that Rickard had been the young American at the party and pointed out that he was listed in *Who's Who in the CIA*. The article maintained that both the National Security Agency and the CIA passed intelligence to the South African government. "The CIA has worked with the South African military, police and intelligence branches for years in a variety of ways: trading information, conducting joint military and security covert operations, and even undertaking secret agreements outside the legislative review processes of their respective countries." ("The Arrest of Nelson Mandela: Uncovering the American Connection", *National Reporter*, Vol. 10, no. 2, Autumn/Winter 1986.)

15 A secret CIA report sent to Washington four months after Mandela's arrest, titled "Country Internal Defense Plan" (a copy of which is now in the National Security Archives in Washington D.C.), laid out in detail Mandela's activities prior to his arrest. (It also described his arrest without mentioning any agency involvement.) Under a section titled, "Past, Present, and Future Threats to Internal Stability", the report said:

> On July 23 1962 Nelson Mandela returned to Bechuanaland where he was met by Cecil Williams, a prominent South African Communist. He drove to Johannesburg in Williams' car. In late July Mandela, acting as chauffeur for Williams, drove to Durban and had at least one meeting with the sabotage committee there. He also met with ANC leaders and announced the ANC was no longer under the Congress Alliance. The rank and file of the ANC did not know that this new tactic had been directed by the SACP and thought instead that Mandela was moving away from the white Communist domination of the Congress Alliance. While returning to Johannesburg from Durban, Mandela was arrested by the South African Police and was subsequently convicted of incitement and illegally leaving the country.

The report also contained detailed information about those Mandela had recruited. "A group of ten men who went to Morocco for training were known as Mandela's men", it said. And: "during the month of November, 1962, 56 students clandestinely escaped from South Africa and South West Africa to Bechuanaland. They are en route to Tanganyika. Of these 27 so far have reached Dar-es-Salaam. There is reliable information to the effect that the ANC had inserted into the first group of 27 a number of students to the Patrice Lumumba University in Moscow."

The report stressed that Communist-supported armed intervention "under the guise of African liberation" should not be allowed to happen. Instead of allowing South Africa's racial majority to become "well-organised, armed and radically indoctrinated," the United States was to exert its influence to create a coalition of moderates to work on a program of agreement. The aim of the agreement would be the gradual incorporation of non-Whites into the political, social and economic fabric of the country. In the early 1960s Nelson Mandela was not regarded as such a moderate.

16 Letter from H. G. Makgothi, Johannesburg, in *New Age*, Thursday 1 November 1962. The following quotation, from a letter by J. J. Mathabathe, appeared in the same publication on 18 October 1962.

17 *New Age*, 15 November 1962.

18 *The World That Was Ours: The Story of the Rivonia Trial* by Hilda Bernstein, S. A. Writers, London, 1989.

19 *New York Times*, 19 October 1989.

20 Both this quotation and the one below are from the *Observer*, 22 April 1973.

Chapter Four

1 State Department Cable, 24 January 1966.
2 Confidential State Department report, 10 October 1966.
3 White House, secret memo, 6 September 1966.
4 *Detention and Torture in South Africa* by Don Foster with Dennis Davis and Diane Sandler, James Currey Ltd, 1987.
5 *No Neutral Ground* by Joel Carlson, Thomas Y. Crowell Company, 1973, pp. 186—7.
6 Statement of Rita Ndzanga to Joel Carlson.
7 *Winnie Mandela: Mother of a Nation* by Nancy Harrison, Victor Gollancz, 1985.
8 Statement to the court by Mendel Levin, Case No: 27/70, The State *v*. Ndou & 21 others.
9 Transcript of Case No: 27/70, The State *v*. Ndou & 21 others.
10 *Part of My Soul* by Winnie Mandela, edited by Anne Benjamin and adapted by Mary Benson, Penguin Books, 1985 p. 104.
11 Ibid.
12 Ibid.
13 Mahanyele did not answer repeated letters and telephone calls asking him to explain his testimony. Eventually he indicated he would be prepared to respond to written questions. He was sent an extensive list, asking him among other things whether he had been forced to give evidence for the State. He did not respond. Five months later he sent a message via his secretary saying that he had decided to remain silent. He is aware that his testimony must therefore speak for itself as must his career.

Though dismissed from his job at USIA, he went on to become one of the most powerful and wealthy blacks in South Africa. As chairman of National Sorghum Breweries — a company with an annual turnover of $100 million — he took control of the country's sorghum — or traditionally brewed — beer market. By the late 1980s he had a seat on the South African President's Economic Advisory Council. He was also a director of Johnson and Johnson S.A, PISA Investments (Phillips in South Africa) and the multi-million dollar York Timber Organisation.
14 Case No: 27/70 The State *v*. Ndou & 21 others.
15 Interview with Indris Naidoo, August 1991.
16 Transcript of Case No: 27/70, The State *v*. Ndou & 21 others.
17 Ibid.

Chapter Five

1 *Part of My Soul* by Winnie Mandela, edited by Anne Benjamin and adapted by Mary Benson, Penguin Books, 1985.
2 Carte Blanche (M—Net), Sunday 26 April 1992.
3 Interview with Peter Davies, Winnie Mandela documentary, 1986.
4 *Sunday Express*, 20 September 1969.
5 Letter from Nelson to Winnie Mandela, 7 March 1981.
6 Interview with Angela Cobbett, August 1991.
7 Interview with Cosmas Desmond, 1 September 1992.
8 Interview with Renfrew Christie, 19 August 1992.
9 *Argus*, 15 January 1970.

10 Interview with Joel Carlson, October 1991.
11 *Inside Boss* by Gordon Winter.
12 Interview with Ray Carter, 18 February 1992.
13 *Encountering Darkness* by Gonville Aubie ffrench-Beytagh, Collins, 1973.
14 Interview with John Horak, *Vrye Weekblaad*, June 19–25, 1992.
15 *Sunday Star*, 27 May, 1980.
16 *Cape Times*, 3 January 1973.
17 Winnie Mandela interview with the *Star*, 30 September 1975.
18 Minutes of a meeting of the Meadowlands Tswana School Board held on 20 January 1976, reproduced in *The South African Institute of Race Relations, Survey of Race Relations, 1976*.
19 Confidential State Department memo, 9.10.71.
20 *Cape Times*, 3 October 1975.

Chapter Six

1 An open letter to Mr John Vorster from Desmond Tutu, 6 May 1976.
2 "One fifth of Soweto is schoolchildren" *Rand Daily Mail*, 18 June 1976.
3 All statements are taken from the *Rand Daily Mail* editions 16–18 June 1976.
4 Interview with Peter Davies, Winnie Mandela documentary 1986.
5 *Herald*, 12 July 1980.
6 Coetzee's decision was reversed on appeal.
7 Interview with former student leader, since active in the ANC, who asked not to be identified, September 1991.
8 *Lives of Courage: Women for a New South Africa* by Diana E. H. Russell, Basic Books, Inc., New York, 1989, p. 102.
9 *Part of my Soul* by Winnie Mandela, edited by Anne Benjamin and adapted by Mary Benson, Penguin Books, 1985, p. 38.
10 Assignment number 04, Anthropology I, student number 3070042, Mrs N. W. Z. Mandela, stamped 1987–8–10, 52 per cent.
11 Assignment number 02, Anthropology I, student number 3070042, Mrs N. W. Z. Mandela, stamped 1979–04–20.
12 Assignment number 03, Anthropology I, student number 3070042, Mrs N. W. Z. Mandela, stamped May 23, 1979.
13 *Observer*, 22 April 1973.
14 *Sechaba*, January 1971.
15 *Cape Times*, 22 November 1980, reports that Winnie's sister Mrs Nancy Vutela died in exile in Botswana.

Chapter Seven

1 Interviews with white shop keepers who wish to remain unidentified, September 1991.
2 Interviews with crèche staff, August 1991.
3 Black Consciousness in South Africa did not exclude Coloureds or Indians.
4 *Call Me Woman* by Ellen Khuzwayo, Ravan Press JHB, Johannesburg, 1985.
5 In January 1992 I was briefly and secretly allowed into the Security Police archives in Pretoria to look at Winnie Mandela's files. I was allowed to make no copies of

documents, but able to take notes. All the details of her bank accounts come from these files. I have no reason to believe they were false.

6 Testimony in Case No: 167/70, The State *v*. Joseph Jabu Sithole & 7 Others
7 South African Press Association reports: 30 August, 8 November, 17 November, 9 December, 27 December.
8 *Volksblad*, 20 June 1985.
9 *Weekend Argus*, N. D.
10 *Citizen*, 6 June 1984.
11 *Weekly Mail*, 8 August 1985.
12 "The Cabinet splits over the stubborn prisoner Mandela", *Weekly Mail*, 6—12 December 1985.
13 *Weekly Mail*, 7—13 and 14—20 February 1986.
14 *Business Day*, 4 December 1985; *Star*, 4 December 1985; *Citizen*, 4 December 1985; *Weekly Mail*, 6—12 December 1985.
15 Interview with Peter Davies, Winnie Mandela documentary, 1986.
16 "The man behind the men behind the bombs", *Weekly Mail*, 10—16 June 1988.
17 *Business Day*, 23 December 1985.
18 *Star*, 23 and 24 December 1985; *Guardian*, 23 December 1985; *Sowetan*, 23 December 1985; Sapa-Associated Press, 23 & 24 December 1985.
19 *Business Day*, 31 December 1985.
20 *Star*, 2 January 1986.
21 *Weekly Mail*, 10—16, 24—30 January and 4—10 April 1986.
22 *Weekly Mail*, 29 January—4 February 1988.
23 Speech before the Ford Foundation, National Press Club, Washington D.C., November 1991.
24 *Sowetan*, 7 April 1986.
25 *Star*, 15 April 1986.
26 *The Times*, 15 April 1986.
27 *Weekly Mail*, 5—11 September 1986.
28 *Star*, 21 April 1986.
29 *Weekly Mail*, 2—9 May 1988.
30 "Donahue", Multimedia Entertainment, Inc., USA, 22 June 1990.
31 Winnie had agree to be interviewed by South African television satellite channel M—Net for its current affairs program *Carte Blanche* following the announcement of her separation from Nelson Mandela. She had imposed terms on the interview. They were that the interviewer not ask her about the separation, the estrangement between her and the United Democratic Front in the late 1980s and allegations regarding the murders of Stompie Seipei and Dr Abu-Baker Asvat.
32 *Statements from the Harare Conference: Children of Resistance: on children, repression and the law in apartheid South Africa*, edited by Victoria Brittain and Abdul S. Minty, Kliptown Books, London, 1988.

Chapter Eight

1 This account is taken from Winnie's sworn testimony in her own defence against four counts of kidnapping and four counts of assault at the Rand Supreme Court, April 1991.
2 Interview with Wordsworth Madikizela, July 1991.

3 Richardson's description of Mandela United was given during his testimony in his own defence in his trial on four counts of kidnapping and assault, one count of murder and one count of attempted murder in the Rand Supreme Court, May 1990.

4 This version has been compiled from interviews with members of the Soweto community and parents of former members who wish to remain unidentified, as well as police and lawyers involved in investigating various crimes committed by members of Mandela United who also wish to remain unidentfied, and testimony from the following cases at the Rand Supreme Court: Case no: 108/90; Case no: 183/89; Case no: 184/89; Case no: 39/88.

5 Interviews with three members of the Wits University faculty who taught Winnie, June 1991 and September 1992.

6 Much has been written and said about the affect of the South African situation on its children. In addition to speaking to a number of human rights lawyers, and listening to the speech by Arthur Chaskalson, Director of the Legal Resources Centre, on kangaroo courts at the South African Bar Conference in Durban, July 1991, I spoke to church members and representatives of the South African Council of Churches. Insights were also offered by the following: *Psychology in Society 8* by Gill Straker and the Sanctuaries Counselling Team, University of Witwattersrand, Dept Of Psychology, 1987, pp. 48–79; *Detention and Torture in South Africa* by Don Foster with Dennis Davis and Diane Sandler, James Currey Ltd, London, 1987; CBS News: 'The Children of Apartheid', produced by Brian Ellis, December 1987. *People and Violence in South Africa*, edited by Brian McKendrick and Wilma Hoffmann, Oxford University Press, Cape Town, 1990; *Statements from the Harare Conference: Children of Resistance: on children, repression and the law in apartheid South Africa*, edited by Victoria Brittain and Abdul S. Minty, Kliptown Books, London, 1988; "The Torture File", *Weekly Mail*, 4–10 October 1985, among other works.

7 Lindi Mangaliso was found guilty of having "planned and arranged" her husband's murder in the early hours of 16 December 1984. Victor Mangaliso, a wealthy businessman, was stabbed twenty-six times while he slept. His wife was found to have paid two assassins to have carried out the murder. The assassins were sentenced to death, and Mrs Mangaliso received twenty years' imprisonment, the judge finding that the circumstances were extenuated by the fact that her husband was a drinker, womaniser and wife-beater. She was freed during a general amnesty in December 1991.

8 SABC Evening News, 3 December 1986; *Citizen*, 4 December 1986; *Weekly Mail*, 5–11 December 1986,

9 According to a high-ranking Security Officer.

10 Psychological report on Jerry Vusi Musi Richardson by Paul Garwood (Clinical Psychometrist) and Midge Doeppel (Clinical Psychologist). Their tests showed Richardson to have a severe personality disorder and possibly be psychotic and schizoid. They revealed him to be anti-social, unable to trust, isolated and lonely, desperately in need of affection. Their report, which was conducted on Richardson's behalf to prove mitigating circumstances lay behind his crimes, was accepted by the Appeal Court in August 1992.

11 "The strange and suspicious history of Winnie's coach" by Johnny Maseko and Thandeka Gqubule, *Weekly Mail*, 3–9 March, 1989.

12 "Richardson the Monster", *Drum*, October 1990.

13 Ibid.

14 Case no: 184/89, The State *v*. J. V. M. Richardson, Rand Supreme Court.

15 Ibid.

16 Case no: 41–1743–88, Johannesburg Regional Court; *Citizen*, 20 and 22 September 1988; *Star*, 22 and 27 September 1988; *Eastern Province Herald*, 22 September 1988; *Weekly Mail*, 23 September 1988; interviews with lawyers and police.

Chapter Nine

1 Testimony of Oupa Alex Seheri, Accused Number 1: Case no: 39/88, Rand Supreme Court.

2 The car had been bought for her by Yusuf Cachalia (Amina's husband), much to his later horror.

3 Judgment (Summary of Fact) in Case no: 39/88, Rand Supreme Court, 17 November 1988. Justice O'Donovan and two assessors, Mr. E. Heller and Miss V. Fortunat.

4 Ibid. Testimony of Aaron Makhunga, Jeremia Nkosi and Collin Dlamini.

5 Ibid. Testimony of Faith Mokhaula.

6 Ibid.

7 Ibid.

8 *Business Day*, 5 March 1987.

9 Interview with member of Attorney General's office involved in the case, June 1991.

10 Statement of Brian Sheer for the prosecution to the court, Case no: 33/89. "My Lord, on the witness list before your Lordship appear two names at numbers 18 and 19. These are the names of Nomzamo Winnie Mandela and Zindziswa Nubutho Mandela. My lord the evidence of these two witnesses in the light of the full admissions that have been made by my learned friends on behalf of accused four and accused five for the purpose of the state has no longer become necessary and the state does not intend calling them as witnesses."

11 *Star*, 26 February 1987.

12 Testimony of Lerotodi Ikaneng, Case Nos: 183/89 and 184/89, Rand Supreme Court.

13 "The fire and the football club", *Frontline*, August/September 1988.

14 Press conference given by Ismail Ayob, 31 July 1988.

15 According to Brown's spokesman, Armstrong Williams, quoted in the *Cape Times*, 3 August 1989.

16 Interview with former State Department official involved in discussions of Brown as suitable candidate for Ambassador to South Africa, December 1991.

17 *Finance* magazine, 5 August 1988.

18 An FBI investigation revealed that Brown's close ties to Umaru Dikko of Nigeria, who fled to London after a 1983 coup and was alleged to have stolen millions of dollars from the State, would hamper his chances of confirmation. It also emerged that US government contracts awarded both to him and to a company in which he was a partner after he left the White House in 1973 would be problematic. To win the former he had represented himself as "economically and socially dis-

advantaged", even though he had just left a $36,000 p.A. White House position. (Argus Foreign Service, 16, 18, 19 and 21 July 1986.)

19 *Business Day*, 17 March 1989.
20 A copy of the contract is in Winnie's Security Police file in Pretoria.
21 *Cape Times*, 25 July 1988.
22 Ikaneng, Case Nos: 183/89 and 184/89.
23 Ibid.

Chapter Ten

1 Interviews with church officials and former residents of the manse who asked not to be identified, January 1992.
2 Testimony of Bishop Peter Storey in Case No: 167/90 – The State *v.* John Morgan and three others, Rand Supreme Court, Friday 15 March 1991.
3 *Weekly Mail*, 17–23 February 1989; *Frontline*, March 1989; Interviews with Security Police and church officials, January 1992.
4 Interviews with Priscilla Jana, August 1991, and Ilona Tipp, June 1991.
5 Testimony of Paul Verryn in Case No: 184/89 The State *v.* J. V. M. Richardson, Rand Supreme Court.
6 Testimony of Xoliswa Falati in Case No: 167/90, Rand Supreme Court.
7 Ibid. Testimony of Thabiso Mono and Kenneth Kgase.
8 Ibid. Testimony of Bishop Peter Story and Winnie Mandela.
9 Ibid. Testimony of Winnie Mandela.
10 Ibid. Testimony of Bishop Peter Storey.
11 Ikaneng, Kgase, Mono & Mekgwe in Case no: 184/89 – The State *vs.* J. V. M. Richardson.
12 Ibid. Kenneth Kgase.
13 Ibid. Testimony of David Ching.
14 Ibid. Paul Verryn.
15 Medical report on Kenneth Kgase by Martin A. Connell, 7 January 1989.
16 Interview with Geoff Budlender, June 1991.
17 Interview with senior police official involved in the case who wishes to remain unidentified, August 1991.
18 This account is based on interviews with lawyers and church members involved.
  One of those I interviewed, who wishes to remain unidentified, was present at every Crisis Committee meeting and kept notes to which I was allowed access.
  Portions of these accounts were corroborated by the court testimony of Storey, Verryn, Mono and Mekgwe.
19 Ayob would say in a letter signed 30 June 1989 that he had not seen Mrs Mandela "since about February 1989".
20 Mono, Mekgwe and Storey in Case No: 184/89.
21 See Note 18, paragraph 2.
22 According to other lawyers involved in the case.

Chapter Eleven

1 Interviews with a number of the late Dr Asvat's relatives who wish to remain unidentified.
2 Interview with Priscilla Jana, August 1991.

3 Interview with Yunus Mayet, January 1992.

4 Interview with Anton Harbor, August 1991.

5 Testimony of Albertina Sisulu, The State *v*. Cyril Mbatha and Nicholas Dlamini, Rand Supreme Court.

6 NBC News Interview conducted by Robin Lloyd, 1 February 1989.

7 Exhibit AE paragraph 2.2 Case No: 167/90, Rand Supreme Court.

8 Ibid. Testimony of Winnie Mandela.

9 Medical card of Katiza Chebekhulu, 30 December 1992.

10 Johannesburg *Sunday Star*, 12 February 1989.

11 Testimony of Witness B and Witness C (held in camera) Case No: 183/89, Rand Supreme Court.

12 Testimony of Dr Patricia Klepp, Case No: 167/90, Rand Supreme Court.

13 Statement of Nicholas Dlamini, 17 February 1989.

14 Statement of Cyril Mbatha, 17 February 1989.

15 The State *v*. Mbatha and Dlamini.

16 *Higher than Hope* by Fatima Meer, Madiba Publishers, 1990.

17 Testimony of Winnie Mandela, Case No: 167/90, Rand Supreme Court.

Chapter Twelve

1 There are two main documented sources for this chapter. The first is the report of the Commission of Enquiry into the death of Clayton Sizwe Sithole. It was submitted to State President F. W. De Klerk by the chairman and sole member of the commission, Judge Richard Goldstone. During the public hearings evidence was heard from twenty-three witnesses, including Constable Jansen, who searched Sithole on his arrival at the police station at John Vorster Square; Captain du Toit, who interrogated Sithole; Dr Krausey, who examined Sithole the day before his death; Warrant Officer Augustyn, to whom Sithole made serious allegations about Winnie and Zinzi; and Constable Powrie, who took Sithole to the shower where he was later found hanged.

  The second source is the transcript of Case No: 184/89 The State *v*. J. V. M. Richardson, Jerry Richardson's trial.

Chapter Thirteen

1 *Drum*, May 1990.

2 *New York Times*, 22 June 1990.

3 Ibid., 23 June 1990.

4 'Donahue', Multimedia Entertainment Inc., 22 June 1990.

5 The account of how Kenneth Kgase's article came to be published in the *Sunday Telegraph* is taken from testimony given on 22 April 1991 by *Sunday Telegraph* journalist Peter Taylor in Case No.: 167/90 The State *v*. John Morgan and 3 others in the Rand Supreme Court.

6 Testimony given by *Johannesburg Star* journalist Pat Devereux in the case mentioned in note 5 provided an account of how the *Star* adapted material from the *Sunday Telegraph*.

7 The direct quotation in the account of this meeting comes from a six-page document prepared by a member of the social work delegate. It is entitled:

Minutes of a Meeting between ANC NEC and Social Service Workers, 28 August
1990.
8 Case No: 108/90 The State *v*. Charles Zwane, Rand Supreme Court.
9 Heads of argument: admissibility of similar fact evidence submitted in Case No:
167/90 The State *v*. John Morgan and 3 others.
10 In June 1993, the Witwatersrand Attorney-General's office announced it was still
considering bringing charges against Winnie in one of these two cases.

Chapter Fourteen

1 Testifying as "Youth X" because at the time he was under eighteen years old,
Rabolou contradicted Winnie's testimony. He said he went to Winnie in
September 1987. She said it was June. In his judgment, Justice Stegmann said, "Mr
Bizos led his evidence with great care and gave him clear opportunities to correct
that statement . . . Youth X, who is by no means unintelligent, failed to take the
opportunities and insisted that the incident had occurred in September 1987. After
the luncheon adjournment, however, Youth X testified that he had been thinking
about his evidence and that it had spontaneously occurred to him that he had erred
and that the incident in 1987 had in fact occurred in June and not in September."
2 Judgment in Case No: 167/90, Rand Supreme Court,
3 Ibid.
4 In August 1991, I travelled to Bloemfontein and Brandfort where I interviewed
township residents, township police, South African Police officers and members
of the Security Police. The various police force personnel (there were eight in all)
that I spoke to in a number of different locations and at different times
corroborated each other on one key issue: everything they told me, they said, they
had told the police in Johannesburg.
5 At the end of the trial, counsel agreed it was common cause that there was "no
room for any connection" between the death of Dr Asvat "and the issues in the
present case." (Judgement in Case No: 167/90, Rand Supreme Court.)
6 Interview with Priscilla Jana, September 1991.

Chapter Fifteen

1 There were two published reports of this incident. The first appeared in *The
Sowetan* on 30 March 1992, the second in the *Sunday Times*, 5 April 1992.

Chapter Sixteen

1 South African *Sunday Times* 11 November 1992.
2 Interview with the South African Press Association, 20 April 1992.
3 Carte Blanche (M–Net television), 26 April 1992.
4 South African *Sunday Times*, 19 April 1992.
5 The estimates of the number of women marchers varied. One had 700 women
taking part. Another said there were only 18. The comission heard that there were
a substantial number of women, but not more than a hundred.
6 *Weekly Mail*, 5–11 June 1992.
7 Ibid. 11–17 September 1992.
8 Ibid.

9 Letter from Messrs Ranoto, Seleka, Kgolane and Phantshang of the Malibongwe Women's project to The Manager, First National Bank, Life Centre, Johannesburg, 8 January 1990.
10 Letter from Cheadle, Thompson and Haysom to The Manager, First National Bank, Life Centre, Johannesburg, 19 February 1990.
11 Letter from Cheadle, Thompson and Haysom to Messrs Webber Wentzel, Johannesburg, 12 October 1990.
12 Letter from Soman Kamdar and Partners to Webber Wentzel, 8 February 1991.
13 Letter from Webber Wentzel to Cheadle, Thompson & Haysom, 4 April 1991.
14 *Weekly Mail*, 9–15 November 1990.
15 Given the option of transferring from social welfare to the ANC's legal department — arguably a more appropriate office for him as a trained lawyer with little social welfare experience — Mpofu had been sacked when he refused to move. His contention was that the proferred move was merely the first step in removing him from the ANC and he would eventually have been fired anyway.
16 *Sunday Star*, 6 September 1992.

Bibliography

Allport, Gordon W., *The Nature of Prejudice*, Addison-Wesley, 1954.

Benson, Mary, *Nelson Mandela*, Penguin, reprinted 1990.

Bernstein, Hilda, *For their Triumphs and for their Tears*, London, IDAF, 1975 (revised and enlarged 1985).

Bernstein, Hilda, *The World that Was Ours: The Story of the Rivonia Trial*, SAW, London, 1989.

Boesak, Allan, *Black and Reformed*, South Africa, Skotaville Publishers, 1984.

Brittain, Victoria, and Minty, Abdul S. (eds), *Children of Resistance*, London, Kliptown Books, 1988.

Carlson, Joel, *No Neutral Ground*, New York, Thomas Y. Crowell, 1973.

Cock, Jacklyn, and Nathan, Laurie (eds), *War and Society*, South Africa, David Philip, 1989.

Cock, Jacklyn, *Colonels and Cadres*, Oxford, OUP, 1991.

Cowell, Alan, *Killing the Wizards*, New York, Simon and Schuster, 1992.

Davenport, T. R. H., *South Africa: A Modern History*, South Africa, Southern Book Publishers, 1988.

Esterhuyse, Willie, and Nel, Philip (eds), *The ANC and Its Leaders*, Cape Town, 1990.

Finnegan, William, *Crossing the Line*, New York, Harper & Row, 1986.

Finnegan, William, *Dateline Soweto*, New York, Harper & Row, 1988.

Foster, Don, *Detention and Torture in South Africa*, South Africa, David Philip, 1987.

Frederikse, Julie, *The Unbreakable Thread*, South Africa, Ravan Press, 1990.

Gandhi, Mohandas K., *Autobiography*, Washington, Public Affairs Press, 1948.

Gastrow, Shelagh, *Who's Who in South African Politics*, Johannesburg, Ravan Press, 1990.

Goulds, Sharon, *In Her Own Time: Winnie Mandela*, Hamish Hamilton Children's Books, 1990.

Harrison, Nancy, *Winnie Mandela: Mother of a Nation*, Victor Gollancz, 1985

Holland, Heidi, *The Struggle*, London, Grafton Books, 1989.

Jeffery, Anthea J., *Riot Policing in Perspective*, South African Institute of Race Relations, 1991.

Johns, Sheridan, and Hunt Davis Jr, R., *Mandela, Tambo and the ANC: The Struggle against Apartheid 1948–1990, a Documentary Survey*, Oxford, OUP, 1991.

Joseph, Helen, *If This Be Treason*, André Deutsch, London, 1963.

Karis, Thomas, and Carter, Gwendolen, *From Protest to Challenge: A Documentary History of African Politics in South Africa 1882–1964* (4 volumes), Hoover Institution Press, Stanford, 1972–7.

Khuzwayo, Ellen, *Call Me Woman*, Ravan Press, Johannesburg, 1985.

Lake, Anthony, *The 'Tar Baby' Option*, New York, Columbia University Press, 1973.

Lekota, Mosiuoa Patrick (Terror), *Prison Letters to a Daughter*, South Africa, Taurus, 1991.

Lelyveld, Joseph, *Move Your Shadow*, London, Michael Joseph, 1986.

Lodge, Tom, *Black Politics in South Africa since 1945*, Ravan Press (South Africa), reprinted 1990.

Luthuli, Albert, *Let My People Go*, Collins, 1962.

Mandela, Winnie, *Part of My Soul*, Penguin, reprinted 1985.

Mandela, Nelson, *No Easy Walk To Freedom: Articles, Speeches and Trial Addresses*, Heinemann, London, 1966.

Mandela, Nelson, *The Struggle is My Life*, Pathfinder Press, 1986.

Manganyi, N. Chabani, and du Toit, Andre (eds), *Political Violence and the Struggle in South Africa*, London, Macmillan Academic and Professional, 1990.

Mathiana, Nomavenda, *Beyond the Headlines*, Johannesburg, Southern Book Publishers, 1990.

Mbeki, Govan, *Prison Writings*, South Africa, David Philip, 1991.

Mbeki, Govan *Learning from Robben Island*, Ohio University Press, 1991.

McKendrick, Brian, and Hoffmann, Wilma (eds), *People and Violence in South Africa*, Cape Town, OUP, 1990.

Meer, Fatima, *Higher Than Hope, Mandela, The Biography of Nelson Mandela*, Madiba Publishers, reprinted 1990.

Mostert, Noël, *Frontiers: The Epic of South Africa's Creation and the Tragedy of the Xhosa people*, Jonathan Cape, London, 1992.

Naidoo, Indres, *Robben Island: Ten Years a Political Prisoner in South Africa's Most Notorious Penitentiary*, Vintage Books, 1983.

Reddy E. S. (ed.), *Nelson Mandela*, London, Kliptown Books, 1990.

Roux, Edward, *Time Longer Than Rope: The Black Man's Struggle For Freedom in South Africa*, University of Wisconsin Press, reprinted 1964.

Russell, Diana E. H., *Lives of Courage*, New York, Basic Books, 1989.

Sampson, Anthony, *Black and Gold*, London, Hodder and Stoughton, 1987.

Schadeberg, Jurgen (ed.), *Nelson Mandela and the Rise of the ANC*, South Africa, Jonathan Ball and Ad Donker, 1990.

Spink, Kathryn, *Black Sash*, London, Methuen, 1991.

Swilling M., Humphries R., and Shubane, K. (eds), *Apartheid City in Transition*, Oxford, OUP, 1991.

The Treason Cage. The Opposition on Trial in South Africa, Heinemann, London, 1958.

Tutu, Desmond Mpilu, *Hope and Suffering*, South Africa, Skotaville, 1983.

Walshe, Peter, *The Rise of African Nationalism in South Africa: The African National Congress 1912–1952*, University of California Press, 1971.

Acknowledgements

The following archives and libraries were used and my thanks are due to: The Government Archive Service, Pretoria; The Rand Supreme Court Archive; The South African Archive, Cape Town; The South African Library, Cape Town; The Argus Library; The Times Media Library; The Mayibuye Centre, University of the Western Cape; The Centre for African Studies Library, University of Cape Town, and the National Security Archive, Washington D.C.

I would also like to thank Kathy Strachan, Paul Lindsay and in particular Tony Karon for their unstinting hard work in helping me research this book.

Finally I am indebted to Mic Cheetham for her loyalty and support.

The author and publisher are grateful to the following for permission to reproduce photographs:

Agence France Presse – pls 13 (© Gideon Mendel), 19 (© Walter Dhladhla), 31 (© Trevor Samson); Associated Press – pls 6, 15 (A. Zieninski/AFRAPIX), 16, 21, 29, 30; Joel Carlson (from his book *No Neutral Ground*) – pls 7, 8; Lesley Lawson – pl. 17; Mayibuye Centre, U.W.C. – pls 1 and 2 (Eli Weinberg), 3, 4, 5 (Mary Benson), 9 (Steve Kgami), 12; Network – pl. 11 (© Gideon Mendel); Popperfoto – pls 10, 14, 23–8; SIPA/Rex Features – pls 18, 20 (J. Kuus); Sygma – pl. 22 (A. Tannenbaum).

Acknowledgement should also be made to the following books for their valuable insights into aspects of South Africa: *Part of My Soul*, Winnie Mandela (edited by Anne Benjamin and adapted by Mary Benson), Penguin Books, 1985; *In Her Own Time: Winnie Mandela*, Sharon Goulds, Hamish Hamilton, 1988; *Higher Than Hope*, Fatima Meer, Madiba Publishers, 1990; *The World That Was Ours*, Hilda Bernstein, SAW, 1989; *No Easy Walk to Freedom*, Ruth First, Heinemann Educational Books, 1965; *Winnie Mandela: Mother of a Nation*, Nancy Harrison, Gollancz, 1985; *Lives of Courage*, Diana Russell, Basic Books, 1989; *No Neutral Ground*, Joel Carlson, Thomas Y. Crowell, 1973; *Call Me Woman*, Ellen Khuzwayo, Ravan Press, 1985.

Every effort has been made to obtain the necessary permissions with reference to copyright material, both illustrative and quoted; should there be any omissions in this respect we apologise and shall be pleased to make the appropriate acknowledgements in any future edition.

Index